Organizational, Legal, and Technological Dimensions of Information System Administration

Irene Maria Portela
Polytechnic Institute of Cávado and Ave, Portugal

Fernando Almeida
Polytechnic Institute of Gaya, Portugal

A volume in the Advances in Systems
Analysis, Software Engineering, and High
Performance Computing (ASASEHPC)
Book Series

Managing Director:	Lindsay Johnston
Production Manager:	Jennifer Yoder
Publishing Systems Analyst:	Adrienne Freeland
Development Editor:	Christine Smith
Acquisitions Editor:	Kayla Wolfe
Typesetter:	Lisandro Gonzalez
Cover Design:	Jason Mull

Published in the United States of America by
Information Science Reference (an imprint of IGI Global)
701 E. Chocolate Avenue
Hershey PA 17033
Tel: 717-533-8845
Fax: 717-533-8661
E-mail: cust@igi-global.com
Web site: http://www.igi-global.com

Library of Congress Cataloging-in-Publication Data

Organizational, legal, and technological dimensions of information system administration / Irene Maria Portela and Fernando Almeida, editors.
    pages cm
 Includes bibliographical references and index.
 Summary: "This book recognizes the importance of information technology by addressing the most crucial issues, challenges, opportunities, and solutions related to the role and responsibility of an information system, highlighting various aspects of the organizational and legal implications of system administration"-- Provided by publisher.
 ISBN 978-1-4666-4526-4 (hardcover) -- ISBN 978-1-4666-4527-1 (ebook) -- ISBN 978-1-4666-4528-8 (print & perpetual access) 1. Management information systems. 2. Computer networks--Management. 3. Computer security. 4. Computer security--Law and legislation. I. Portela, Irene Maria, 1965- II. Almeida, Fernando, 1979-
 T58.64.O74 2014
 658.4'038011--dc23
                            2013020688

This book is published in the IGI Global book series Advances in Systems Analysis, Software Engineering, and High Performance Computing (ASASEHPC) (ISSN: 2327-3453; eISSN: 2327-3461)

British Cataloguing in Publication Data
A Cataloguing in Publication record for this book is available from the British Library.

All work contributed to this book is new, previously-unpublished material. The views expressed in this book are those of the authors, but not necessarily of the publisher.

Advances in Systems Analysis, Software Engineering, and High Performance Computing (ASASEHPC) Book Series

Vijayan Sugumaran
Oakland University, USA

ISSN: 2327-3453
EISSN: 2327-3461

MISSION

The theory and practice of computing applications and distributed systems has emerged as one of the key areas of research driving innovations in business, engineering, and science. The fields of software engineering, systems analysis, and high performance computing offer a wide range of applications and solutions in solving computational problems for any modern organization.

The **Advances in Systems Analysis, Software Engineering, and High Performance Computing (ASASEHPC) Book Series** brings together research in the areas of distributed computing, systems and software engineering, high performance computing, and service science. This collection of publications is useful for academics, researchers, and practitioners seeking the latest practices and knowledge in this field.

COVERAGE

- Computer Graphics
- Computer Networking
- Computer System Analysis
- Distributed Cloud Computing
- Enterprise Information Systems
- Metadata and Semantic Web
- Parallel Architectures
- Performance Modeling
- Software Engineering
- Virtual Data Systems

IGI Global is currently accepting manuscripts for publication within this series. To submit a proposal for a volume in this series, please contact our Acquisition Editors at Acquisitions@igi-global.com or visit: http://www.igi-global.com/publish/.

Titles in this Series

For a list of additional titles in this series, please visit: www.igi-global.com

Service-Driven Approaches to Architecture and Enterprise Integration
Raja Ramanathan (Independent Researcher, USA) and Kirtana Raja (Independent Researcher, USA)
Information Science Reference • copyright 2013 • 411pp • H/C (ISBN: 9781466641938) • US $195.00 (our price)

Progressions and Innovations in Model-Driven Software Engineering
Vicente García Díaz (University of Oviedo, Spain) Juan Manuel Cueva Lovelle (University of Oviedo, Spain) B. Cristina Pelayo García-Bustelo (University of Oviedo, Spain) and Oscar Sanjuán Martínez (University of Oviedo, Spain)
Engineering Science Reference • copyright 2013 • 388pp • H/C (ISBN: 9781466642171) • US $195.00 (our price)

Knowledge-Based Processes in Software Development
Saqib Saeed (Bahria University Islamabad, Pakistan) and Izzat Alsmadi (Yarmouk University, Jordan)
Information Science Reference • copyright 2013 • 318pp • H/C (ISBN: 9781466642294) • US $195.00 (our price)

Distributed Computing Innovations for Business, Engineering, and Science
Alfred Waising Loo (Lingnan University, Hong Kong)
Information Science Reference • copyright 2013 • 369pp • H/C (ISBN: 9781466625334) • US $195.00 (our price)

Data Intensive Distributed Computing Challenges and Solutions for Large-scale Information Management
Tevfik Kosar (University at Buffalo, USA)
Information Science Reference • copyright 2012 • 352pp • H/C (ISBN: 9781615209712) • US $180.00 (our price)

Achieving Real-Time in Distributed Computing From Grids to Clouds
Dimosthenis Kyriazis (National Technical University of Athens, Greece) Theodora Varvarigou (National Technical University of Athens, Greece) and Kleopatra G. Konstanteli (National Technical University of Athens, Greece)
Information Science Reference • copyright 2012 • 330pp • H/C (ISBN: 9781609608279) • US $195.00 (our price)

Principles and Applications of Distributed Event-Based Systems
Annika M. Hinze (University of Waikato, New Zealand) and Alejandro Buchmann (University of Waikato, New Zealand)
Information Science Reference • copyright 2010 • 538pp • H/C (ISBN: 9781605666976) • US $180.00 (our price)

Large-Scale Distributed Computing and Applications Models and Trends
Valentin Cristea (Politehnica University of Bucharest, Romania) Ciprian Dobre (Politehnica University of Bucharest, Romania) Corina Stratan (Politehnica University of Bucharest, Romania) Florin Pop (Politehnica University of Bucharest, Romania) and Alexandru Costan (Politehnica University of Bucharest, Romania)
Information Science Reference • copyright 2010 • 276pp • H/C (ISBN: 9781615207039) • US $180.00 (our price)

www.igi-global.com

701 E. Chocolate Ave., Hershey, PA 17033
Order online at www.igi-global.com or call 717-533-8845 x100
To place a standing order for titles released in this series, contact: cust@igi-global.com
Mon-Fri 8:00 am - 5:00 pm (est) or fax 24 hours a day 717-533-8661

Table of Contents

Section 1
The Role and Responsibility of the System's Administrator

Section 2
Legal and Regulatory Frameworks

Section 3
Privacy and Security

Section 4
Survey and Case Studies

Detailed Table of Contents

Section 1
The Role and Responsibility of the System's Administrator

Chapter 1
> *Filipe Moreira, Higher Polytechnic Institute of Gaya, Portugal*
> *Joel Luz, Higher Polytechnic Institute of Gaya, Portugal*

Chapter 1 presents an overview of the role and responsibilities of the system's administrator. The authors also presented some suggestions and tools that might help IT teams improve their daily work from the technical and organizational points of view.

Chapter 2
> *Michele Tomaiuolo, University of Parma, Italy*

Chapter 2 presents several mechanisms and models for the establishment of secure delegations in open interconnected information systems environments. The considered models include Role-Based Access Control, Trust Management, and Federated Identity.

Chapter 3
> *José Monteiro, Higher Polytechnic Institute of Gaya, Portugal*
> *Mário Lousã, Higher Polytechnic Institute of Gaya, Portugal*

Chapter 3 looks at the factors that influence the career of the systems administrator in the context of the organization. The main goal of this chapter is to provide a contribution to the future systems administrators, employers, and scholars to better understand what factors influence the figure of the systems administrator.

Section 2
Legal and Regulatory Frameworks

Chapter 4

Peter J. Wasilko, The Institute for End User Computing, Inc., USA

Chapter 4 provides a global understanding of the legal aspects of information systems administrative functions within the organization. This chapter describes how prudent technological choices can facilitate future regulatory compliance, drastically reduce legal costs, and allow agile strategic responses to emerging business risks.

Chapter 5

Joanna Kulesza, University of Lodz, Poland

Chapter 5 analyzes the due diligence standard in public international law. The author discusses the possibility of introducing an international due diligence standard for Internet Service Providers (ISPs).

Chapter 6

Gonçalo S. de Melo Bandeira, Escola Superior de Gestão, IPCA, Portugal

Chapter 6 helps one to understand the problem of the question of criminal liability and legal persons in Portuguese cybercrime laws. The chapter clarifies the notion of legal persons and presents some holes in the Portuguese law that enable some "legal persons" to not be blamed for cybercrimes.

Chapter 7

Irene Portela, Polytechnic Institute of Cávado and Ave, Portugal

Chapter 7 discusses the role of CNPD ("Comissão Nacional de Proteção de Dados") in case of violation of privacy, like dissemination or revelation of personal data by a public/private organization or entity.

Section 3
Privacy and Security

Chapter 8

Fawzy Soliman, University of Technology Sydney, Australia

Chapter 8 looks to the cloud system as an enabler of global competitive advantages. Typically, the goal of cloud systems is to provide easy and scalable access to computing resources and IT services, but when we use it for innovation we should also include the ability of the system to assist the innovator in assessing the knowledge transferred. Additionally, this chapter also discusses the various success factors of cloud systems implementations.

Chapter 9 looks to the main challenges introduced by cloud computing in terms of governance, legal, and public policy factors. The right addressing of these aspects is a fundamental condition for successful deployment, whether done by the in-house IT department or outsourced to cloud server providers.

Chapter 10 analyzes US and European Information Security (InfoSec) and Information Assurance (IA) related social publications and standards and discusses the perception of the disciplines in academic and industry works. The chapter highlights the importance of clear and precise definitions of InfoSec and IA and a need for the definitions to promote open-mindedness among practitioners and researchers.

Chapter 11 proposes a conceptual framework for big data analysis. The idea behind this chapter is to look for the main challenges and issues that will have to be addressed to capture the full potential of big data.

Section 4
Survey and Case Studies

Chapter 12 provides a discussion about the importance of the organizational context and the role of network administrator performed in an organization. These two elements are evaluated, and the authors look at how the organizational culture can impact the degree to which security can be successfully maintained.

Chapter 13 discusses the main results and findings of the 2011 survey of information security and information assurance professionals. These results helped to identify a commonly accepted perception of information assurance and clarified the goals of the discipline.

Fernando Almeida, University of Porto, Portugal
José Cruz, University of Porto, Portugal

Chapter 14 analyzes the most common security threats of VoIP solution in a corporate environment. Additionally, this chapter proposes several security policies and practices that could have been adopted to mitigate the security vulnerabilities introduced by VoIP.

Pedro Sousa, Higher Polytechnic Institute of Gaya, Portugal
José Costa, Higher Polytechnic Institute of Gaya, Portugal
Vitor Manso, Higher Polytechnic Institute of Gaya, Portugal

Chapter 15 presents a practical approach for data breach cases in ERP systems. This chapter is based on a case study scenario where a major data breach happens in one institution of the public sector, a municipally, in Portugal.

Foreword

The management of IT systems is a subject with a history spanning almost 40 years; yet it is not a subject well known to business leaders. System administration is considered to be a technical subject, too low level for consideration by businesses. That perception is beginning to change today, largely due to an awareness of the services provided in the so-called public cloud. It is a perception that has to change in order for businesses to exploit the benefits of online services safely and economically.

This book presents some of those issues and challenges faced by businesses in the context of the IT landscape today. It offers managers an opportunity to understand some of the technical challenges presented by their IT systems at a conceptual level.

As online services become an essential backbone to businesses of all kinds, the infrastructure behind those businesses becomes an increasingly important part of the value chain. That means leaders need to get on board and understand IT services at a level where they can utilize infrastructure in a strategic role. The authors in this volume have covered some of those challenges here, and I add only a few simple words of encouragement to both sides of the business-IT divide, to build the bridge between technology and business and usher in the third wave of information technology.

Mark Burgess
Oslo University College, Norway
2013

Mark Burgess *is professor of Network and System Administration at Oslo University College. He was the first professor with this title. Mark obtained a PhD in Theoretical Physics in Newcastle, for which he received the Runcorn Prize. His current research interests include the behaviour of computers as dynamic systems and applying ideas from physics to describe computer behaviour. Mark is the author of the popular configuration management software package Cfengine and is the founder, chairman, and CTO of the Cfengine company. He led theoretical and practical contributions to the theory of automation and policy-based management, including the idea of Operator Convergence and Promise Theory. He is the author of numerous books and papers on Network and System Administration and has won several prizes for his work.*

Preface

The focus of this book is to discuss the main issues, challenges, opportunities, and solutions related to the role and responsibility of the system's administrator. Therefore, we intend to discuss the mission and challenges of a system's administration in the 21st century, the importance of proper information security policy, the drivers and barriers to address a completely safe and reliable ICT system, and the organizational and legal implications of system administration. Furthermore, we intend to present some practical solutions that would make it possible to implement a reliable system administration policy.

Networking and IT professionals today have a tremendous responsibility when it comes to managing the network of an organization. The complexity of information management is huge, particularly in large organizations. The data explosion continues to drive the demand for increased storage capacity and a parallel need to secure that information. Companies are facing increased security threats from both within the organization and externally. A company's data is one of its most valuable assets, and organizations need to implement a thorough security plan taking all aspects of securing the data into account. Each point in the storage infrastructure provides a different security threat that must be dealt with using the most appropriate technologies available. Some examples of these security domains include data protection, authentication of devices and users, key management, and end-to-end data integrity.

Currently, all organizations have a system administrator, whose role is mainly developed in the dark to avoid data leaks, safeguard the integrity of databases, etc., which is part of the organization's policy, but when there is a failure, a breach of competition rules, a violation of confidentiality, the responsibility is in the administrator. In fact, the system administrator has access to very sensitive and important information inside an organization. Together, with the CIO of a company, they may define and apply a global Information Security Policy that must be followed by all employees. This Information Security Policy typically contains operational policies, standards, guidelines, and metrics intended to establish minimum requirements for the secure delivery and utilization of IT services. Secure service delivery and utilization requires the assurance of confidentiality, integrity, availability, and privacy through the management, and business processes that include and enable security processes, the physical security requirements for information systems, the ongoing personnel awareness of security issues, and monitoring for compliance.

The whole system of an organization is based on the myth that the organization's privacy is properly addressed and assured by the company. However, this assumption is absolutely an illusion. Security breaches and data loss can happen in very sophisticated National Defense systems, small business, and organizations. A significant part of these security pitfalls may occur due to information disclosures or bad business practices, which result essentially from human errors, negligent behavior, and criminal acts.

At the same time, very often organizations are spending "enough" money on security, but spending it in the wrong places or otherwise inappropriately. This occurs for two main reasons: they do not understand what security risks are associated with their business strategies, and they do not have a systematic way to intelligently secure their entire enterprise.

This book is organized in four sections composed by 15 chapters that intend to smoothly introduce and discuss the main ideas related with the current and future challenges faced by network administrators.

Chapter 1 presents an overview of the role and responsibilities of the system's administrator. The authors also advance with some suggestion and tools that might help IT teams to improve their daily work from the technical and organizational points of view.

Chapter 2 presents several mechanisms and models for the establishment of secure delegations in open interconnected information systems environments. The considered models include Role Based Access Control, Trust Management and Federated Identity.

Chapter 3 looks at the factors that influence the career of the systems administrator in the context of the organization. The main goal of this chapter is to provide a contribution to the future systems administrators, employers, and scholars to better understand what factors influence the figure of the systems administrator.

Chapter 4 provides a global understanding between the connection of legal aspects and information systems administration functions within the organization. This chapter describes how a right technological choice can facilitate future regulatory compliance, drastically reducing legal costs and opening new ways for agile strategic responses to emerging business risks.

Chapter 5 analyzes the due diligence standard in public international law. The author discusses the possibility of introducing an international due diligence standard for Internet Service Providers (ISPs).

Chapter 6 helps one to understand the problem of the question of criminal liability and legal persons in Portuguese cybercrime laws. The chapter clarifies the notion of legal persons and presents some holes in the Portuguese law that enable some "legal persons" to not be blamed for cybercrimes.

Chapter 7 discusses the role of CNPD (*Comissão Nacional de Proteção de Dados*) in case of violation of privacy, like dissemination or revelation of personal data by a public/private organization or entity. For that, the author seeks to assess the legal responsibility of the System Administrator in a case of dissemination or revelation of personal data to the market by a public or government entity like the online "Portal of Portuguese Treasury."

Chapter 8 looks to the cloud system as an enabler of global competitive advantages. Typically, the goal of cloud systems is to provide easy and scalable access to computing resources and IT services, but when we use it for innovation we should also include the ability of the system to assist the innovator in assessing the knowledge transferred. Additionally, this chapter also discusses the various success factors of cloud systems implementations.

Chapter 9 looks to the main challenges introduced by cloud computing in terms of governance, legal, and public policy factors. The right addressing of these aspects is a fundamental condition for successful deployment, whether done by the in-house IT department or outsourced to cloud server providers.

Chapter 10 analyzes US and European Information Security (InfoSec) and Information Assurance (IA) related social publications and standards and discusses the perception of the disciplines in academic and industry works. The chapter highlights the importance of clear and precise definitions of InfoSec and IA and a need for the definitions to promote open-mindedness among practitioners and researchers.

Chapter 11 proposes a conceptual framework for big data analysis. The idea behind this chapter is to look for the main challenges and issues that will have to be addressed to capture the full potential of big data.

Chapter 12 provides a discussion about the importance of the organizational context and the role of network administrator performed in an organization. These two elements are evaluated, and the authors look at how the organizational culture can impact the degree to which security can be successfully maintained.

Chapter 13 discusses the main results and findings of the 2011 survey of information security and information assurance professionals. These results helped to identify a commonly accepted perception of information assurance and clarified the goals of the discipline.

Chapter 14 analyzes the most common security threats of VoIP solution in a corporate environment. Additionally, this chapter proposes several security policies and practices that could have been adopted to mitigate the security vulnerabilities introduced by VoIP.

Chapter 15 presents a practical approach for data breach cases in ERP systems. This chapter is based on a case study scenario where a major data breach happens in one institution of the public sector, a municipally, in Portugal.

We hope that this book will provide an important resource and support to disciplines (post-graduate studies) of Management, Enterprise Information Systems, Information Systems Management, and Management Information Systems in general. It intends to serve as guidance for top managers and Information Technologies (IT) professionals (system developers and IT specialists).

Irene Portela
Polytechnic Institute of Cávado and Ave, Portugal

Fernando Almeida
Polytechnic Institute of Gaya, Portugal

Section 1
The Role and Responsibility of the System's Administrator

Chapter 1
The Role and Responsibilities of the System's Administrator

Filipe Moreira
Higher Polytechnic Institute of Gaya, Portugal

Joel Luz
Higher Polytechnic Institute of Gaya, Portugal

ABSTRACT

In this chapter, the authors present an overview of the role and responsibilities of the system's administrator. They start with giving a background description on how this activity has been changing within the last decades considering not only the roles but also how the educational background changed and the new challenges regarding high-level IT management. After this contextualization, the authors reproduce some thoughts and experiences shared by experienced IT professionals giving their vision on how the industry has been changing and what would be the future of system administrators. They advance some suggestions and tools that might help IT teams improve their daily work from the technical and organizational point of view and highlight some future points of research concerning educational paths.

INTRODUCTION

Thanks to the evolution of critical activities within enterprise context, system's administration has a particular importance because corporative activities tend to be directly or indirectly dependent on data networks. Naturally, not only system's administrators but also manufacturers, facing new issues related with heterogeneity and systems flexibility, have found new challenges regarding network management systems. Factors like the increasing creation of new services, the need to provide quality of service for all the organization and also the requirement of "managing people" takes the network administration to face a whole bunch of new "activities", roles and responsibilities transposed to IT Professionals, namely system's / network administrators. In this chapter we will approach the "social" and "technical point of view of these professionals,

DOI: 10.4018/978-1-4666-4526-4.ch001

understanding who are they, what they do and how they roles have changed through the last years. To fulfill this objective it will be presented not only the "background literature" about the theme but also some statements of IT professionals working in the industry for more than fifteen years.

It is a matter of fact that system administration is a mix of technical and sociological skills. Because of the broad branch of activities that these professionals face it is not easy to define their activity specifically. Certain positions maybe more social, others more technical and even though we are talking about the same professional category. Just as a point of start, when we talk about system's administrators we are not excluding network administrators from this discussion. Obviously, from the semantic point of view, someone who is a system administration is a person that manages an array of systems, software, which might be Customer Relationship Management – CRM - solutions, operating systems, helpdesk platforms, etc. However we are not going to split this role from the network management as it is commonly seen together and, generally, share the same definitions only changing the scope: software (systems) and hardware (network).

BACKGROUND

So, what is the job of a system administrator? This professional builds and manages IT infrastructures taking care of security issues, software and hardware management / deployment. It's also common to deliver to this IT staff some development / programming roles specially on automating management roles (ie. scripting) though they are not Software Engineers (Kichel, 2003). One of the main requirements of a system's administrator is to be versatile with a wide variety of skills. The best system administrators are often quite general, both theoretically and practically. From making or repairing wiring cable installations, installing operating systems or software

applications, correcting problems and errors in the systems to developing scripts, software, planning, constructing and managing databases and also training company users, their main objective could be resumed as: to automate a large number of common tasks and increase the overall work performance in the organization.

From the 1980 / 1990 decade the system's administrators that were present on lots of companies were the persons who "understood" about computers which the main role were to fix computers and put it back to work. Their profile were not clear, and they did not have extensive knowledge but only basic knowledge of a dozen of applications (word processor, spreadsheet, databases, etc.) and some basic knowledge of hardware were sufficient for the everyday tasks. This was the picture of lots of companies and public institutions back then. The evolution of this professional role is highly linked with Internet growth and the companies need to have multiple systems in heterogenic ecosystems. From the end of the 1990 decade through the new millennium the presence of these IT Staff in the companies developed to persons who had to own general understanding, theoretical and practical, of very diverse areas from networking technologies, operating systems, applications. Also, the new paradigm asks for knowledge on programming in a wide variety of programming languages comprehensive knowledge of both network and hardware, Internet technologies, databases construction, etc. Obviously, in bigger companies, nowadays, it is common to see that this generic profile divides itself in sub-profiles such as operating systems administrator, database administrators, security specialists, helpdesk staff, etc. As we said before we are not excluding network administrators from this logic but with the evolution of IT careers it is imperative to understand that there are some particularities that distinguishes these two professionals. Network management is to manage services, devices and network systems on a certain infrastructure. It clearly depends on how big is a company to have different staff doing the system's administration and network administrator jobs. These two categories are clearly connected because it is not possible for a system's administrator to manage a Server OS without knowing, at least, how the network is configured and implemented.

From the technical point of view, due to the vast scope of duties, systems, devices, manufacturers and companies, it is not doable do present on this chapter specific management tools, "tricks" or "how-to's" that a system's administrator follows nowadays. However, independently from the "way they do" there are certain performance indicators / policies that any CEO wants to be fulfilled in their company without even knowing their IT Staff. Obviously we have to talk about management models and compare, at least two of them: proactive and reactive models.

From the point of view of companies that are highly dependent on IT infrastructures, given the multiplicity of environments, systems management is a costly activity not only human but also economic. In this way it is common to observe a major concern by the concepts of performance especially on what refers to the most "common" of the term, (i.e., processor speed, bandwidth being used on the network, RAM being consumed in a given set of virtual machines, etc.). Despite the importance that the "pure performance" has to an organization it is also not less important ensuring "business continuity". A few minutes of downtime, depending on the aggregated services, it may be very serious from the financial, competitive, but also on the operation point of view of the organization. According to Imoniana (2006) it is common to see the adoption of a reactive management model only in small organizations that do not justify the existence of an IT department because of its dimension or core business . Moreover, in organizations of medium and large, this is a completely rejected idea for obvious reasons. First, the infrastructures that these organizations depends on, immediately creates the need to avoid any occurrences and, of course, given the business area will be a priority to ensure low response times.

This type of management is, in its turn, called the "Proactive Model Management" and has a set of confidence measures (Patterson, n.d.):

- **Failure Rate:** Average number of failures for a given period of time;
- **Mean Time to Failure (MTTF):** Mean time to failure occurring;
- **Mean Time to Repair (MTTR):** Mean time to repair;
- **Mean Time between Failures (MTBF):** Mean time between the occurrence of failures.

This management model assure that IT staff is alerted before a system or asset needs to be fixed (i.e. an e-mail server that is almost out of storage). It guarantees that IT does not contribute to the decrease of general staff productivity and minimizes costs being able to decrease avoidable IT Specialists support. Keeping all network assets on detailed monitoring is very difficult and time consuming to the system's administrator and the amount of data that must be analyzed is huge (Sata Technologies, 2011). To do this, IT professionals must adopt solutions that help capture as much data so it is easy to understand and reflect the actual state of the network. The proactive monitoring allows the administrator to be notified of potential problems before it happens so corrective measures can be taken. From the point of view of the quality of IT service, it becomes very interesting to use tools that notify the administrator about the failure of a link, or lack of disk space on a server even before end users notice the problem (Rodrigues, 2010). Daily monitoring and statistical resources are used to track changes behavior and to anticipate failures and performance loss. This task is carried out by Network Management System's – NMS. This is intrinsically connected with the way how organizations and their System's Administrators manage IT-related risk issues. In this field there are frameworks, good practices and guides such as COBIT or ITIL, which we will discuss on the solutions and recommendations section of this chapter. The National Institute of Standards and Technology - NIST - suggests that Risk Management is an iterative process that is present through all SDLC (system development life cycle).

So what is risk management and how important is it for system's administrators and organizations in general? Risk Management in the IT industry is the array of processes that balances the weight of operational and economic costs of protective measures to achieve business alignment with the organizational mission (Stoneburner, Goguen & Feringa, 2012). To achieve such objectives we have different key roles where the system's administrators assume an important duty. Forgetting the high level management roles from Chief Executive Officers – CEOs, Chief Technology Officers – CTOs, or Business and Functional Managers we can describe these system's administrator duties as "IT Security Practitioner" and regular IT systems users as Security Awareness Trainers. The first ones are people who are responsible for the security requirements implementation and for the proper use of risk management processes to identify and mitigate new potential risks. This may occur when the IT environment changes, for instance, when the there is a network expansion, introduction to new technologies, etc. On the other side, Security Awareness Trainers, are the people who use IT systems according to the organizational rules and guidelines. These actors play an important role in the risk mitigation of a certain organization protecting its IT resources. However this is only possible when application users receive security awareness training. "One of the best ways to make sure company employees will not make costly errors in regard to information security is to institute company-wide security-awareness training initiatives that include, but are not limited to classroom style training sessions, security awareness Website(s), helpful hints via e-mail, or even posters" (SANS Institute, 2009). Security awareness training can pay off by training

users on what they can do to prevent malicious activity and what to do in the event of such activity. Of course security awareness training is not the be-all-end-all, it is a significant layer of security to add to existing security measures (Rothman, 2007). This makes us a bridge to why system's administrator should be not only a "system's guru" but also a "people manager". A recent SOPHOS study on employee usage behavior indicates us that 96 percent of respondents (IT professionals) do not trust their end users to make sound IT security decisions. Some important results show us that 48% of respondents fix security issues caused by end user negligence at least once a week, 26% of respondents say senior management commits the worst IT security offenses and 19% of respondents say that IT commits the worst IT security offenses (SOPHOS, 2012). These results points us to the importance of IT education inside organizations and obviously IT education of system's administrators.

According to Burgess and Koymans (2007) for several years academically inclined system administrators have struggled to identify the role and place of System Administration within the fields of Computer Science and Engineering. This is true and reminds us of what we said before: back in the 80s "system's administrators" were people who "knew about computers." The same authors defend that from the academic point of view computer science derives from two main areas: mathematical logic and electrical engineering however computing phenomena show us that there are lots of IT related staff that never learned the subject at a higher education level. The truth is, even nowadays, you will find lots self-taught people who achieved their job by their own determination and we are not talking about people who "just know about computers."

System's's and Network administration areas, even today, are weak points of higher studies programmes so this is a growing area at this level (Burgess & Koymans, 2007). Obviously that we are not forgetting the existence of certification courses carried out by the main players of IT players such as CISCO, Microsoft, Avaya or Blue Coat but these courses teaches their technology lacking a more embracing methodology. There are many points of view about learning methodologies but, in a general way, it might be described as a group of three aspects Education, Training and Self-Learning. So this points us to the importance of higher degree courses in the System's Administration field but in some way these people will be, someday, "teachers". When we describe them as teachers, we are not saying that they are going to be college teachers. As system's administrators, this staff will have to educate their end users of how to use their systems and what would be the best practices.

It's common, for a system's administrator, to see his quotidian as "we against them". It's necessary to remember that home computer user is often said to be the weakest link in computer security. People tend to use their job IT resources as they use their own equipment at home. IT Staff must understand this behavior to best educate end

users and best produce guidelines and rules. End users tend to describe themselves as proficient in IT resources. A study about computer use indicates us that the percentage of people that considers themselves as knowledgeable, very knowledgeable or expert are (Aytes & Connolly 2004) (see Figure 1):

- E-mail use: 93%
- Protecting against viruses: 69%
- Protecting against computer crash: 70%
- Protecting against interception of financial information: 50%

These are very "positive" results however, in the same study, when analyzed some key security-related practices they are very revealing (See Figure 2).

- Share passwords – 25% (results for occasionally, frequently and all the time)
- Voluntary change passwords – 58% (results for never)

Figure 1. End users perception about IT issues

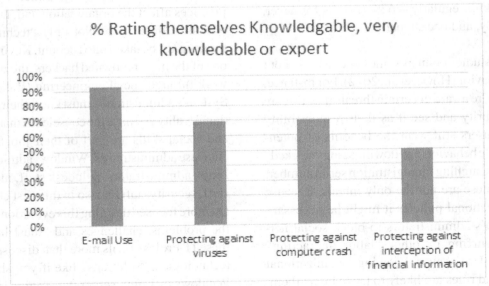

Figure 2. Key security practices adopted by end-users

Activity	Never	Rarely	Occasionally	Frequently	All the Time
Share passwords	22%	53%	20%	3%	2%
Voluntarily change password*	27%	24%	29%	9%	11%
Open e-mail attachments w/out virus checking – unknown source	58%	18%	14.5%	6%	4%
Open e-mail attachments w/out virus checking – known source	25%	19%	18%	23%	25%
Backup regularly*	6%	21%	35%	24%	14%

* = Higher frequency on these items indicates more secure behavior

- Open e-mail attachments without virus checking from unkown source – 24,5% (results for occasionally, frequently and all the time)
- Open e-mail attachments without virus checking from known source – 66% (results for occasionally, frequently, and all the time)
- Backup regularly – 62% (results for never, rarely, and occasionally)

Other studies point us some conclusions about user's behavior (Howe, et al., 2012). For instance, when they're aware of certain threats they do care about security and see it as their responsibility whoever users still want the benefits of potentially unsafe behavior (e.g. downloading "cracked" software, searching for registration serial number, etc.) but these are not the only threats. Because of organizational policies it might be necessary for system's administrators to block social networking surfing or other "labor distracting" Websites. Users even knowing organizational policies and rules are likely to try to break them. So the main point of these IT Professionals would

be to educate end users and make them to really understand the "why's" and possible results of such behavior.

Sans Institute points us some crucial keys for system's administrators (Baker, 2001). Educating end users is not easy and often requires good social skills so these professionals really need to understand that security, policies and good practices affect the organization and, for obvious reasons, affect them. Not only "technological" threats must be taken into account. Kevin Mitnick, one of the most renowned hackers, did most of his work through social engineering (Baker, 2001). System's administrators must know their organizational reality and have the conscience that technical and social skills are part of their job. There are database administrators, Windows administrators, Linux administrators, helpdesk staff, monitoring staff, security staff, etc. so in this first chapter we are more focused defining this evolution knowing the problems, challenges and "must have's" of these IT Professionals more than discuss specific technological "solutions" like if you should use Windows or Linux servers, if Nagios is the best Infrastructure Monitoring platform or not, what are the best network architecture for a certain reality and so on but there are some "technological factors" that a system's administrator must take into consideration.

No single company is willing to do bad calculations about network and system designs so to best design any service system's administrators must understand how it works and, if necessary, consider the best way to scale it across multiple locations and machines. On the other side, load testing lets the IT staff knowing specifically how the system reacts on very specific conditions depending on what kind of service they are deploying. It would be a good policy to question vendor's predictions about equipment and system performance. For the best IT practices, International Organization for Standardization (ISO) suggests functional areas to best perform on any IT infrastructure. Fault Management is the process of identifying and correcting network problems (Cisco, 2012). Faults typically manifest themselves with errors transmission or hardware failures and result in unexpected downtime, performance degradation or loss of data. Understandably, this is the most important area of network management. On the other side, configuration management is a process related to the startup, shutdown and modification. Networks and systems are constantly adjusted when they are added, removed, reconfigured or updated. For this process to be led successfully system's administrator needs topological information about the network, information on device configuration and control of network components. Also performance management involves measuring the performance of a network and its resources in terms of utilization, throughput, error rates and response times. With this information the administrator can reduce and / or prevent overcrowding and inaccessibility of the network. This monitoring provides qualitative and relevant information and regards the "health" and performance of the devices so the devices can be "rebalanced" according to its degree of utilization. On the other side, accounting management is the process that involves monitoring the use of resources by each user in order to allocate the same usage of your network. This kind of information helps the network administrator to allocate the correct type of resources to users as well as make a correct planning of network growth. This type of management is possible by monitoring login and logout records and by checking the use of the network to determine the use of a certain user. The last point that ISO points us is security management that ensures the overall network security including protecting sensitive information via control points of access to that information. The protection of sensitive data is indeed a mandatory requirement. This process can be successful thanks to a safety management system well designed and implemented.

So, we already presented the evolution of system's administrator roles in the past decades, their need for "management skills", the "educational state of art" and the ability to teach and educate end users to use IT resources. But we have to analyze an important aspect: every system's administrator is different from one to another due the obvious condition of human being. Authors suggest some stereotypes for these IT professionals based on their roles. The installer, the repair person, the hero, etc. these are "funny" descriptions for some types of professionals. As humans we work to and for humans so non-IT personnel often rejects big technological changes as implementing bleeding edge technological solutions because its seen as complicated and commonly unfinished "products" but not only non-IT personnel resists to technology change. Even some system's administrators are happy with their current bandwidth, network topology, current operating system, etc. and this is intrinsically connected to the fact that they feel secure and comfortable with their current systems. In resume system's administrators may play many roles based on organizational, technical and social needs but are always conditioned to their education background, to what kind of end users they have to manage and, obviously, to what kind of high level IT policies are implemented on their organization.

Next, we will present "real-life" situations. Thoughts, issues and suggestions of IT professionals that are on the market trying to best know the "on-job" reality.

EDUCATION, ROLE EVOLUTION AND FUTURE CHALLENGES

Professionals Vision

Depending on many factors such as geographic location, type o industry or education background it is possible to find system's administrators with wide range of role and responsibilities. In order to "take the pulse" of these IT professionals we obtained some of their thoughts. Trying to make it as embracing as possible these system's administrators are from public sectors and also private held companies.

As we presented before the "system's administrators" profession is relatively new and still lacking of some "patterns" on the education background, roles and duties, plus in most countries it is not a regulated activity such as lawyers, doctors or even engineers. In the other side, recognizing the wide array of IT related professions some organizations such as ACM (Association for Computing Machinery) present their "guidelines" such as ethic and deontological codes to IT professionals in general.

We talked with a 22 years experience system's administrator working on a European city council. He points us some interesting points that reaffirm what we discussed on the previous point. Regarding the background education, "back then it wasn't necessary to have any specific degree. We are talking about a hiring system that puts you on a certain career category based on your educational

history. For example, if you were competing for an architect position you needed a degree in architecture, if you were competing for an engineer position you needed a degree in engineering… if you were competing for a system's operator as it was called before you just needed to prove that you knew about computers on a written test."

So, the educational background, in cases like this was ignored and the future professional only needed to prove their knowledge. So how was these staff seen 20 years back? "In the beginning we were only "operators." So any activity that needed a computer such basic stuff as writing a document was our duty. With the career evolution this category was extinct. Eventually some of us became IT Technicians. We were the "fireman's" of the city council. You see, if a computer, printer or other device stopped working we should fix it, if someone didn't know how to work with a certain piece of software we should guarantee that he/she learned how to work with it." Obviously that we are talking about a very specific reality: public sector – city councils. But it's interesting to see how this relates with other literature (see the Additional Reading Section). This people "saw" the birth of "system's administrator" profession. Even if it is way distant from the duties and requirements that nowadays we consider as "the minimum" to have a profession like this. Nowadays computer science related courses have a high degree of attendants being an educational programme that, generally, guarantee a high rate of employability. "(…) people with degrees on computer science working at city councils are a relatively recent fact. With the evolution of computer systems some city councils understood that it would be necessary to have people who developed software to their needs in the staff."

This lead us to discuss the roles and how it was the "division" process between the older "system's operators" and the new "computer scientists" arriving at the scene. Even if we are describing a specific reality this is transversal to public and private sectors: the arriving of high degree IT staff. "The history was: first system's operator then IT technician. Other colleagues are now on the high degree careers where you need a degree in computer science." However the roles are different "some of them are purely programmers developing software solutions regarding the city council needs and it is not a rare situation to verify that they are not very comfortable on networking areas specially if we are talking about juniors, others are "system's administrators". I mean, they manage windows and linux servers, they do scripting to automate tasks, they know about virtualization, about VOiP, they do networking tasks such as configuring routers, firewalls and switches but I would say that the main difference is: they have the big picture. They plan and design all the infrastructure".

Nowadays it is possible to find various "categories" of system's administrators, and interestingly, sometimes they share the same duties and have different educational degrees. An IT Engineer, Datacenter Director at a private held company shares an identical point of view "I've a degree in Electronic and Automation Engineering. I started at the company on the helpdesk giving support to other staff. Eventually the company believed on my potential and started to pay me certification courses. I'm talking about Cisco, Microsoft, BlueCoat, etc. certifications. Today I've more certification courses than the faculty classes I had. I work every day with senior and junior IT Staff and they don't necessarily have a degree on Engineering areas but they all start to do likely the same tasks that I did when I started here." At a first glance it might look that the educational point it's not important but it is a completely wrong idea. "I'm not expecting to teach junior staff to do subnetting, to explain them what is a router or switch or even to explain them how does an e-mail server work." However even from high degree educational levels it is not uncommon to observe the same difficulties between juniors: "I had people who really did not know what is a VLan and they came from technical high school

courses and also from college. I was surprised how could a junior IT Engineer not know these things. They knew how to code in different programming languages, but I always got puzzled on how they could develop software if they didn't know basic concepts of networking and system's administration."

In the previous section, we said that a system's administrator also manages people. This lead us to talk about ethics and how important it is to guarantee it in educational programmes. While information technologies are a great advantage for organizations, accelerating their growth, it can also be a big risk. It also opens doors to the world and valuable information of a certain organization can be reached. Because information is an asset, it makes sense the study of ethics in information technology. The ethics are not just a simple statement of rules of behavior, it is the development of an ethic social function. It is essential that professionals in information technology have a strong sense of moral ethics so the application of their knowledge is as correct as possible. This can be especially critical as our Datacenter Director describes: "We had software that stored user's passwords on its database in plain text. At that time we had a junior system's administrator that had access to this software database. Obviously, that being a corporate software it would not be critical that system's administrators knew user's passwords. The problem was that we didn't have any specific policy for the password constitution and this system administrator tried all these passwords with personal e-mails of our staff, paypal accounts, etc. Eventually he got some matches and did some bad use of it as if it was not bad enough to have this behavior."

The ethics development applied to information technology, addresses the need to establish a social context into a society that is more complex, less secure and more vulnerable. Given the global nature of the Computer Revolution we must think the future of ethics will have a global character. It will be global on a double meaning:

it will embrace the entire globe and will address the totality of actions and human relationships. Possibly, this global ethic would be a computing ethic because it will be originated by the information revolution. This reveals how important it is for future system's administrators and end users to be educated not only technically but also regarding the ethic problematic. Fortunately, based on a study made by the *San Sebastian* University in Spain, students feel that "ethic training" is essential in the line of computer training. These students also differentiate between legal aspects and ethical aspects indicating that the most does not prefixes the legal aspects to the knowledge of ethical aspects. Regarding the same study only 26% of respondents did not recognize advantages on an "ethical behavior."

We already talked about the roles and responsibilities, the educational background of these professionals but we did not explained the "confusion" about the designation or, if you prefer, the title. Industry players as CISCO, Microsoft, HP, etc. have certificate programmes that everyone can attend to be "certified" on a certain technology. There are some well-known certifications in the industry as the CCNA or MCSE but the way how IT Managers see it may be changing. Obviously that assuring that someone has the knowledge on a certain technology is important but we had the chance to ask a Technical Coordinator from a service provider IT company and "it is not everything. As partners of certain manufacturers we have benefits to have a number of our IT staff certified. First of all, if your company is a service provider this certifications give you credibility among your costumers and it is not uncommon that a costumer prefer a team constituted by IT Certified professionals instead of professionals with a high educational degree. If they mix the two together, better. If not they prefer the certified ones" however this is not just a knowledge factor because "there are benefits having your IT Staff certified, for example because the free licenses that manufacturers offer". Back in 2005

the Quebec Court of Appeal denied the Microsoft motion regarding the use of "Engineer" title between MCSE certified staff. The Superior Court decided that only engineers, members of Ordre d'ingenieurs could use the title. Microsoft suggested partners to use the acronym instead. This situation shows an interesting fact: given the multiple IT Professions it is sometimes hard to give a title or description to it. The Datacenter director explains that "I'm an Engineer because I've a degree on Engineering. But often you hear people presenting themselves as IT Engineers without having completed High School. I really don't care about titles but most on people knowledge and attitude. However I recognize that higher level studies are very "programming-centric" and there's a lack of College programmes for System's / Network Administrators."

This vision goes the same way of some master courses in Europe like in Oslo University College where students can attend to the Master programme in Network and System Administration recognizing that today, system administration is normally learned without any systematic training. It is passed on randomly, rather than being taught systematically. This is slowly changing, but the courses available are still mainly product specific certifications sold by companies with a vested interest in their products.

About the future of system's administrators we have got some different visions. As you may have noticed we have been describing the education and role evolution almost on the first person and confronting it with other data as studies or manufacturer's issues. Regarding the future of system's administrators and the so-called cloud "one of the most important administrative tasks will be managing Internet bandwidth and connectivity. If everything is running in the cloud, then a saturated Internet connection could prove to be catastrophic. As such, I expect traffic shaping and prioritization to become an important skill for IT pros. Of course, if you practiced shaping traffic to the rhythm of Beethoven's Ninth, then you're already well on your way to success" (Simple Talk, 2011). Obviously, it is not possible to ignore the cloud. If we think about small organizations they are already using it. They have storage in the cloud, they have mail in the cloud, Websites are not hosted inside their IT Infrastructure so the future as system's administrator might be changing. We asked our datacenter director and his vision goes on the same way because "if we think about system's administrator as a profession that might exist in every single company I believe that this is changing. I don't see the cloud as a "job quitter" but it might change the roles of system's administrators to something closer to the business management area."

The suggested paradigm would be something "hosted outside" with system's administrators playing a role of strategic decision on what technologies should companies use regarding their needs or requirements more than an "IT geek" taking care of all the servers, all the services, being alert with the status of their storage cluster's or interface's bandwidth. Not that it will cease but IT as a service might be the future since non-IT companies do not want to think about the physical infrastructures but more on what services are being provided independently of the environment.

A new paradigm that is emerging is Bring Your Own Device – BYOD. This is one of the most important trends affecting the corporate world. High-level managers but also general employees want to use their own devices at their job. Personal mobile phones, tablets or laptops are being introduced into the corporate reality. End-users point to this as a productivity and mobility increaser while system and network administrators have to face it as a new challenge. "With BYOD, IT must approach the problem differently. Devices are evolving so rapidly that it is impractical to pre-approve each and every device brand and form-factor. It is also somewhat impractical to expect IT organizations to have the same level of support for each and every device that employees may bring to the workplace" (Cisco, 2012). System's /

network administrators have to take into how they will identify devices on their network but also the person who is using it. On the other hand, though we are talking about employees own devices it would be mandatory to network admins to have the ability to push updates to that devices or even revoke access granting ways of wiping part or all data that is contained on a specific device. But not only employees must be tracked and controlled. Nowadays guests are commonly offered Internet access so access policies and properly network design must be assure to grand that each user or group of users only access to the resources that it is supposed. Plus, with these all new devices "you need to ensure your Wireless LAN (WLAN) infrastructure can support growing numbers of mobile devices and bandwidth-hungry, delay-sensitive applications, while delivering predictable connectivity and service levels, and high quality of experience (QoE)" (HP, 2013).

Solutions and Recommendations

Taking into account our last section, system's administrators have some tools that improve their day to day activity. Beginning with the management area, we said before that system's administrators should manage themselves, other users and the implemented technology. Frameworks like COBIT or ITIL helps the organization to align their business with their IT. The ITIL emerged after the recognition of organizations from their dependence on IT to achieve the fulfillment of its objectives (Oracle, 2009). This growth stems from the growing need for IT services in the quality area that helps to achieve the customer's objectives and expectations. Service management is directed at both the supply chain and support of its IT services. Here ITIL, which was created as a set of best practices of systematic and consistent operations, takes its role. ITIL provides a working basis for all activities of an IT department, integrates itself as part of a service provisioning based on IT department infrastructure. A company with a well-organized IT department not only brings benefits as an infrastructure and more fitting service, but also helps people develop their tasks related to the business more efficiently. The ITIL implementation does not necessarily need to be performed in its full extension, ie the company can establish maturity levels for these implementations (Dias, n.d.). The idea is just that this implementation is not done on a massive scale, but slowly, because as I already mentioned, this type of change will often against the way people perform their tasks.

This work base is divided into processes enabling a mature and efficient basis. Each of these processes covers various tasks of the department, such as service development, management and infrastructure assistance and service providing. Also The COBIT framework was created with a strong focus on the business, processes and performance measuring (Frank, 2011). It is designed to serve not only IT service providers, users and auditors, but also to serve as a guide for managers. Its main objective is to provide the information that organization needs to achieve its objectives. Cobit applicability areas are the focus on IT governance, plan alignment, strategy and IT. IT has to be prepared for any business requirement guaranteeing business evolution and continuity. This strategic alignment has the objective of gathering value to services and products of the company, helping the competitive positioning and aiding the costs optimization (Pereira & Neves, 2010). These frameworks work as a strong point of management and information control. Implementing these frameworks in an organization should be a considered and wade decision because of its extensiveness, complexity and because the process is quite expensive. Many organizations fail to implement the projects as ITIL or COBIT (Custy, n.d.). This happens because these frameworks refer to what organizations should do, but does not say how they should implement. There are many reasons for these implementations to fail. Reasons such as resistance to change, or-

ganizational culture and business alignment are factors to be taken into account in the process of implementing any of these guidelines and not only system administrators play an important role but also every IT System user (Custy, n.d.). It's recommended that system's administrators may have training on these frameworks as it will contribute for the alignment with business goals and, at the same time, improve IT processes as well assuring that tasks will be measurable and controllable.

Taking into account the BYOD paradigm, different organizations might adopt different scenarios from the total limitation of "strange" devices into the organization to a clear embrace of devices and resources. To grant a smooth BYOD implementation the focus should be the architecture. Organizations and system's / network administrators have to analyze the deepness of integration. Cisco suggest three different approaches: native where "applications running on the device communicate directly with the application server in the host data center (or cloud)", native device experience is provided, maximum performance is granted and data is local. Browser architecture where "any device with a standard HTML browser capability can be used to access the application. The disadvantages are that much like native mode, data may be exchanged and stored directly on the BYOD device" and finally a completely virtualized architecture where end-users would not have any corporate data on their devices, granting the maximum security but might be compromised due to the lack of the native OS being and obstacle to end-users. This decision of what kind of architecture must be used should be deeply analyzed by the IT Teams regarding the corporate policies. There are no perfect solution to BYOD implementation since it must be adequate to every reality (Cisco, 2012).

On the technical field, in order to create systems to support network management, network management software manufacturers developed complete information systems taking into account the network environment to manage. Designed for exclusive use of the systems management, manufacturers soaked their information systems into the network management applications itself, as if the generated information wasn't important *per se* but only into a complete suite. System's administrators would benefit from this software implementation. Examples of it would be Nagios a complete network management suite, highly configurable and with a strong community of users using it (Koira & Soidridine, 2012). On the other side, software like Spiceworks, take the network management to complete helpdesk, buy management and internal portal suite (Spiceworks, n.d.). Others such as Cacti are very specific, as in this case the main goal is to observe bandwidth utilization though it is possible to improve these applications with external plugins or own development. A great plus for the organization is the fact that, these software are mainly freeware and, in some cases, open source providing a great opportunity to minimize costs. The increasing dependence of multiple domains of management and multiple network service providers have been forcing management applications manufacturers to rethink their strategies in order to respond to their customers. Long-term scalability, flexibility, ability to accommodate new devices and high level of integration are main goal of these suites. Aiding the everyday tasks system's administrators may also use other tools to provide a better service. From ticketing platforms such as osTicket, FusionTicket or GLPI or JIRA all of them free and with different capabilities such as scalability, high level of integration and network inventory. These are mainly integrated systems with centralized ticket repository and automated processes that logs every inquiry and streamlines support workflow ensuring Service Level Agreement - SLA is met. The advantage of these solutions are the possibility of the avoidance of email management, in other works, centralizing all support issues on one platform enhances the response speed and the issues tracking on the other hang it permits

to keep the track of the communication with the costumer which is very benefic in organizations with multiple helpdesk operators. Finally the time management that these platforms allow are very important taking into consideration the correct SLA dates accomplishment, the efficient resource management and the possibility to assign similar answers to identical problems (Webhosting Help Guy, n.d.). Many of these tools integrate knowledge base modules and this is very important to keep monitoring IT knowledge and projects and in this field wiki platforms may be a great add-on to the organization such as Plone, MediaWiki, Joomla, etc.

FUTURE RESEARCH DIRECTIONS

To provide the best background to future system's administrators from the technical field to the management field it will be necessary that colleges understand the opportunity of this unexplored field at that level. Burges and Koymans (2007) defends that the students that are typically attracted by the Network and System Administration programme in Holland are the ones who are looking for a way to work with computers that is not about programming and have rarely any background in UNIX systems. It would take some time and some programmes to study this profile but it is interesting to note that the educational path is somewhat disconnected regarding the profession and has a high level of fragmentation. Starting from the education prism we have a whole branch of research directions from the ethics topic to the implementation of Information Technology Service Management that sometimes is considered a high level management tool and is slightly forgotten on more technical programmes. It would be important to organizations / colleges to study the new trends of system's administration trough market and industry studies regarding the possible new paradigms such as the cloud and how this may influence the common roles of system's administrators and their organizations. System and Network administration is an "unexplored world" comparing it with the maturity of other computer science fields. Taking into consideration our chapter, future research on this area should embrace not only the technical paradigms and tools but also the business management and people management state of art to provide a sustained background based on the duties, roles and challenges that we discussed.

Obviously, we are not forgetting the educational field. As discussed before this is the foundation of system's administrator's knowledge though the path is not clear enough, at least on college programmes. It would be necessary for these institutions to design new programmes regarding the specificities of the profession. Manufacturers certification courses are a good starting point and exploring the weaknesses of it would contribute to build up new college degrees regarding system and network administration. Other factors such as the approximation of companies to the college courses providing internship opportunities, promoting projects that might embrace both academic and business areas simply contributing to better construct programmes based on the industry necessities. It would be interesting to promote studies that could allow a better analysis on how little internships along the Bachelor of Arts or Master's Degrees can be more productive than a massive internship at the end of these courses from the knowledge acquirement point of view.

CONCLUSION

System administration roles changed through the past decades. From the "geek" and sometimes unqualified professional nowadays we have a whole branch of IT professions, being highly specialized and with educational paths mainly rolled out by manufacturers. The complexity has been increasing with the dependency of organizations on IT assets. Non-IT companies has their business based on other objectives rather the technological ones even if it is dependent from each other. System's administrators must realize that their role and technological decisions must be based on the organizational business goals and not the technology *per se*. The future may reserve challenges regarding the cloud and it is changing the way how companies understand their infrastructures and their needs: human and technological.

Computer networks are an extremely important asset of communication in modern society. On businesses and governments, much of the information and transactions are taken using computer networks, particularly the Internet, as a means of communication. Currently, the cloud is so fundamental that most users already consider computers as mere access equipment. In fact, networks have become part of everyday life for many areas of modern life so system's administrators must understand the security, performance, configuration and business alignment issues.

Even if the educational path is not truly defined as other computer science fields it should start from the "official" educational programmes such as colleges. This will lead the new professionals to a better background regarding the emerging needs without invalidating specific technologies and manufacturers certifications paths. From daily basis point of view system's administrators has tools that help the monitor, control and document the entire IT department activity which will embrace business processes and good practices sustained by IT management standards. This chapter tried to give an overview through system's administration field regarding the past, the present and the future "giving the word" to some IT professionals and relating it with industry issues. The future may pass through a more analytical and "scientific" approach when all the industry and educational fields converge to a more accurate path on how this IT staff is trained and align to.

REFERENCES

Anderson, N. (2012). *Cisco bring your own device - Device freedom without compromising the IT network*. Cisco.

Aytes, K., & Connolly, T. (2004). Computer security and risky computing practices: A rational choice perspective. *Journal of Organizational and End User Computing, 16*(3), 22–40. doi:10.4018/joeuc.2004070102.

Baker, B. (2001). *Security education for users: A starting place for network administrators*. SANS Institute InfoSec Reading Room.

Burgess, M., & Koymans, K. (2007). *Master education programmes in network and system*. Paper presented at 21st Large Installation System Administration Conference, LISA 2007. Dallas, TX.

Cisco. (n.d.). *Network management system: Best practices white paper*. Retrieved October 24, 2012, from http://www.cisco.com/en/US/tech/tk869/tk769/technologies_white_paper-09186a00800aea9c.shtml

Custy, J. (n.d.). *Practical IT service management: Rapid ITIL without compromise*.

Dias, R. (n.d.). Aplicações do ITIL. *TechNet Blogs*. Retrieved November 23, 2012, from http://blogs.technet.com/b/rodias/archive/2007/03/05/aplica-ccedil-otilde-es-do-itil.aspx

Frank, S. (2011). IT organization assessment—Using COBIT and BSC. *Cobit Focus, 1*.

Howe, A., Ray, I., Roberts, M., Urbanska, M., & Byrne, Z. (2012). The psychology of security for the home computer user. In *Proceedings of IEEE Symposium on Security and Privacy*. IEEE.

HP. (2013). *Unleash the full potential of BYOD with confidence*. HP.

Imoniana, J. (2006). Workability of a management control model in service organizations: A comparative study on reactive, proactive and coactive philosophies. *Journal of Information Systems and Technology Management, 3*(1), 35–52. doi:10.4301/S1807-17752006000100003.

Kichel, M. (n.d.). *Administração de sistemas de informação I*. Retrieved November 11, 2012, from http://d.yimg.com/kq/groups/22104202/1070702132/name/SI01+-+Conceitos+Basicos.PDF

Kora, A., & Soidridine, M. (2012). Nagios based enhanced IT management system. *International Journal of Engineering Science and Technology, 4*(3), 1199–1207.

Network Administrators Past, Present, and Future. (2011). *Simple talk: SQL server and. net articles, forums and blogs*. Retrieved November 7, 2012, from http://www.simple-talk.com/sysadmin/general/network-administrators-past,-present,-and-future/

Oracle. (2009). *ITIL best practices with oracle enterprise manager 10g and oracle siebel help desk*. Oracle.

Patterson, D. (n.d.). *I/O 2: Failure terminology, examples, gray paper and a little queueing theory*. Retrieved November 3, from http://www.cs.berkeley.edu/~pattrsn/252S01/Lec06-IO2.pdf

Pereira, M., & Neves, R. (2010). *Aplicação do cobit em empresas de médio porte*.

Rodrigues, R. (2010). *Integração das ferramentas nagios e cacti como solução de monitoramento de recursos computacionais em redes*.

Sata Technologies. (2011). *Reactive versus proactive management*. Sata Technologies.

SOPHOS. (2012). *Sophos survey reveals need for IT security education within organizations: Antivirus, endpoint, disk encryption, mobile, UTM, email and web security.* Retrieved November 1, 2012, from http://www.sophos.com/en-us/press-office/press-releases/2012/04/sophos-survey-reveals-need-for-it-security-education-within-organizations.aspx

Spiceworks. (n.d.). *Free help desk software, help-desk support & help ticket tools from spiceworks.* Retrieved October 24, 2012, from http://www.spiceworks.com/free-help-desk-software/

Stoneburner, G., Goguen, A., & Feringa, A. (2012). *Risk management guide for information technology - Recommendations of the national institute of standards and technology.*

Webhosting Help Guy. (n.d.). *Support ticket systems: 5 tools for managing customer support.* Retrieved November 23, 2012, from http://Webhostinghelpguy.inmotionhosting.com/Website-optimization/support-ticket-systems-5-tools-for-managing-customer-support/

ADDITIONAL READING

Ahmad, I., & Ranka, S. (2012). *Handbook of energy-aware and green computing.* Boca Raton, FL: Chapman & Hall/CRC.

Burgess, M. (2003). On the theory of system administration. *Science of Computer Programming, 49*(1).

Campi, N., Bauer, K., & Bauer, K. (2009). *Automating linux and UNIX system administration.* Berkeley, CA: Apress.

Collings, T. (2005). *Red hat linux networking and system administration.* Indianapolis, IN: Wiley.

Deutscher, J.-H., & Felden, C. (2010). Concept for implementation of cost effective information technology service management (ITSM) in organizations. In *Proceedings of the IEEE/IFIP Network Operations and Management Symposium Workshops,* (pp. 167-168). IEEE.

Easttom, C. (2006). *Computer security fundamentals.* Upper Saddle River, NJ: Pearson Prentice Hall.

Esmaili, H., Gardesh, H., & Sikari, S. (2010). *Strategic alignment: ITIL perspective.* Paper presented in 2010 2nd International Conference on Computer Technology and Development. New York, NY.

Farrokhi, B., Bogorodskiy, R., & Pradeep, D. (2008). *Network administration with FreeBSD 7: Building, securing, and maintaining networks with the FreeBSD operating system.* Birmingham, UK: Packt Pub..

Hall, A. (2003). *Managing people.* Maidenhead, UK: Open University Press.

Hoe, A., Ray, I., Roberts, M., & Urbanska, M. (2012). *The psychology of security for the home computer user.* Paper presented at 2012 IEEE Symposium on Security and Privacy. San Francisco, CA.

Institute for Career Research. (2005). *Career as a computer network architect administrator: Connecting computers within an office and around the world.* Chicago, IL: Institute for Career Research.

Institute for Career Research. (2009). *Careers in computer network administration.* Chicago, IL: Institute for Career Research.

IT Governance Institute. (2007). *COBIT 4.1.* Rolling Meadows, IL: IT Governance Institute.

Klosterboer, L. (2008). *Implementing ITIL configuration management.* Upper Saddle River, NJ: IBM Press.

LaRose, R., Rifon, N., Liu, X., & Lee, D. (2005). *Understanding online safety behavior: A multivariate model.* Paper presented at the International Communication Association, Communication and Technology Division. New York, NY.

Limoncelli, T., Hogan, C. J., & Chalup, S. R. (2007). *The practice of system and network administration.* Upper Saddle River, NJ: Addison-Wesley.

Long, J. O. (2008). *ITIL version 3 at a glance.* New York: Springer.

Moisand, D., Garnier, L., & Lambert, D. (2010). *CobiT.* Paris: Eyrolles.

National Learning Corporation. (2006). *Network administrator.* Syosset, NY: National Learning Corp..

Orebaugh, A., & Pinkard, B. (2008). *Nmap in the enterprise: Your guide to network scanning.* Burlington, MA: Syngress Pub..

SANS Institute. (2001). *Security education for users: A starting place for network administrators.* Retrieved November 5, 2012, from http://www.sans.org/reading_room/whitepapers/infosec/security-education-users-starting-place-network-administrators_600

Stoneburner, G., Goguen, A., & Feringa, A. (2002). Risk management guide for information technology systems (Nist special publication 800–830). Washington, DC: National Institute of Standard Technology.

Valade, J. (2005). *In linux.* Upper Saddle River, NJ: Addison-Wesley.

KEY TERMS AND DEFINITIONS

Information Technology Service Management: Array of processes and guidelines that aim to enable IT services satisfying business requirements and aligning it with organizational goals.

Network Management System: System that is constituted by software and hardware which the main goal is to provide information about an IT infrastructure monitoring its assists.

Service Level Agreement: Level of service that is part of a certain service contract (i.e. time to respond to an IT Issue).

Ticketing System: Software that allows to manage a helpdesk providing control about SLA, resource management and customer relationship.

Chapter 2
Trust Management and Delegation for the Administration of Web Services

Michele Tomaiuolo
University of Parma, Italy

ABSTRACT

The availability and adoption of open protocols allow applications to integrate Web services offered by different providers. Moreover, simple services can be dynamically composed to accomplish more complex tasks. This implies the delegation of both tasks and permissions. In fact, delegation is intertwined with some notion of risk, on the one hand, and trust, on the other hand. Well founded socio-cognitive models of trust may orient managers and system administrators to delegate tasks and goals to the most trusted entities, after conscious evaluation of risks and gains associated with the decision. This chapter presents different mechanisms and models that have been proposed for establishing secure delegations in open environments. They include Role-Based Access Control, Trust Management, and Federated Identity. Complex frameworks and live systems have been realized according to these models. However, their administration remain a challenging task. Ongoing research works in various fields, such as Automated Trust Negotiation, promise to simplify the practical realization and configuration of delegation-based systems.

1. INTRODUCTION

The adoption of a Service-Oriented Architecture based on Web services has definitely many benefits, above all from the point of view of interoperability among diverse systems. Web services offer a paradigm based on self-contained components, with a public description of their interface. Thus, modular applications can be developed on the basis of services hosted on the Internet and invoked though open standard protocols. This way, it is possible to select and compose services at runtime, crossing boundaries among underlying technologies and among organizations. Consequently, the

DOI: 10.4018/978-1-4666-4526-4.ch002

number of platforms hosting and providing open services is growing, together with the number of systems developed through the composition of simpler services. Through service composition, applications can combine simpler services together in order to provide a certain useful functionality, even if no single Web service can satisfy the functionality by itself.

This trend has triggered several initiatives, platforms and languages to simplify the integration of existing heterogeneous systems. Despite all the efforts, however, the realization of service composition through manual configuration is still a challenging task, for both systems developers and system administrators.

The service composition problem becomes more complex when the use of workflows involves many layers of services. In this scenario, at each level an agent is responsible for managing its workflow. It can possibly subdivide its complex task into sub-tasks and set up a negotiation process with some agents responsible for the execution of simpler Web services. From the perspective of this example, two main abstract roles can be distinguished: the Service Manager and the Workflow Manager. In a typical peer-to-peer architecture, each agent can play different roles at different times. Each Service Manager is associated to one or more Web services and is responsible for the interaction with them. The Workflow Manager has the goal of supporting its user in the process of building a workflow, composing external Web services and monitoring their execution. The Workflow Manager assumes the role of the delegate agent in a delegation protocol.

However, the dynamic composition of services provided by many different sources can be a cumbersome task. Therefore, the aid of software tools is critical for building composite Web services. Efforts for realizing automated or semi-automated workflow composition have been conducted in different branches of artificial intelligence, including planning and theorem proving. Those efforts generally assume that the description of each Web service includes its preconditions and postconditions. Thus, it is theoretically possible to compose a number of services, in such a way to satisfy the final user's own constraints and goals. Being the service descriptions public, this process of dynamic composition of services can also be automated, even without a precise preconfigured workflow. Preconditions play the role of local constraints for the planning process.

It's easy to see that the problem of service composition in dynamic and open environments is quite complex. However, matching explicit preconditions and effects may represent only a part of the problem. Particular attention has also to be devolved to the management of delegation chains and underlying trust relations, which often remain implicit. In fact, apart from the formal correspondence of preconditions and effects with final requirements, it is important to acknowledge the aspects of security and trust. In the end, the delegation of tasks and goals cannot come into effect unless it is associated with a corresponding delegation of privileges, for accessing needed resources and completing assigned tasks.

This chapter describes the advantages and issues related to the use of delegation in the composition of Web services. The "Background" section starts with a brief description of protocols for REST-style and SOAP-style Web services. Though they provide mechanisms for service composition, some analysis is always required for determining trust relations, which need to be at the basis of delegation decisions. For managers and system administrators, it is important to delegate tasks and goals to trusted partners, evaluating risks and gains of each decision. Socio-cognitive models of trust can be used to better evaluate and construct such relations.

The following section deals with "Delegation Models and Systems". It describes the main models of integration of security policies and mechanisms defined in different domains, including Role Based Access Control, Trust Management and Federated Identity. Then some major systems based on delegation of access rights are discussed. A case study is presented in greater detail, regarding the development of a delegation library for Web services.

In this rapidly evolving context, some aspects are object of ongoing research. They are described in the "Future Research Directions" section. Among the most promising fields, which may simplify the practical realization of delegation-based systems, Automated Trust Negotiation certainly deserves the attention of developers and administrators. Oblivious Attribute Certificates and other cryptographic techniques may greatly improve such negotiations, since they can be used to develop trust reciprocally, without disclosing sensitive attributes.

Finally, some concluding remarks are provided, about the status of the field and the open challenges for system administrators.

2. BACKGROUND

The benefits of Web services, and Service Oriented Architectures in general, are well known. In particular, the adherence to open protocols greatly improves the interoperability among diverse systems. The popularity of service-based systems is intertwined with the growing trend toward Cloud Computing, which basically considers computing and storage capabilities as a commodity. Both trends guide towards more simplified and efficient data exchange and system integration activities. Also, both the service-based componentization of business applications, and the availability of scalable computing platforms, push organizations to adopt the most effective solution for each block in the workflow of the whole system.

With regard to security, a lot of efforts have been devoted to develop adequate standards by various organizations such as W3C, WS-I, OASIS, etc. A basic way of achieving security for Web services is relying on a secure transport layer, typically HTTPS and TLS. However, a message-level security is required in the case of architectures in which intermediaries can manipulate messages on their way. This was the rationale for the definition of new specifications, such as WS-Security. By using the XML-signature and XML-encryption specifications, WS-Security defines a standard way to secure SOAP messages, independently from the underlying transport protocol. As far as the REST-style is concerned, the security model is not as highly-developed as the security model for SOAP. The administration of individual Web services requires the configuration of security mechanisms at various levels, possibly including TLS, WSDL and WS-Policy.

Nevertheless, both in the REST-style and SOAP-style Web services, the focus is on individual Web services. In the context of a Service-Oriented Architecture, the access issues in composed services or in the presence of intermediaries between the requesters and the resources still deserve more consideration. In such complex cases, the careful management of the delegation flow is one of the main challenges for system administrators.

While the management of delegation decisions may require configuring security policies and issuing appropriate certificates and security tokens, the delegation process at its roots needs to be founded on an explicit model of trust. In fact, open systems can be described as environments where independent entities cooperate or compete, each one persecuting its own different interests, yet collaborating to achieve common goals. In this context, the delegation of goals and tasks is a key concept. But delegation is usually associated with a risk. And the decision of facing this risk is necessarily related to some form of trust.

Trust is an important aspect of human life, and it has been studied under different points of view, for example in the context of psychological and sociological sciences, or to draw specific economical models. Both Luhmann (1979) and Barber (1959), just to take two famous examples, analyze trust as a social phenomenon. In particular, Luhmann argues that trust is a fundamental instrument to simplify life in human society, ending with the idea that human societies can exist only on the base of trust. Barber associates the idea of trust with some expectations about the future: about the persistence of social rules, about the technical competence of the partners, and about the intention of the partner of carrying out their duties, placing others' interests before their own.

On the other side, other researchers analyze trust mainly in its psychological forms. Deutsch (1962) describes trust in terms of personal beliefs and perceived/expected benefits.

Gambetta (2000) is the first to give a definition of trust which is more grounded in mathematics, as a "subjective probability with which an agent assesses that another agent or a group of agents will perform a particular action…." This definition appears more useful than the previous ones in the context of computer systems. In fact it is founded on the mathematical concept of "probability," and this makes trust a quantifiable concept.

Yet, as Castelfranchi and Falcone (2001) argue, the definition of trust as a "subjective probability" hides too many important details, thus being too vague to be applied in real cases. Instead, they present trust using a socio-cognitive approach, providing a deep analysis of a party's believes, and the way they can influence trust. In particular, they list the beliefs about competence, disposition, dependence and fulfillment as important components of trust in every delegation, even towards non-cognitive software service providers. Instead, delegation towards people, organizations and social entities requires the delegating entity to hold additional believes about willingness, persistence and self-confidence of the partner, at least about the specific domain of the delegation.

Then, using the socio-cognitive approach, trust can be evaluated as a continuous function of its constituents (Castelfranchi & Falcone, 2003), more precisely of the certainty of its constituent beliefs. But, though trust is a continuous function, the decision to delegate is necessarily discontinuous in its nature. The delegating entity can just decide to delegate or do not delegate, and this decision has to take into account not only the degree of trust, but even other factors. These factors, including the importance of the goal, the perceived risk of frustrating the goal, the increased dependence on the trustee, and all other costs or possible damages associated with the delegation, will all influence a threshold function which will be eventually compared with the degree of trust for deciding whether to delegate or not.

Following this approach, security is deeply intertwined with both the degree of trust and the threshold function. In fact, security can certainly influence positively the trust on the partner, especially if security includes auditing mechanisms, certifications and confidentiality at the transport layer, which can help to associate a principal with its own actions and social behaviors. An even stronger degree of trust can be achieved when social interactions are founded on "contracts", i.e. signed documents that will make some party responsible for its own actions against an authority, a trusted third party able to issue norms, and to control and punish violations.

On the other hand, security mechanisms can be useful to limit the costs of a failed delegation. For example, delegation often comes in the twofold aspect of delegation of duties (performing actions or achieving goals), and delegation of corresponding permissions (rights to access the needed resources). In this case authorization mechanisms can be used to grant to the delegated entity only a limited number of access rights to valuable resources, thus limiting the damage that could be received from a misbehaving partner. In this way, security can be useful to reduce the threshold, and thus it can make delegation possible in a larger number of cases.

Moreover, when proper authorization mechanisms are available, delegation can be modulated according to the degree of trust, starting from the delegation of a single action, granting only the smallest set of strictly needed access rights, up to the delegation of a full goal, without specifying a plan or some needed actions to achieve it, and providing access to the largest set of available resources.

3. DELEGATION MODELS AND SYSTEMS

This section presents various systems allowing delegation of access rights for easing the tasks of system administrators, especially when authorization issues cross organizational boundaries.

In fact, cooperation and agreements among companies and institutions are making virtual organizations both a reality and a necessity. But they'll never spring into success if existing technologies will not match their needs. Particularly in the case of knowledge-based organizations, the continuous production of valued information poses a heavy burden on system administrators, who have to deal with security issues at an increasing pace. A centralized approach to the administration of system security can hardly scale to the most complex and dynamic settings.

Delegation of authorization to local resource managers can instead help to manage the complexity of the whole administration job. On the one hand, delegation can be used to empower directly interested people in securing the sub-systems they rely on and they know better. On the other hand, it can reduce the scope of a possible breech due to a policy misconfiguration or a violation due to a user's malicious behavior.

Yet, the principle of delegation is not new and it is not a silver bullet, by itself. In fact, the interoperation among diverse mechanisms and policies has usually to overcome a number of serious issues. Those include technology mismatches, possibly caused by syntactic or semantic differences among policy and access control systems. Moreover, the heterogeneity often emerges from different underlying resource management and business

models, and their background of culture, strategy and vision. Thus, at the very least, delegation among diverse security realms needs a common set of protocols and mediation mechanisms to overcome the heterogeneity of existing policies and mechanisms, without ambiguity.

Since reimplementing all existing security infrastructures is often undesirable or simply infeasible, federated security is nowadays considered the key to build global security infrastructures, integrating already deployed security systems. This way, users are not obliged to adopt some out of the box solution for their particular security issues, to rebuild the whole system or to make it dependent upon some global authority, for gaining interoperability with others. Instead, they are provided with means to manage the trust relations they build with other entities operating in the same, global environment. In particular, the idea at the basis of Trust Management is to make systems interoperate in the virtual world, just in the same manner as people collaborate in the real world, i.e. on basis of evolving trust relations.

This section provides an overview of some attempts in this direction, including distributed Role- and Attribute-Based Access Control, Trust Management principles, security protocols for the federation of the information systems of different organizations. The analysis of those systems is accompanied by hints about the practice of their administration, especially in the context of a Service Oriented Architecture.

3.1. RBAC Model

For the administration of open and interconnected systems, delegation is a requirement. In fact, a system administrator is not necessarily entitled to know the internal structure and roles of a partner organization. In any case, it is difficult to propagate information about people involved in a certain project timely and across organizational boundaries. It is often more convenient to leave the duty of assigning local roles and access rights for local resources to a local system administrator, instead of relying on centralized and remote administration.

A widely accepted scheme defines authorization in terms of Role-Based Access Control (RBAC) (Sandhu, Coyne, Feinstein, & Youman, 1996). In this scheme, which is quite conventional nowadays, permissions are not assigned directly to users, but to roles. Those roles are then assigned to users, according to their tasks. Hence users acquire their own permissions indirectly, as they are associated to assigned roles. This level of indirection separates the assignment of permissions to roles, and of roles to users. Thus, it eases the management of access control by system administrators.

There are many variations of RBAC in the literature, but typically roles are structured hierarchically, with senior roles being at higher level than junior roles and thus extending their set of access rights. A basic RBAC model, often called RBAC96, is introduced by Sandhu et al. (Sandhu, Coyne, Feinstein & Youman, 1996). A RBAC infrastructure based on X.509 is proposed by Chadwick et al. (2003). It stores a user's roles into an attribute certificate. Among the systems aimed at the protection of Web services, X-RBAC is developed by Bhatti et al. as a framework for the specification of access control policies based on XML. Another role-based access control system for Web services is proposed by Feng et al. (2004), as an extension to RBAC96. These systems can be used to define policies specifically for complex scenarios. Nevertheless, practice has demonstrated that administration of large and distributed systems through a Role-Based Access Control (RBAC) approach may remain a challenging task (Ferraiolo, Kuhn & Chandramouli, 2007).

Various alternatives, designed for use in larger systems, are defined as distributed extensions to RBAC (dRBAC). Other systems, based on Attribute-Based Access Control (ABAC), assign attributes to users, which can be certified by specific authorities and later verified against access control policies. These alternatives often use the idea of delegation of access rights (Bandmann, Dam & Firozabadi, 2002) for making the duties of systems administrators more manageable. In fact, delegation can subdivide and decentralize access control tasks among various entities. Delegation has been applied to a wide range of applications and it is often considered as an effective mechanism to enhance the scalability of a distributed system. Related to RBAC, a role-based delegation mechanism is described by Na and Cheon (2000). Another mechanism for role delegation is proposed by Zhang et al. (2001), as an extension to the RBAC96 model called RDM2000.

Freudenthal et al. (2002) argue that dRBAC should add some new features to previous approaches:

- Third-Party delegations allow some entities to delegate roles in different namespaces. This mechanism, related to the "speaks for" relationship in the Taos system, does not add any new functionality, as the same results can be obtained using anonymous intermediate roles, but improves the expressiveness and manageability of the system;
- Valued attributes allow authorities to add attributes and corresponding numeric values to roles. This way, access rights for sensible resources can be modulated according to some attributes. The same result could be obtained by defining different roles for different levels of access rights, but this would multiply the number of needed roles;
- Finally, continuous monitoring is needed, to verify the actuality of trust relationships. Typically, this feature is based on a pub-

lish/subscribe protocol to advertise the status updates of relevant credentials, which can be either revocable or short-lived.

3.2. Trust Management Model

In contrast with the traditional approach to system security, based on Certification Authorities as trusted third parties, other solutions are possible. Trust Management is a different approach to distributed administration.

In fact, Trust Management (TM) is based on the concept of local trust, local names and delegation of access rights through delegation chains. In particular, in TM systems, the manager of local resources is considered as the ultimate source of trust about them, and it is provided with means to carefully administer the flow of delegated permissions. No a-priori trusted parties are supposed to exist in the system, in general, as this would imply some "obliged choice" of trust for the user, and without choice there is no real trust.

Following the approach of Li, Grosof & Feigenbaum (2000), a generic system can be described as a community of peers, where each node is able to play the role of a controller or a requester. If an entity ultimately controls access to resources, being able to authorize or refuse requests for their usage, it plays the role of a controller; if an entity requests to access resources controlled by other entities, it plays the role of a requester. To have a sound system, all these peers should adhere to the principles of trust management. In (Khare & Rifkin, 1997) these rules of thumb are summarized as:

1. **Be Specific:** "Alice trusts Bob" is a too vague concept; it has to be better quantified in expressions as "Alice trusts Bob to read file.txt in her home directory today";

2. **Trust Yourself:** All trust decisions should be founded on sound, local believes; when possible, trusted third parties should be avoided, especially if their mechanisms and policies are not known;

3. **Be Careful:** Even the best implementation can be violated if users behave superficially and expose reserved data.

Applying these rules requires each service provider to be described as an authority, responsible for protecting its local resources and for managing its trust relations. This modus operandi provides a solid ground for the definition of trust relations among providers and consumers of services.

Distributed RBAC can be realized also on the basis of a TM system, if local names are interpreted as distributed roles (Li, 2000). Distributed authorization mechanisms are especially useful in the case of federated security systems, which can rely on a number of standardized technologies. In the case of Service Oriented Architecture, federation can be realized using various combinations of WS-* specifications, SAML, XACML, OpenID and OAuth.

A number of architectures have been proposed for TM, including the Simple Distributed Security Infrastructure (SDSI) introduced by Rivest and Lampson (1996), and the Simple Public Key Infrastructure (SPKI) introduced by Ellison et al. (1999). They start from the observation that what computer applications often need is not to get the real-life identity of keyholders, but to make decisions about them as users (e.g. to grant access to a protected resource or not). More appropriately, Trust Management systems focus on principals and authorization. In general, a principal is any entity that can be taken accountable for its own actions in the system. In systems relying on asymmetric cryptography, principals could also be said to "*be*" public keys, i.e., if each principal has its own public key, then the principal can be identified directly through its own public key and rights to access system resources can be bound to the same key.

In a typical TM scheme, local names defined by a principal can be used on a global scale, if they are prefixed with the public key (i.e. the principal) defining them (Rivest & Lampson, 1996). Then, each principal can issue a Name Certificate to associate some name (in the issuer's namespace) with its intended meaning (either a public key or another name). A Name Certificate creates a name→subject bound and is defined as a 4-tuple: (issuer, name, subject, validity). There's no limitation to the number of keys which can be made valid meanings for a name. So in the end, a Name Certificate can be used to define a named group of principals. Li, Grosof & Feigenbaum (2003) interpret these named groups of principals as distributed roles, paving the way for a dRBAC (distributed Role-based Access Control) paradigm.

An example of a delegation chain, realized through local name certificates, is shown in Figure 1.

Another basic concept of TM systems is the Authorization Certificate, meant to create a straight authorization→subject bound (Ellison et al., 1999). It is defined as a 5-tuple: (issuer, subject, authorization, delegation, validity). Through an Authorization Certificate, a manager of some resources can delegate a set of access rights to a trusted subject. On its turn, this newly empowered principal can issue other certificates, granting a subset of its access rights to other entities. When finally requesting access to a resource, the whole certificate chain must be presented.

Li, Grosof and Feigenbaum (2003) discuss the importance of Authorization Certificates. Even recognizing that Authorization Certificates can improve the flexibility and granularity in permission handling, authors argue that most use cases can be satisfied by using local names and Name Certificates, only. In their perspective, local names are the distributed counterpart of roles in Role-Based Access Control (RBAC) frameworks. In fact, Name Certificates can be organized in a chain to link local roles, for delegation of access rights. Like roles, local names can be used as a level of indirection between principals and permissions. Both a local name and a role represent at the same time a set of principals, as well as a set of permissions granted to those principals. But, while roles are usually defined in a centralized fashion by a system administrator, local names, instead, are fully decentralized. This way, they better scale to Internet-wide peer-to-peer applications.

3.3. Federated Identity Management

Typical access to Web services on the Internet is controlled on the basis of some identity management. The possibility of Single Sign-On is a further improvement over this basic scheme, since a user can login at a site, and then use services provided at different sites, while preserving security requirements. Identity federation schemes conveniently

Figure 1. A delegation chain: $Role_m$ is granted indirectly from $K_{manager}$ to K_{client}

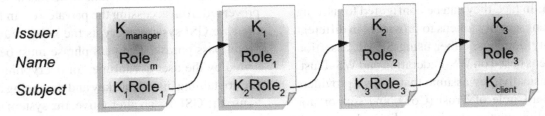

decentralize identity management and login services among various identity providers (Shin, Ahn & Shenoy, 2004). Such federated identity services usually allow trusted service providers, also in different security domains, to verify sensitive attribute and login information about a requester. Thus, a service provider can grant or refuse access to local resources on the basis of a user's status and attributes. For the practical realization of identity federation systems, various standard specifications are available, including SAML (Security Assertion Markup Language) (Hallam-Baker & Maler, 2002), WS-Federation (Hondo, Maruyama, Nadalin & Nagaratnam, 2006) and Liberty ID-FF (Identity Federation Framework). Those standards define how to handle an opaque security token issued to a particular user. Thus, their usage is important for improving interoperability, while preserving a certain level of privacy.

When the overall system architecture include some form of service composition, with providers taking actions on behalf of a user, then providers need to possess and show required access rights. Moreover, these privileges should be associated with a particular session, varying according to the final user's attributes and roles. In such a context, management and delegation of access rights is an indispensable aspect of the system, to control access to final services from intermediaries that must receive and use appropriate privileges from a responsible principal. The cited specifications about identity management depend on a strong assumption of generic "trust" among providers. Instead, they do not detail delegation mechanisms for transferring privileges from a user, behaving as a principal in the system, to an intermediate service provider, accessing some resources on his behalf. In fact, they can be configured for issuing different security tokens to providers in different security domains, either using SAML assertion or tokens based on WS-Federation and WS-Trust. But basically they assume that known providers are in a Circle of Trust (CoT), and support for delegation mechanism is quite limited.

Nevertheless, basic standards for the federation of Web services platforms can pave the way for more complex systems, which may introduce more advanced delegation and distributed RBAC mechanisms. SAML assertions, for example, are very generic and extensible, and can be used to encode delegation of access rights among cooperating parties. These delegations may be orchestrated by some acknowledged and trusted certification authorities, which can sign the appropriate assertions for attesting delegation (Gomi, Hatakeyama, Hosono, & Fujita, 2005), or they can occur in a completely distributed choreography, on the basis of local relations developed according to Trust Management principles. This latest case will be discussed at the end of this section, along with the description of the dDelega library.

3.4. Delegation-Based Systems

Among the examples of security systems allowing the distributed delegation of access rights, it is worth mentioning the Grid Security Infrastructure (GSI), which is the security layer realized for the Globus Toolkit (Welch et al., 2003). Differently from other solutions based on Trust Management, the GSI essentially relies on X.509 Identity Certificates, issued by traditional authorities as trusted third parties. Additionally, GSI introduces X.509 Proxy Certificates as an extension to X.509 Identity Certificates. Those certificates must be signed using a user's own credentials, instead of involving a CA. They allow the issuer to delegate some subset of his rights to some other entity created dynamically. The Globus Toolkit normally stores the user's private key locally, in a file. Other users of the same local machine are prevented from accessing the private key. In fact, the core GSI system encrypts the key through a secret pass phrase. The pass phrase must be inserted by the user at runtime, for decrypting the file containing his private key and thus being able to use the GSI. As an alternative, the system may be configured for using smart cards. This way, a user's private key is not stored in the local file system and it is better protected against unauthorized access from a malicious user. Version 4 of GSI can also be configured for using SAML AuthorizationDecision assertions, in two ways: (*i*) SAML AuthorizationDecision assertions can be issued by the CAS (Community Authorization Service) to communicate the rights of CAS clients to services; (*ii*) the SAML AuthorizationDecision protocol can be used to integrate a third party authorization decision service, such as PERMIS.

PERMIS (PrivilEge and Role Management Infrastructure Standard) is an authorization infrastructure supporting both Role-Based and Attribute-Based Access Control (Chadwick et al., 2008). With PERMIS, administrators assign attributes and roles to users by issuing proper Attribute Certificates. The whole infrastructure also relies on traditional X.509 Certification Authorities for assigning public keys. The administrator of a certain service provider can then use these attributes and roles, for defining the security policies regulating access to local services. The access control for a service is performed by the local PEP (Policy Enforcement Point), which asks a PDP (Policy Decision Point) for the list of required credentials. The PDP is provided as a standalone authorization server. It is a Web Service implemented as a Java based application, running with an embedded Apache Axis2 container. It can be configured to provide different services, including authorization decision, credential validation, obligation enforcement. It handles three protocols: XACML, XACML over SAML, Ws-Trust and SAML. Other components involved in the operation are the CIS (Credential Issuing Service) and the AR (Attribute Repository), from which credentials can be collected. Policies are distinguished as Credential Validation Policies, to define the trusted authorities for each attribute, and Access Control Policy (ACP), to define the access rights associated with each attribute. Mahmud et al. (2010) present a security scenario involving a sensor network in an e-health environment. Security

policies for the e-health scenario are designed and enforced through PERMIS. Policies are based on a classical RBAC model, using X.509 Attribute Certificates and configured as a PMI (Privilege Management Infrastructure).

Shibboleth (Cantor, 2005) is a system for realizing the federation of security infrastructures. Shibboleth has been integrated into other frameworks, including PERMIS and the Globus Toolkit for realizing grid applications. It is deployed at various collaborating institutions, based on SAML formats and protocols. An important feature is the clear separation between (*1*) the authentication process, that is performed by an IdP (Identity Provider) service and assigns some attributes to an acknowledged user, and (*2*) the authorization process, that is performed by service providers on the basis of those proven attributes. This way, it is possible to use Shibbolet for Single Sign On (SSO) among different sites, removing the need to maintain user names and passwords at those sites. Shibboleth is independent of the local authentication mechanisms, though they can be described in SAML assertions and later used for deciding about authorization. A Shibboleth IdP may be configured to use multiple authentication methods at one time. In a request message, a service provider may supply a list of acceptable SAML authentication mechanism. If at least one of those mechanisms is supported by the IdP, then it can be used. If acceptable authentication mechanisms are not specified by the service provider, then the mechanism configured as default is used. To realize the SSO functionalities, the user's session is taken into consideration before other evaluations. If such session exists and its active authentication mechanism matches the requirements of the service provider, then the login handler of the existing session is used. Shibboleth itself does not support the delegation of access rights among users and processes, but it has been integrated into other frameworks, including PERMIS and the Globus Toolkit for realizing grid applications.

A number of other systems have been proposed, especially in the field of Web Services. In fact, access control in Service Oriented Architectures is already becoming an important topic of many recent researches. The various security standards proposed and most of the studies carried out in the context of Web services focus mainly on the access control policies for single Web services (Bhatti, Joshi, Bertino & Ghafoor, 2003; Bertino, Squicciarini, Paloscia & Martino, 2006; Bhargavan, Corin, Fournet & Gordon, 2007). In particular, Bhargavan et al. (2007) address the problem of securing sequences of SOAP messages exchanged between Web services and their clients. By constructing formal models they investigate the security guarantees offered by the WS-Trust and WS-SecureConversation specifications, which provide communicating parties with mechanisms to establish shared security contexts and thus to secure SOAP-based sessions. She, Thuraisingham and Yen (2007) propose a delegation-based security model to address problems such as how much privilege to delegate, how to confirm cross-domain delegation, how to delegate additional privilege. The proposed model extends the basic security models and supports flexible delegation and evaluation-based access control. But all Web services participating in this composition have to agree on a single token-based authorization mechanism, i.e. a hierarchical access control framework is provided. Bussard, Nano & Pinsdorf (2009) present a delegation framework for the delegation of access rights in multi-domain service compositions. The approach is based on an abstraction layer, called abstract delegation, which harmonizes the management of heterogeneous access control mechanisms and offers a unified user experience hiding the details of different access control mechanisms. Other systems, including the case study which will be discussed in the next subsection, follow a different approach. In an open distributed system, in fact, each service

or resource can be considered as a trust domain on its own, and access control may be enforced on the basis of chains of delegation certificates.

3.5. Case Study: dDelega as a Generic Delegation Library

This section discusses the main advantages and the main issues to face for realizing generic security mechanisms for Web services, based on peer-to-peer delegation. In particular, it presents dDelega, a generic security library distributed as open source software (available at https://github.com/tomamic/dDelega). It can be used for issuing and verifying chains of delegation certificates, to eventually associate a particular request for a service with some roles and permissions. At its core, it defines an abstract Certificate class, extended by concrete classes representing Name Certificates, Authorization Certificates and Oblivious Attribute Certificates. Certificates are encoded as SAML assertions, with the possible inclusion of XACML policies, as these languages are expressive, flexible and extensible. SAML and XACML are readily integrated into a Service Oriented Architecture, yet they may serve in different application scenarios. In fact, dDelega is the result of ongoing work started with the development of a security layer for JADE, one the most widespread FIPA-compliant multi-agent systems (Poggi, Tomaiuolo & Vitaglione, 2005).

dRBAC

In TM systems based on asymmetric cryptography, principals can be identified directly by their public key. This may also be obtained in SAML. In fact, being designed to foster interoperability among very different security systems, SAML offers a variety of schemes for creating security assertions. In particular, there are a number of possible ways to represent a subject, including a

SubjectConfirmation object to represent a subject as the holder of a certain public key (which is a principal in a TM system).

One of the main aims of dDelega is to implement a distributed RBAC access control system, along the lines discussed in (Li, 2000). For this purpose, local names are particularly important, as they allow each principal to manage its own name space, which, on the other hand, is also one of the foundations of "federated identity" and SAML. In fact, while it is possible to use X.509 distinguished names with SAML, it also supports a number of other heterogeneous naming schemes. In this sense, its reliance on XML provides intrinsic extendibility through schemas and namespaces.

In dDelega, assigning a local name to a public key, or to a set of public keys, is as simple as defining a role through a SAML assertion. In fact in SAML names and roles are not considered globally unique by design. And also assigning a named principal to a local name, or to a role, is perfectly possible. In particular, though not being foreseen in the specifications, it is perfectly possible to organize some SAML assertions into a certificate chain.

Ellison et al. (1999) note that, according to the X.509 PKI model, the issuer has the ability to eventually decide the conditions under which the certificate must be considered valid, and the enabled uses of the public key. But while the issuer must certainly be able to define the limits of its delegation, it is the final user who definitely takes a risk by accepting the certificate. Thus, if the relying party has to place some confidence in the certificate, it may need additional information about the assertion itself. In fact SAML allows the authentication authority to specify which mechanisms, protocols, and processes were used for the authentication.

Fine Grained Delegation

With regard to the use of SAML as a representation of an Authorization Certificate, it would be important to have access rights, or permissions, associated with the subject. In dDelega, this is achieved through the integration of an XACML policy into a SAML assertion. The precise way to accomplish this is described in a separate profile of the standard (Anderson & Lockhart, 2004). From the Trust Management perspective, the conjunction of SAML and XACML, in particular the inclusion of XACML policies and authorization decisions into SAML assertions, provides a powerful tool for the delegation of access rights.

From this point of view, the fact that logic foundations of the XACML language exist is very important, as they provide XACML with a clear semantic. The problem is to find algorithms through which the combination of permissions granted in a chain of certificates could be computed in a deterministic way, as it is already possible in TM. In fact, even if the semantic of a XACML policy is logically sound, nevertheless subtle problems can appear when different policies, linked in a chain of delegation assertions, have to be merged. One major problem is about the monotonicity of authorization assertions, which cannot be guaranteed in the general case. Using XACML authorization decisions as SAML assertions, it is possible to assert that access to a particular resource is denied, instead of permitted. Though being a perfectly legal and meaningful concept, the denial of a permission (a "negative permission") is not desirable in decentralized environments. In this case, a service provider can never allow access, as it cannot be sure to possess all issued statements. On the other hand, the non-monotonicity of the system can also lead to attacks, as issued assertions can be prevented to reach the provider, this way leading it to take wrong authorization decisions. Therefore, it is necessary to define a specific profile of SAML and XACML which could enable the secure delegation of permissions in decentralized environments, especially dealing with the case of "negative permissions".

Threshold Subjects

In SPKI, threshold subjects are defined as a special kind of subjects, to be used only in Authorization Certificates. Li, Grosof and Feigenbaum (2003) question the usefulness of this construct, arguing it is used as an alternative to simulate conjunction and disjunction of subjects. Moreover, they provide an intuitive meaning for threshold subjects when used in Name Certificates. XACML does not support threshold subjects in their general case, but conjunction of multiple subjects is possible in dDelega. In particular it is possible to associate multiple subjects per access request, as the request could originate from a user, but it could also be mediated by one or more middle agents. The XACML Multi-Role Permissions profile specifies a way to grant permissions only to principals playing several roles simultaneously. In dDelega, this kind of policy can be defined by using a single Subject in its Target, but adding multiple Subject-match elements to it.

Additionally, a Role Assignment policy can be used to define the associations between roles and principals. Restrictions can be specified about the possible combinations of roles, thus limiting the total number of roles played by a principal. In principle, this way the disjunction of some roles could also be imposed. However, this use could be complicated in decentralized environments, as it could invalidate the monotonicity of the system. In fact, showing more credentials should never lead to obtaining less permission.

Oblivious Attribute Certificates

The set of APIs supporting Oblivious Attribute Certificates is homogeneous with the rest of the dDelega library and the whole Java environment. In particular, the package for OACerts, just like the other packages of dDelega, can be used in different contexts, including applications not based on Web services. OACerts are implemented as a subclass of the dDelega Certicate class, and represented as SAML assertions.

With respect to implemented protocols, they are organized to guarantee simplicity and extensibility. The protocols are divided in two categories, according to their scope. The first category, descending from the VerifyScheme class, is meant to be used by a receiver, when it needs to match an oblivious credential against an access policy, before disclosing a resource according to the DirectShow or the ZeroKnowledge schemes. The second category allows (*1*) a provider to encrypt a resource to be sent to a requester; and (*2*) the requester to decrypt the resource, if the access policy is satisfied.

4. FUTURE RESEARCH DIRECTIONS

While Trust Management efforts are related to the protection of local resources, it has to be noted that credentials may convey sensitive data, as well. This data, including attributes, names and roles, needs to be protected at the same manner as other resources. Automated Trust Negotiation (ATN) (Winsborough & Li, 2000), in fact, enables interacting parties to establish trust incrementally, possibly starting as strangers and reaching some level of trust by disclosing credentials and policies iteratively. Various negotiation strategies are possible, as discussed by Winsborough & Li

(2000), ranging from an eager strategy, in which credentials are disclosed as soon as it is permitted by the access control policy, to a parsimonious strategy, in which credentials are disclosed only after ensuring that a successful result will be reached. Yu, Winslett and Seamons (2003) describe the Disclosure Tree as a family of strategies, which are proven to be interoperable with each other, i.e. interacting parties can choose each one a different strategy in the family and participate together to a negotiation.

Like credentials, policies may convey sensitive data and thus may need protection, too. The problem is discussed by Seamons, Winslett and Yu (2001) and by Yu and Winslett (2003). Winslett et al. (2002) introduce TrustBuilder as a modular system which can be used to perform customizable trust negotiation protocols. Lee and Winslett (2008) discuss the integration of TrustBuilder into a Service Oriented Architecture, in particular for realizing a Security Token Service which can carry on a Trust Negotiation conforming to WS-Trust specifications.

The various open issues of ATN, related to the protection of credentials and possible stall situations in the protocols, are addressed by a number of cryptographic protocols. For example, protocols for solving cyclic dependencies in disclosure policies include Oblivious Signature Based Envelopes (Li, Du & Boneh, 2005), Hidden Credentials (Bradshaw, Holt & Seamons, 2004), Oblivious Commitment Based Envelopes (Li & Li, 2005), and secret handshakes (Balfanz et al., 2003). Other protocols, focused instead on the separation of credential disclosure from attribute disclosure, include Private Credentials (Brands, 2000), Anonymous Credentials (Belenkiy et al., 2009), and OACerts (Li & Li, 2005).

In particular, to avoid the disclosure of sensitive information and help solving possible deadlocks during a Trust Negotiation, Li and Li (2005) present a family of protocols based on the concept of Oblivious Attribute Certificate (OACert). Instead of storing a user's attribute values in the clear, an OACert stores a cryptographic commitment of such attributes. Thus, the certificate alone does not allow anyone to gather information about the attribute values. Nevertheless, in a typical zero-knowledge scheme, OACerts may allow a certificate holder to satisfy some policy, disclosing some certificates but not the sensitive information associated with its attributes.

An OACert is an assertion about the certificate holder, digitally signed by some trusted party. Each OACert contains one or more attributes. When the commitment system is secure, the certificate does not leak any information about sensitive attribute values. Since the protocol guarantees the separation of credential disclosure from attribute disclosure, the content of an OACert can be made public. The sender can show its OACert without having to worry about the privacy of its attributes. An attribute value in an OACert can be used in different ways to (*1*) open the commitment and thus reveal the attribute value; (*2*) prove that an attribute value satisfies a condition, using a Zero-Knowledge Proof protocol and without revealing more information; and (*3*) guarantee that the requester obtains a resource only when its attribute values satisfy an access control policy.

5. CONCLUSION

Delegation of tasks and goals among services is a powerful technique for realizing complex applications. However, it is also a complex process, which needs to overcome interoperability issues, and needs to be founded on a clear notion of trust. In fact, effective delegations of tasks often need to be associated with corresponding delegations of access rights. The risks of a delegation have to be taken into account, along with foreseen advantages. Among the available mechanisms for establishing secure delegations in open environments, this chapter has analyzed Role Based Access Control, Trust Management and Federated Identity. They are all quite different approaches, but they pave the way to some form of delegation and trust among interconnected systems. Trust Management makes trust decisions more explicit, and thus it offers a more clear model of delegation for system administrators. Various security frameworks and complex systems have been analyzed, underlying the adherence to a particular scheme of access control. The configuration of delegation based systems remains a challenging task, above all if delegation decisions may happen at runtime in an open environment. Thus, research conducted in the field of Automated Trust Negotiation should be followed with attention, as it may provide simplified and automated procedures for realizing future delegation based systems.

REFERENCES

Anderson, A., & Lockhart, H. (2004, September). *SAML 2.0 profile of XACML*. OASIS Standard.

Balfanz, D., Durfee, G., Shankar, N., Smetters, D., Staddon, J., & Wong, H. C. (2003). Secret handshakes from pairing-based key agreements. In *Proceedings of the IEEE Symposium on Security and Privacy*, (pp. 180-196). IEEE.

Bandmann, O., Dam, M., & Firozabadi, B. S. (2002). Constrained delegation. [IEEE.]. *Proceedings of Security and Privacy*, *2002*, 131–140.

Barber, B. (1959). *The logic and limits of trust*. New Brunswick, NJ: Grammercy Press.

Belenkiy, M., Camenisch, J., Chase, M., Kohlweiss, M., Lysyanskaya, A., & Shacham, H. (2009). Randomizable proofs and delegatable anonymous credentials. In *Proceedings of Advances in Cryptology - CRYPTO 2009 (LNCS)* (*Vol. 5677*, pp. 108–125). Berlin: Springer. doi:10.1007/978-3-642-03356-8_7.

Bertino, E., Squicciarini, A. C., Paloscia, I., & Martino, L. (2006). Ws-AC: A fine grained access control system for web services. *World Wide Web (Bussum)*, *9*(2), 143–171. doi:10.1007/s11280-005-3045-4.

Bertino, E., Squicciarini, A. C., Paloscia, I., & Martino, L. (2006). Ws-ac: A fine grained access control system for web services. *World Wide Web (Bussum)*, *9*(2), 143–171. doi:10.1007/s11280-005-3045-4.

Bhargavan, K., Corin, R., Fournet, C., & Gordon, A. D. (2007). Secure sessions for web services. *ACM Transactions on Information and System Security*, *10*(2), 8. doi:10.1145/1237500.1237504.

Bhargavan, K., Fournet, C., Gordon, A. D., & Corin, R. (2007). Secure sessions for web services. *ACM Transactions on Information and System Security*, *10*(12).

Bhatti, R., Joshi, J. B., Bertino, E., & Ghafoor, A. (2003). Access control in dynamic XML-based web-services with x-rbac. In *Proceedings of the International Conference on Web Services*, (Vol. 3, pp. 23-26). ICWS.

Bradshaw, R. W., Holt, J. E., & Seamons, K. E. (2004). Concealing complex policies with hidden credentials. In *Proceedings of the 11th ACM Conference on Computer and Communications Security (CCS'04)*, (pp. 146-157). ACM.

Brands, S. A. (2000). *Rethinking public key infrastructures and digital certificates: Building in privacy*. Cambridge, MA: MIT Press.

Bussard, L., Nano, A., & Pinsdorf, U. (2009). Delegation of access rights in multi-domain service compositions. *Identity in the Information Society*, *2*(2), 137–154. doi:10.1007/s12394-009-0031-5.

Cantor, S. (2005). *Shibboleth architecture: Protocols and profiles.* Retrieved from http://shibboleth. Internet2.edu/shibboleth-documents.html

Castelfranchi, C., Falcone, R., & Pezzullo, G. (2003). Belief sources for trust: some learning mechanisms. In *Proceedings of the 6th Workshop on Trust, Privacy, Deception and Fraud in Agent Societies*. IEEE.

Chadwick, D., Zhao, G., Otenko, S., Laborde, R., Su, L., & Nguyen, T. A. (2008). PERMIS: A modular authorization infrastructure. *Concurrency and Computation, 20*(11), 1341–1357. doi:10.1002/cpe.1313.

Chadwick, D. W., & Otenko, A. (2003). The PERMIS X. 509 role based privilege management infrastructure. *Future Generation Computer Systems, 19*(2), 277–289. doi:10.1016/S0167-739X(02)00153-X.

Deutsch, M. (1962). Cooperation and trust: Some theoretical notes. In *Nebraska Symposium on Motivation*. Nebraska University Press.

Ellison, C., Frantz, B., Lampson, B., Rivest, R., Thomas, B., & Ylonen, T. (1999). *SPKI certificate theory*. IETF RFC 2693.

Falcone, R., & Castelfranchi, C. (2001). Social trust: A cognitive approach. In *Trust and deception in virtual societies* (pp. 55–90). Dordrecht, The Netherlands: Kluwer Academic Publishers. doi:10.1007/978-94-017-3614-5_3.

Feng, X., Guoyan, L., Hao, H., & Li, X. (2004). Role-based access control system for web services. [IEEE.]. *Proceedings of Computer and Information Technology, 2004*, 357–362.

Ferraiolo, D., Kuhn, D. R., & Chandramouli, R. (2007). *Role-based access control*. Artech House.

Freudenthal, E., Pesin, T., Port, L., Keenan, E., & Karamcheti, V. (2002). dRBAC: Distributed role-based access control for dynamic coalition environments. [IEEE.]. *Proceedings of Distributed Computing Systems, 2002*, 411–420.

Gambetta, D. (2000). Can we trust trust? In *Trust: Making and breaking cooperative relations*. Academic Press.

Gomi, H., Hatakeyama, M., Hosono, S., & Fujita, S. (2005, November). A delegation framework for federated identity management. In *Proceedings of the 2005 Workshop on Digital Identity Management* (pp. 94-103). ACM.

Hallam-Baker, P., & Maler, E. (2002). *Assertions and protocol for the oasis security assertion markup language (saml)*. OASIS Committee Specification.

Hondo, M., Maruyama, H., Nadalin, A., & Nagaratnam, N. (2006). *Web services federation language*. WS-Federation.

Khare, R., & Rifkin, A. (1997). Weaving a web of trust. *World Wide Web Journal, 2*(3), 77–112.

Lee, A. J., & Winslett, M. (2008). Towards standards-compliant trust negotiation for web services. In *Proceedings of the Joint iTrust and PST Conferences on Privacy, Trust Management, and Security (IFIPTM 2008)*. IFIPTM.

Li, J., & Li, N. (2005). OACerts: Oblivious attribute certificates. In *Proceedings of the 3rd Conference on Applied Cryptography and Network Security (ACNS)* (LNCS), (vol. 353, pp. 3010-3017). Berlin: Springer.

Li, N. (2000). Local names in SPKI/SDSI. In *Proceedings of Computer Security Foundations Workshop, 2000* (pp. 2-15). IEEE.

Li, N., Du, W., & Boneh, D. (2005). Oblivious signature-based envelope. *Distributed Computing, 17*(4), 293–302. doi:10.1007/s00446-004-0116-1.

Li, N., Grosof, B. N., & Feigenbaum, J. (2000). A practically implementable and tractable delegation logic. [IEEE.]. *Proceedings of Security and Privacy, 2000,* 27–42.

Li, N., Grosof, B. N., & Feigenbaum, J. (2003). Delegation logic: A logic-based approach to distributed authorization. *ACM Transactions on Information and System Security, 6*(1), 128–171. doi:10.1145/605434.605438.

Luhmann, N. (1979). *Trust and power.* New York: Wiley.

Mahmud, H., Didar-Al-Alam, S. M., Morshed, M. S., Haque, M. O., & Hasan, M. K. (2010). Designing access control model and enforcing security policies using permis for a smart item e-health scenario. *International Journal of Engineering Science, 2*(8).

Na, S., & Cheon, S. (2000). Role delegation in role-based access control. In *Proceedings of the Fifth ACM Workshop on Role-Based Access Control* (pp. 39-44). ACM.

Pedersen, T. (1991). Non-interactive and information-theoretic secure verifiable secret sharing. In *Proceedings of Advances in Cryptology — CRYPTO '91 (LNCS) (Vol. 576,* pp. 129–140). Berlin: Springer.

Poggi, A., Tomaiuolo, M., & Vitaglione, G. (2005). A security infrastructure for trust management in multi-agent systems. [LNCS]. *Proceedings of Trusting Agents for Trusting Electronic Societies, 3577,* 162–179. doi:10.1007/11532095_10.

Rivest, R. L., & Lampson, B. (1996). *SDSI - A simple distributed security infrastructure.* Crypto.

Sandhu, R. S., Coyne, E. J., Feinstein, H. L., & Youman, C. E. (1996). Role-based access control models. *Computer, 29*(2), 38–47. doi:10.1109/2.485845.

Seamons, K. E., Winslett, M., & Yu, T. (2001). Limiting the disclosure of access control policies during automated trust negotiation. In *Proceedings of the Network and Distributed Systems Symposium.* IEEE.

She, W., Thuraisingham, B., & Yen, I. L. (2007). Delegation-based security model for web services. In *High Assurance Systems Engineering Symposium, 2007* (pp. 82-91). IEEE.

Shin, D., Ahn, G. J., & Shenoy, P. (2004). Ensuring information assurance in federated identity management. In *Proceedings of the Performance, Computing, and Communications,* (pp. 821-826). IEEE.

Welch, V., Foster, I., Kesselman, C., Mulmo, O., Pearlman, L., & Tuecke, S. … Siebenlist, F. (2004). X.509 proxy certificates for dynamic delegation. In *Proceedings of the 3rd Annual PKI R&D Workshop.* Gaithersburg MD: NIST Technical Publications.

Welch, V., Siebenlist, F., Foster, I., Bresnahan, J., Czajkowski, K., & Gawor, J. … Tuecke, S. (2003). Security for grid services. In Proceedings of High Performance Distributed Computing, 2003 (pp. 48-57). IEEE.

Winsborough, W. H., & Li, N. (2000). Automated trust negotiation. In *Proceedings of DARPA Information Survivability Conference and Exposition,* (vol. 1, pp. 88-102). IEEE Press.

Winslett, M., Yu, T., Seamons, K. E., Hess, A., Jacobson, J., & Jarvis, R. et al. (2002). Negotiating trust in the Web. *IEEE Internet Computing, 6*(6), 30–37. doi:10.1109/MIC.2002.1067734.

Yu, T., Winslett, M., & Seamons, K. E. (2003). Supporting structured credentials and sensitive policies through interoperable strategies for automated trust negotiation. *ACM Transactions on Information and System Security*, 6(1), 1–42. doi:10.1145/605434.605435.

Zhang, L., Ahn, G. J., & Chu, B. T. (2003). A rule-based framework for role-based delegation and revocation. *ACM Transactions on Information and System Security*, 6(3), 404–441. doi:10.1145/937527.937530.

ADDITIONAL READING

Abadi, M. (1998). On SDSI's linkd local name spaces. *Journal of Computer Security*, 6(1-2), 3–21.

Aura, T. (1998). On the structure of delegation networks. In *Proceedings of the 11th IEEE Computer Security Foundations Workshop* (pp. 14-26). IEEE Computer Society Press.

Blaze, M., Feigenbaum, J., Ioannidis, J., & Keromytis, A. (1999). *The KeyNote trust-management system version 2*. IETF RFC 2704, September 1999. Retrieved November 20, 2012, from http://www.ietf.org/rfc/rfc2704.txt

Blaze, M., Feigenbaum, J., & Lacy, J. (1996). Decentralized trust management. In *Proceedings of the 17th Symposium on Security and Privacy* (pp. 164-173). IEEE Computer Society Press.

Bonatti, P. A., & Samarati, P. (2002). A uniform framework for regulating service access and information release on the web. *Journal of Computer Security*, 10(3), 241–272.

Diffie, W., & Hellman, M. E. (1976). New directions in cryptography. *IEEE Transactions on Information Theory*, 22(6), 644–654. doi:10.1109/TIT.1976.1055638.

Forman, G. (2003). An extensive empirical study of feature selection metrics for text classification. *Journal of Machine Learning Research*, 3, 1289–1305.

Foster, I., Kesselman, C., & Tuecke, S. (2001). The anatomy of the grid-enabling scalable virtual organizations. *International Journal of High Performance Computing Applications*, 15(3), 200–222. doi:10.1177/109434200101500302.

Gavriloaie, R., Nejdl, W., Olmedilla, D., Seamons, K., & Winslett, M. (2004). No registrations needed: how to use declarative policies and negotiation to access sensitive resources on the semantic web. In *Proceedings of the European Semantic Web Symposium*. Heraklion, Greece: IEEE.

Gutmann, P. (2000). *X.509 style guide*. Retrieved April 20, 2009, from http://www.cs.auckland.ac.nz/~pgut001/pubs/x509guide.txt

Gutmann, P. (2004). *How to build a PKI that works*. Paper presented at the 3rd Annual PKI R&D Workshop. Gaithersburg, MD.

Halpern, J., & van der Meyden, R. (1999). A logic for SDSI's linked local name spaces. In *Proceedings of the 12th IEEE Computer Security Foundations Workshop* (pp. 111-122). IEEE.

Housley, R., Polk, W., Ford, W., & Solo, D. (2002). *Internet X.509 public key infrastructure certificate and CRL profile*. IETF RFC 3280, April 2002. Retrieved April 20, 2009, from http://www.ietf.org/rfc/rfc3280.txt

Kohnfelder, L. (1978). *Toward a practical public cryptosystem*. (Bachelor's thesis). MIT, Cambridge, MA.

Lewis, J. (2003). *Reinventing PKI: Federated identity and the path to practical public key security*. Retrieved April 20, 2009, from http://www.burtongroup.com/

Li, J., & Li, N. (2006). OAcerts: Oblivious attribute certificates. *IEEE Transactions on Dependable and Secure Computing*, 3(4), 340–352. doi:10.1109/TDSC.2006.54.

Li, N., Mitchell, J. C., & Winsborough, W. H. (2002). Design of a role-based trust management framework. In *Proceedings of the IEEE Symposium on Security and Privacy*, (pp. 114–130). IEEE.

Moses, T. (2005). *eXtensible access control markup language (XACML) version 2.0*. Retrieved April 20, 2009, from http://docs.oasis-open.org/xacml/2.0/access_control-xacml-2.0-core-spec-os.pdf

O'Riordan, C. (2006). *Transcript of opening session of first international GPLv3 conference*. Retrieved April 20, 2009, from http://www.ifso.ie/documents/gplv3-launch-2006-01-16.html

Open, I. D. (2007). *OpenID authentication 2.0*. Retrieved April 20, 2009, from http://openid.net/specs/openid-authentication-2_0.html

Ragouzis, N., Hughes, J., Philpott, R., Maler, E., Madsen, P., & Scavo, T. (2008). *Security assertion markup language (SAML) V2.0 technical overview*. Retrieved April 20, 2009, from http://www.oasis-open.org/committees/download.php/27819/sstc-saml-tech-overview-2.0-cd-02.pdf

Saltzer, J. H., & Schroeder, M. D. (1975). The protection of information in computer systems. *Proceedings of the IEEE*, 63(9), 1278–1308. doi:10.1109/PROC.1975.9939.

Schneier, B. (2002). *Crypto-gram newsletter*. Retrieved April 20, 2009, from http://www.schneier.com/crypto-gram-0208.html

Seamons, K. E., Winslett, M., & Yu, T. (2001). *Limiting the disclosure of access control policies during automated trust negotiation*. The Internet Society.

Spector, A. Z. (1989). Achieving application requirements. In S. Mullender (Ed.), *Distributed Systems*, (pp. 19-33). New York: ACM Press. DOI=http://doi.acm.org/10.1145/90417.90738

Stallman, R. M. (1997). The right to read. [from http://www.gnu.org/philosophy/right-to-read.html]. *Communications of the ACM*, 40(2), 85–87. Retrieved April 20, 2009 doi:10.1145/253671.253726.

Walker, J. (2003). *The digital imprimatur: How big brother and big media can put the internet genie back in the bottle*. Retrieved April 20, 2009, from http://www.fourmilab.ch/documents/digital-imprimatur/

Winsborough, W. H. (2002). Towards practical automated trust negotiation. In *Proceedings of the 3rd International Workshop on Policies for Distributed Systems and Networks* (pp. 92–103). IEEE Computer Society Press.

Winsborough, W. H., & Li, N. (2002). Protecting sensitive attributes in automated trust negotiation. In *Proceedings of WPES*, (pp. 41–51). ACM. ISBN 1-58113-633-1

Winsborough, W. H., & Li, N. (2006). Safety in automated trust negotiation. *ACM Transactions on Information and System Security*, 9(3), 352–390. doi:10.1145/1178618.1178623.

Winslett, M., Ching, N., Jones, V. E., & Slepchin, I. (1997). Using digital credentials on the world wide web. *Journal of Computer Security*, 5(3), 255–266.

Yu, T., Ma, X., & Winslett, M. (2000). Prunes: An efficient and complete strategy for automated trust negotiation over the Internet. In *Proceedings of the 7th ACM Conference on Computer and Communications Security*, (pp. 210–219). ACM. ISBN 1-58113-203-4

KEY TERMS AND DEFINITIONS

Automated Trust Negotiation: A negotiation process which allows unknown users to establish a level of trust in an incremental way through the exchange of credentials. Automated Trust Negotiation can be used to to automate trust building, guiding the disclosure of credentials according to privacy policies and negotiation strategies. The process is typically aimed at accessing some resource or some service.

Delegation: A mechanism for assigning the responsibility for completing a task, or satisfying a goal, to another entity. The delegation process may cascade across several levels, and may require a corresponding delegation of access rights.

Digital Certificate: A digital document in which a issuer attests, via a digital signature, the association of one or more attributes to an entity, defined as the subject of the certificate.

Federated Identity: The means of linking a person's identity and attributes, stored across multiple distinct identity management systems. Often Federated Identity is associated with an implementation of the Single Sign-On (SSO) scheme.

Role-Based Access Control (RBAC): An access control scheme in which permissions are not assigned directly to users, but to roles. Those roles are then assigned to users, according to their tasks. Hence users acquire their own permissions indirectly, as they are associated to assigned roles. This level of indirection separates the assignment of permissions to roles, and of roles to users. Thus it eases the management of access control by system administrators.

Single Sign-On: A mechanism for establishing trust about a user's authentication process, performed at a certain site, across multiple identity management systems, also owned by different organizations. In this sense, SSO is an aspect of a federated identity management system. In particular, it provides interoperability among the authentication mechanisms of different systems.

Trust: The perceived probability that another agent will perform a particular action. This probability may be evaluated as a continuous function of the certainty of its constituent beliefs. The constituents and their importance may vary, according to the different existing socio-cognitive models of trust.

Trust Management: A system for the symbolic representation, creation and management of social trust. In particular, trust can be used for controlling access to protected resources. A request for accessing a resource is accepted only if accompanied with sufficient credentials, according to a local policy. Trust, quantified as a set of access rights, can be further delegated to other agents, creating trust networks. A chain of credentials may be used to represent the trust flow, from the resource manager to the agent requesting access.

Chapter 3
Academic and Professional Qualifications of the Systems Administrator Required to Work in the Organizational Context

José Monteiro
Higher Polytechnic Institute of Gaya, Portugal

Mário Lousã
Higher Polytechnic Institute of Gaya, Portugal

ABSTRACT

This chapter presents the factors that influence the career of the systems administrator in the context of the organizations, namely the roles and the responsibilities. The objective is to provide a contribution to the future systems administrators, employers, and academics to better understand what factors influence the role of the systems administrator. The approaches to identify the main concepts are based on the past experience of the authors in the information technology systems area, a systematic study of professional groups, and a study about academic entities. As a result, the authors present a conceptual view to frame the roles and responsibilities of the systems' administrator in the context of his/her instruction and the organizations where he/she works.

INTRODUCTION

In the context of Information Systems (IS), the role of the Systems' Administrator (SA) is seen by the other actors who interact with him/her as an expert in computer systems, capable of solving all computer problems. This inaccurate generalization, derived from common sense, does not match the today's reality. This "person" is in charge of a broad set of responsibilities and roles that fit (in) the goal of ensuring that the information systems of a given organization is responding adequately to the requests of the users.

DOI: 10.4018/978-1-4666-4526-4.ch003

The complexity of the issues that involve computer systems is extensive. For this reason there are doubts about who should manage systems and if they should meet or not, for example, competencies of software development, planning and implementation of information systems, resolution (repair) of hardware problems or software, extensive knowledge of operating systems or even computer security.

Assuming that the domain of all these areas is not an imperative, it is comfortable for the SA and the beneficiaries of his activity to be well prepared in all the areas mentioned above. However, in a more realistic scenario, it is impractical to carry out all these activities with the same level of expertise.

This way, it is understood that the SA should meet a set of skills in the management and maintenance of computer systems and information, including the ability to diagnose and predict problems, sometimes under pressure. These variables may have less or more importance whether the system is critical or not to the operation of the organization. Additionally the management of the systems implies the planning, the development and the exploration of the information system.

Another aspect for discussion is on the extension of the "power" of the SA. In a society where IT systems have an increasing importance, who are the individuals that have "free access" to the data and information (McNutt, 1993)? To delimit the scope of the topics of this chapter the ethical aspects will not be studied. Following this approach we intend to present the figure of SA along two lines of thought: (1) the roles that fit the profile, and (2) the responsibilities in the information systems' domain. To characterize the SA, we will present the roles in the context of the Informatics Science (ISc) and Computer Science (CSc) and the context of action of the SA according to the size of the organization. We will also present how SA obtains skills and how they relate to the areas of expertise. In terms of responsibilities, we will introduce a mapping that illustrates the relationship between the roles played by the SA and the domain of responsibilities in terms of decision taking. The explanation will be complimented with a conceptual view to help futures SA and employers to better understand the roles and responsibilities of the SA.

METHODOLOGICAL APPROACH

The methodology used to write this document was supported by four factors: (1) the past experience of the authors in the field of IT systems; (2) a literature review, particularly in the field of IT systems administration; (3) a review about professional careers and recruitment on IT systems; (4) a research of fields of studies on IT systems.

We designed a methodological framework (Figure 1) to guide the document presentation and help to classify the factors that characterize the role of the SA. Two main vectors have driven the explanation: (1) the roles that fit the profile of the SA; (2) the responsibilities in the IS domain.

Starting with the roles of the SA, we identified the factors and the paths in terms of studies that contribute to the acquisition of the skills in ISc and CSc areas in order to understand what roles can be played by an SA. In a second step based on the resultant categories of roles, we determined how the roles fit in the context of the size of the organizations. In a third step, related with the roles and aiming to respond to IT needs in terms of the human resources in the organizations, we identified the academic fields of study (named by academic branches) that provide skills to instruct IT specialists. On the side of responsibilities, we identified the areas of expertise as the areas where organizations have needs of IT professionals. At the end we identified a core of responsibilities and provided a conceptual view to illustrate the relationships between the factors that characterize the figure of the SA in the context of the organizations (roles and responsibilities).

Figure 1. Methodological framework

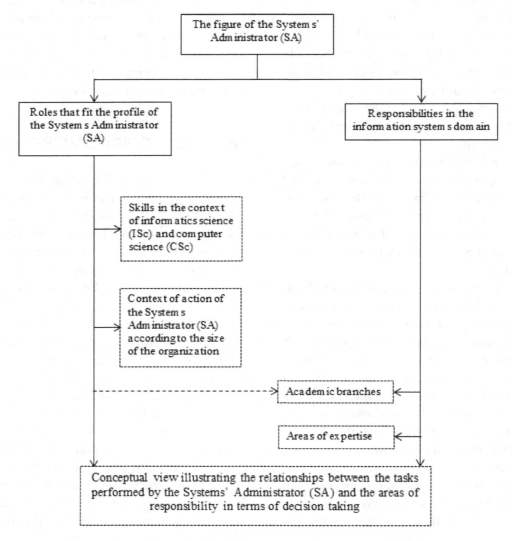

Our approach has followed a high-level view and avoids entering in detailed descriptions of particular cases. Below we present a methodological map to illustrate what has been reported before.

HOW DOES THE SYSTEMS ADMINISTRATOR ACQUIRE HIS SKILLS?

In terms of roles, the SA tends to provide specialized and technical services where the main objects are the Information Technologies (IT), the Information Systems (IS) or, informatics in general. Many SA do not have a formal education, they are self-taught. There are people that become SA after work or obtain education in other areas (Frisch, 2002). In some cases, their informatics abilities started in high school or professional education training. Others attended one or more training certifications from one or more brands of informatics systems to reinforce or complement their SA skills. Regarding the industry, some of the most important players in informatics systems as Microsoft Corporation, Sun Microsystems, Cisco Systems, Oracle Corporation, Apple Computers,

Google Inc., Yahoo! Inc., offer certification training programs to qualify people in their systems, and become "systems administrator". In those cases, the term "systems administrator" is delimited by the promoter of the program to a particular certification system. These programs take no longer than a year and are focused on a specific system or technology. On the other hand, university and polytechnic institutions offer academic degrees in computer science, informatics Science or management information systems (MIS) that lead students to acquire SA skills. The courses involve technical and non-technical abilities and, depending on the program, is complimented with knowledge about project management, business functions and communication skills. At later stage the graduates can obtain their certification by submitting to an exam to be admitted to a national professional board or to become a member of a professional associa-

tion (Chalupa, 2007). In Table 1 we present six attributes to take into consideration regarding the evaluation of how a SA has built his career and how he has obtained his skills.

In the section below, we present each attribute domain and value:

- **Education Type:** This attribute considers only formal or non-formal education. By formal education we understand the education that each citizen has to meet according to national rules. There are different kinds of education or qualification systems according to each country. So, to promote the education of its citizens, each country has defined by law what are the mandatory principles and the rules for each cycle of studies and what is the certification obtained at the end of the cycle. As non-for-

Table 1. Attributes of the systems administrator career

Education Type	Training / Education Options	Precedence	Entity	Certification Type	Skills Obtained Conducing To...
Non-formal education.	Self-taught.	n/a	n/a	n/a	Non specialized
Non-formal education.	Specialized short-term training.	Usually not required.	Employers; training entities.	Non-recognized certificate.	Expert in... (a system or technology)
Non-formal education.	Technical certification program.	Requisites defined by brands and industry.	Brand academies; commercial systems developers.	Brand / industry recognized certificate. Usually required a classification of 70% or more to obtain the certificate.	Systems' administrator on... (may vary according to the organization and certification)
Formal education.	High-school or equivalent.	Basic education.	Vocational and professional schools.	Program certificate by national authorities and(or) with regional recognition (e.g.: European Union; United States, etc.).	Technician
Formal education.	University / polytechnic.	High school to be admitted to university or polytechnic; academic degree to be admitted to a professional board exam or post-graduate levels.	Universities / Higher education institutions / Polytechnics schools.	Program certificate by national authorities and (or) with regional recognition (e.g.: European Union; United States, etc.).	Engineer or technical engineer in... (depend on the regional model, polytechnic graduation should be differentiated from university graduations)

mal education we classify all other alternatives that provide theoretical or practical experience. In parallel with the education or qualification system or after completing studies, each citizen has the possibility of attending courses or studies to improve skills, academic experience and(or) professional experience. The non-formal education studies are defined by private entities and the target publics are small groups with particular interests in a certain fields of studies. The certification level, when exists, is defined by the entities that create and promote the studies. In short, non-formal education is a complimentary alternative to formal education;

- **Training / Education Options:** This attribute has been classified according to five categories: (1) self-taught; (2) specialized short-term training; (3) technical certification programs; (4) high-school or equivalent; (5) university / polytechnic. Self-taught refers to a person who acquires new skills without a mediator by himself/herself. Specialized short-term training and technical certification programs categories includes people that choose a specific training to increase his own competencies. These main differences in these categories are the certification acceptance and the purposes. Technical certification programs are promoted by industry and oriented to form specialists on IT systems represented by a certain brand. Taking as an example an organization that has a system based on Cisco Systems technologies, certainly it will prefer professional that has a Cisco Certification, rather than a professional that has a generic network certification. The category high-school or equivalent refers to the path that a common citizen takes to obtain a professional qualification of middle level. In the present context, the qualification is in CSc or ISc.

The last category, university / polytechnic, refers to the people that have finish mandatory education and intend to have a higher education instruction oriented to CSs, ISc or MIS;

- **Precedence:** The attribute precedence consists on mandatory requirements that a candidate has to meet to be admitted to a qualification program or a training course. This attribute is not easy to define, due the variables implied on each training/education option. To present a clear explanation, we start from education type: (1) in formal education the rules to be admitted to a program are universal, available to public domain and defined by education authorities. We have classified the categories in basic education (referring to the basic educational level), high school (referring to vocational or professional studies options). However the educational path does not stop with graduation. After graduation, new skills can be obtained throughout Master Science (MSc) degree, Doctorate (PhD) degree or Postdoctoral. The paths to these academic degrees were not considered in this work, because it would lead us to a philosophical discussion about academic and professional path. (2) In non-formal education type, excluding the self-taught, the requirements (we prefer to call them requirements instead rules, because, in this case, rules are not universal) to be admitted to courses or programs are defined by each entity, organization or brand representative. In the short-term training, usually there are no pre-requisite categories or, the existent pre-requisites are circumstantial. In the case of the technical certification programs, rules and admitting are defined and publicized by industry representative brands (e.g.: Microsoft IT Academy Program, Cisco Networking Academy, Primavera Academy);

- **Entity:** This attribute has been classified in four main categories: (1) employers and training entities. Refers to the training promoted by employers, promoted by employers recurring to an external and specialized training entity, promoted by a training entity (includes professional or academic groups); (2) brand academies and commercial systems developers, refer to companies well implemented on market and in the industry of systems that already have implemented their own academic structures, to form and certify professionals, whose value is recognized by market and employers; (3) vocational and professional schools, refer to entities public or private which offer programs oriented to students that intend to be professionals on IT systems branches; (4) universities / polytechnics schools, refers to entities that provide superior qualifications to students that want improve their skills is CSc or ISc;

- **Certification Type:** The certification type attribute has been divided into three main categories: (1) non recognized certificate, referring to the participation certificates or, in general, the certificates that are not emitted by recognized accreditation system; (2) brand / industry recognized certificate, refer to certificates which are not a "standard de jure", but are a "standard in fact". They have good acceptance by the market. They are emitted by brand academies according to each particular rule system. As the main relevant characteristics of these certificates (not all) are the high difficulty of the examinations and the mandatory classification of 70% or more; (3) a program certified by national authorities, referring to the certificates emitted by national education authorities. The recognition of these certificates, in some cases, extends the limits of the country borders to large regional contexts (e.g.: Europe or North America), through accreditation systems (e.g.: ECTS - European Credit Transfer and Accumulation System) subscribed by a large number or countries;

- **Skills Obtained Conducing To…:** This attribute should be regarded as the result of each path, individually, leads to. The attribute has been classified in four main levels concerned the career of SA: (1) expert in…, represented by professionals that act on systems' administration area with non-relevant capabilities or responsibilities; (2) system administrator on…, refers to professionals specialized in IT system brands and with other generic informatics skills; (3) technician, refers to professionals that are beginning their career and have not yet developed scientific knowledge or relevant experience in IT systems; (4) engineer or technical engineer in…, refers to professionals that have higher education degree or advanced studies on IT systems. Depending on the academic path, the graduates on polytechnic institutions may be differentiated from the graduates on universities. The first are viewed as operational and the second ones are viewed as modelers or conceptualizers.

Before the end of this section, it is important to refer that the formal education could be complemented with non-formal education. It is very common, to fill new professional requirements, that SA professionals need to get new specialized training. Usually, it is obtained through self-taught, specialized short-term training and(or), technical certification programs. Certification and training are very important to the IT team, namely SA. In the organizational context education, training, and certification are factors of credibility.

THE ROLES AND TASKS OF THE SYSTEMS ADMINISTRATOR

In a broad sense SA could perform a very diverse set of tasks into their daily activity. Depending on the size of the organization, the availability of the human resources and the IT/IS needs, those tasks could be more or less complex and in a small or large number. We considered two distinct contexts of organizations: (1) small organizations; (2) large organizations.

Starting from the context of the small organizations, due to the predictable shortage of human resources, it is understandable that more polyvalence is required to perform an infinite number of tasks. Usually, the SA takes care of hardware, system software, software applications, network infrastructure, does backups, helps users, and performs a non-referenced set of tasks. In large companies, the complexity of the systems and the requirements of the business makes it more relevant to focus on high-level and specialized tasks (e.g.: planning, design, modeling). In organizations that have their business around the World, the role of SA may be assumed by a group of people instead of a single person, due the distributed context. Without defining a specific business or organizational context, Haber et al. (2011) point out some tasks of the SA: handling data, managing, designing and operating the IT systems (Haber, Kandogan, & Maglio, 2011). These "hi-level" tasks embrace a very diverse and more focused technical tasks. For example, database administration is a specialization of data administration. Another one is the design of the data systems to represent the business specificities (Edlund & Lövquist, 2012).

We conceived the roles of the SA as a pentagram, represented in Figure 2 that includes the main categories of tasks referred above. The roles are: (1) management; (2) design; (3) security; (4) operation; (5) training.

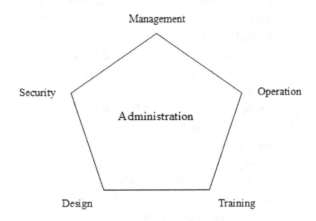

Figure 2. Categories of the roles of the systems administrator

- **Management Role:** Consists on performing tasks that guarantee the proper operation of the systems, e.g. analyze logs, take preventive actions, plan updates, take corrective actions, add or revoke users' permissions, add or remove devices;
- **Design Role:** Consists on designing and planning systems and software development to meet the business needs, e.g. modeling databases, modeling and developing software applications, identify relevant systems, design IS architecture;
- **Security Role:** Consists on performing the tasks that help to prevent the accidental loss of data, data deletion or system intrusion, e.g. monitoring network access, monitoring and perform backups, monitoring the data consistency, define and update security policies, implementation of encryption mechanisms, define authentication procedures;
- **Operation Role:** Consists on performing tasks related with processing data, operation of data servers, systems configuration, e.g. bulk operations, server and services administration;

- **Training Role:** Consists on "instruction" and training of the users of the systems, e.g. promote best practices, instruct users, instruct technicians.

Regarding the overall organizations and the very diversified contexts in which IT systems are administrated, the discussion of phenomena in order to the business model will lead us to an undeterminable number of business models and a predictable impossibility to study a relevant sample. In order to frame the roles of the SA according to the organization's size we have considered the main categories of the roles of the SA (Figure 3) for the organization.

We start from the principle that the large organizations have greater probabilities of acting in a global market compared to a small organization, requiring, for example geographically distributed facilities or offices. Additionally it is expected that they have distributed IT systems with middle or high complexity. On the other hand, small organizations have more probability of having less human resources, and IT systems with low complexity.

The layout of the categories presented in Figure 2 has been taken into consideration to be the core categories of roles of the SA. The trilogy: management, operation and security, is vital to guarantee the minimum conditions for a system to work well. In a small organization, most of the times, due to a shortage of resources, SA have to take care of the operation of the system, manage the system and, very important, to ensure that security backups are made and data are protected. As organizations become larger, IT needs of the organization may extend the SA roles to conceptual (design) and (or) to instruction (training) roles in addition to core roles. Figure 3 represents how the size of the organization tends to extend SA roles and its conceptualization and the educational level tend to grow as well. In synthesis, we found a relation between the size of the organization, the diversity of roles of the SA and the educational skills.

Figure 3. Context of the roles of the systems administrator in organizations

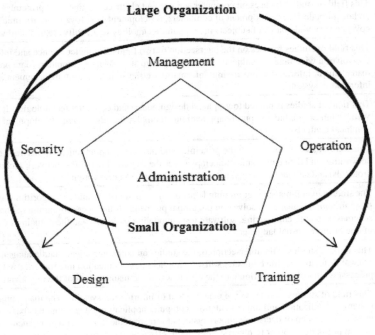

THE SYSTEMS' ADMINISTRATOR AND INFORMATION TECNOLOGIES / INFORMATION SYSTEMS AREAS OF EXPERTISE

There is a wide set of possibilities of specializations in the areas of the CSc and ISc. The continuous advances of science and technology motivate the interest for new branches of studies and lead to a decrease in the interest in the branches that lost their relevance. In parallel, in the professional context, the scenario is the same, new recruitment areas of expertise emerge and others tend to disappear. We identified two determinant factors to justify the existence of many different specializations in the referred areas: (1) Academic factor - opportunities of research in order to promote science advances and prepare students with scientific and professional capabilities to satisfy the needs of professionals in the referred areas; (2) Market factor - the organizations' needs to recruit IT professionals.

The changes influenced by these two factors, make it very difficult to fully determine the areas of expertise without being very imprecise or the expertise becoming obsolete in the short-term. Nevertheless, in the case of the academic factor, changes are not so critical. The scientific areas were guided by academic referentials, adopted in several countries as the main reference. They allow us to present a set of branches that lead future SA to obtain expertise in a wide range of specific branches (e.g.: IT developer, IT analyst, programmer, project manager, IT security, database manager, IT/IS consultant,...). In Table 2 we propose a synthesis of branches of studies in the CSc / ISc areas that we consider relevant to describe the areas of expertise of the SA. We have

Table 2. Branches of studies in computer science / informatics science and the correspondent specific branches

Branch of Studies	Range of Specific Branches
Computer engineering	This field of studies focuses on computer science and electrical engineering principles. It emphasizes the architecture, design, development of computers, development of software, algorithmic problem solving. It covers a very wide range of subjects in computer technology (e.g.; software and hardware).
Computer Information Science	This field of studies focuses on the intersection of two fields: computer science and information management. It involves a wide range of subjects, like techniques to store data on computers, data processing, data management, information processing, information retrieval, information management and theories of information systems.
Computer multimedia	This field of studies is related to graphical design, video and computer technologies. It could be extended to Web design or graphic computing applications. It emphasizes the design, development and the produce of graphical contents.
Computer networks and data communication	This field of studies focuses on the principles and theories of communication between computers. Computer networking and data communication emphasizes the design of networks, network architecture, communication protocols, and network topology, network security and data encryption.
Computer programming	The studies in computer programming focus on the domain of techniques, algorithms and the use of programming languages to solve computational problems. It involves programming concepts, notational schemas, software engineering, software tests, modeling problems and the domain of the syntax and semantics of one or more formal languages.
Computer science for management	This field of studies is the intersection of the studies on computer science and management of organizations science. It focuses on the computer software applications, application integration, database management, data processing, in order to contribute to the efficiency of the management of the organizations.
Information systems management	This field of studies focuses on the management of information systems. The main subjects are related to systems modelization and implementation, computer application integration, database management, data processing, design of decision-support systems for management, project management, to solve information system problems in order to make systems more efficient to organizations.

supported our proposal in (1) scientific references: CORDIS framework (CORDIS: FP6), FRASCATI manual (Revised field of science and technology (FOS) classification in the Frascati Manual (OECD), 2007), and (2) in research work on the academic offer of top universities (QS World Universities Ranking) in the Computer Science Technologies and Engineering areas, namely the Massachusetts Institute of Technology (MIT), University of Cambridge, Harvard University, University of Oxford. We also extend our research to the University of Minho and University of Porto (Portugal), having in consideration our background affiliation as authors.

The proposal presented in Table 2 is not static and does not intend to be a closed set of domains. It may suffer changes with new advances on computer science that open new fields of studies, namely on computerized systems. Nevertheless, its relevance is justified by the need of a reference to the current and future systems administrators in terms of choosing a specific branches. The organization of the branches covers a wide set of subjects as engineering, information, multimedia, networks, programming and management and are justified by increasing importance that systems based on computers have assumed nowadays on these particular areas. As for the different structures of the academic referentials that support our research, the scope of each branch can be object of discussion. However, our approach, in general, matches the current context of studies in European Union and in United States.

How do the different branches of studies fit in the areas of expertise? The educational programs combine different scientific areas, some more relevant to the program than others, and a wide range of subjects divided by course. Due to the extensive set of program subjects, the students or researchers are organized according to the area of expertise where they, individually feel more oriented (Burgess & Koymans, 2007). This "self-vocational" orientation leads the future IT specialists to seek for job offers in the areas where they have been specialized, using spontaneous applications or by answering to recruitment offers of the employers. The dilemma is: who determines the areas of expertise, the academic background of the individual or the needs of the market, in particular, the industry of technologies?

With the demands of the world's economy in permanent "stress", academic institutions can no longer live isolated from the market. The present conjuncture demands that, in order to attract students, the academic institutions have to improve their studies offer to meet the students' expectations in terms of education and employability. This leads to an adjustment to meet the market needs in terms of specialized professionals. In that sense there is an adjustment between the academic offer and the market needs in terms of specialists. We observed that the academic offer changes are diluted with time, while the market needs are more spontaneous. By comparison, the determination of areas of expertise is less consensual than the branch of studies. Some barriers were identified: (1) each particular country has its own labor regulations and jobs definitions, (2) the terminology adopted is also very diversified in the different IT areas, (3) the needs of recruitment of IT companies and the terminology adopted are in constant change, (4) the terminology in the context of the professional paths of each program degree outcomes.

To propose the areas of expertise in Table 3 were consulted professional orders, professional groups, and international recruitment agencies (ACM), (IEEE), (LOPSA), (OE), (USENIX). The criteria to present the synthesis of areas of expertise were based on the roles of the SA and the object of his actions, the computer systems.

THE RESPONSIBILITIES AND DECISION TAKING OF THE SYSTEMS' ADMINISTRATOR

The term responsibility implies being accountable or, when things go wrong, taking the blame for something. A free translation from the dictionary points responsibility as "the fact of having a duty

Table 3. Areas of expertise in the context of computer science / informatics science

Areas of Expertise	Related Activities
Computer network security administrator	To guarantee the security of the computers, networks and data throughout the implementation of prevention and correction methods to avoid computer damage, data corruption, data loss, intrusion of the systems and to guaranty data privacy.
Computer programmer and developer	To program, to solve real problems using one or more programming languages. To use, develop or reuse methods, techniques, algorithms, standards procedures in order to produce software modules or software applications.
Computer systems analyst	To analyze existing computer systems in an organization and design new systems that meet the specific information needs of the organization.
Content multimedia developer	To develop, design, manipulate and produce graphical contents. The contents include the treatment of the textual information, image editing and manipulation, audio editing and manipulation, video editing, manipulation, and creation.
Database systems manager	To install, to configure and to maintain database systems updated. It is also relevant to domain one or more variants of Structure Query Language (SQL), to monitoring, perform regular maintenance of database system, to do regular analysis of critical databases performance, provide suggestions or implement security measures to protect the database system.
Information systems manager	To implement, maintain, and update systems; to perform and implement schedule backups, verify the consistency of the backups, to define and implement security policies; to guarantee the correct licensing of the software; to evaluate user needs and system functionality and providing the appropriate support and advice; plan solutions to critical situations, training the users and the support staff; plan budget needs to maintain systems updated in order to meet the business needs.
Web manager and developer	To design, host and maintain Web pages and their graphical features; to develop applications that emphasis business logic, create conditions to manipulate data throughout a Web interface; to customize the Web users' experience; to define system policies in order to guarantee secure conditions for the users and the system.

to deal with something". Regarding the context of the SA activities in an organization, this "person" has a duty to deal with the systems he/she is the responsible for, in order to respond effectively and efficiently to the needs of the organization.

Responsibility implies taking decisions, namely the right decisions. To take the right decisions it is necessary to be prepared, to be capable and master a set of skills that will be the core functions in an organization. So, decision taking implies being ready for something, knowing a broad set of pros and cons to judge with wisdom each new situation.

As referred before, the SA has associated a set of roles. Such roles do not mean that the SA must be an expert in all areas related to the roles. However, it is recommended that at least one role should fit in the area of expertise of the SA. That lead us to what should be the responsibilities of

the SA and what spectrum of the decisions that can be taken. In a broad sense, everything that is done according to the SA free will in the context of work should be considered of his/her own responsibility. This conception of responsibility is common to most of the activities performed by any other employee in the organizations. Nevertheless, what is being analyzed is the set of responsibilities of the decisions that affect systems analysis, performance, development, management, security, and overall influence in systems outcomes, and not the responsibilities from the execution of tasks. At this point it matters to refer the differences among roles and responsibilities. We refer to the roles as something directly related to the qualitative perspective of performing something. On the other hand, we understand the responsibility as an abstraction of the duty to control and make systems work efficiently. The decision-taking will be the first step of the consequence of having responsibility. The impact of the decision will be revealed on systems' performance and efficiency.

To classify in detail all the responsibilities of the SA is a path with non-returning back. It implies taking into consideration particular characteristics of the organizations, understanding the employers' perspectives, understanding the SA perspective. Our approach is to contribute with a first step in this subject.

In order to better exemplify the context of the responsibility and the decision taking in the context of the SA we present four categories of responsibilities that aim to be the synthesis of the large number of different conceptualizations (SA-BOK, Systems Administration Body of Knowledge).

- **Administrate:** In the IT context, to administrate a system can be referred as the responsibility to define the tactics and the policies of the system (e.g.: network administration - Figure 4). Nevertheless, other perspectives should be presented. Regarding the scenario of the large organizations, due to the wide variety of responsibilities, most of the times, it is necessary to have more than one IT specialist and a defined hierarchy of IT responsibilities to guarantee the necessary quality to support the systems. This means that the responsibility of the administrator is comparable to a mid-level manager. In broad sense, our conviction is that the administration responsibility is the core responsibility of the SA;

- **Manage:** The management responsibility in the IT context is comparable to a top-level decision, which places the SA as the responsible person for the definition of the strategic subjects of the system (e.g.: database systems manager, information systems manager - Figure 4). For an example, it is the SA who decides how and when a back-up should be performed and what databas-

es are affected. The SA defines the strategy of the system and the strategic alignment with business strategies to respond to the business needs. He/She defines the strategy of the system and the strategic alignment with business strategies to respond to the business needs. A complementary perspective, regarding small organizations, is the problematic of the strategic alignment between IT systems and the business which is less critical than in the large organizations. Most of the organizations do not consider strategic alignment as a priority or do not even know what it means. In the small organizations context, our belief is that the responsibility of the SA is more related to the management of the systems and less with the administration;

- **Develop:** The responsibility of the development of the systems is less consensual to frame in the context of the SA. By principle, a developer is seen as an operational. Regarding the size of the organizations, in the small organizations it is common that the person who administers or manages a system, is the same that develops all or part of the system (e.g.: content management systems developer, Web systems manager and developer - Figure 4). On the opposite sense these responsibilities in case of the large organizations, are distributed by different and specialized individuals or even by specialized teams. We understand that the SA should have capabilities of development, and in particular should be able to develop small applications to solve very particular problems of interoperability among systems;

- **Analyze:** Not less important than administering, a SA should have good skills of analysis. However, that should not be confused with the responsibility of being an analyst. This responsibility fits in the context of the role of design, fits in the diagnostic of the problematic situations and also in the context of the development (analysis is required). The SA, due to the responsibilities of administrator, manager and developer, should assume the responsibility of being an analyst. Our belief is that this responsibility is transversal to IT/IS systems (e.g.: computer systems analyst - Figure 4). We do not consider a core responsibility of the SA.

A CONCEPTUAL VIEW ABOUT THE ROLES AND THE RESPONSIBILITIES OF THE SYSTEMS ADMINISTRATOR

To complement the explanations presented in the document about the subjects related to the role of the systems administrator, we have conceived a conceptual view of the roles and the responsibilities of the SA. In this conceptual view we present: (1) the link between the SA and the organization; (2) the categories of the SA roles and their relation with the size of the organizations; (3) a category of the skills of the SA, their relations and the academic branches of studies that contribute to skills; (4) the relation of organizations and the needs of professionals in IT experts; (5) the relation of the organizations and the needs of recruitment on IT areas; (6) the categories of responsibilities that define a SA. With this view we aim to demonstrate that the roles and the responsibilities of the SA are a consequence of a chain of factors, some of them strongly associated. We also have the intention to provide a first step to stimulate the discussion about the definition of the concepts of the roles and the responsibilities of the SA. Below we present a synthesis of each item of the conceptual view:

- **The Link of the SA with the Organization:** In the context of this document the SA was treated as an employee of an organization. However this is not what happens in every situation. There are cases, namely in small

organizations in which the role of the SA is delegated on an enterprise that performs IT services by outsourcing. In this case, to delimitate the context of the explanation, we have considered that the SA only exists in the organizations and not by outsourcing. Nevertheless, as this context was not studied, it cannot be discarded in future works;

- **The Categories of the SA Roles and their Relation with the Size of the Organizations:** The diverse type of organizations makes it very difficult to clearly identify the roles of the role of the SA in each different case. Additionally, the business changes and subsequent concepts could make the work very extensive and useful. To contextualize the SA in the organization, we have used the attribute size. In particular, the two extremes (large and small) and its characteristics allow us to face the situation in two distinct perspectives: the perspective of the small organizations that need an operational and polyvalent SA and the perspective of the large organizations that need a more executive and conceptualizer SA. In this context we identified a core set categories of roles (security, operation, management) that are transversal to different types of organizations and two additional categories of roles that occur mainly in the large organizations (training using and design). Nevertheless, the core categories of roles are the reflection of the size of the organization based on the needs of the roles played by the SA (more operational in small organizations or more executive in large organizations).

- **The Category of Skills of the SA, How they Relate, and What Academic Branches of Studies Contribute to Which Skills:** As previously stated the educational, vocational, and the training path are relevant to determine the skills of the SA. Due to the differences among national teaching sys-

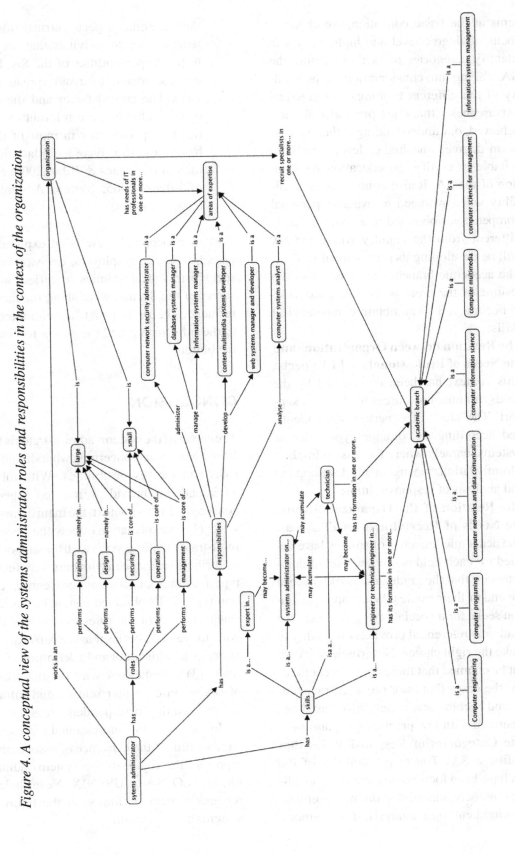

Figure 4. A conceptual view of the systems administrator roles and responsibilities in the context of the organization

tems at the basic education, we chose to focus on degree level and higher levels to identify categories of skills to define the SA. Taking into consideration the possibility of the different trainings and practical experiences that a professional has achieved, our understanding is that the program degrees and higher levels are more reliable to certify the educational formation of the SA. It also confers more credibility when we need to evaluate personal competencies obtained in a country that is different from the country where the SA will be developing its professional activity. The academic branches are a result of the resume of the areas where the candidates to become a SA can obtain competencies/skills;

- **The Relation between Organizations and the Needs of Professionals in IT Experts:** This context has been delimitated by the needs of human resources for internal support. The areas of expertise were identified according to common typologies of systems, namely where there is an implicit administration, management, development and analysis of responsibilities;

- **The Relation of the Organizations and the Needs of Recruitment in IT Areas:** The academic branches of studies have defined for each field of studies a set of competencies that the graduates should reach at the end of their studies. When an organization seeks for a specialist in given area, the academic referential provides credibility to make the right choice. Nevertheless, it cannot be claimed that there are no exceptions. For the cases that have preceded the studies and become academics, there have been identified with low practicing capabilities;

- **The Categories of Responsibilities that Define a SA:** The responsibilities of the SA have been focused on technical capabilities, namely administration, management, development and analysis. Furthermore,

there are other aspects, intrinsic for the systems of human activities that are relevant to the responsibilities of the SA, but were not considered to avoid spread the subjects. The ethical factor and the integrity of the individual are relevant characteristics to a person that in most of the cases has access to private and classified information (Fagernes & Ribu, 2007; Schedule of Ethics, 2005; System Administrators' Code of Ethics).

This conceptual view is an exploratory approach to guide employers, decision-takers, IT specialists and academics to reflect about the career of the SA and what about the factors that influence the person that has unlimited access to the information and the power to "switch off the button."

CONCLUSION

The career of the systems administrator is far away from a consensus concerning what should be their roles and the responsibilities. With this work, we intended to provide a first step to generate a consensus. In this context, the main contributions were: (1) an explanation of how the systems' administrator acquires skills with the support of a set of attributes associated with the career (education type, training/education options, entity, certification type, skills obtained conducing to…); (2) a categorization of the roles to conceptualize the wide range of activities that are performed by the systems' administrator and a definition of the core roles; (3) a framework with the main branches of studies in computer science and Informatics science and the correspondent areas.

In the context of professional representation, were identified the existence of associations that represent the figure of the systems administrator, like LOPSA or USENIX. Nevertheless still remains a fuzzy definition of the figure of the systems administrator.

In the context of the academic instruction, we have registered the offers to develop studies as Master of Science in diverse areas of computer administration and systems administration. The training and the certification of the systems' administrators, beyond the added value to their professional skills and competencies, is a factor of credibility. More than the trust on the IT team, the systems' administrator is "the man of the systems" and should inspire credibility.

As limitations we identified the lack of scientific references dedicated to the role of the systems' administrator. The bibliographical references to the systems' administrator were found, mainly, in the context of other subjects: administration of a particular operative system, administration of a database management system, or even, in the context of systems' implementations. Other references were found on Websites of professional associations or groups of practitioners, most of them very sparse and sometimes divergent. A possible explanation is the fact that the systems' administrator is, most of the times, connoted with computer and electrical sciences or just a computer science engineer.

REFERENCES

ACM. (n.d.). Retrieved 11 22, 2012, from http://www.acm.org

Burgess, M., & Koymans, K. (2007). Master education programmes in network and system administration. In *Proceedings of the 21st conference on Large Installation System Administration Conference* (pp. 215-229). Dallas, TX: USENIX Association.

Chalupa, S. R. (2007). Systems administration as a self-organizing system: The profissionalization of the SA via Interest and advocacy groups. In Bergstra, J., & Burgess, M. (Eds.), *Handbook of network and system administration* (pp. 961–968). London: Elsevier Science.

CORDIS: FP6. (n.d.). Retrieved 10 22, 2012, from http://cordis.europa.eu/fp6/fp6keywords.htm

Edlund, S., & Lövquist, A. (2012). *The role of system administrators in information systems success*. (MSc Thesis). Uppsala University, Uppsala, Sweden.

Fagernes, S., & Ribu, K. (2007). Ethical, legal and social aspects of the systems. In Bergstra, J., & Burgess, M. (Eds.), *Handbook of network and system administration* (pp. 969–999). London: Elsevier Science.

Frisch, A. (2002). *Essential system administration: Tools and techniques for linux and unix administration* (3rd ed.). Sebastopol, CA: O'Reilly Media, Incorporated.

Haber, E. M., Kandogan, E., & Maglio, P. P. (2011). Collaboration in system administration. *Communications of the ACM, 1*(54), 46–53. doi:10.1145/1866739.1866755.

IEEE. (n.d.). Retrieved 10 29, 2012, from http://www.ieee.org

LOPSA. (n.d.). Retrieved 11 17, 2012, from https://lopsa.org/

McNutt, D. (1993). Role-based system administration or who, what, where, and how. In *Proceedings of the Seventh System Administration Conference (LISA '93)* (pp. 106-112). Monterey, CA: USENIX.

OE. (n.d.). Retrieved 11 11, 2012, from http://www.ordemengenheiros.pt

QS World Universities Ranking. (n.d.). Retrieved 11 12, 2012, from http://www.topuniversities.com/university-rankings/world-university-rankings/2012/subject-rankings/technology/computer-science-information-systems

SA-BOK, Systems Administration Body of Knowledge. (n.d.). Retrieved 11 24, 2012, from http://www.sysadmin.com.au/sa-bok.html

Schedule of Ethics. (2005). Retrieved 11 24, 2012, from http://www.sage-au.org.au/sites/sage-au.org.au/files/attachments/SAGEAU/schedule_of_ethics-2005-10-03.pdf

System Administrators' Code of Ethics. (n.d.). Retrieved 11 15, 2012, from https://www.usenix.org/lisa/system-administrators-code-ethics

UNESCO. (2007). *Revised field of science and technology (FOS) classification in the frascati manual* (OECD). Retrieved 11 20, 2012, from http://www.uis.unesco.org/ScienceTechnology/Documents/38235147.pdf

USENIX. (n.d.). Retrieved 11 15, 2012, from https://www.usenix.org/

ADDITIONAL READING

Bernestein, A. B. (2004). *Guide to your career* (5th ed.). New York: Princeton Review.

Blank-Edelman, D. N. (2000). *Perl for system administration: Managing multi-platform environments with perl*. Sebastopol, CA: O'Reilly Media, Inc..

Burgess, M. (2000). Theoretical system administration. In *Proceedings of the Fourteenth Systems Administration Conference (LISA XIV)* (pp. 1-14). New Orleans, LA: LISA.

Burgess, M. (2003). On the theory of system administration. *Science of Computer Programming, 49*, 1–46. doi:10.1016/j.scico.2003.08.001.

Burgess, M., & Koymans, K. (2007). Master education programmes in network and system administration. In *Proceedings of the 21st Conference on Large Installation System Administration Conference* (pp. 215-229). Dallas, TX: USENIX Association.

Carter, G. (2003). LDAP system administration. Sebastopol, CA: O'Reily Media, Inc.

Chalupa, S. R. (2007). Systems administration as a self-organizing system: The professionalization of the SA via interest and advocacy groups. In Bergstra, J., & Burgess, M. (Eds.), *Handbook of network and system administration* (pp. 961–968). London: Elsevier Science.

Firesmith, D. G., & Henderson-Sellers, B. (2001). *The OPEN process framework: An introduction*. London: Addison Wesley.

Freeland, C., & McKay, D. (2002). *The complete systems administrator*. OnWord Press.

Greg, R., & Brian, M. (2012). *Microsoft system center 2012 configuration manager: Administration cookbook*. Birmingham, AL: Packt Publishing.

Haeder, A., & Burleson, D. (2004). *Conducting the network administrator job interview: IT manager guide with Cisco CCNA interview questions*. New York: Rampant TechPress.

Hrebec, D. G., & Stiber, M. (2001). A survey of system administrator mental models and situation awareness. In *Proceedings of the 2001 ACM SIGCPR Conference on Computer Personnel Research* (pp. 166-172). San Diego, CA: ACM.

Inc.Bizmanualz.com. (2005). Bizmanualz(tm) computer & network policies, procedures & forms. New York: Bizmanualz.com.

Kemp, J. (2009). *Linux system administration recipes: A problem-solution approach*. New York: Springer-Verlag.

Limoncelli, T., Hogan, C. J., & Chalup, S. R. (2007). *The practice of system and network administration* (2nd ed.). Reading, MA: Addison Wesley.

Limoncelli, T. A. (2005). *Time management for system administrators*. Sebastopol, CA: O'Reilly Media, Inc..

MacKey, D. (2003). *Web security: For network and system administrators*. New York: Course Technology.

Naghibzadeh, M. (2011). Operating system: Concepts and techniques. Bloomington, IN: iUniverse Books.

Pokorny, J., Repa, V., Richtai, K., Wojtkowski, W., Linger, H., & Barry, C. et al. (2011). *Information systems development: Business systems and services: Modeling and development*. London: Springer.

Regan, S. (2005). *Apple training series: Mac OS X system administration reference*. Berkley, CA: Peachpit Press.

Rosenblatt, G. B. (2009). *Systems analysis and design*. Boston: Course Technology, Cernage Learning.

Rountree, D. (2010). *Security for Microsoft windows system administrators: Introduction to key information security concepts*. London: Elsevier Inc..

Schneider, L. (n.d.). *Tech careers, system administrator*. Retrieved 11 03, 2012, from http://jobsearchtech.about.com/od/careersintechnology/p/SysAdmin.htm

Vacca, J. R. (2005). *Computer forensics: Computer crime scene investigation* (2nd ed.). Boston: Charles Media, Inc..

Willis, J. (2008). *MCSA 100 success secrets Microsoft certified systems administrator certification, training, boot camp, courses and exam 100 most asked questions to implement, manage, and maintain windows OS*. Emereo Publishing.

Winsor, J. (2003). *Solaris operating environment administrator's guide* (4th ed.). New York: Prentice Hall.

Wylie, K. (2003). *SWOT analysis of Cisco systems, inc*. Munich, Germany: GRIN Publishing GmbH..

Yang, J., Ginige, A., Mayr, H. C., & Kutsche, R.-D. (2009). *Information systems: Modeling, development, and integration*. Berlin: Springer. doi:10.1007/978-3-642-01112-2.

KEY TERMS AND DEFINITIONS

Academic Branches of Studies: Sub-areas of studies of the areas of computer science / informatics science areas.

Areas of Expertise: Areas where the systems administrator obtain its specialization.

Conceptual View: A view of the main concepts about a specific subject.

Information Systems: In the context of this document, a system to manage information supported by computer systems.

Responsibilities of the Systems Administrator: The duty to deal with the systems which he is the responsible person.

Roles of the Systems Administrator: The roles assumed by systems administrator in the context of its professional activities.

Section 2
Legal and Regulatory Frameworks

Chapter 4
Beyond Compliance:
Understanding the Legal Aspects of Information System Administration

Peter J. Wasilko
The Institute for End User Computing, Inc., USA

ABSTRACT

This chapter focuses on the relationship between law and information systems administration. It highlights how technological choices can facilitate regulatory compliance, reduce legal costs, and allow agile responses to emerging risks. The reader should not regard this chapter as a comprehensive introduction to all of the world's criminal and civil IT related statutes, regulations, and case law. It should be used as a basis for discussions with local counsel.

BACKGROUND ON THE NATURE OF LAW

Law is the medium through which political decisions are promulgated and implemented and through which private obligations are established and enforced. It can take the form of explicit statutes, regulations, and contracts or it can arise implicitly from the Common Law tradition of past judicial and regulatory enforcement opinions in law and equity. It can be substantively related to issues at hand or procedurally based in the rules of the legal system. This procedural dimension governs:

- **Standing:** Who has the right to litigate.
- **Venue:** Which tribunal will decide a matter.
- **Choice of Laws:** Which jurisdiction's law will be used.
- **Motion Practice:** What requests to make by what deadlines at various stages in a dispute.
- **Rules of Evidence:** What proof can be offered.
- **Published Tribunal Specific Practice Rules:** How parties must conduct themselves.
- **Unpublished Tribunal Specific Practice Norms:** Informal rules and patterns of behavior.

DOI: 10.4018/978-1-4666-4526-4.ch004

Cases often encompass several areas of substantive law raising numerous procedural issues. We speak of tribunal rather than court and adjudicator rather than judge, as many matters are resolved through administrative proceedings under executive branch agencies and commissions, negotiation and settlement, and Alternative Dispute Resolution (ADR) mechanisms like mediation & arbitration outside of the court system.

Formal litigation need not resolve all of the issues "at bar" in a given case if its outcome can be determined without addressing them. If multiple judges hear a case, each is free to issue his or her own opinion—either concurring with the majority on its result under a different interpretation of law, or dissenting to argue against the majority position in the hope that it might be judicially or legislatively overturned. This can occur on an issue-by-issue basis, thus reducing or increasing the precedential value of the majority decision on each point. Portions of opinions going beyond purely legal arguments to stake out Public Policy positions or to suggest how cases ought to be argued before and decided by future courts are called dicta.

While published laws, rules, and options are in-principle intended to offer guidance to ordinary lay people, their use of language assumes readers are familiar with the legal interpretations of terms of art and with legal principles expressed by allusion to famous cases. Thus, the correct interpretation of legal language depends on mastery of its historical context, coupled with the skill set to track down unfamiliar references and to read between the lines (This last facet comes into play in recognizing those hopefully rare instances influenced by extra-legal considerations in which a judicial or regulatory opinion does not reflect the actual decision-making process through which it was reached).

Legal Risk

One cannot take legal writing at face value. It is critical to seek legal help when you feel that you have been wronged, need to know your rights and obligations, or need to make long-range plans. Ideally, you will want clearly articulated answers that let you avoid disputes or reliably predict their resolution. Few areas of law are this highly predicable leading us to recognize the notion of Legal Risk.

"Legal risk is the danger that when relevant laws are applied to a course of action, they will have negative or unforeseen consequences affecting one's rights and obligations. It can stem from uncertainties over what the law will be and how it might be applied. Since each possible course of action will raise multiple issues each of which could play out several different ways, one must consider all plausible permutations to develop a range of scenarios that can be ranked in a game theoretical sense by likelihood and severity of impact. This is the essence of legal analysis and planning..." (Wasilko, 2011, p. 476).

Such analysis combines rigorous attention to detail at multiple levels with an instinctive understanding of the psychology and politics needed to read people and play to their often-unstated motivations. Some representations fall more on the logical side, while others turn more on human factors. Seasoned lawyers are equally adept at both. Lawyers' secondary skills include proficiency with legal research & writing, a baseline mental model of a range of legal topics, familiarity with legal procedures, and access to a social network of colleagues. Their exacting use of language whose legal effect may deviate from its apparent semantics has deep historical roots that defy simplification (Mellinkoff, 1963, sec. 87, 116, 130–131).

The degree of legal risk inherent in different situations varies dramatically with their complexity, the relative stability of the areas of law they implicate, their political ramifications, and the degree to which they turn on subjective or disputable facts. The greater the risk, the greater the need for legal guidance and the less likely that it will offer a satisfying degree of certitude. At the opposite end of the spectrum, are simple questions with definitive answers for which a self-help book, such as "Forming an LL.C." may well be adequate (Spadaccini, 2007).

The Process of Lawyering and Value of In-House Counsel

Lawyering can be viewed as akin to a vigorous Code Review, with an eye toward provable correctness. Your counsel will be able to spot potential legal problems and suggest ways to minimize their impact. This is similar to Chess with its combinatorial explosion of potential moves and countermoves, but with rules that are subject to ongoing change. Beyond the political aspects of shifting law and interpretation, there is a major psychological component to legal gamesmanship that closely parallels Poker with elements of uncertainty and bluff. Outside of a relatively small subset of "bright line" legal problems, one is dealing with a sea of what-ifs trading business goals off of a desire to minimize legal exposure.

For technical people, this endemic uncertainty and intrinsic risk in any course of behavior is maddening. Outside counsel (i.e. independent law firms) are delighted to dive as deeply into this Rabbit's Hole as a client's legal budget permits. Often clients wind up periodically asking, "Has anything changed?" only to be billed to hear, "Not that we know of, yet."

Given the oversupply of legal talent in metropolitan areas, the most economical approach is to employ in-house counsel whose financial interests are those of your organization. Since younger lawyers (and even many older ones) are heavily interested in technology, even a small enterprise should be able to recruit one to work closely with its Systems Administrator in ongoing issue spotting. If needed, outside counsel can be engaged on a limited basis to deal with matters in which they specialize, under the direction of one's in-house counsel.

Now we can consider those areas of law effecting one's decision making as a Systems Administrator and explore some technical and social strategies to minimize their legal risks to both the Admin and his or her organization. Because, the law may have shifted between the time of this writing and its publication, accordingly it cannot be emphasized too strongly that this text should not be regarded as offering legal advice with respect to the reader's individual circumstances. While there are some situations in which an organization's in-house or outside counsel can ethically represent both the business entity and its employees, there are others in which a Systems Administrator will face personal risk that would necessitate seeking independent legal advice.

AREAS OF RESPONSIBILITY

Systems Integrity

Systems Administrators play key roles in legal compliance both with regard to the IT functions under their immediate purview and on a deeper level in maintaining the integrity of their organizations' business records with respect to all technologically mediated activities. This places the Systems Administrators in a unique position to implement measures to expose insider malfeasance.

One's greatest technical challenge is to preserve the integrity of the information systems in one's charge. It is critical to know with relative certitude that they have not been compromised thus insuring that the access control policies governing their use have been properly applied. It is critical that Intrusion Detection measures are in place to immediately flag and respond to any attempts at subverting security protocols. This often involves operating system level services to mirror or checksum critical files on a remote system, monitor open ports, running processes, and resource utilization patterns to reliably detect any unexpected activity.

Once this baseline is established to guard against elements of the OS being modified on or off line, security extensions can be put in place to establish the true provenance of all monitored actions.

Workflow and business logic can then be designed by others to document compliance with any rules pertaining to their respective areas of responsibility. Human Resources might set up a Whistleblower policy through which complaints would be sent via digitally signed and encrypted emails to a designated mail account. From there they could be forwarded to multiple officers and directors who would be required to send out digitally signed acknowledgements, building a documentation trail from the complaint to its resolution. The exact structure of such business processes and the appropriate level of redundancy needed to guard against compromise by those in the chain of responsibility is most likely outside the scope of a System Administrator's duties.

Security considerations aside, being able to establish that the resulting records are authentic and were produced in the ordinary course of business allows one to introduce their substantive contents into evidence, even if the individuals who entered them can no longer be located or recall the facts they documented. Failure to produce such records if required by a court can expose a firm to legal sanctions, as we shall see in our discussion of e-discovery. Thus, it is vital to put the tools in place and to educate the responsible parties on their proper use.

User Education

The Systems Administrator's educational role goes beyond instruction in the use of deployed technology. It further encompasses making sure that users are employing sound authentication strategies, are cognizant of "Social Engineering" attack vectors, and are actively reporting any suspicious incidents. This is more than just a matter of prudent security policy since it could prove dispositive in shielding one's organization from legal liability.

Users must also be trained in how to comply with relevant Criminal and Civil laws vis-à-vis your firm's and third parties' Intellectual Property Rights, regulatory reporting frameworks, privacy rules, and how to respond to third party and government information requests and demands for access to data in your systems or its removal from public view. Under the United States' Computer Fraud and Abuse Act (CFAA) ("18 USC § 1030 - Fraud and related activity in connection with computers," 2012) employee violations of your organization's computer usage policies or of the contractual clauses in online service usage agreements might be construed as Criminal activity.

One must consider local law when communicating with employees and users to insure that they will be deemed to have received legally effective notice of what you have to tell them. This can take the form of a click-through license for most generic Terms of Service and End User License Agreements. Jurisdictions may diverge on which terms of such agreements will be enforceable, but as a rule of thumb the more you can do to establish that the terms were both reasonable and understood, the greater the likelihood of their being enforced. This is why some implementations of click-through agreements require you to wait several seconds or to scroll through the full text of the agreement before they will permit you to accept their terms.

For multinational entities, local law in a number of jurisdictions may require communications in a language other than English. France, Belgium, Quebec, Spain, Mongolia and Turkey have strict rules on which language must be used. Nations like Chile, Macedonia, Poland, and Russia will invalidate untranslated documents. In many other jurisdictions, regulatory filings must be made in the native language and in even more places using the wrong language will lead to an antagonistic bias from local tribunals. Donald C. Dowling, Jr. explores all of these issues in much more depth in "English Is Not Your Exclusive Company Language" (Dowling, 2012).

HR departments are generally on top of these issues, but Systems Administrators need to track them as well since their usage guidelines are often incorporated by reference into other contracts and policies; and they may even come into play in complying with notice provisions in software license agreements.

CLASSIFYING INFORMATION ASSETS

Once we set up our infrastructure to control access and log activities, we can think about how to classify the information assets within the firm.

- **Public Resources:** Many items have no monetary value, consisting of nothing more than local copies of email newsletters, Web pages, freely redistributable pdfs, and the like. While it may make sense to maintain local copies of them in case the originals go offline, their only possible legal significance would be in establishing knowledge of their existence or contents.
- **Business Records:** The preservation of business records is critical in documenting regulatory compliance and as evidence in the event of litigation.

- **Personally Identifying Information:** Such as customer lists, addresses, ages, phone numbers, email addresses, credit card numbers, bank accounts, and the like need to be closely guarded against external leakage and internal abuse.
- **Email:** Messages sent to and from one's organization as well as any email accounts it might provide to third parties are potentially subject to regulation.
- **User Content:** A category embodying most social media ranging from blog posts and comments to media assets embedded in online games by their players.
- **Software (and Media) Assets:** These are mostly computer programs and supporting Media like artwork that are generally acquired through a license that the Systems Administrator will be expected to adhere to both directly and indirectly through the activities of his or her users.
- **Trade Secrets:** A category that is somewhat amorphous and can consist of intangible business or technological knowhow whether or not embodied in code.

Saving too much information can be as big a mistake as not saving enough, since it will be subject to costly electronic discovery in the event of litigation; this is why we speak of the need for firms to have a Defensible Deletion Policy.

Mitigating the Ramifications of Seizures

Ideally, you will structure your system to isolate different classes of information from one another and segregate them by user jurisdiction, so that you can vary your IT policies to comply with conflicting national laws. If one country's investigators arrive demanding to seize all digital media and systems bearing User Content, you can direct them to just that server and its backups without having all of the other aspects of your business taken offline. (This is of course assuming that officials will accept your assertion that the data is indeed so segregated, but even if they do not, taking this precaution should speed up the eventual return of any media and devices seized.).

If your organization is dealing with considerable amounts of user content or has well-funded, highly zealous, or politically connected enemies then it pays to mirror all of your data operations in multiple jurisdictions so you can redirect your DNS pointers away from any location that is forced to go dark.

If you send employees abroad, it is better to not have them carry any data that might be subject to seizure by customs. Instead, either separately ship media with the data in encrypted form to their destination or have them pull it down from the cloud to be decrypted on site with a password that is transmitted to them once they arrive in country. If you or your staff travel with encrypted data you may be asked to decrypt it at the border. Moreover, it may be illegal to cross a boarder with or ship overseas some types of cryptography software and hardware subject to control by The Export Administration Regulations of the Bureau of Industry and Security in the U.S. Department of Commerce. ("U. S. Bureau of Industry and Security - Policies and Regulations," 1918)

Privacy Regulations

Privacy legislation varies dramatically across national boundaries. The founders of the United States never contemplated an explicit privacy right when they set up the Constitution and the Bill of Rights. Rather than introducing a Right to Privacy through the constitutional amendment process, it was instead created by judicial fiat—limiting it to those areas where there was a reasonable expectation of privacy.

In practice, through litigation and legislation, this core protection has come to cover physical sexual encounters, birth control, abortion, medi-cal records and doctor-patient communications (although healthcare "reform" may soon threaten medical privacy rights), some other personal information, and privileged communications with spouses, lawyers, and clergy. In general, your obligation to protect privacy is largely limited to:

- **Medical Records:** Under the Health Insurance Portability and Accountability Act (HIPPA) ("Understanding Health Information Privacy," 2007).
- **Contact Information Related to Minors:** Under the Children's Online Privacy Protection Act (COPPA) (Electronic Privacy Information Center, 2012).
- **Personally Identifying Information:** Such as that described by the Identity Theft and Assumption Deterrence Act of 1998 under the Code of Federal Regulations and several state privacy laws("e-CFR," n.d., sec. Part 313 – Privacy of Consumer Financial Information).

In contrast, the European Union takes privacy to be a fundamental right, and offers dramatically greater protection for the subjects of data collection under The Data Protection Directive – Directive 95/46/EC (European Parliament and Counsel of the European Union, 1995). This has dramatic implications for multinational enterprises that want to be able to share customer records with third parties and business units outside of EU jurisdictions. The US and EU have established a safe harbor program, whereby your organization can pay a fee and self-certify that you are maintaining high enough privacy standards to meet minimal EU standards allowing you to move data freely. (U.S. Department of Commerce, 2012)

You may or may not be required to publish a formal Privacy Policy if you maintain a public facing Internet presence, but if you do, there is a high probability that you will be compelled to abide by it. This presents a business planning challenge since your organization will need to balance its lawyers' desire to make no privacy guarantees against its marketers' desire to offer them to attract users.

Another hassle has been the UK Cookie Law (Information Commissioner's Office, 2012), which led to a proliferation of annoying cookie management notices at a time when most reasonably intelligent end users have long since learned how to manage cookies. Also unclear is how to deal with other forms of client side persistent storage like Flash-based mechanisms. Equally troubling is the open question of whether Websites outside the UK will be expected to comply, although the act seems to be drawing a significant backlash from Web developers worldwide.

AN OVERVIEW OF INTELLECTUAL PROPERTY

The law recognizes several ways to protect the product of one's mental labor flowing from both common law and statute. We will now consider their attributes and impact.

Copyright

In order to encourage writers to share their ideas, Copyright Law gives them the right to control how their works are disseminated. In the US, copyright is controlled by Title 17 of the United States Code (U.S. Copyright Office, 2011). Copyright vests when an author fixes his or her ideas in a medium (i.e. expresses them as text, audio, graphics, animation, or video such that they can be faithfully reproduced). There is no need to do anything beyond the act of recording expressions to receive a copyright interest in them. In most nations, additional benefits can be obtained by paying a nominal "registration" fee and submitting a copy of the work to a governmental entity like the Library of Congress in the United States. This procedure makes it easier to sue and recover damages from anyone making unauthorized cop-

ies. While the life of a copyright in the US is ostensibly supposed to run for the life of an author plus 75 years, special interests consistently succeed in lobbying Congress to extend copyright terms so that additional works no longer enter the Public Domain, insuring that properties like early Mickey Mouse cartoons effectively remain under copyright in perpetuity. Thus, you cannot safely assume that older works are freely available for use.

It should also be noted that Copyright applies to the expression of ideas but not the ideas themselves; and where an idea is represented in a medium so constrained as to exclude meaningful variations in its expression, the idea and expression are said to "merge" precluding protection. (e.g., if in the assembly language of a given CPU, there might only be one way to code an algorithm, that code could be legitimately copied verbatim).

Copyright can also be applied to aggregations of data and the "organization and structure" of larger composite works like computer programs, so infringement can be found in the absence of literal copying. Authors often insert minor errors in factual databases or maps to make it possible to prove when they have been copied.

Websites themselves can be protected under the doctrine of "compilation copyright" to obtain the benefits of registration without having to make an additional filing corresponding to every minor edit. That said, making material available on a public Web server would be held to grant users implicit permission to view and archive it. It would not convey the additional right to convert it into a book and market it. In some jurisdictions, hot linking to individual images or embedding portions of a site may not be legally permissible and there are periodic efforts to preclude even the most basic act of linking without permission (Associated Press, 2003).

Copyright also carries Fair Use exemptions to permit direct quotations in scholarly works, critiques and reviews, parodies, and software backups. Fair Use is a nebulous area that is evaluated on a case-by-case basis using a multi-factored test that looks at such aspects as how much of a work is being used, whether the use is in education or a profit making endeavor, what impact the use has on the market for the work, etc.

While a given use may be deemed fair, it may still be illegal to extract the copy for that use under the Digital Millennium Copyright Act (DMCA), also known as the WIPO Copyright and Performances and Phonograms Treaties Implementation Act of 1998, if the copy is protected by technological means (i.e. some form of Digital Rights Management). The DMCA and subsequent litigation must also be taken into consideration before trafficking in any "circumvention" technology even at the level of linking to a site with instructions on how to thwart DRM. (U.S. Copyright Office, 1998) At the time of this writing, the DMCA exemption for jail breaking US cell phones has been revoked, so you should have employees traveling overseas purchase a local phone if they can't buy one in an unlocked state.

Licensing

To monetize copyrights, it is necessary to license them out. A license is a contract conveying a set of rights, in this case reproduction rights. The art of licensing lies in carving up IP Rights by market, distribution method, period of distribution, and any other imaginable facet to maximize their value.

When a copyrighted work is reproduced in an artifact like a book, disk, or preloaded MP3 player that is *sold* to someone, its author's interest in that copy is extinguished by the First Sale Doctrine. This notion, which is extended to incorporate the transmittal of whatever IP Rights are needed to use that particular copy, is the legal basis on which book owners and Used Book Stores are permitted to resell texts and on which Libraries are permitted to loan out copies of books, music, and videos. This right to dispose of purchased copies has been somewhat constrained by the concept

of Artistic Rights embodied in the international Berne Convention, which empowers a creator to prevent his or her work from being distorted or mutilated by subsequent owners.

Big content publishers would very much like to avoid the loss of control conveyed by the First Sale Doctrine, particularly where they use differential pricing across global markets. At the time of this writing the US Supreme Court has ruled that the First Sale Doctrine applies to copies purchased abroad making it likely that congress may address this issue.

Many publishers, particularly of software, try to avoid the ramifications of selling a copy by characterizing their sales as a shrink-wrapped-license. Under this model, ownership of the physical artifact is ostensibly retained by the publisher. The copy being purchased, can be thought of as being offered on a long term loan with attendant rights to access the content so long as a litany of license terms (which in the software case, generally include a prohibition on reverse engineering the product) are adhered to.

Such license terms may or may not be enforceable, the license to use the copy may or may not be deemed transferable, and a breach of any given license term may or may not lead to civil and criminal liability. Thus, it is to the Systems Administrator's advantage to keep End Users in full compliance unless one's organization has received explicit written permission from the copyright holder to deviate, or is sizable enough to embark on litigation over such matters.

Infringement

It is crucial to institute some form of Software Asset Management to insure that none of the End Users under your purview are using illegal copies of proprietary software on the job, as criminal copyright liability might attach to you even if you are not directly aware of the violation. (Collins, 2012) With the Business Software Alliance offering sizable financial bounties for employees to report the illegal use of software, it is highly likely any illegal software use will be reported. (Business Software Alliance, 2012) If you find yourself working for an employer that condones such behavior, or if you discover that a system under your management is harboring illegal copies, you should seek independent legal advice on how best to rectify the situation.

Even when using licensed software, a given usage might not be covered by the license. These can take the form of incompatibilities between licenses as might preclude the incorporation of GPL libraries into property code or of usage restrictions, as would be the case if one wanted to use the version of Microsoft Office™ that is bundled with a Microsoft Surface™ tablet for Business Use.

It is not sufficient to audit the software being used by your organization if it provides any form of file storage or exchange to its customers. Sadly, there is legal precedent for authorities to seize a firm's servers if they contain illegal End User uploaded content.

To address the common case of allegations of copyright infringement, the DMCA established a "safe harbor" provision to protect Web hosting services and forum operators who promptly "take down" any infringing content upon "notice" from rights holders. It also provides a mechanism to permit content restoration upon receipt of a "counter notice" challenging the claim while its validity is assessed. This regime has had a chilling effect since the easier course of action is to treat all notices as representing valid claims rather than to try to provide some form of in-house due process to customers. (Seltzer, 2010)

Digital Music Rights

Before incorporating music in Web content, you should be aware that there are different licensing regimes in place depending on whether you wish to stream a song in real time or distribute a re-playable copy. Depending on the work and its intended use, you may be able to seek a compulsory license or have to negotiate with a rights management agency or music label. If you are part of a startup that wants to get into the online music distribution business, you need to make sure it has top entertainment lawyers on staff and a deep enough capital reserve for a prolonged negotiating process. If the organization is relatively small or even midsized relative to a Microsoft or Apple, its odds of success are quite low and you should probably start circulating your resume (Braun & Castle, 2004).

If you need to use existing music as a background to Webcasts, your first choice should be pre-packaged audio loops explicitly licensed for that purpose like those in Apple's Garage Band and similar software. If only a popular song will do, you need to engage an entertainment lawyer to secure its use.

However, if your organization just wants a punchy signature theme, it really should not be looking at licensing it from the music industry. Instead, for a fraction of the legal fees you could find an unknown local artist to create a totally original track as a one-time "work for hire" which would make your organization the copyright holder of record, further enhancing the potential to use that tune as an audio trademark.

Patents

Patents are the most pernicious form of intellectual property because they grant the right to block the use of innovations even if they are discovered independently. Under copyright, if two developers read about a new data structure in an academic text, they can both freely encode identical programs to implement it without conflicting with each other's rights. If a third developer refactors one of these programs, renames the variables to enhance their clarity, and adds some explanatory comments, his or her work will be deemed sufficiently transformational as to be permitted.

However, if someone filed a Software Patent on the idea of using such a data structure, even if it had not been reduced to actual running code, he or she would receive a government granted monopoly on its use. This would permit the patent holder to exclude all others from practicing the patented idea, even if they had invented it first, invested substantial resources in its discovery, and had no knowledge of the patent in question.

The Constitutional basis advanced by the Founders for granting such patent monopolies was to trade their economic benefits for the public disclosure of the discoveries they embody to advance the progress of the useful arts. In any public policy analysis, we must therefore focus on the degree to which the patent system is incentivizing patent holders to make meaningful disclosures and to develop useful technologies that would not have be developed in its absence. As the pace of innovation has quickened and the scope of covered subject matter has grown, many have come to question whether the patent system is still performing this intended function (Jaffe & Lerner, 2006).

In the US, Software and Business Method Patents have become pervasive and could cover many things one might come up with as a Systems Administrator, and almost any sizable piece of software is all but guaranteed to infringe on a number of patents. The language used to define patent claims is all but impenetrable and sufficiently removed from that of computer scientists and programmers as to require the mediation of expert patent researchers. Most patents lack enough detail to permit "a practitioner of the art" to actually implement the claimed innovation.

Even worse, this year's move in the US from "First To Invent" to "First to File" will make it harder for small innovative firms to compete with established firms that have large in-house legal departments, while encouraging everyone to file claims on ever more trivial ideas lest someone

beat them to the patent office ("Public Law 112 - 29 - Leahy-Smith America Invents Act," 2012).

The US Patent and Trademark Office views Patent Applicants as its primary customers and treats the number of new patents and the speed with which they are issued as its key metrics. Such policies, coupled with the fact that previously inapplicable solutions often become broadly obvious as soon as a requisite enabling technology becomes available resulting in their never being documented in the academic literature, have led to an explosion in low quality patents.

Wealthy players can afford to tweak and resubmit rejected applications repeatedly until some variant passes muster. This creates an environment in which mega-corporations can use patent litigation to stymie each other's attempts to introduce superior products and bully small firms into abandoning their business plans or agreeing to be acquired.

Once issued, patents can change hands often being collected by so-called Patent Trolls who leverage the expense of defending patent litigation to extract license fees in what amounts to a legal extortion racket. People often conflate Patent Trolls with Non Practicing Entities (NPEs). This erroneous distinction casts Universities, Standards Bodies, R&D Consortia, and Patent Pools in the same light as litigious shell companies exploiting low-quality patents that ought never have been issued.

The question of whether a rights holder is abusing the system is only tangentially related to NPE status since the best way to monetize IP, whether for good or ill, is often through the use of a dedicated NPE with the resources and expertise to pursue licensing and litigation.

Non-Value-Contributing Entities

I therefore propose that we speak instead of Non-Value-Contributing Entities (NVCE's), which can be identified with a five prong factual analysis suitable for determination by a jury and incorporation into future IP Reform legislation:

- Is the rights holder actively developing a product or service based on the claimed technology?
- Did the rights holder participate in or fund the R&D leading to the patent grant?
- Is the rights holder sharing revenue from the patent with the original innovators and/or their employers as opposed to purchasing IP on the cheap to capture most of its value?
- Are the claims in the patent grant sufficiently narrow and clear as to allow a practitioner to implement a novel and useful solution to a real problem?
- Is the rights holder engaged in pro-active technology transfer to identify willing licensees, to teach them the claimed art, and to help them integrate it into their businesses?
- Is the rights holder acquiring patents to fund pre-competitive research, to help craft Industry Standards, or to perhaps establish Patent Pools clearing all of the IP Rights needed to legally practice its technology without fear of litigation?

If the answer to all of these questions is no, then the rights holder is a Non-Value-Contributing Entity whose actions impede technology diffusion, deter investment, and run at cross-purposes with the Constitutional basis for allowing patents. This definition filters out Original Innovators, Pre-launch Businesses, Universities, R&D Consortia, Standards Bodies, and Patent Pools who use the law as intended, making it possible to target only the subset of NPEs that abuse the legal system for potential reform legislation like a Looser Pays Legal Fees with Treble Damages rule.

Such reform could eliminate some of the worst abuses of the patent system, although a strong case can still be made that for both technological and economic reasons, Software Patents in any form serve to so disproportionately impede innovation in practice, as to fail to rise to the Constitutional

threshold for patent protection. Other possible reforms might include a much higher bar for patentability coupled with statutory defenses for independent discovery, noncommercial use, and/or widespread industry practice.

Absent reform, the unmanageable legal risk that any useful piece of software, whether commercial or free, may violate many patents threatens to exclude all but large deeply capitalized commercial players who can afford to battle NVCE's from participating in the market making Software Patents a threat to your employer and to your ability to legally do your job.

Links to many of the relevant statutes and rules can be found at the US Patent Office Website (Office of Patent Legal Administration, 2009).

Trademarks

Trademarks as formalized under the Lanham Act ("U.S. Trademark Law," 2012) are a far more benign and socially valuable form of IP, that protects consumers from being deceived as to the source and origin of products and services. Your role here is to make sure that your End Users are not referencing other corporate marks in any content they store and disseminate using your systems, without properly attributing them to their owners. You should also maintain archival copies of your organization's Web site and sales correspondence that can be referred to in establishing the date on which new marks like tag lines and logos are first "used in commerce" in the event that your organization subsequently decides to register them. In the United States, "Intent to Use" Trademarks can also be pre-registered prior to their actual use for the added convenience of avoiding the need to "rebrand" a product or service in the event that a desired mark is not available.

That said, as with copyright, registration is not required to establish a legally defensible interest and under the "common law" (i.e. the accumulated precedence of centuries of individual cases) using a mark in the course of one's business itself establishes a "common law trademark" to the extent that one's customers come to uniquely identify that mark with your business.

A trademark can be lost if its holder fails to defend it in the face of violations by other businesses or its use to describe similar good and services. This is why you will see language like "Kleenex® Brand Tissue, Registered Trademark of Kimberly-Clarke Worldwide, Inc." used in an effort to discourage the public from treating the term "Kleenex" as a generic synonym for tissue. When a trademark losses its association with its source in the minds of consumers we speak of it as trademark dilution and if unmitigated it could result in a loss of the mark under the common law.

Bearing this in mind, if you find yourself operating a very small organization, you may want to take the initiative in periodically searching the Internet for unattributed use of its marks. Since it is easy for anyone to search the PTO trademark database, you should consult it before using any potential marks to make sure they are not already registered. ("Trademark Electronic Search System (TESS)," 2013)

If your organization has available funds and is of any appreciable size, it will want to outsource policing its IP Right to a firm dedicated to performing that function. Regardless, it should only take your legal counsel a few minutes to prepare simple written guidelines on proper trademark use in your jurisdiction; you should then have all of your users read and acknowledge them.

Trade Secrets

Trade Secrets are perhaps the most appealing form of IP since they do not entail any marginal upfront registration costs and are largely self-enforcing if you choose your personnel wisely. Trade Secrets can have a very broad scope, but unlike patent protection, this is not an exclusionary right that prevents others from coming up with the same ideas through legitimate means.

The key to establishing a Trade Secret claim is to identify not widely known subject matter that leads to a commercial advantage and then taking affirmative measures to prevent its disclosure. If reasonable measures have been taken and a competitor uses improper means (e.g. bribing your employees or using surveillance gear) to acquire the secret, it will be subject to legal sanctions. Nimmer provides an excellent overview of these considerations (Nimmer, 1985, chap. 3).

Firms engaging in outright industrial espionage may also face criminal charges in addition to civil liability for stealing trade secrets.

Non-Disclosure Agreements

When pitching new business ventures, procuring outsourcing options, or beta-testing a new technology it is often necessary to share business practices or provide access to one's IT infrastructure that could potentially expose trade secrets. The standard way to address this concern is through a non-disclosure agreement whereby in consideration for sharing secrets in support of the overall project, the receiving party undertakes to protect the secret.

EMPLOYMENT LAW

Non-Compete Clauses

Hand-in-hand with maintaining thorough NDAs, it is critical to build that obligation into employment contracts and their non-compete clauses, which excluding the use of your firm's trade secrets, must generally be limited in terms of scope to specific markets and periods of time with respect to your employees general skills. For example, your firm:

- Cannot prohibit you from coding in Ruby.
- Could prevent you from working for its arc rival for a period of time that will vary depending on the precedents in your jurisdiction.
- Could prevent you from launching a competing startup in the same city.
- Might be able to prevent you from launching a competing venture in the same region.
- Probably cannot keep you from launching a competing venture on the opposite coast.
- Cannot prevent you from working as a Systems Administrator.
- Could prevent you from re-implementing its secret Page Ranking Algorithm until such time as the firm publishes the algorithm or others discover it on their own making it public knowledge.
- Might be able to prevent you from creating a New Page Raking Algorithm within the next five years.
- Could not prevent you from ever working on page ranking.

The more reasonable an employment contract is, the more likely it is to be enforced, whereas agreements calling everything a trade secret and trying to sideline former employees from practicing their trade are unlikely to prove enforceable. States will also widely differ in this area of law. California regards non-compete clauses as Unfair Business Practices immiscible with its Tech Sector and punishes firms trying to impose them on its residents, while many other states would be happy to enforce them (Gansle & Garber, 2012).

Enforcing broad non-compete clauses is bad public policy and you should avoid perspective employers who attempt to get you to agree to them.

Employee / Independent Contractor Distinctions

A number of statutes impose costs on employers that are not incurred when outsourcing tasks to Independent Contractors. The distinction turns on the degree of control that you have the right to exercise over the performance of the work in question. The IRS has become increasingly aggressive in sanctioning employers who miss-categorize employees as contractors, so if you have any doubts as to the status of one of your reports, you should ideally file Form SS-8 to seek a formal determination (Internal Revenue Service, 2010).

The more closely you supervise the work and control where it takes place, the more likely it will be deemed traditional employment. If instead, you limit your control to evaluating a small number of deliverables prepared when and where a worker with other clients sees fit, the more likely it will be deemed an independent contractor relationship. Loosely supervised part time telecommuting relationships are harder to classify, although the IRS will try to argue that they are traditional employment.

SOCIAL MEDIA, ADVERTISING, AND ACCESSIBILITY

Social media use by employees is a particularly thorny source of disputes. A mean spirited tweet or blog posting can be ascribed to one's employer and lead to claims of a hostile workplace environment. Many employers have asked for the passwords to employees social media accounts so they can monitor them. Some states like California are beginning to put breaks on this practice since it can unduly burden after hours freedom of speech (Lazzarotti, 2012). You will want to work with your counsel to lay out proper social media usage guidelines vis-à-vis the workplace.

You must also note that you may be required by law to make your Website, ecommerce, and social media services accessible to the disabled and to retain a log of all Instant Messages sent on the job as part of one or more mandatory record retention schemes.

Federal Trade Commission Rules

Under 16 C.F.R. Part 255: Guides Concerning the Use of Endorsements and Testimonials in Advertising, the Federal Trade Commission requires that any bloggers endorsing products disclose any consideration like free merchandise that they may have received in consideration for their reviews. This is relevant both if you personally control a blog hosting such reviews or if your organization has engaged in any efforts to solicit them on third party Websites (Federal Trade Commission, 2009).

Another source of concern is the FTC's Greenwashing Guidelines which may make it ill advised to tout the eco-friendliness of your Web hosting platform (M, 2012).

Online Censorship

A number of nations have seen social media as a dangerous force to be censored. At the time of this writing, Syria has cut off the Internet (Prince, 2012), Germany has asked Twitter to bar a NeoNazi (chillingeffects.org, 2012), India has criminalized hate speech ("Section 153A - Indian Penal Code (IPC)," n.d.), and Google is restructuring its blogging platform to selective block content where required ("Google-hosted blog content to be censored on country-by-country basis," 2012). So you will want to put similar technological levers in place to enable you to do likewise.

KNOWABLE RISKS

Beyond keeping hardware and software up to date, allocating resources, and vetting new solutions, the key role of the Systems Administrator lies in working out how to deploy technology and personnel to best mitigate the risk of business process disruption. In the absence of legal considerations, most approaches should be rather obvious.

You should maintain the ability to recreate legacy hardware and software configurations if an upgrade goes wrong or it becomes necessary to troubleshoot why a past version of the system did something unexpected. The law is unsettled as to whether you can legally emulate defunct systems even if you legally own ROMs for them and some modern OS Licenses prohibit virtualization. You may wish to run new configurations of particularly sensitive applications in parallel with older ones for a time to compare and validate their results.

You should have fall back systems in place both for load balancing in the case of distributed denial of service attacks to customer facing systems, and to maintain smooth operation if one or more devices experience hardware failures or power disruption in the case of a natural disaster. The design of fault tolerant systems that can cope with hardware and software glitches is a rich field of study.

You should cross-train personnel and devise ways to hold passwords in escrow to insure that they can be recovered if one or more key employees become unavailable. This aspect of risk management is sometimes called your Bus Number (i.e. the number of key employees whose premature deaths under a bus would be sufficient to kill your business). Thus if an organization has a single systems administrator in sole possession of all of its passwords and operational know how, its

Bus Number is one, leaving it highly vulnerable. The higher your Bus Number the better. It is, of course, also desirable to establish Bus Numbers for all of the discrete sub-processes within your organization, but your focus will be on those that are IT related. There is of course a tension between wanting high Bus Numbers for business continuity low ones with respect to any Trade Secrets.

You should establish system supported checks and balances to reduce the risk of being blindsided if one or more employees turn against your organization, possibly colluding to defeat your security protocols. Fans of the Survivor™ franchise will appreciate the risk of even the best alliance being subverted by a few key defections. If a single employee has unilateral access to your records, he or she would have the power to blindside your organization. This risk can be mitigated by ensuring that all critical actions are logged and that multiple employees need to cooperate to perform those actions or alter the logs. This could lead to scenarios where logs are automatically transmitted to a remote site subject to modification only by a different set of employees than those whose actions are being monitored. Likewise, instead of having a single employee enter a password, several could be required to cooperate in entering password segments to unlock sensitive functions. Combining automatic logging and notifications with multiple factor identification, segmented passwords, and thorough employee background screening can greatly reduce an organization's blindside risk and potential legal exposure in the unlikely event of an actual blindside.

Should you experience an internal or external data breach a number of state laws and federal regulations may require its disclosure, both to those users whose data may have been accessed and to your investors & regulators. At the first sign of a lawsuit you need to issue a Litigation Hold instructing all of your users not to delete or alter any potential evidence. By keeping emails limited to discrete topics with standardized subject lines you can go a long way to reducing the costs of eDiscovery.

All of these tactics entail introducing redundancies into your IT and business processes, which will of course, carry their own costs in terms of added personnel and equipment and potentially in employee dissatisfaction if the climate becomes too paranoid.

WITHDRAWAL AND DISSOLUTION THRESHOLDS

Legal Risk looks at the obligations imposed on a venture by current law and the potential ramifications of changes to law and policy. This is quite distinct from the ordinary business risks that would persist in the absence of any legal uncertainty.

Withdrawal and Dissolutions Thresholds exist with respect to any given jurisdiction or line of business, where the legal prohibitions, imposed obligations, reporting requirements, procedural red tape, tax policy, personal liability, political climate, labor relations, and overall level of Legal Risk reach the point at which their economic costs and the mental stress they induce become unbearable.

At these points, one must decide whether it is possible to reconfigure the business to push back the threshold. If the risks are concentrated in a jurisdiction to which alternatives exist, one can relocate the activity. If the risk is broadly associated with a given line of business across jurisdictions, and that activity is not essential to the overall survival of the enterprise, one can withdraw from engaging in it anywhere. However, if the risky activity lies at the core of one's business and the risk is indeed too great to ride out in the hope of a tolerable outcome, one must dissolve the business. From a strictly legal perspective, withdrawal is the act of ceasing operations and contacts with a jurisdiction and dissolution is the formal act of going out of business and terminating the existence of any associated corporate entities.

This analysis is distinct from the closely related question of whether it might be possible to use Bankruptcy Proceedings to reorganize your business, since we are concerned here with anticipating risky situations before they degenerate into concrete circumstances precluding you from meeting your immediate obligations. In short, an enterprise that heeds its withdrawal and dissolution thresholds should be able to address its problems at an earlier stage of their development.

Individuals in your enterprise, fearing that your venture's Legal Risks might spill over on to them, have personal thresholds at which point they will seek other work, a prolonged sabbatical, or early retirement. Indeed, this second-order effect must be taken into consideration in evaluating your organization's risks, as it might lead to a staffing crisis, if for example a jurisdiction assigning personal liability to Systems Administrators for innocent regulatory compliance errors or illegal activity on the part of their end users.

As a Systems Administrator, your goal is to help structure systems and agreements to minimize regulatory drag and legal risk and thus keep your organizations Withdrawal and Dissolution Thresholds as far away as possible.

Sadly, this exercise can quickly transition into a zero sum game when creating functional redundancies to evade a looming Withdrawal Threshold in one jurisdiction motivates you to start shifting business functions elsewhere, thus substituting one set of regulators for another and at least temporarily increasing your short term legal risk. Alternatively, it might induce you to outsource infrastructure to the Cloud or to engage a Software-as-Service provider risking a loss of privacy and complicating your contractual relationships.

Even with highly redundant well-managed information systems, operated by loyal cross-trained staff in full compliance with all relevant oversight guidelines, some risks are more politi-cal in nature. Thus with an unanticipated sweep of a regulatory pen, with the drafting of an ill-considered clause in an obscure law or treaty, with a result driven legal holding, or an unfavorable tax treatment, the entire economic viability of one's line of business or an entire industry can be destroyed by regulators, politicians, judges, and taxing authorities.

The Risk of a Dystopian Future

Given current trends and the predilection for governments to demand ever-greater levels of control, it is very easy to posit plausible *1984* scenarios that might feature such horrors as:

- National firewalls to balkanize social media.
- Mandatory GPS Tags on all communications.
- Criminalization of the use of steganography and encryption technologies.
- Outlawing of anonymity services.
- Regulating wifi hotspots.
- Outlawing "mesh networks".
- Regulation of the trade of computer programming.
- Treaty negotiated transnational control of the Internet.
- Regulation of all devices connected to the Internet to mandate the use of trusted hardware and operating systems supporting hardware backed digital rights management.
- Global speech codes precluding language offensive to members of certain religions or other protected groups.
- Registration of bloggers and imposition of civil and criminal liability on them for any comments damaging to politicians or businesses.
- Automatic warrantless filtering and surveillance of all digital traffic.
- Registration of all Internet users with universal biometric based national logins tying all online activity to specific citizens in most nations.

Should such a dark future unfold, open interpersonal communications would be relegated to the use of non-networked computers dependent on the physical exchange of data bearing media using traditional Cold War era spy craft. Large organizations will then fall back to the use of private networks, where they remain legal, with satellite links "routing around" regulated zones to connect any remaining islands of freedom. Many politicians would salivate at the thought of seizing such power. Moreover, many of the very precautions you must take today move in this direction. Nevertheless, one hopes there is still time for Legal and IT professionals to recognize the grave danger such a course represents and take measures to mobilize the public to stand against it.

The Icelandic Modern Media Initiative is one such ray of hope offering to institute a Web of End User friendly legal reforms that promise to draw considerable economic activity to its emerging zone of Freedom (McCarthy, n.d.).

Solutions and Recommendations

Most firms and systems administrators will want to avoid being drawn into the political sphere—a luxury they cannot afford in today's world. Measures are proposed and promulgated without adequate consideration of their ramifications and with little or no reasoned public debate. Primary responsibility for formulating firm policy in these areas rests with the CIO and senior management. Systems administrators need to proactively support them in identifying emerging political opportunities and threats, in assessing their implications, and in communicating their firms' positions to legislators, administrative tribunals, and the public at large. It is far easier and more economical to head off bad legislation and rule making than to try to mitigate their impacts.

More concretely, this policy monitoring role might take the form of a standing agenda item for monthly IT Staff meetings to maintain a prioritized 'hot list' of pending political and regulatory issues in support of an ongoing process of scenario building. The systems administrator can then flesh out these documents with time, cost, and resource allocation estimates that the CIO and senior management can draw on to lobby for preferred outcomes.

Administrators need to constantly monitor technical, managerial, and legal news feeds always looking for ways to better compartmentalize and refactor the systems in their care. While IT related Legal Risks may seem daunting, incorporating to limit civil liability, using common sense, and planning can keep them in check.

REFERENCES

18, USC § 1030 - Fraud and related activity in connection with computers. (2012). Retrieved March 21, 2013, from http://www.law.cornell.edu/uscode/text/18/1030

Associated Press. (2003). *German parliament sends Google tax to committee*. Retrieved November 30, 2012, from http://www.myfoxdc.com/story/20245195/german-parliament-sends-google-tax-to-committee

Braun, D. A., & Castle, C. L. (2004). The phonograph record industry. In *Entertainment Law* (3rd ed., pp. 3–75). New York: New York State Bar Association.

Business Software Alliance. (2012, April 17). *BSA's guide to software piracy and the law*. Retrieved March 21, 2013, from http://sc-cms.bsa.org/~/media/10A2E6D161594C499AC16F68C7E57A65.ashx

chillingeffects.org. (2012, September). *German police ask Twitter to close account -- Chilling effects clearinghouse*. Retrieved November 30, 2012, from https://www.chillingeffects.org/notice.cgi?sID=625342

Collins, G. (2012, June 13). *Five steps to simplify software asset management | Guest opinions.* Retrieved November 30, 2012, from http://www. itbusinessedge.com/cm/community/features/ guestopinions/blog/five-steps-to-simplify-soft- ware-asset-management/?cs=50612

Dowling, D. C. Jr. (2012). English is not your exclusive company license. *NYSBA Journal, 84*(9), 46–51.

Electronic Privacy Information Center. (2012). *Children't online privacy proteciton act.* Retrieved November 30, 2012, from http://epic.org/privacy/ kids/

European Parliament and Counsel of the European Union. (1995, October 24). *Directive 95/46/EC.* Retrieved November 30, 2012, from http://eur-lex.europa.eu/LexUriServ/LexUriServ. do?uri=CELEX:31995L0046:en:NOT

Federal Trade Commission. (2009, October 5). *FTC publishes final guides governing endorsements, testimonials.* Retrieved November 30, 2012, from http://www.ftc.gov/opa/2009/10/ endortest.shtm

Gansle, G., & Garber, J. R. (2012, July 26). Non- compete provisions in California: Unenforceable and affirmative liability for unfair business practices | News & events. *Dorsey & Whitney.* Retrieved November 30, 2012, from http://www.dorsey.com/ eU_LE_noncompete_california_072612/

Google-hosted blog content to be censored on country-by-country basis. (2012, February 6). Retrieved March 21, 2013, from http://www. out-law.com/en/articles/2012/february/google- hosted-blog-content-to-be-censored-on-country- by-country-basis/

Internal Revenue Service. (2010, January 13). *Independent contractor (self-employed) or employee?* Retrieved March 21, 2013, from http:// www.irs.gov/Businesses/Small-Businesses-&- Self-Employed/Independent-Contractor-(Self- Employed)-or-Employee%3F

Jaffe, A. B., & Lerner, J. (2006). *Innovation and its discontents: How our broken patent system is endangering innovation and progress, and what to do about it.* Princeton, NJ: Princeton University Press.

Lazzarotti, J. (2012, September 30). *California becomes third state to limit access to employees and students' social media accounts: Workplace privacy, data management & security report.* Retrieved November 30, 2012, from http://www. workplaceprivacyreport.com/2012/09/articles/ workplace-privacy/california-becomes-third- state-to-limit-access-to-employees-and-stu- dents-social-media-accounts/

M, E. (2012, October 9). *FTC's greenwashing guidance.* Retrieved November 30, 2012, from http://westreferenceattorneys.com/2012/10/ ftcs-greenwashing-guidance/

McCarthy, S. (n.d.). *Icelandic modern media initiative.* Retrieved March 21, 2013, from https://immi.is/index.php/projects/immi

Mellinkoff, D. (1963). *The language of the law.* Boston: Little, Brown.

Nimmer, R. T. (1985). *The law of computer technology.* Warren Gorham & Lamont.

Office of Patent Legal Administration. (2009, November 7). *Laws, regulations, policies & procedures.* Retrieved November 30, 2012, from http://www.uspto.gov/patents/law/index.jsp

Prince, M. (2012, November 29). How Syria turned off the internet. *CloudFlare blog*. Retrieved November 30, 2012, from http://blog.cloudflare.com/how-syria-turned-off-the-Internet

Public Law 112 - 29 - Leahy-Smith America Invents Act. (2012). Retrieved November 30, 2012, from http://www.gpo.gov/fdsys/pkg/PLAW-112publ29/content-detail.html

Section 153A - Indian Penal Code (IPC). (n.d.). Retrieved November 30, 2012, from http://www.vakilno1.com/bareacts/IndianPenalCode/S153A.htm

Seltzer, W. (2010, March 30). *Free speech unmoored in copyright's safe harbor: Chilling effects of the DMCA on the first amendment*. Retrieved November 29, 2012, from http://papers.ssrn.com/abstract=1577785

Spadaccini, M. (2007). *Forming an LLC*. Irvine, CA: Entrepreneur Press.

Title 16: Commercial Practices, Part 313—Privacy of Consumer Financial Information. (n.d.). Retrieved November 30, 2012, from http://www.ecfr.gov/cgi-bin/text-idx?c=ecfr,sid=1e9a81d52a0904d70a046d0675d613b0,rgn=div5,view=text,node=16%3A1.0.1.3.37,idno=16,cc=ecfr

Trademark Electronic Search System (TESS). (2013, March 21). Retrieved March 21, 2013, from http://tess2.uspto.gov/

U. S. Bureau of Industry and Security - Policies and Regulations. (1918, December 1). Retrieved November 29, 2012, from http://www.bis.doc.gov/policiesandregulations/index.htm#ear

Understanding Health Information Privacy. (2007, August 13). Retrieved November 30, 2012, from http://www.hhs.gov/ocr/privacy/hipaa/understanding/index.html

U.S. Copyright Office. (1998). *Circular 92: Appendix B*. Retrieved November 30, 2012, from http://www.copyright.gov/title17/92appb.html

U.S. Copyright Office. (2011). *Copyright law of the United States*. Retrieved November 30, 2012, from http://www.copyright.gov/title17/

U.S. Department of Commerce. (2012, April 11). *Export.gov - Main safe harbor homepage*. Retrieved December 1, 2012, from http://export.gov/safeharbor/

U.S. Trademark Law. (2012, August 9). Retrieved November 30, 2012, from http://www.uspto.gov/trademarks/law/Trademark_Statutes.pdf

Wasilko, P. J. (2011). Law, architecture, gameplay, and marketing. In Business, Technological, and Social Dimensions of Computer Games: Multidisciplinary Developments (pp. 476–493). Academic Press.

ENDNOTES

[1] This type of analysis played a central role as the organizing theme of Ayn Rand's prescient 1957 novel, *Atlas Shrugged*, which considered the societal ramifications of runaway regulation in pursuit of social justice. The novel is also the source of the catch phrase, "Who Is John Galt?" found in many blog comments related to recent business closings that resulted from the kind of withdrawal and dissolution analysis described herein.

Chapter 5
Due Diligence in Cyberspace

Joanna Kulesza
University of Lodz, Poland

ABSTRACT

Within the chapter, the author discusses the possibility of introducing an international due diligence standard for Internet Service Providers (ISPs). She analyzes the due diligence standard in public international law as the common element of two accountability regimes binding upon states: the regime of state responsibility for the breach of an international obligation and international risk-liability for transboundary harm. They are both aimed at preventing transboundary harm originating from state territory. Such harm may presently be inflicted also with the use of cross-border electronic networks. Since the Internet is considered a global resource, the analysis provided is based upon international environmental law doctrine with its detailed due diligence standard and principle of prevention. The author goes on to propose their application to cyber-security. The idea argued within the chapter is for the development of an international cyberspace-specific due diligence standard and possibly a liability mechanism, as based on the multistakeholder principle recognized within Internet governance. The author aims to answer the question of whether a due diligence standard for cyberspace may and if so ought to be introduced through particular obligations laid upon Internet Service Providers, in particular Critical Internet Resources operators and introduction of an international ISP liability fund.

INTRODUCTION

Internet creates significant risk of transboundary harm. Insufficient security of its components, such as root-servers and other Critical Internet Resources (further herein: CIRs) (COE, 2012), faulted by Internet Service Providers, may cause damage to international and state security or cause significant transboundary harm. Presently interna-

tional law lays upon states no particular obligation relating to cybersecurity directly or indirectly aimed at preventing that risk and minimizing the threatening damage. It does however contain a generally recognized due diligence standard in transboundary harm prevention where lack of due diligence of state organs in preventing significant transboundary harm may bring international responsibility to that state. Existing international treaties on international environmental law transfer significant part of that risk liability onto businesses

DOI: 10.4018/978-1-4666-4526-4.ch005

benefiting from the created risk. Although the international due diligence standard cannot be directly applied to private parties, states are under international obligation to introduce national laws aimed at preventing significant transboundary harm binding private actors. The contents of those laws are funded upon the international due diligence standard, which allows to identify obligations resting upon states. This chapter is an attempt at applying those general due diligence obligations to prevention of transboundary harm in the cyber-realm. The practical application of such seemingly academic exercise comes to foreground in the context of prevention of international terrorist acts conducted or initiated online. International community recently directed its attention towards legal possibilities of holding states "sponsoring" cyberterrorism accountable for their omissions in preventing such attacks initiated from their territories or conducted with infrastructure located therein. Identifiable international obligation of states in preventing transboundary harm affected through cyberthreats is soon to be transposed into national obligations of companies operating CIRs. Since international law offers models for private liability schemes, they are likely to be applied also towards cybersecurity and cyberterrorism prevention.

Usually listed among asymmetric threats, the term cyberterrorism covers threats to international peace and security originated with the use of devices connected to the global computer network and relying upon the Internet Protocol (TCP/IP) and protocols compatible with it. A Draft Convention on Cyber Crime and Terrorism from the U.S. Hoover Institute described this activity as "intentional use or threat of use (...) of violence, disruption or interference against cyber systems, when it is likely that such use would result in death or injury of a person or persons, substantial damage to physical property, civil disorder, or significant economic harm" (Sofaer, 2000). In particular damage attempted or done to the functioning of "critical infrastructures" or CIRs

constitutes international cyberterrorism[1]. The cited document defines "critical infrastructure" as "interconnected networks of physical devices, pathways, people and computers that provide for timely delivery of government services; medical care; protection of the general population by law enforcement; firefighting; food; water; transportation services, including travel of persons and transport of goods by air, water, rail or road; supply of energy, including electricity, petroleum, oil and gas products; financial and banking services and transactions; and information and communications services"[2]. Therefore diligent administering of those resources and their protection against harmful unauthorized interference is the necessary condition for preventing significant transboundary harm. For entities administering such systems any legal obligations to act diligently may originate solely from national laws. Those however are being shaped by international consensus and international obligations of states. States are obliged to show due diligence in preventing ok transboundary harm and to introduce national laws meeting that standard. For that reason the background of the existing due diligence standard in international law must be considered when ISP risk-liability is to be discussed.

STATE RESPONSIBILITY VS. INTERNATIONAL LIABILITY IN INTERNATIONAL LAW

Contemporary international law, as recapitulated by the International Law Commission (further herein: ILC), foresees for two seemingly separate regimes: that of state responsibility for internationally wrongful acts and that on international liability for harm caused through acts not prohibited by international law. Both regimes have been summarized in corresponding soft law documents, attempted to capture contemporary international rules: the 2001 ILC Draft Articles on Responsibility of States for Internationally Wrongful Acts and the 2006 Draft Principles on the Allocation of Loss in the case of Transboundary Harm Arising out of Hazardous Activities respectively (ILC, 2001 and 2006). They summarize the results of an academic and political debate dating back to 1949[3] on the needed shape and scope of international responsibility of states and include general principles and obligations of states in respect of all the activities conducted within their territories.

A scrupulous distinction between the two abovementioned regimes, as formulated by the ILC and disputed by academics, is claimed to be based on the character of a state act giving grounds to its accountability (Boyle, 1990). An action or omission of state contrary to its international obligations puts it in breach of international law and subject to international responsibility, as described in the 2001 ILC Draft Articles (WCD, 2012a). The regime of state responsibility does not itself define those international obligations, the breach of which brings such legal consequences. It only describes the existing, common rules to be applied to any breach of an international obligation, regardless whether it is treaty-based or customary. Therefore the state responsibility regime may be described as secondary, while each set of international rules, the breach of which evokes state responsibility, will be than designated as primary (Combacau & Alland, 1988).

When discussing the issue of state responsibility, the question on transboundary harm and damage arises.[4] Criticized by legal scholars[5] the ILC decided not to include damage as a necessary prerequisite for state responsibility.[6] The very breach of an existing international obligation theoretically may be considered sufficient grounds for state responsibility,[7] regardless whether it brought damage to a legitimate interest of another state. Depending on the nature of a particular primary regime however, transboundary damage or harm may present itself a necessary element for assessing the breach of a particular obligation of prevention resulting in state responsibility for an unlawful act. This is most likely the case, when a state is to be held responsible not for its actions, but for its omissions. Therefore should a state be internationally obliged to act in order to prevent damage or harm, and failed to meet that obligation by e.g. not taking appropriate measures, it may be held internationally responsible.[8]

The 2006 ILC Draft describing the international liability regime focuses on the legal consequences of acts not prohibited by international law. Significant transboundary damage may result in so-called risk-liability.[9] ILC emphasized the distinction between the two regimes, however legal scholars claim the division ambiguous.[10] Boyle describes international liability as a set of primary obligations resting upon states, including precautionary measures in e.g. oil transportation, nuclear energy production or damages done in outer space exploration. He sees the secondary state responsibility regime as applicable in cases where states fail to meet so defined primary obligations.[11] In other words, the contemporary risk liability regime focuses on the primary obligation of states to cooperate in prevention of significant transboundary harm and to compensate significant transboundary damage.[12] The secondary international responsibility mechanism for unlawful conduct is to be applied to those states, that fall short of meeting the primary prevention and liability obligations, as specified by the ILC in its 2001 and 2006 drafts respectively. States will therefore face international responsibility for the breach of any international obligation to prevent significant harm, regardless whether contractual or customary.

A joint feature of the two regimes and key to responsibility for transboundary harm is the concept of due diligence, designated to assess state efforts in transboundary harm prevention and potential responsibility for omissions. As such it allows to identify a model of an appropriate state reaction to most categories of threats of transboundary harm. State obligation to prevent harm will be assessed according to a due diligence standard, which ought to be identified as crucial to ascertaining international risk-liability or responsibility for state omissions contrary to international obligations. Although the contents of the standard are always case-specific, basic traits of this flexible international law instrument may be identified.

Due Diligence in International Law

The due diligence standard originates from the 1872 Alabama claims arbitration (Bingham, 2005) and commonly appears in numerous international law regimes.[13] Shaw follows the ILC to define due diligence as the standard that is accepted generally as the most appropriate one.[14] *Restatement* describes due diligence in more detail, as a state obligation to take such measures, as may be necessary in particular circumstances, allowing to ensure that activities in state jurisdiction or control are conducted so as not to cause significant injury abroad and conform to the generally accepted international rules and standards.[15] Similarly, Okowa (2009) defines due diligence as the contents of a reasonable conduct, generally accepted within international law instruments, dependant on the means at the disposal of the particular state. She summarizes the current academic debate and state practice on the minimum level of due diligence as states' obligation to exercise "diligent control over the sources of harm under their jurisdiction and control".[16] Failing to meet the due diligence standard ought to be recognized as failing to meet the standard of conduct expected of a reasonable government in certain circumstances and might result in international responsibility of that state.[17] As Okowa rightfully notes, appropriateness of state conduct depends not only on regional or international standards, but also on the economic situation of a particular state, its capacities and practices.[18] The due diligence standard in international law is not and ought not be a uniform set of rules, principles or obligations.[19] It is designed to be a flexible tool, and

as such it accumulates as much significance, as it does uncertainty.

Due diligence standard is a non-absolute one.[20] It should always relate to two basic elements: factual circumstances of the situation in question and actual state capabilities.[21] Assessment of those two elements must be objective, based upon existing international law obligations - a sole claim of the state at fault seems far insufficient. Traditionally the role of assessing state compliance with international law falls within the competence of international courts and tribunals.[22] Attempting to describe the general traits of a non-diligent state behavior the Mexico-United States General Claims Commission in the Neer Case used terms such as "bad faith, willful neglect of duty" and "an insufficiency of governmental actions so far short of international standards that every reasonable and impartial man would readily recognize its insufficiency".[23]

All those critical elements of an international due diligence standard are amended and completed by detailed prerequisites defined within individual areas of international law. Through contract and custom numerous criteria were developed to allow states to identify the amount of their input and efforts needed to meet the expectations of the international community and avoid international responsibility. The general considerations made above, originating from the long-lasting jurisprudence, seem best completed by the stipulations of recent treaties on international environmental law where the most detailed set of guidelines for the contemporary due diligence standard can be found. Cyberspace is often considered a global resource therefore references to its protection in a way similar to one agreed among states towards the environment is often made.

DUE DILIGENCE IN INTERNATIONAL ENVIRONMENTAL LAW

Shaw argues that the standard for international environmental liability ought not be generally[24] identified as a strict nor an absolute one, meaning states ought not be held liable regardless of their fault.[25] Therefore the proof of fault in environmental law ought be based on a due diligence standard assessment – liability shall be dependent on failing to meet the prerequisites set by such a particular standard.[26] He describes the due diligence appropriateness test by identifying it as states' obligation to collaborate in good faith and in an attempt to prevent significant transboundary harm, while using the assistance of relevant international organizations.[27] Obligations of a state may be deemed fulfilled once it takes appropriate legislative, administrative or any other suitable action,[28] including introducing monitoring and authorizing mechanisms.[29] The operation of such mechanisms is to be based on appropriate risk and impact assessment.[30] Should this analysis provide information on possible risks, states potentially endangered must be informed and consulted on the most appropriate means of diminishing the risk or damage incurred.[31] The flexibility of the due diligence test in international environmental law is well envisaged in the final element of the test: the obligation of balancing the interests of all parties involved before inducing the risk.[32]

This duty of environmental impact assessment is raised by Okowa to the status of an international environmental law principle,[33] along with two other: the principle of sustainable development and the precautionary principle.[34] The former[35] obliges the states to consider environmental protection in all their actions[36] while the latter[37] relates to the obligation of environmental impact assessment and necessitates national authorities to conduct all necessary research, regardless of their cost, to prevent environmental degradation.[38] Those obligations however are not aimed at restraining states from taking actions that hold immanent risk to the environment – their sole purpose is to minimize the possible harm brought thereby.[39] Such non-restraining character of the principles is assured by the introduction of the de minimis test. It requires states not to prevent all harm, but only

that which is appreciable, significant or substantial,[40] as referred to in the 2006 ILC Draft Principle 1. This Principle sets the scope of application of the document solely to "transboundary damage caused by hazardous activities not prohibited by international law", where " 'hazardous activity' means an activity which involves a risk of causing significant harm".[41] Making the due diligence standard a flexible one however, the ILC left the particular decision on harm "significance" in each case up to the proceeding judges, as "a determination has to be made in each specific case. It involves more factual considerations than legal determination."[42] Although the ILC decided not to provide a generic list of such activities, making the principles defined therein applicable to all instances of transboundary harm, it defined the characteristics of such activities in much detail.[43]

Identifying case-specific due diligence standard is crucial to enforcing individual obligations based upon its obedience. The standard may be ascertainable as an element of a binding international obligation of states in particular circumstances, recognized within a treaty or as an element of international custom. International law practice leaves the identification of detailed obligations entailing due diligence to individual liability regimes, just as is the case with oil transport or nuclear energy production. Those often resolve to laying the economic consequences of transboundary harm occurred upon private parties, operating risk-originating activities. Applicability of those mechanisms for transboundary harm in cyberspace must therefore be analyzed.

DUE DILIGENCE IN CYBERSPACE

The due diligence standard is an imminent element of states obligation to preserve other states from transboundary harm originating from their jurisdictions or entities under their control[44]. As noted by Boyle, ILC attempted to avoid terminological confusion when referring to attribution of harmful activities in its work on state liability.[45] Therefore the term "attribution" used for state responsibility for acts contrary to international law is avoided in the 2006 ILC Draft Principles and as an effect of numerous attempted word-ings,[46] it refers to state "jurisdiction", "territory" and "control" as basic criteria for international liability. ILC define s "state of origin" as the state within whose territory, under whose jurisdiction or control the hazardous activities[47] are carried out. International liability is therefore bound not to state actions, but to its omissions – failures to prevent or at least minimize the risk of significant transboundary harm by inadequately controlling entities causing risk of such harm within state territory, jurisdiction or control.[48] A mechanism designated to aid states in meeting these goals resolves to state monopoly in authorizing private entities running risk-generating enterprises.[49] In order to assess whether a state met its prevention and risk-assessment obligations, the due diligence standard is evoked.

Principles of cyberthreats prevention can be identified through an analysis of numerous international law documents on transboundary harm liability, including the 2006 ILC Draft and numerous treaties embodying the developments of international environmental law, the youngest branch of international law. The operation of critical infrastructure and in particular CIRs may originate significant transboundary harm, either through its negative impact onto the flow of infor-mation or Internet accessibility, or through physi-cal consequences of an infrastructure malfunction operated with the use of electronic networks, such as power plants or water management systems. It is one of the reasons why cyberspace is willingly compared to universal shared resources, including the natural environment.

Cyberspace holds one unique characteristic when compared to other global resources. Internet has been designed as a decentralized network. It cannot be subjected as a whole to territorial state sovereignty, therefore it abstracts in its architec-ture from traditional, territorial and geographi-cal divisions of powers and competences. This characteristic of cyberspace creates the biggest challenge for effective international cooperation on prevention of transboundary cyber-threats. CIRs are managed by private entities and unlike with other risk-generating activities are not subject to state authorization nor to state control. The basic principle of multistakeholderism in Internet governance, necessitates intense international cooperation among various stakeholder groups, including business, civil society and academia, next to governmental representatives, to ensure the effective protection of cyberspace (Kulesza, 2012). Regardless of intergovernmental accords, network architecture makes it extremely difficult to engage state authorities in effective coopera-tion on network security, since administration of crucial network resources rests at the hands of private entities and business.

The issue of network security in its interna-tional aspect came to the attention of the United Nations in 2003 during the first World Summit of Information Society (WSIS) in Geneva[50]. In its 2005 report the WSIS inspired Working Group on Internet Governance (WGIG) defined Internet governance as "the development and application by Governments, the private sector and civil soci-ety, in their respective roles, of shared principles, norms, rules, decision-making procedures, and programs that shape the evolution and use of the Internet"[51]. This brief definition is the cornerstone of the contemporary debate on the appropriate model of governing the global network. Three groups of stakeholders: national governments, business represented among others through ISPs and civil society, including non-governmental organizations and academia, are perceived equal partners. Therefore it is upon their consensus that any effective management of the global resource that is the Internet may be affected. That consen-sus needs to cover all areas of impact the global network has on contemporary policies. Follow-ing the WGIG guideline: "Internet governance includes more than Internet names and addresses" but also "other significant public policy issues, such as critical Internet resources, the security and safety of the Internet, and developmental aspects and issues pertaining to the use of the Internet"[52]. Therefore the principle of multistakeholderism, crucial to Internet governance, must be applied also when addressing cybersecurity challenges. Any obligations of providing stability and resiliency of the network must be shared among governments and private entities, as is the case with other activities, originating significant risk of transboundary harm.

Forever more intergovernmental organizations deal with this challenge. They include the Council of Europe, European Union as well as the North Atlantic Treaty Organization (NATO).

The most comprehensive study of due diligence assessment of transboundary risk in cyberspace was included in a report of the Council of Europe (further herein: CoE)[53] followed by the Declaration by the Committee of Ministers on Internet governance principles, and the Recommendation on the protection and promotion of the universality, integrity and openness of the Internet both adopted by the Committee of Ministers on 21 September 2011 (WCD, 2012). Although non-binding, the documents introduce particular state obligations in respect of transboundary harm in cyberspace, while focusing on the obligation of states to cooperate in order to prevent, appropriately manage and respond to "Internet disruptions and interferences".[54] In order to achieve such aim CoE encourages all states to cooperate with each other and with other stakeholders in order to ascertain and take "all reasonable measures to prevent, manage and respond to significant transboundary disruption of and interference with the stability, robustness, resilience and openness of the Internet, or at any event minimise the risk and consequences thereof". The rights, responsibilities and duties of states in respect of CIRs, next to the obligation of international cooperation, include also the obligation of a multistakeholder cooperation[55] and the imple-

mentation of reasonable legislative, administrative or other measures, including the establishment of suitable monitoring mechanisms.[56] CoE encourages states also to engage in further dialogue on the development of a suitable liability mechanism for transboundary harm in cyberspace.[57] Prevention and control should be introduced also through the elaboration of joint standards and exchange of best practices,[58] exchange of information[59] and joint coordination of actions aimed at preventing such harm,[60] including mutual assistance.[61] CoE proposes the introduction of a particular set of preventive measures relating to CIRs, including "the development and application of standards, policies, procedures or practices".[62] Particular attention should be given to the methodology of consultations aimed at the identification of "appropriate responses to specific issues that may arise in respect of the management" of CIRs.[63]

Similar obligations, although defined in less detail, are present also in the revised Council Framework Decision 2005/222/JHA of 24 February 2005 on attacks against information systems[64]. The 2012 "Tallin manual" published by NATO includes a comprehensive analysis of responsibility in international law in the face of state omissions resulting in infringement of sovereignty of any third part, presuming the existence of an international obligation to present due diligence in preventing attacks thereon (NMILCW, 2012). Also the White House in its 2011 Strategy for Cyberspace calls for international cooperation on establishing what the minimal standards of network security are (ISC, 2011). General guidelines formulated within those documents recommend applying the due diligence standard known to international law to any transboundary harm originated through online activities. The general references to best available practice and exchange of knowledge are abundantly made. Yet despite numerous references to due diligence, no proposals on the consequences of lack of due diligence are presented. International liability for transboundary harm in cyberspace is the most challenging part of the analogy so willingly named.

Compensation of Transboundary Harm: ISP Liability Fund?

Compensating transboundary damage originated online would require a unique approach. As much as existing notions of transboundary harm liability may be applied directly to states not showing due diligence in preventing harmful or hazardous activities disrupting the stability or resiliency of the network, proposing a feasible financial compensation scheme for damage so affected requires new consensus-seeking.

Presently international law recognizes three basic liability regimes for transboundary harm, relating to, respectively: international maritime oil transport, production and use of nuclear energy and space exploration. As Gehring and Jachtenfuchs rightfully note, states are reluctant to accept liability for transnational environmental damage, laying most of the burden on the industry running the risk-generating enterprises.

The initial blueprint for all transboundary harm liability regimes was the maritime oil transport scheme, developed following the 1967 Torey Canyon incident.[65] The Inter-governmental Maritime Consultative Organization (IMCO),[66] entrusted with the task of elaborating a model of international compensation for transboundary harm done by oil-tankers paved the way for any further negotiations on similar transboundary harm liability issues. During the IMCO negotiations[67] it became clear that states controlling oil-tankers fleets were reluctant to carry any direct liability for harm caused through oil-tanker disasters.[68] State representatives agreed only to transfer all the liability onto the oil-tankers industry, as the ones generating profit from the risk-originating activities. At the same time coastal states, most likely to suffer from oil-tankers disaster, opted for a strict liability as a guarantee of compensation.[69] As a result the ship owners' strict liability model was supplemented by an oil pollution compensation fund, fueled by the industry representatives. States were considered only a guarantee of compensation, should strict liability of the individual party show insufficient (ICE, 1972). No subsidiary liability of the flag ship state nor state participation in the fund was acceptable to the negotiating governments[70] and so was this "privately financed voluntary compensation scheme"[71] accepted by the industry (Cristal, 1970/71). The direct result of such a liability scheme was the vigorous development of oil-transport insurance industry, providing private companies, compelled to participate in such an inauspicious liability regime, with the necessary financial safeguard (Gehring, 1993). The focus on private parties' strict liability leads some authors to denote the occurring "shift from international liability, mitigated by private remedies, to private liability".[72] Such a model of direct and strict private liability, although placing a heavy burden upon the industry, might seem fit for the current era of globalization, where powerful international companies are participating in international policy-shaping more actively than numerous under-developed states. At the same time it practically unburdens states from direct economic liability for risk-originating activities they authorize, making state-authorization insignificant (Abeyratne, 2010). The complex state liability scheme, although in line with the 2006 ILC Draft Principles, through its intricacy makes it additionally difficult to execute any state liability, leaving affected states at the resort of due diligence based international responsibility of the originating state.

This basic scheme of exclusive private liability served as a blueprint for liability regimes applicable to maritime and inland transportation[73] of dangerous goods as well as a convention on oil drilling[74] and was the background for liability schemes in nuclear energy production and space exploration.

The nuclear liability scheme, as prescribed by the 1960 Paris Convention is also based on strict liability of the nuclear installation operator, while the operators' insurance is no longer voluntary. Since states continued to disagree upon any state-funded compensation for nuclear damage, the Paris Convention (Annex II) includes a direct reference to state responsibility as the appropriate mechanism for reviewing compensation claims on nuclear damage (Gehring, 1960). Regarding the fact, that state responsibility is never strict, the due diligence standard to be examined upon its application designates the mechanism as potentially ineffective and therefore providing no economic security against nuclear damage. Two additional instruments assuring nuclear liability were introduced,[75] binding liability with the authorizing state. Should the privately fueled fund show exhausted, nuclear installation licensing state would be complementarily liable. Should this mechanism also show insufficient, the treaty-based mechanism would activate a third "layer of compensation",[76] co-funded by all Paris Convention state-parties.[77] The nuclear industry liability scheme provides for a limitation of claimed amounts and no direct nor strict state liability on one hand,[78] unlike the oil liability regime however, puts certain, supplemental financial obligations on state parties.

Key to the existing liability schemes is state authorization of risk-generating activities. Whether it is running a nuclear power plant or oil transportation, conducting such activities requires state authorization and following a series of intergovernmental treaties states hold monopoly on controlling them. The case is fundamentally different with Internet governance. As already mentioned, the Internet was intentionally designed as structure resistant to central, governmental control, intended to keep this global resource outside political and governmental influence. The 1997 Clinton/Gore White Paper and the following creation of ICANN were intended to hand over the decisive power over the electronic resource to an independent, non-commercial entity. As the criticism of ICANN grows and states find forever more reasons to control the cyberspace, the 1997

model of multistakeholder governance faces more challenges. Radical modification thereof would not be feasible, since even though the criticism of ICANN/U.S. hegemony over Internet resources is not unfounded, it served well the Internet evolution and paved the way for the global information society. At the same time keeping international law out of the debate on cyberspace, its security and state sovereignty no longer seems possible nor justified.

Introducing a liability fund for transboundary damage originated in cyberspace based on the principles known to international law, should it show at all possible, would change the entire business landscape of Internet services. It would require risk assessment for new technologies introduced and would significantly raise the costs of running a company offering ISP services, in particular operating CIRs, such as name Domain Name System (DNS) root-servers or managing Internet Exchange Points (IXPs). The evolution of the concept of international liability shows that introducing any financial support for risk-originating activities always met with understandable opposition from the business sector. Initiating negotiations on any ISP liability for transboundary damage would require introducing rigorous limitations of activities accounted for within such a regime and supporting companies with appropriate risk assessment tools and information. Although a distant perspective, a risk liability ISP fund should be kept in mind when discussing transboundary liability for cyberspace harm.

Although the existing transboundary harm prevention regimes foresee for authorization of risk originating activities, lack of enforceable authorization mechanism in place is not effective ground for releasing a state from responsibility. States are to be held liable for harmful consequences originating from their territories, regardless of the method used by them to prevent such harm from arising. Even though states are not capable of authorizing any ISP activity, they may be held liable or responsible for the damage caused by insufficient protection of the electronic infrastructure within their territory or control, once evidence is shown that due diligence was not provided in securing it. International liability results from state omission and is territorially ascertainable, therefore insufficient security of elements of the network located within state territory rather than lack of control over particular activities of individuals residing within state borders that will be the potential source of transboundary harm liability. At the same time due diligence in preventing transboundary harm may not result in the breach of basic human rights, in particular the individual right to privacy, by state authorities attempting to identify any possible risk. Any state surveillance should be restricted to enactment and effective execution of feasible national criminal legislation envisaging a compromise between human rights and international security Identifying the contents of such consensus must be the scope of a multistakeholder debate (Rush et al, 2006).

SOLUTIONS AND RECOMMENDATIONS

Transboundary Risk Control and Prevention: Due Diligence in Cyberspace

It would seem easiest to review the scope of duties resting upon states, as it is national authorities that are bound by due diligence requirements in other areas of international law. Therefore when assessing the due diligence in cyberspace, all general due diligence principles would be applicable. For states due diligence would be defined as failing to meet the standard of conduct expected of a reasonable government in certain circumstances, rather than its malice, negligence or recklessness.[79] Appropriateness of state conduct would than depend not only on regional or international standards, but also on its economic situation, its factual capacities and local or regional practices (rather ethical than technical ones, since technical practices need to meet a global standard for the Internet to function properly, be it one set within the IETF's RFCs)[80]. It would always involve two basic elements: factual circumstances of the situation in question and actual state capabilities,[81] while the assessment of those two elements must be objective. At the very first glance it seem apparent that the regional practice of human rights protection (in particular the right to privacy) would be of crucial importance, since the current disaccord on human rights practice would meet its very first global forum with the due diligence cyber-security standard.

Moreover due diligence in cyberspace would include states' obligation to collaborate in good faith and in an attempt to prevent significant transboundary harm, while using the assistance of relevant international organizations.[82] Just as is the case with international environmental law, also with respect to cybersecurity, obligations of a state may be deemed fulfilled once it takes appropriate legislative, administrative or any other suitable action,[83] including introducing monitoring and authorizing mechanisms.[84] In international environmental law the operation of such mechanisms is to be based on appropriate risk and environmental impact assessment.[85] Appropriate measures for assessing the risk of introducing new elements or tools applicable to the operation of the cyberspace need to be elaborated, should the due diligence standard be grounds for state accountability. It ought to be noted however, that the past developments of the Internet, ones that led to its tremendous success, disregarded that rule.[86] Should a due diligence standard for cyberspace be introduced, at least crucial modifications of the Internet backbone structure would require risk-assessment. Only than could states and possibly other stakeholders be contractually bound by the due diligence obligation. Then, once informed of possible risks, they would be obliged to notify and consult other potentially endangered stakeholders.[87] The development of this element of a due diligence test seems to be approaching with the propagation of the view that cyber-security may only be granted through international cooperation and consultation[88] - a view common also to environmental law (USCPRa/USCPRb 2012; Evans, 2010).

The flexibility of the due diligence test in international environmental law, phrased as the obligation of balancing the interests of all parties involved before inducing the risk,[89] seems well fit with the multistakeholder principle of Internet governance. A common consensus of all stakeholders is crucial for defining the limits of due diligence in cyberspace. The multistakeholder principle means that all the power and initiative of regulating the Net may not lay in the hands of the governments, but neither may all the responsibility for its protection.

When seeking such a proper multi-stakeholder balance for network security liability other international environmental law due diligence elements, fitting well with the nature of the electronic global asset that is the Internet, ought to be considered: the principle of sustainable development and the precautionary principle. In cyberspace terms the former would mean an obligation to consider cyber-security in all undertakings of the due-diligence obliged stakeholder. The latter would relate to the obligation of risk assessment and necessitate to conduct any research needed, regardless of its cost, to prevent significant transboundary harm in cyberspace. The burden of research cost would need to be divided among the states and other stakeholders involved, as set through a comprehensive regime, following multilateral negotiations.

The international environmental law *de minimis* test might also be well applied to cyberspace. It would require states (or – following a relevant agreement – other stakeholders) not to prevent all harm, but limit the risk of undertakings which might bring appreciable, significant or substan-tial harm[90] as referred to in the *2006 ILC Draft Principles* Principle 1.

FUTURE RESEARCH DIRECTIONS

Currently the question of ISP liability may be analyzed together with issues of international liability, assuming that electronic infrastructure used for the performance of activities originating risk, especially CIRs, are a composite of such an activity and require the same level of due diligence as the activity itself. At the same the principles of prevention of transboundary harm online and for preserving the stability and resiliency of the network are similar in all functions of the CIRs, regardless of the activity for which they are deployed. Therefore identifying a uniform due diligence standard for ISPs operating CIRs would seem practical.

There is no treaty-based hard-law international obligation to preserve the stability and security of cyberspace. Nevertheless obligations of prevention and precaution acknowledged in international law allow to ascertain state responsibility for harmful acts, originated from within its territory. Cyberspace-specific details of due diligence need to be further elaborated among all the stakeholders within the Internet governance arena: states, business and civil society. They would include engaging in platforms for versatile multistakeholder cooperation, not limited to intergovernmental organizations, such as the UN or Council of Europe, observatories and think-tanks combining the efforts of international experts in various relevant fields. The unique forum for Internet governance dialogue – the UN sponsored Internet Governance Forum has been unable to gain political significance since its creation in 2005 as it holds no decisive power. It might however show a good forum for furthering the discussions present in its forum from its very creation, leading up to elaborating a binding set of principles, shared among the different stakeholders. Future research direction cover therefore international cooperation among all stakeholders in order to establish the specific procedures of exchanging information and good practice examples on securing the global network.

Regarding various national efforts on combating online crime and terrorism, individual obligations of ISPs towards granting security of the network are to be expected to appear in national acts of law in the near future. That will create a challenge particularly for transnational companies, if they do not originate from commonly approved business standards, based on an international accord. Similar obligations of professional due diligence may presently be derived from national legal acts dealing with fair trade practices. The commercial law prerequisite of business due diligence is recognized in numerous national legal systems. On the international level it will cover an obligation to provide best professional knowledge and awareness in technical developments related to cyber security. Lack of knowledge or recklessness will not be considered a plausible excuse for lack of liability in case of harm caused thereby.

Deriving such a standard from the existing achievement of international public law requires a reference to the basic principles of due diligence, as recognized by contemporary international customary law. Since failing to meet the due diligence standard might lead to state responsibility for its omission, the current international law regime would require states, rather than any other stakeholder to undertake direct specific actions aimed at preventing transboundary damage. The multistakeholder principle ought to allow to distribute this obligation evenly among all stakeholders and help further develop a more balanced, possibly treaty-based transboundary harm liability scheme for the Internet, engaging all stakehold-

ers. Introducing different obligations for various categories of stakeholders it would engage them all within one international law instrument. Binding states the document would oblige them to enforce through national laws appropriate safeguards for Internet traffic. Open for signature to ISPs it would allow them to gain the trust of their customers by presenting to them the status of a member to the cybersecurity treaty, giving them particularly significant business advantage. The membership might be confirmed by the declaration of adherence managed by the secretariat of the convention bureau or other treaty-based body. Not meeting the obligations defined within the treaty might result in suspending the particular entity in their rights as member to the treaty or withdrawing the certificate of the treaty-based body. As the case of privacy protection shows, providing security standards recognized by the users is bound to prove significant in gaining business advantage by individual service vendors.

CONCLUSION

The growing significance of online communications brings a pressing need for securing the network that is crucial to the information society. Due diligence standard recognized in international law allows to identify the obligations resting upon states when it comes to national legislature and practice on securing the sovereignty of other states. Due diligence in respect of resiliency and stability of the network as proposed by the CoE puts the general due diligence standard in more detail with respect to online traffic. Similarly as was the case other risk generating industries, although the obligation to prevent transboundary harm rests upon states, they are not able to guarantee for its fulfillment without extensive industry cooperation. In other areas of international law states have managed to secure their power over authorizing any risk-generating activity and transfer significant amount of liability for damages to private parties. The polluter pays principle present in international environmental law obliges businesses originating risks of transboundary harm to provide risk assessment analysis and cover for liability funds in case of an accident.

Also in cyberspace enacting any due diligence obligations requires intensified state cooperation with private business. The obligation to show due diligence, resting upon states means the need for them to engage in close cooperation to prevent transboundary damage with all other parties concerned. This facet of multistakeholderism is new to the international due diligence standard so far restricted only to states as decision makers and authorization powers. It is a natural consequence of the specific traits of the multilayered and multistakeholder cyberspace.

Since the Internet may be regarded as a global resource,[91] an international obligation of preserving its stability and resiliency[92] together with a call for a uniform set of values for all its users are being expressed forever more strongly (IRP, 2012; APC, 2012). A due diligence standard is crucial for its preservation as it is key to asserting accountability for failure to protect network security and prevent harm.

REFERENCES

Abeyratne, R. (2010). The deepwater horizon disaster - Some liability issues. *Tulane Maritime Law Journal, 125*(35).

APC. (2012). *Association for progressive communication with its APC internet rights charter.* Retrieved October 13, 2012, from http://www.apc.org/en/node/5677/

Bingham, T. (2005). The Alabama claims arbitration. *The International and Comparative Law Quarterly, 54*, 1–25. doi:10.1093/iclq/54.1.1.

Birnie, P. W., Boyle, A. E., & Redgwell, C. (2009). *International law & the environment.* Oxford, UK: Oxford University Press.

Boyle, A. E. (1990). State responsibility and international liability for injurious consequences of acts not prohibited by international law: A necessary distinction? *The International and Comparative Law Quarterly, 39*(1), 21–24. doi:10.1093/iclqaj/39.1.1.

Brownlie, I. (2008). *Principles of public international law.* Oxford, UK: Oxford University Press.

Clifford, M. (Ed.). (1998). *Environmental crime: Enforcement, policy and social responsibility.* Gaithersburg, MD: Aspen.

COE. (2010). *International and multi-stakeholder co-operation on cross-border internet.* Retrieved from http://www.coe.int/t/dghl/standardsetting/media/mc-s-ci/Interim%20Report.pdf

COE. (2012). On the definition of CIRs see generally: CoE internet governance and critical internet resources. *Council of Europe.* Retrieved October 13, 2012, from http://www.umic.pt/images/stories/publicacoes5/Internet%20governance_en.pdf

Combacau, J., & Alland, D. (1988). Primary and secondary rules in the law of state responsibility: Categorizing international obligations. *Netherlands Yearbook of International Law, 81*, 95–107.

Combacau, J., & Alland, D. (1995). Primary and secondary rules in the law of state responsibility: categorizing international obligations. *Netherlands Yearbook of International Law, 16*(81), 88–107.

CRISTAL. (1970/71). Contract regarding an interim supplement to tanker liability for oil pollution (CRISTAL) 1971. *Journal of Maritime Law & Commerce, 2*, 705.

Evans, M. (2010, March 8). Cyberwar declared as China hunts for the west's intelligence secrets. *The Times*. Retrieved October 13, 2012, from http://technology.timesonline.co.uk/tol/news/tech_and_Web/article7053254.ece

Gehring, T., & Jachtenfuchs, M. (1993). Liability for transboundary environmental damage towards a general liability regime. *European Journal of International Law, 4*, 92–106.

(1960). Convention on third party liability in the field of nuclear energy. *European Yearbook, 6*, 268.

(1977). Convention on civil liability for oil pollution damage resulting from exploration for and exploitation of seabed mineral resources. *ILM, 16*, 1451.

Godt, C. (1997). *Haftung für ökologische schäden: Verantwortung für beeinträchtigungen des allgemeingutes umwelt durch individualisierbare verletzungshandlungen*. Berlin: Duncker & Humblot.

Handl, G. (1980). State liability for accidental transnational environmental damage by private persons. *The American Journal of International Law, 74*, 525–535. doi:10.2307/2201649.

ILC. (2001) II (2) *yearbook of the international law commission* 31 ff. Draft Articles on State Responsibility: Titles and texts of articles adopted by the Drafting Committee, International Law Commission, UN Doc. A/CN.4/L.472, hereinafter cited as *2001 ILC Draft Articles*.

ILM. (1984). Draft convention on liability and compensation in connexion with the carriage of noxious and hazardous substances by sea. *ILM, 23*, 150.

IRP. (2012). *Internet rights and principles coalition with its charter of human rights and principles for the internet*. Retrieved October 13, 2012, from http://Internetrightsandprinciples.org/node/367

ISC. (2011). *International strategy for cyberspace*. The White House. Retrieved October 17, from http://www.whitehouse.gov/sites/default/files/rss_viewer/international_strategy_for_cyberspace.pdf

Kulesza, J. (2012). *International internet law*. London: Routledge.

Malanczuk, P. (1997). *Akehurst's modern introduction to international law*. London: Routledge.

NMILCW. (2012). *NATO tallinn manual on the international law applicable to cyber warfare*. Retrieved October 13, from http://www.ccdcoe.org/249.html

Okowa, P. N. (2000). State responsibility for transboundary air pollution. In *International Law*. Oxford, UK: Oxford University Press.

Pisillo-Mazzeschi, R. (1992). The due diligence rule and the nature of international responsibility of states. *Jahrbuch fur Internationales Recht. German Yearbook of International Law, 35*(11), 9–51.

Rush, M. A., & Paglia, L. G. (2002). Balancing privacy, public safety, and network security concerns after September 11. *Information Systems Security, 11*(2), 15–24. doi:10.1201/1086/43320.11.2.20020501/36765.4.

Seibt, C. H. (1994). *Zivilrechtlicher ausgleich ökologischer schäden*. Tubingen: Mohr Siebeck.

Shaw, M. N. (2003). *International law*. Cambridge, UK: Cambridge University Press. doi:10.1017/CBO9781139051903.

Sofaer, A. (2000). A proposal for an international convention on cyber crime and terrorism. *Hoover Institute*. Retrieved October 13, 2012, from: http://iis-db.stanford.edu/pubs/11912/sofaergoodman.pdf

Trouwborst, A. (2006). *Precautionary rights and duties of states*. The Hague, The Netherlands: Brill. doi:10.1163/ej.9789004152120.i-352.

USCPR. (2011a). *The US cyberspace policy review*. Retrieved from http://www.whitehouse.gov/assets/documents/Cyberspace_Policy_Review_final.pdf

USCPR. (2011b). *International strategy for cyberspace*. Retrieved from http://www.whitehouse.gov/sites/default/files/rss_viewer/international_strategy_for_cyberspace.pdf

WCD. (2012). *Declaration by the committee of ministers on internet governance principles*. Retrieved October 13, 2012, from https://wcd.coe.int/ViewDoc.jsp?id=1835773

ADDITIONAL READING

Benedek, W., Bauer, V., & Kettemann, M. (Eds.). (2008). *Internet governance and the information society: Global perspectives and European dimensions*. Utrecht, The Netherlands: Eleven International Publishing.

Bidgoli, H. (2006). *Handbook of information security: Threats, vulnerabilities, prevention, detection, and management*. New York: John Wiley & Sons.

Campbell, D. (2006). *The internet: Laws and regulatory regimes*. Salzburg, Germany: Yorkhill Law Publishing.

Cornish, P., Livingstone, D., Clemente, D., & Yorke, C. (2010). *On cyber warfare: A Chatham house report*. London: Chatham House. Retrieved October 13, 2012, from http://www.chatham-house.org.uk/publications/papers/view/-/id/967/

Delibasis, D. (2006). State use of force in cyberspace for self–defence: A new challenge for a new century. *Peace Conflict and Development: An Interdisciplinary Journal, 8*. Retrieved October 13, 2012, from http://www.peacestudiesjournal.org.uk/dl/Feb%2006%20DELIBASIS.pdf

Delibasis, D. (2007). *The right to national self–defense: In information warfare operations*. Suffolk, VA: Arena Books.

Drake, W. J. (Ed.). (2002). *Internet governance: Creating opportunities for all*. New York: United Nations Publishing.

Drake, W. J. (Ed.). (2005). *Reforming internet governance: Perspectives from the working group on internet governance (WGIG)*. New York: United Nations Publishing.

Gelbstein, E., & Kurbalija, J. (2005). *Internet governance: Issues, actors and divides*. Msida: Diplo Foundation.

Hoffer, S. (1998). *World cyberspace law*. New York: Juris Publishing Inc..

Jorgensen, R. F. (Ed.). (2006). *Human rights in the global information society*. Cambridge: MIT Press.

Joyner, C. C. (2005). *International law in the 21st century: Rules for global governance*. Oxford, UK: Rowman & Littlefield.

Kamal, A. (2005). *The law of cyber–space*. Geneva: United Nations Institute of Training and Research.

Kramer, F. D., Starr, S. H., & Wentz, L. (2009). *Cyberpower and national security*. Dulles: Potomac Books Inc.

Mathiason, J. (2004). A framework convention: An institutional option for internet governance. *Internet Governance Project Papers*. Retrieved October 13, 2012, from http://dcc.syr.edu/mis-carticles/igp–FC.pdf

Mathiason, J., Mueller, M., Klein, H., & Holitscher, M. (2004). *Internet governance: The state of play*. Internet Governance Project Papers IGP04–001. Retrieved October 13, 2012, from http://www.Internetgovernance.org/pdf/ig–sop–final.pdf

Mayer–Schönberger, V., & Ziewitz, M. (2007). Jefferson rebuffed: The United States and the future of internet governance. *Columbia Science and Technology Law Review*, *8*, 188–228.

Mueller, M. L. (2004). *Ruling the root: Internet governance and the taming of cyberspace*. Cambridge, MA: MIT Press.

Mueller, M. L. (2010). *Networks and states: The global politics of internet governance*. Cambridge, MA: MIT Press.

Personick, S. D., & Patterson, C. A. (Eds.). (2003). *Critical information infrastructure protection and the law: An overview of key issues*. Washington, DC: National Research Council, The National Academies Press.

Schmitt, M. N. (2001). Computer network attack: The normative software. *Yearbook of International Humanitarian Law*, *4*, 53–85. doi:10.1017/S1389135900000829.

Segura–Serrano, A. (2006). Internet regulation: A hard–law proposal. *The Jean Monnet Working Papers*. Retrieved October 13, 2012, from http://ideas.repec.org/p/erp/jeanmo/p0183.html

Shapiro, A. L. (1998). The disappearance of cyberspace and the rise of code. *Seton Hall Constitutional Law Journal*, *8*, 703–723.

Smith, G. J. H. (2007). *Internet law and regulation*. London: Sweet & Maxwell.

Uerpman–Wittzack, R. (2010). Principles of international internet law. *German Law Journal*, *11*(1), 1245–1263.

van Schewick, B. (2010). *Internet architecture and innovation*. Cambridge, MA: MIT Press.

Weber, R. H. (2010). New sovereignty concepts in the age of internet. *Journal of Internet Law*, *14*(8), 12–20.

KEY TERMS AND DEFINITIONS

Critical Infrastructure: Interconnected networks of people and devices allowing for the delivery of information society services and fulfillment of governmental obligations, including firefighting, transportation services, supply of water or energy or banking services.

Critical Internet Resources: Elements of Internet infrastructure critical for its secure and stable functioning. They include, but are not limited to name root servers, Internet's backbone structures and the domain name system, addresses and Internet transmission protocols. The catalogue of CIRs remains disputable, since CIRs are sometimes considered elements of national critical infrastructure, especially if they are used to operate elements of that infrastructure, such as power plants of water supply systems.

Due Diligence: An international law standard requiring state authorities to show conduct expected of a reasonable government in certain circumstances. Lack of due diligence, affected through omissions of state organs, may result in international responsibility of that state.

International Internet Law: Public international law framework for InternetInternet

Governance, aimed at applying existing international law instruments to the cyberspace, with due regard to its transboundary characteristic.

Internet Governance: Multistakeholder management of resources of the global electronic network, including, but not limited to the management of the Domain Name System, root-servers and InternetInternet Exchange Points.

Multistakeholderism: Key principle of InternetInternet governance, requiring joint management of InternetInternet resources by governments, business and the civil society in their respective roles.

Transboundary Harm: Risk of damage occurring outside the state where a risk-originating activity is carried out. By contrast, the term "damage" refers to actually affected economic, social, environmental or other negative consequences to the interests of another state or shared resources.

ENDNOTES

1. Id., Article 3 pt. 1) (g).

2. Id., Article 1 pt. 7).

3. The ILC was given the task of researching and summarizing the state responsibility principles in international law in 1954, following a GA resolution 799(VIII) from 7 December 1953, although at its very first session in 1949 state responsibility was named one of the issues the ILC ought to be dealing with. In 1978 ILC was authorized to examine state liability (II (2) *Yearbook of the International Law Commission* 149 ff.)

4. The ILC Draft Principles introduce a distinction between „harm" and „damage", where the former describes the reference "only to the risk of harm and not to the subsequent phase where harm has actually occurred. The term "damage" is employed to refer to the latter phase. The notion of "transboundary damage" is introduced to denote specificity to the harm, which occurred. *2006 ILC Draft Principles* commentary (11) on Principle 1 at 120.

5. Boyle at 16.

6. See *ILC Draft Articles*, commentary (9) on Article 2 at 36.

7. See *2001 ILC Draft Articles*, commentary (6) on Article 31 at 92, where the ILC explains that harm might be a necessary element, required by a primary rule, however should the primary rule oblige the state only to prevent a happening or introduce a certain national regulation, the omission to do so will also result in international responsibility, although no harm to another states' interests was done.

8. *2001 ILC Draft Articles* (supra 92 at 38) mention the Teheran case where ILC found Iran failed to provide sufficient diplomatic protection for US diplomats, although obliged to do that in the light of e.g. Vienna Convention and customary law.

9. "Responsabilité pour risqué crée" as defined by the *2006 ILC Draft Articles* (supra 422 at 155). The ILC mentions also other designations used to describe strict liability: "liability without fault" (responsabilité sans faute), "negligence without fault", "presumed responsibility", "fault per se", "objective liability" (responsabilité objective).

10. Boyle supporting Brownlie (supra 99 at 13) and Akehurst (supra 101 at 13).

11. Boyle at 15-16.

12. *See Draft Principles*, Principle 3. The details of the obligation of prevention are set in the *2001 ILC Draft Articles on Prevention*.

13. Due diligence is the focal point of all international environmental law regulations, originating from the principle of good neigh-

borliness, that set limits to the sovereignty of state at the line of other states' interests. It was later transformed into Principle 21 of the 1972 Declaration of the UN Conference on the Human Environment ("Stockholm Declaration") and repeated in Principle 2 of the1992 Rio Declaration on Environmental Development. It also appears in numerous EC documents, such as the 1979 ECE treaty (Article 2) or the 1980 EEC Council Resolution on Transboundary Air Polution by Sulphur Dioxide and Suspended Particulates. So defined due diligence standard takes into account the means at the disposal of particular states, bound thereto (see Okowa, 2000). *State Responsibility* for *Transboundary Air Pollution* in. *International Law*, Oxford: Oxford University Press, p 79). It also appears in the regime for protecting aliens and representatives of foreign states (see e.g. Pisillo-Mazzeschi at 22), as well as in regulations on terrorist attack prevention (see: Pisillo-Mazzeschi at 31- 32) generally referred to as an obligation to protect the security of foreign states.

14 SHAW, *at* 855.

15 Restatement (Third) of Foreign Relations of the United States, Section 601.

16 OKOWA, *at* 79.

17 OKOWA, supra 91 *at* 83.

18 OKOWA, *at* 83.

19 OKOWA, *at* 83.

20 OKOWA, supra 81 *at* 81, referring to Counter-Memorial of the Republic of Hungary.

21 As in the Salvador Prats Case, where the Mexico-United States Mixed Claims Commission held that: "The duty of protection on the part of the government (…) only goes as far as permitted by possibility" (see: OKOWA, supra 84 *at* 81).

22 OKOWA mentions here also the general acceptance of surrendering such an assessment to external verification by reference to international law standards, following the argument raised by France in the 1995 Nuclear Tests Cases (France claimed to have met the due diligence standard by providing a prior environmental impact assessment). OKOWA, *at* 82.

23 OKOWA, supra 86 at 82.

24 He denotes important exceptions, such as article II of the Convention on International Liability for Damage caused by Space Objects, providing for the absolute liability of the originating state (SHAW, *at* 854).

25 SHAW, *at* 853.

26 SHAW, *at* 855.

27 SHAW, *at* 861.

28 *1998 ILC Draft Articles,* Article 5.

29 *1998 ILC Draft Articles,* Article 6.

30 *1998 ILC Draft Articles,* Article 7.

31 *1998 ILC Draft Articles,* Article 8 and 17.

32 *1998 ILC Draft Articles,* Article 9.

33 A soft-law principle rather than a "general principles of law recognized by civilized nations" as referred to in Article 38 of the ICJ statute, at 87.

34 OKOWA, at 83-84.

35 As identified within Article 4 of the Rio Declaration: „In order to achieve sustainable development, environmental protection shall constitute an integral part of the development process and cannot be considered in isolation from it".

36 As rightfully denoted by OKOWA this reaffirms the relativity of the due diligence standard to the actual capacity of state resources. at 83.

37 As defined in Principle 15 of the Rio Declaration: „In order to protect the environment the precautionary approach shall be widely applied by states according to their capabilities."

38 As noted by OKOWA this principle is subject to academic debate and various interpretations. at 84, supra 97.

39 OKOWA, supra 107 *at* 87.

40 OKOWA, supra 108 and 109 *at* 88.

41 *2006 ILC Draft Principles*, Principle 2, pt. (c).

42 *2001 ILC Draft Articles on Prevention*, commentary (4) to Article 2, at 152.

43 Such a list would naturally be under-inclusive and would have to be amended on regular basis in the light of changing technology. The present broad definition allows more flexibility in the application of the articles, as "the risk that flows from an activity is primarily a function of the particular application, the specific context and the manner of operation", which is impossible to capture in a generic list. *2006 ILC Draft Principles*, comment (3) on Principle 1, at 117.

44 According to the 2001 Draft on state responsibility states are responsible for acts "attributable" to them. Those two terms cover different sorts of activities. State conduct traditionally plays a key role in the state responsibility regime, as defined by the 2001 ILC Draft. A state may be held internationally responsible when an act (action or omission) contrary to its international obligations may be attributed thereto under international law. Attribution has been defined by the ILC with much scrutiny, however the construct still raises numerous practical concerns. *2001 ILC Draft Articles*, Article 2 and Chapter 2 (articles 4 – 11).

45 Boyle, at 21.

46 Boyle (at 21) refers to "assignment of obligations" in Article 3 of the 1986 version of the draft, that has been eventually replaced with the definition of the "state of origin" in Article 2 of the *1998 ILC Draft*.

47 *ILC Draft Principles*, Article 2 (d). In Principle 2 the "hazardous activity" is defined as "an activity which involves a risk of causing significant harm".

48 Such an obligation – an obligation to prevent – was initially defined in Article 3 of the *1998 ILC Draft Articles*, which obliges States to take all appropriate measures to prevent or to minimize the risk of significant transboundary harm. The details of the obligation were elaborated on in *2001 ILC Draft Articles on Prevention*.

49 *ILC Draft Articles* Article 7 and *ILC Draft Articles on Prevention* Article 6.

50 World Summit on the Information Society, *Tunis Agenda for the Information Society*, WSIS-05/TUNIS/DOC/6(Rev. 1)-E, pt. 58.

51 WGIG Report, pt. 10.

52 WGIG Report, pt. 12.

53 *CoE Report*.

54 Further herein: *CoE Report*, Principle A.2.

55 *CoE Report* Principle A.1 and A.3.

56 *CoE Report* Principle A.4.

57 *CoE Report* Principle A.5.

58 *CoE Report* Principle B.1.

59 *CoE Report* Principle B.2.

60 *CoE Report* Principle B.3.

61 *CoE Report* Principle B.4.

62 *CoE Report* Principle C.

63 *CoE Report* Principle C.

64 OJ L 69, 16.3.2005, p. 67–71.

65 Gehring & Jachtenfuchs, at 97.

66 Since 1982 the International Maritime Organisation (IMO).

67 Negotiations on what later became the International Convention on Civil Liability for Oil Pollution Damage, 1969, 9 ILM (1970) 45.

68 Gehring & Jachtenfuchs, at 98.

69 Gehring & Jachtenfuchs, at 98.

70 Only residual liability, if any, should be placed on the authorizing state. Gehring & Jachtenfuchs, *at* 97, citing Barboza.

71 Gehring & Jachtenfuchs, at 99.

72 Gehring & Jachtenfuchs, at 97.

73 Convention on Civil Liability for Damage Caused During Carriage of Dangerous

Goods by Road, Rail and Inland Navigation Vessels, 1989, United Nations Economic Commission for Europe Doc. ECE/TRANS/84 (including explanatory report).

[74] See Gehring & Jachtenfuchs, supra 39-41 *at* 99.

[75] In the Convention of 31 January 1963 Supplementary to the Paris Convention of 29 July 1960 on Third Party Liability in the Field of Nuclear Energy, 2 ILM 685.

[76] Gehring & Jachtenfuchs, *at* 101.

[77] Gehring & Jachtenfuchs, *at* 101.

[78] Proposals for introducing direct state liability have been made after the Chernobyl incident, without tangible results as of yet. See: Gehring & Jachtenfuchs, supra 52 *at* 101.

[79] OKOWA, *at* 79.

[80] Internet Engineering Task Force (IETF) operates through Requests for Comments (RfCs) – non binding technical standards introduced by and enforced through the voluntary practice of network engineers, often responsible within their professional capacities for the proper functioning of the World Wide Web.

[81] See the Salvador Prats Case, where the Mexico-United States Mixed Claims Commission held that: „The duty of protection on the part of the government (…) only goes as far as permitted by possibility" (see: OKOWA at 81 supra 84).

[82] SHAW, at 861.

[83] *1998 ILC Draft Articles,* Article 5.

[84] *1998 ILC Draft Articles,* Article 6.

[85] *1998 ILC Draft Articles,* Article 7.

[86] May the introduction of the new gTLDs serve as the most current example of introducing a technical solution without a detailed analysis of its impact.

[87] *1998 ILC Draft Articles,* Article 8 and 17.

[88] Vinton Cerf proposed creating a "cyber fire-department" in response to the current global cyber-threats, emphasizing that no state is capable of effectively facing them alone. This statement seems confirmed by the NATO and EU circulated warnings on the needed protection of secret intelligence material against cyber attacks originating from China. Warnings were based on the conclusion that the EU system was vulnerable since security efforts rested within the scope of individual responsibility of each member state.

[89] *1998 ILC Draft Articles,* Article 9.

[90] OKOWA, supra 108, 109 *at* 88.

[91] That is the view of the CoE; see: *CoE Internet governance and critical Internet resources,* 6 (2009).

[92] Expressed in numerous soft-law documents, most recent and crucial of which include: *International and multi-stakeholder co-operation on cross-border Internet,* Interim report of the Ad-hoc Advisory Group on Cross-border Internet to the Steering Committee on the Media and New Communication Services incorporating analysis of proposals for international and multi-stakeholder co-operation on cross-border Internet.

Chapter 6
Criminal Liability of Organizations, Corporations, Legal Persons, and Similar Entities on Law of Portuguese Cybercrime:
A Brief Discussion on the Issue of Crimes of "False Information," the "Damage on Other Programs or Computer Data," the "Computer–Software Sabotage," the "Illegitimate Access," the "Unlawful Interception," and "Illegitimate Reproduction of the Protected Program"

Gonçalo S. de Melo Bandeira
Escola Superior de Gestão, IPCA, Portugal

ABSTRACT

In Portugal, and in much of the legal systems of Europe, "legal persons" are likely to be criminally responsibilities for cybercrimes, for example, "false information," "damage on other programs or computer data," "computer-software sabotage," "illegitimate access," "unlawful interception," and "illegitimate reproduction of protected program." However, there are exceptions to the "question of criminal liability" of "legal persons." Some "legal persons" cannot be blamed for cybercrime. The

DOI: 10.4018/978-1-4666-4526-4.ch006

legislature did not leave! These "legal persons" are the following ("public entities"): legal persons under public law, which include the public business entities; entities utilities, regardless of ownership; or other legal persons exercising public powers. In other words, and again as an example, a Portuguese public university or a private concessionaire of a public service in Portugal cannot commit any one of the highlighted cybercrimes. Fair? Unfair. All laws should provide that all legal persons (rectius organizations) can commit cybercrimes.

1. INTRODUCTION

Criminal liability is the highest penalty that the modern democratic, free and true "rule of law," gives to individuals and their organizations and/or "corporations, legal persons and similar entities." Whether from the point of view of criminal law or from criminology perspective, or even in a trend of criminal policy, there is already a consensus, quite broad (Dias & Andrade, 1984; Dias, 2007). Quite broad consensus—in doctrine, jurisprudence, and legislation—on the necessity, appropriateness, and proportionality to consecrate the criminal liability of organizations—"corporations, legal persons and similar entities" (Bandeira, 2011a, 2011b; Guinter, 2009; Keulen & Gritter, 2010). Only a few voices in a few countries, like some doctrine in Germany, are still defending the old principle of "*societas delinquere non potest*" (Bandeira, 2004). But, even here, they have other type of sanctions. The criminal law—which is constitutional law—should always be a "law of minimum intervention." A *ultima ratio law*. The criminal law, among other things, has to take into account the general and special positive preventions, but also the retribution and Justice. Some part of the criminal law must also look for a restorative Justice.

However, in the context of the Portuguese legal system, is scheduled to criminal liability of organizations ("corporations, legal persons and similar entities") on different places of legislation, and in particular in the designated "law of cybercrime."[1] And this responsibility can in particular be for the following crimes: "False

information"[2]; the "Damage on other programs or computer data"[3]; the "Computer-software sabotage"[4], the "Illegitimate access"[5], the "Unlawful interception" and "Illegitimate reproduction of the protected program"[6]. It turns out that, with regard to the "criminal responsibility" of organizations, "corporations, legal persons and similar entities," the "Law of Cybercrime" makes a reference to the portuguese Penal Code.[7]

We need to see also some of the possible legal consequences in relation to issues that are related to system administration information within organizations. And this, or that, is right in the middle of "corporations, legal persons and similar entities," "organizations." You need to check to what extent cannot exist here and there, an interception among the following three groups of questions. 1) "Management Information System" within organizations, *id est*, the "corporations, legal persons and similar entities"; 2) Responsibility/liability of the criminal organizations, *id est*, the "corporations, legal persons and similar entities" in the context of so-called "Cybercrime Law"; 3) Crimes of "False information"; "Damage on other programs or computer data"; "Computer-software sabotage"; "Illegitimate access"; "Unlawful interception"; and "Illegitimate reproduction of protected program."

It is also crucial, of course, to realize how it works—from the strict point of view of legal technique and criminal—the nexus of imputation of criminal liability to "organizations," i.e., the "corporations, legal persons and similar entities." We refer to the respective criminal liability for crimes of "False information," "Damage on other programs or computer data," "Computer-software sabotage," "illegitimate access," "Unlawful interception," and "illegitimate reproduction of protected program."

At the end, we have the conclusions and constructive suggestions, but not before finally realizing what type of "organizations"—"corporations, legal persons, and similar entities," through a poor administration of the information system, can commit crimes that are in the "Cybercrime Law."

After all, we are talking about fundamental rights and duties.

1.1. Introduction of Reference of the Article 12 of the Convention on Cybercrime According to CCC(2001)[8]

Article 12: Corporate Liability

1. Each Party shall adopt such legislative and other measures as may be necessary to ensure that legal persons can be held liable for a criminal offence established in accordance with this Convention, committed for their benefit by any natural person, acting either individually or as part of an organ of the legal person, who has a leading position within it, based on:
    a. A power of representation of the legal person;
    b. An authority to take decisions on behalf of the legal person;
    c. An authority to exercise control within the legal person.
2. In addition to the cases already provided for in paragraph 1 of this article, each Party shall take the measures necessary to ensure that a legal person can be held liable where the lack of supervision or control by a natural person referred to in paragraph 1 has made possible the commission of a criminal offence established in accordance with this

Convention for the benefit of that legal person by a natural person acting under its authority.
3. Subject to the legal principles of the Party, the liability of a legal person may be criminal, civil or administrative.
4. Such liability shall be without prejudice to the criminal liability of the natural persons who have committed the offence...." COE (2001)[9].

This is the article 12. of the Convention on Cybercrime. But, as we will see, the problem in Portugal is not the article 12 of the Convention on Cybercrime. The problem is quite different: the article 11 of the Portuguese criminal code that we must apply also to the cybercrimes. The article is similar but at the same time very different.

2. THE CRIMINAL LIABILITY OF INDIVIDUAL'S AND "LEGAL PERSON'S" ("ORGANIZATIONS," "CORPORATIONS," "COLLECTIVE ENTITIES," "LEGAL ENTITIES," AND SIMILAR) CRIMES DEFINED AND PUNISHED BY THE DESIGNATED "LAW OF CYBERCRIME"

Thus, as mentioned previously, and once the "Law of Cybercrime" refers to the "penal code,"[10] we put our attention on this same Portuguese Penal Code. It is through this code that we will see how it establishes the nexus required imputation of criminal liability of "legal persons"[11] in relation to crimes that are foreseen and punished through the "Law of Cybercrime" (in Portugal as a country from the European Union, EU). Which, incidentally, also as we have seen implements international and European standards for the domestic Portuguese legal system.[12] Crimes, as already mentioned before, are: "False information," the "Damage on other programs or computer data," the "Computer-software sabotage," the "Illegitimate access," the "Unlawful interception" and the "Illegitimate reproduction of the protected program."

2.1. Article 11 of the Portuguese Penal Code

Article 11 of the Portuguese Penal Code reads as follows:[13]

Liability of natural and legal persons" §

1. Except as provided in the following paragraph and in cases specified by law, only natural persons are liable to criminal responsibility.

2. Legal persons and similar entities, other than the State, other public bodies and international organizations under public law, are responsible for the crimes referred to in articles 152.°-A e 152.°-B, articles 159.° e 160.°, from article 163.° to 166.°, being the victim a minor, and in articles 168.°, 169.°, from 171.° to 176.°, from 217.° to 222.°, 240.°, 256.°, 258.°, from 262.° to 283.°, 285.°, 299.°, 335.°, 348.°, 353.°, 363.°, 367.°, 368.°-A and 372.° to 374.°, when committed:

   a. In their name and in the collective interest in them by persons who occupy a leading position, or

   b. For those who act under the authority of the persons mentioned in the previous paragraph because of a violation of the duties of supervision or control of their responsibilities.

3. For the purposes of the criminal law the public entities expression covers:

   a. Legal persons under public law, which include the public business entities;

   b. Entities utilities, regardless of ownership;

   c. Other legal persons exercising public powers.

4. It is understood that occupy a leading position the organs and representatives of the legal person and who it has authority to exercise control over their activity.

5. For the purposes of criminal liability to similar entities from the legal persons are considered the civil societies and the associations of fact.

6. The liability of legal persons and similar entities is deleted when the agent acted against the express orders or instructions of those eligible.

7. The liability of legal persons and similar entities not exclude the individual liability of its agents nor depends on the liability of these.

8. The fission and fusion do not determine the extinction of criminal liability of the legal person or similar entity, accounting for the crime:

   a. The body corporate or similar entity in the merger if effected, and

   b. Legal persons or similar entities that resulted from the breakup.

9. Notwithstanding the right of return, persons who occupy a leading position are jointly liable for the payment of fines and damages in the legal person or similar entity is convicted, respect to crimes:

   a. Practiced during the exercise of his office, without your express opposition;

   b. Practiced previously, if it was his fault that the assets of the legal person or similar entity became insufficient for the payment; or

   c. Practiced previously, when the final decision to implement it has been notified during the exercise of his office and they are attributable to lack of payment.

10. As several persons responsible under the preceding paragraph, their liability is joint.

11. If fines or damages are applied to an entity without legal personality, for them the common heritage and, in his absence or insufficiency, severally, the assets of each of the members.

2.2. Quick note to Article 11 of the Portuguese Penal Code: Introduction

Article 11 of the Penal Code is not the only legal provision ("rule of law") which allows to impute criminal liability to "legal persons" within the Portuguese legal system (de Albuquerque, 2010). There are other cases.[14] At all, the "Law of Cybercrime" (2009) that we are looking, unlike the previous "Computer Crime Law" (1991) that was before the reform of Portuguese Penal Code concerning this matter (2007),[15] refers to Article 11 of the Portuguese Penal Code.

There is consensus, in most jurisdictions in Europe and worldwide, the criminal liability of individuals differs from criminal liability of "legal persons." There is a real autonomy. Thus, the criminal liability of "legal persons" shall not exclude criminal liability of the respective agents. The Portuguese Constitution (CRP) is not therefore in any way violated. There is no violation of the principle of "*ne bis in idem.*"[16]

2.3. The Crimes Defined and Punished in the "Law of Cybercrime,"[17] Especially within the Social and Economic Criminal Law: The Case of the Importance of "Company," "Corporation," "Organization"

Nobody can deny that there may be cases of "cybercrimes" in the context of different national criminal laws and, in very broad sense, in many areas such as: the economy and society in general, management, the environment, consumption, the tax; in securities markets and/or other financial instruments, medicine, biology, public health, at work, competition, industrial property, in sport, culture, among others. If we want, we can say that the "cybercrime" may be economic, social, political, cultural and even "mental." Now, as we

have seen before—and nobody can deny not only in the economic-capitalist system—entrepreneurs and "companies," "corporations," acquire also a central role in all this dialectic.

However, it is easy to impute responsibility for crimes to "firms" ("companies," "corporations"), in particular, responsibility/liability for "cyber crimes"? *Id est*, of course, of "collective entities" or "legal entities," also called "legal persons" or, for example, how to become more appropriate, "organizations" (i.e., "corporations or statutory corporations or even public companies")? No, we think it is not easy… We can already say that, from a technical-legal and legal-criminal point of view, is not easy to sue (proceed, in Court) "companies," "corporations," a liability for crimes (in Portugal), including liability for "cybercrimes." It is not at all easy.

2.4. Some Results about the Difficulty of Attributing/Imputation Crimes, Including "Cybercrimes," on the "Companies," "Corporations," "Organizations," under the Jurisdiction of the Portuguese Law and in this Case, through the Adoption of European Legislation[18]

Strange as it may be, and is valid for at least the entry into force of the new wording of art. 11 of the Portuguese Penal Code, i.e., since the end of 2007 and the present moment we are writing this work, is easier—from the standpoint of legal imputation of criminal responsibility a company practicing a "cybercrime" p. and p. under the "Law of Cybercrime" (e.g., arts. 3, 4, 5, 6, 7, and 8)—than, for example, a crime of "speculation," punished in the art. 35 (and art. 3) of the "Legal and Economic Offences Against Public Health" (R.I.A.E.C.S.P.). And who referred to such difference of this crime—with regard to the establishment of its nexus imputation—we could mention many others that appear on both pieces of legislation apply when confronting art. 11 of the Portuguese Penal Code and art. 3 of "R.I.A.E.C.S.P."

Too much sui generis, and this is valid for at least the start in force of the "new version" of art. 11 of the Penal Code, i.e., since the end of 2007 and the present moment we are writing this text: it is easier—from a perspective of allocating criminal legal responsibility, a company operating an offense of "False information" and will be punished through Penal Code (e.g. "Law of Cybercrime" and art. 11 of the Penal Code), than, for example, a crime of tax fraud p. and p. in art. 103 (and art. 7) of the law of "General Tax Infractions."[19]

Who appoints the differential examples described above, the crime of tax fraud or the crime of "speculation" - as to the application of the respective *link* allocation - could point to many others that appear on both pieces of legislation when we expose the art. in comparison 11. of the Penal Code and art. 35. of R.I.A.E.C.S.P. or art. 7. do R.G.I.T. (General Tax Infractions, i.e., "*Regime Geral das Infracções Tributárias*").

It could be provided here other further examples of dissimilarities between standards of legal imputation of criminal liability companies and collective bodies and/or legal persons and/or organizations. Even in the field of offenses and/or offense against society (administrative offences or "against-ordinance"). What in our modest understanding has no sense and violates some constitutional principles as the essential principle of universality (art. 12./2 of the Portuguese Constitution) or the principle of equality (art. 13. CRP), among others basic foundations of the social democratic, free and true "rule of law."

Prompting the need to avoid the constant changes in legislation, it is urgent to correct this nature in terms of legislation and where the divergence of the legislative process is performed from a constitutional perspective, and therefore criminal and legal and scientific.

According to the n. 2 and n. 3 of art. 11. Penal Code, companies that can not commit the crimes of corruption of the Portuguese Penal Code are those that are capable, from a legal perspective, to be included in the following tables: "a) Legal persons of public law, in which include the public business entities, b) Entities utilities, regardless of ownership, c) Other legal persons exercising public powers." This is a juridical scandal. This brings heavy and strong constitutional problems!

Thus, not all "corporations" ("organizations"), by logical reasoning, are capable of practicing "cybercrimes" provided for and punished under the present articles 3, 4, 5, 6, 7, and 8 of the "Law of Cybercrime."

The "Entities utilities, regardless of ownership," the opposite of many other companies cannot make the "cybercrimes" provided for and punished under articles 3, 4, 5, 6, 7, and 8 of the "Law of Cybercrime." And "cannot" why? Because the law itself does not allows, in a clear and unequivocal. This is what the law requires and not fencing with interpretive techniques which have no foundation least minimal verbal or symmetry in the letter of the law: cf. art. 9./2 of the Portuguese Civil Code. It is the letter of the law that is perhaps wrong and violates the CRP (Portuguese Constitution). Or, if not wrong, you can at least call in error. Clearly the composition of the art. 11 of the Penal Code was wrong here and clashes with the restrictive nature of the exception to the principle of responsibility modeled on international texts. Although we can accept, of course, that the design part of the legislature has been different. But it is not transparent. It is very opaque. On the contrary, is unclear. Albeit everyone believes that the work of the revision of the Portuguese Penal Code was very hard. But even worse is when the reform is a historic setback, however unintentionally. For others in the future will have to correct the errors. Moreover, the words of the law in art.11 of the Penal Code describe "Other legal persons exercising public powers." It does not describe it "acted without or with public powers" and even the text is not transparent with regard to public undertakings and entities utilities. In this paper, we refer to the relevant legislation that defines these legal definitions. When in doubt before the letter of the law - we cannot forget - and according to the Constitution, we must choose the interpretation most favorable ("perhaps more constitutional") to the defendant, whether the same is organizational and/or collective or singular. Here is the center of the Criminal Legal Sciences Social State of Law, democratic, free and true. Do not try to get another illegitimate way! On the other hand, is really against the Constitution, as stated elsewhere in this paper, that the designated public organizations (and/or, in this case, "public entities") even if they are "acting under public powers" are excluded the outset, the entire criminal legal responsibility. As we said before, this is a juridical scandal. Will still sense this privilege, when the State, public enterprises or the "public-private partnerships" behave, often as true major players sometimes monopolistic, the game of economic and financial capitalist system, and many of these cases, "only" speculative capitalism and even, e.g., in violation of "Law of Cybercrime," public financial standards, market, consumer and/or environmental, tax, among others?

For that matter here of a more technical point of view, we can also say that not all "corporations" (e.g. "Legal persons," "companies," governed by public law and/or "organizations" in public law, "statutory organizations and corporations"), therefore, are likely to commit, e.g., "cybercrimes."

Contradictory as it may seem, and is valid for at least the entry into force of the new wording of art. 11 of the Portuguese Penal Code, it is easier[20] for a "corporation" and/or "company" practice a "cybercrime"[21], than, for example, a crime of speculation in the art. 35. (and art. 3) of the "Legal and Economic Offences Against Public Health" (R.I.A.E.C.S.P.). And who referred to such difference of this crime—and the establishment of the corresponding bond allocation/imputa-

tion—could mention many others that appear on both pieces of legislation when we expose the art. in comparison with 11 of the Penal Code and art. 3.[22] Not to mention, e.g., in the current Portuguese "General Rules of Administrative Offences (Against-Ordinances)" (R.G.C.O., i.e., "*Regime Geral das Contra-Ordenações*") and in its art. 7, which establishes a narrow model (perhaps one of the closest models!) allocation (imputation) of responsibility for administrative offense "collective bodies" and/or "legal persons" and/or "organizations," "corporations," when it refers only to "organs" (e.g. board of directors).

By bizarre that it can also emphasize, as already stated in another place in this text, and this is valid for at least the entry into force of the new wording of art. 11. of the Penal Code, is easier—from the standpoint of allocating (imputing) legal responsibility criminal, a "company," a "corporation," operating a "cybercrime," than, e.g., a crime of tax fraud p. and p. in art. 103 (and 7) of the "General Administration of Tax Offences" (R.G.I.T., i.e., "*Regime Geral das Infracções Tributárias*")[23]!

Although the reasoning remains the same, it is still jarring in terms of scientific and legal-criminal. This of course if the law has the same aspiration to be taken seriously as science. Or did not? Because if not, Sociology—herself indispensable condition that combined with other sciences—will eventually supplant and even crush the Law, "for the good and for the evil of the rule of law," social democratic, free and true. Space and time, this, which should be based on a series of constitutional principles, including the principle of legality and the principle of criminal guilt among others. Or guarantees as the presumption of innocence or the right to defense and the contradictory.

"Legal persons" ("corporations") governed by public law and/or organizations in public law ("statutory organizations and corporations"), which include the public business; entities utilities, regardless of their ownership, and other legal persons (and/or organizations) who exercise "public powers," "powers of "government"

("State" power") cannot practice "cybercrimes" provided for and punished, either in arts. 3 to 8 of the Portuguese "Cybercrime Law."[24] Now that's what really is happening: art. 11 of the Portuguese Penal Code.

In our point of view, not only has no meaning the exceptions pointed in terms of criminal liability of "legal persons" and/or organizations (e.g. corporations and statutory organizations), as this is a probable violation, not to say "provocation" of the principle of universality, as provided in art. 12/2 of the Portuguese Constitution (C.R.P.): "2. Legal persons shall enjoy rights and are subject to duties compatible with their nature." But also, extensively, the principle of equality provided for in art. 13 of the Portuguese Constitution (C.R.P.). Or even, as is evident, and even proclaimed themselves "apostles of religious and financial capitalist economic system" of their own "sacred, free and fair competition between companies in the markets." Not to mention the ethical example that should, or should be given to all others, from the so-called "public corporations" (statutory corporations).

3. SOLUTIONS AND RECOMMENDATIONS

The solution and recommending is to have a legislative change on art. 11 Portuguese Penal Code. And all similar articles should be equal on the rules of imputation. The aim is finished with the ("very strange") exceptions that are part of the law in force in Portugal regarding the criminal liability of "legal persons." These "legal persons" are the following ("public entities"): legal persons under public law, which include the public business entities; entities utilities, regardless of ownership; or other legal persons exercising public powers. The cybercrimes do not respect borders. These crimes are world crimes or global crimes. Thus a Portuguese public university or a private concessionaire of a public service in Portugal, cannot commit (in Portugal) any one of cybercrime pointed, but can commit it in another legal system of another country. See the juridical problem? Just as a "legal person" from another country can commit in Portugal from abroad, where is punishable. The Internet enables and enhances that. All laws should provide that all legal persons can commit cybercrimes.

4. FUTURE RESEARCH DIRECTIONS

If the cybercrimes are world crimes or global crimes, then this problem has to be studied in a world way or a global way. This will be the future investigation. The case of the Portuguese legislation is a paradigmatic case of (very) national specificities. National specificities those can even be legitimate in democratic rule of law, but precluding legislation cybercriminal to be effective. All laws should provide that all legal persons can commit cybercrimes.

There is another important issue that must be considered: it is not enough that there is criminal liability of organizations, corporations, legal persons and similar entities. We need to adapt criminal procedural law (criminal procedure) in practical terms (Andrade, 1992; Dias, 1974; da Silva, 2009).

5. CONCLUSION

The cybercrimes of "false information," "damage on other programs or computer data," "computer-software sabotage," "illegitimate access," "unlawful interception," and "illegitimate reproduction of protected program" should be treated as crimes of the world or global crimes. Cybercrimes are not crimes from Portugal, or crimes from Europe. The Portuguese law, on this issue, is not the correct law in force. These are crimes from the world, "the world of cybercrime." In the future, especially in this case as is "the world of cybercrime," we need to change (also) the Portuguese national law to build a real law from the world without an offshore side (v.g. starting in Europe).[25] All laws should provide that all legal persons (*rectius* organizations) can commit cybercrimes.

REFERENCES

Andrade, M. C. (1992). *Sobre as proibições de prova em processo penal*. Coimbra, Portugal: Coimbra Editora.

Bandeira, G. M. (2004). *Responsabilidade penal económica e fiscal dos entes colectivos, à volta das sociedades comerciais ou sociedades civis sob a forma comercial*. Coimbra, Portugal: Editora Almedina.

Bandeira, G. M. (2011a). *Abuso de mercado e responsabilidade penal das pessoas (não) colectivas, "contributo para a compreensão dos bens jurídicos colectivos e dos "tipos cumulativos" na mundialização*. Curitiba, Brazil: Editora Juruá.

Bandeira, G. M. (2011b). Abuso de informação, manipulação do mercado e responsabilidade penal das "pessoas colectivas" – "Tipos cumulativos" e bens jurídicos colectivos na "globalização." Lisboa, Portugal: Editorial Juruá. Guinter, J. (2009). Criminal liability of legal persons in Estonia. Juridica International, 16. Retrieved from http://www.juridicainternational.eu/public/pdf/ji_2009_1_151.pdf

da Silva, G. M. (2009). *Curso de processo penal*. Lisboa, Portugal: Editora Verbo.

De Albuquerque, P. P. (2010). *Comentário do código penal à luz da constituição da república e da convenção europeia dos direitos do homem*. Lisboa, Portugal: Universidade Católica Editora.

Dias, J. F. (1974). *Direito processual penal*. Coimbra, Portugal: Coimbra Editora.

Dias, J. F. (2007). *Direito penal, parte geral, tomo I: Questões fundamentais, a doutrina geral do crime*. Coimbra, Portugal: Coimbra Editora.

Dias, J. F., & Andrade, M. C. (1984). *Criminologia: O homem delinquente e a sociedade criminógena*. Coimbra, Portugal: Coimbra Editora.

Keulen, B. F., & Gritter, E. (2010). Corporate criminal liability in The Netherlands. Electronic Journal of Comparative Law, 14(3). Retrieved from http://www.ejcl.org/143/art143-9.doc

ADDITIONAL READING

AA.VV. (1998). *Direito penal económico e Europeu: Textos doutrinários (Vol. I)*. Coimbra, Portugal: Coimbra Editora.

AA.VV. (1999). *Direito penal económico e Europeu: Textos doutrinários (Vol. 2)*. Coimbra, Portugal: Coimbra Editora.

AA.VV. (2009). *Direito penal económico e Europeu: Textos doutrinários (Vol. 3)*. Coimbra, Portugal: Coimbra Editora.

AA.VV. (2010). *Que futuro para o direito processual penal?* Coimbra, Portugal: Coimbra Editora.

Andrade, M. C. (2004). *Consentimento e acordo em direito penal (consentimento para a fundamentação de um paradigma dualista)*. Coimbra, Portugal: Coimbra Editora.

Correia, E. (1963). *Direito criminal*. Coimbra, Portugal: Livraria e Editora Almedina.

Jescheck, H., & Weigend, T. (1996). *Lehrbuch des strafrechts § allgemeiner teil § fünfte auflage, Berlin*. Alemanha, Portugal: Duncker & Humblot.

Portela, I. M. (2009). *O combate ao branqueamento e capitais e o financiamento do terrorismo à luz do USA patriot act 2001*. Curitiba, Brazil: Editora Juruá.

Roxin, C. (1993). *Strafverfahrensrecht: Eine studienbuch*. München, Germany: C. H. Beck.

Sieber, U. (2012). *Straftaten und strafverfolgung im internet*. München, Germany: Beck.

Siracusano, G. Tranchina, & Zappalà. (1996). Diritto processuale penale. Milão, Italy: Giuffrè.

ENDNOTES

[1]   Art. 9. Portuguese Law n. 109/2009, de 15/9, transposing into national law the Council Framework Decision 2005/222/JHA, of the Council of 24 February on attacks against information systems, and adapting the law to the Convention on Cybercrime of the Council of Europe. See also the Proposal for a Directive of the European Parliament and of the Council on attacks against information systems and repealing Council Framework Decision 2005/222/JHA, COM(2010) 517, at http://ec.europa.eu/dgs/home-affairs/policies/crime/1_en_act_part1_v101.pdf ; and the "Opinion of the European Economic and Social Committee on the "Proposal for a Directive of the European Parliament and of the Council on attacks against information systems and repealing Council Framework Decision 2005/222/JHA," *COM(2010) 517 final—2010/0273 (COD)*, (2011/C 218/27), at http://eur-lex.europa.eu/LexUriServ/LexUriServ.do?uri=OJ:C:2011:218:0130:0134:EN:PDF.

[2]   Art. 3. portuguese Law n. 109/2009, of 15/9, "Cybercrime Law."

[3]   Art. 4. portuguese Law n. 109/2009, of 15/9, "Cybercrime Law."

[4]   Cfr. art. 5. portuguese Law n. 109/2009, of 15/9, "Cybercrime Law."

[5]   Cfr. art. 6. portuguese Law n. 109/2009, of 15/9, "Cybercrime Law."

[6]   Cfr. art. 7. portuguese Law n. 109/2009, of 15/9, "Cybercrime Law."

[7]   The art. 9th. the "Law of Cybercrime" states: ("corporations") "Legal persons and similar entities are criminally responsible for crimes under this Act and under the limits of liability system under the Penal Code.." That is, there is a reference to art. 11 ("Liability of natural and legal persons") - "corporations" or "organizations" - of the Portuguese Penal Code. At present, the Portuguese Penal Code was changed to Law n. 56/2011 of 15 November - effective from December 15, 2011.

[8]   See http://conventions.coe.int/Treaty/en/Treaties/Html/185.htm, 22/3/2013. Portugal is one of the member countries of the Council of Europe and signed and ratified the referred Convention on Cybercrime (the Convention on Cybercrime is available in Portuguese at http://www.coe.int/t/dghl/standardsetting/t-cy/ETS_185_Portugese.pdf, 22/3/2013).

[9]   See the Explanatory Memorandum of the Convention on Cybercrime explaining article 12, available at http://conventions.coe.int/Treaty/en/Reports/Html/185.htm, 22/3/2013: "Corporate liability (Article 12) § 123. Article 12 deals with the liability of legal persons. It is consistent with the current legal trend to recognise corporate liability. It is intended to impose liability on corporations, associations and similar legal persons for the criminal actions undertaken by a person in a leading position within such legal person, where undertaken for the benefit of that legal person. Article 12 also contemplates liability where such a leading person fails to supervise or control an employee or an agent of the legal person, where such failure facilitates the commission by that employee or agent of one of the offences established in the Convention. § 124. Under paragraph 1, four conditions need to be met for liability to attach. First, one of the

offences described in the Convention must have been committed. Second, the offence must have been committed for the benefit of the legal person. Third, a person who has a leading position must have committed the offence (including aiding and abetting). The term "person who has a leading position" refers to a natural person who has a high position in the organization, such as a director. Fourth, the person who has a leading position must have acted on the basis of one of these powers – a power of representation or an authority to take decisions or to exercise control – which demonstrate that such a physical person acted within the scope of his or her authority to engage the liability of the legal person. In sum, paragraph 1 obligates Parties to have the ability to impose liability on the legal person only for offences committed by such leading persons. § 125. In addition, Paragraph 2 obligates Parties to have the ability to impose liability upon a legal person where the crime is committed not by the leading person described in paragraph 1, but by another person acting under the legal person's authority, i.e., one of its employees or agents acting within the scope of their authority. The conditions that must be fulfilled before liability can attach are that (1) an offence has been committed by such an employee or agent of the legal person, (2) the offence has been committed for the benefit of the legal person; and (3) the commission of the offence has been made possible by the leading person having failed to supervise the employee or agent. In this context, failure to supervise should be interpreted to include failure to take appropriate and reasonable measures to prevent employees or agents from committing criminal activities on behalf of the legal person. Such appropriate and reasonable measures could be determined by various factors, such as the type of the business, its size, the

standards or the established business best practices, etc. This should not be interpreted as requiring a general surveillance regime over employee communications (see also paragraph 54). A service provider does not incur liability by virtue of the fact that a crime was committed on its system by a customer, user or other third person, because the term "acting under its authority" applies exclusively to employees and agents acting within the scope of their authority. § 126. Liability under this Article may be criminal, civil or administrative. Each Party has the flexibility to choose to provide for any or all of these forms of liability, in accordance with the legal principles of each Party, as long as it meets the criteria of Article 13, paragraph 2, that the sanction or measure be "effective, proportionate and dissuasive" and includes monetary sanctions. § 127. Paragraph 4 clarifies that corporate liability does not exclude individual liability.."

[10] The art. 9th. the "Law of Cybercrime" and the art. 11. of the Portuguese Penal Code.

[11] In this text, the term "legal persons" also means, always, "and similar entities," "organizations," "corporations," "collective entities," "legal entities."

[12] Council Framework Decision 2005/222/JHA, of the Council of 24 February on attacks against information systems, and adapting the law to the Convention on Cybercrime of the Council of Europe.

[13] Amended by Law n. ° 59/2007 of 4 September.

[14] e.g., Decree-Law n. 28/84 of 20 January, "Legal and Economic Offences Against Public Health" (RJIAECSP) with amendments to Law n. 20/2008 of 21 April, or the Law n. 15/2001 of 5 June (RGIT) with amendments to Law n. 20/2012, of 14 May, starting in force on May 15, 2012.

[15] Law n. 109/91 of 17 August, which had the following "rule of law," legal provision:

"Article 3. § Criminal liability of legal persons and equivalent: § 1 - The legal persons, companies and associations mere fact are criminally responsible for the crimes provided for by law, when committed in their name and in the collective interest for their organs or representatives. § 2 - Liability is excluded when the agent acted against the express orders or instructions of those eligible. § 3 - The responsibility of the entities referred to in paragraph 1 shall not preclude the individual responsibility of the respective agents. § 4 - The entities referred to in paragraph 1 jointly liable under civil law for payment of fines, compensation and other benefits for officers who are convicted of offenses covered by this law.."

[16] Which translates literally from latin as "not twice in the same." Means that no legal action can be instituted twice for the same cause of action: Cfr. "*Acórdão do Tribunal Constitucional português*" ("Judgment of the Portuguese Constitutional Court") n. 213/95.

[17] As we saw before, "False information," the "Damage on other programs or computer data," the "Computer-software sabotage," the "Illegitimate access," the "Unlawful interception" and "Illegitimate reproduction of the protected program."

[18] As we have already seen before in this text.

[19] R.G.I.T., i.e., *Regime Geral das Infracções Tributárias*.

[20] It is easier… from the standpoint of allocating legal responsibility criminal.

[21] Cfr. art. 9. portuguese Law n. 109/2009, de 15/9, "Cybercrime Law."

[22] Of R.I.A.E.C.S.P. - "Legal and Economic Offences Against Public Health."

[23] Law n. 15/2001 of 5 June (RGIT) with amendments to Law n. 20/2012, of 14 May, starting in force on 15 May 2012.

[24] Law n. 109/2009, of 15/9, "Cybercrime Law."

[25] See the press release of the European Parliament regarding "Hacking IT systems to become a criminal offence," dated 27 March 2012, available at the Internet address, http://www.europarl.europa.eu/news/en/pressroom/content/20120326IPR41843/html/Hacking-IT-systems-to-become-a-criminal-offence, 22/3/2013. Such press release expressly mentions liability of legal persons.

Chapter 7
Redressing Violations of Privacy:
The Case of Portuguese "E-Invoice"

Irene Portela
Polytechnic Institute of Cávado and Ave, Portugal

ABSTRACT

The chapter discusses the role of CNPD (Comissão Nacional de Proteção de Dados) in case of violation of privacy, like dissemination or revelation of personal data by a public/private organization or entity. About this subject, the CNPD can issue a recommendation to the Portuguese Treasury to take some measures to strictly protect the security of the personal information using the Portuguese "E-Invoice." Portuguese people must be protected against the misuse of personal data by the use of the "E-Invoice." A Security System Administrator continuously monitors the network and all data traffic to prevent any misuse or abuse of the system. A prerequisite for trust and acceptance of these information systems is that appropriate data protection measures are implemented against possible misuse of personal data decreasing the risks in its utilization. Protective measures should be taken by the Treasury referring additional procedures against the misuse of data because the administrative control system is inefficient regarding unauthorized access, disclosure, misuse of localization data or loss, modification, and appropriation of information linked with the use of the Portuguese "E-Invoice."

INTRODUCTION

This chapter seeks to assess the legal responsibility of the System Administrator in a case of dissemination or revelation of personal data to the market by a public or governmental entity like the online "Portal of Portuguese Treasury." This matter is discussed in three parts: Firstly, it is explained who are the principal stakeholders (the tax payers, the Treasury, the system administrator of the portal and the CNPD). The second part presents a perspective of applying with correction

DOI: 10.4018/978-1-4666-4526-4.ch007

the principle of proportionality. For example, the E-Invoice project should be abandoned when it is proved that its use is groundless and excessive by breaching privacy rights, or only when it compromises the purpose for which the project was created. Therefore, the principle of proportionality can explain with accuracy the responsibilities of the System Administrator and the CNPD before the control of the personal data flow in an organization. In a third part, the difference between the security policy of the E-Government and the E-Invoice is presented. An Administrative Security system continuously monitors the network and all data traffic to prevent any misuse or abuse of the system. A prerequisite for trust and acceptance of these information systems is that appropriate data protection measures are implemented against possible misuse of personal data decreasing the risks in its utilization.

THE PORTUGUESE "E-INVOICING SYSTEM"

Noting that there is a relation between the grey economy and public finances, the Portuguese Government, in the purpose of reducing the public debt, has implemented a system of controlling the taxpayers by an E-Invoice system. By the Decree-Law number 198/2012, of August 24, which had entered into force on January first of 2013, the Portuguese Government has issued the "E-Invoice." This system provides a deduction from the IRS collection due by taxable persons of an amount corresponding to 5% of the value added tax (hereinafter 'VAT'- IVA in Portugal) borne by each member of the household, with the overall limit of 250 euros free.

To provide that the above conditions are met, the invoice with VAT included received by the Tax and Customs Authority (AT in Portugal) must be framed in the following sectors of activity: (a). maintenance and repair of motor vehicles; (b). maintenance and repair of motorcycles, parts and accessories; (c). accommodations, catering and similar services; (d). activities of hairdressing salons and beauty institutes. In these invoices it must stating the tax identification number of purchasers who must therefore always require to issuers their inclusion. It should be noted that, in accordance with Law, since the first of January of 2013 it is compulsory to invoice issue, even in cases where final consumers does not request it. The tax return (IRS) of the household should be delivered within the time limits laid down in article 60 of the IRS Code by electronic transmission of data, in April (only taxpayers that have received or have been placed at their disposal incomes in categories A and H and in may, in all other cases. The Authority of the Treasury had foreseen by the law a value of the incentive that is calculated automatically, until 31 January of the year following the issue of invoices, and based on the elements that are reported by service providers or by purchasers. Throughout the year, taxpayers may, at any time, follow the evolution of the value of the incentive through the online service, "Finance Portal."

The Authority of the Treasury allows visualizing the amount of the incentive on the "Finance Portal," until the day 10 of February of the year following the year of invoice issue. If the taxpayers are not agree about the calculation of the amount of the incentive they can present an administrative claim, by the end of March of the year following the invoices issue, in accordance with article 68 of the code of tax proceedings and processes (Tax Procedural Code), mutatis mutandis. The invoices which have not been communicated regularly to the Authority of the Treasury by issuers should be collected in the "Finance Portal" by purchasers, and only in such cases, they should keep them in their possession for a period of 4 years, counted from the end of the year in which the acquisition occurred. The Authority of the Treasury can act in cases of verified discrepancy between the elements reported by acquirers and issuers. If there is an evidence of that the invoices do not correspond to the services framed in these activities, this authority has the right to investigate about the confirmation of the accuracy of the operation. The incentive is not covered by the limits listed in the table of paragraph 2 of article 88 of the code of the IRS (tax benefits-EBF-limits taking into account levels of income).

To implement this "E-Invoice" Portuguese Government has promoted awareness campaigns about motivating consumers for asking an electronic "invoice." So the electronic invoice is an explicit request by the payment service user for the purchase of goods or services. Just after the execution of the payment transaction, the supplier of the services/goods had to issue an electronic invoice regardless the amount (for example, an invoice about taking a coffee). This was a governmental measure to pursue transparency in trade relationships, interoperability, efficiency and cost-savings, financial control and audit-ability/integrity on prompt payment operations in compliance with VAT rules. The Government had an enormous amount of solid arguments to implement these measures of tax transparency and combating grey economy.

In a different aspect about the "E-Invoice," the Council Directive 2006/112/EC of 28 November 2006 (EC, 2006) on the common system of value added tax lays down conditions and rules concerning VAT with respect to invoices, in order to ensure the proper functioning of the internal market (EC, 2006). In accordance with Article 237 of that Directive, the Commission had presented a report which identifies, in the light of technological developments, certain difficulties regarding to electronic invoicing and which, in addition, identifies certain other areas in which the VAT rules should be simplified with a view to improve the functioning of the internal market. Since the record keeping must be sufficient to allow that Member States control the goods moving temporarily from one Member State to another, it should be made clear that record keeping includes valuation details about these goods moving tempo-

rarily between Member States. Also, transfers of goods for valuation purposes to another Member State should not be regarded as a supply of goods for VAT purposes. The rules concerning the VAT chargeability on intra- Community supplies of goods and on intra-Community acquisitions of goods should be clarified in order to ensure the uniformity of the information submitted in recapitulative statements and also to allow the information exchange by means of those statements. It is furthermore appropriate that the continuous supply of goods from one Member State to another over a period of more than one calendar month should be regarded as being completed at the end of each calendar month. To help small and medium-sized enterprises that encounter difficulties in paying VAT to the competent authority before they have received payment from their customers, Member States should have the option of allowing VAT to be accounted using a cash accounting scheme which allows the supplier to pay VAT to the competent authority when he receives payment for a supply and which establishes his right of deduction when he pays for a supply. This should allow Member States to introduce an optional cash accounting scheme that does not have a negative effect on cash flow relating to their VAT receipts. To provide legal certainty for businesses regarding invoicing obligations, it should be clearly stated which Member States invoicing rules are applied (EC, 2010). About the model of Portuguese example of Public E-Procurement and the adoption of "E-Invoicing," the Commission said "in 2009, with the adoption of a new legal framework applicable to the public procurement process in Portugal, the public institutions started a new era for the dematerialization. The establishment of mandatory and widespread use of electronic procurement platforms in public sector to support the tendering and awarding processes gave a new dynamic to this market, and changed the mindset about dematerialization in public procurement processes, beyond the benefits that come from this measure. Objective rules were established about the requirements to be met by solutions that support these procurement processes, increasing awareness of various stakeholders on issues like security and information encryption, digital signatures, timestamps, interoperability, among others. In 2005, very ambitious goals were set concerning the use of E-Procurement in Europe, to be achieved by 2010. However, at that date, the overall rate of use at EU level was between 5% and 10%. Portugal is clearly demarcated from the rest of EU countries in this area, reaching a rate of procedures performed by electronic means of 75%" (EC, 2008).

Additionally, within the context of E-Procurement, specific guidelines were created regarding the use of electronic invoicing in Portugal: "About the issue of invoice, the procedures required by the law in force for the electronic invoice must be observed" at article 22 (DL, 2008) at the Decree Law 143-A/2008. In addition to the well-known advantages of dematerialization, by reducing the cost associated with the management and treatment of the chapter, these projects demonstrated the added value of integrated management of full procurement cycle, with all the potential in terms of traceability and security that comes with it. Additionally, they provided very significant gains also in the dematerialization of the approval processes associated with each step of the cycle, and in terms of minimizing duplication of data entry in multiple systems, through the development of integration with internal systems of each entity. In terms of electronic invoicing, this last point seems to be of great importance to improve the efficiency of financial processes at the level of classification, accounting and document payment, for example.

In this new system, with the exchange of information between traders/producers and Finance, the state will have access to information about the life and habits of the citizens, but on the other side traders also have access to the number of taxpayers and other personal data. Seller may issue electronic invoices for any purchases of Products made using the Internet, e-mail or any other computer based on electronic communications. Electronic invoicing—"E-Invoice"—is electronic transfer of invoicing information (billing and payment) between business partners (supplier and buyer). This may mean access or disclosure, alteration or destruction of information between traders/enterprise/businesses/banks. This breach of confidentiality between the users of the online tax portal raises issues to be considered when at a Government level the administrator of the system may not control the information about the tax flows ; in particular (data flows in general), it is relevant considering problems that may arise when using private data or business information.

THE ROLE OF THE SYSTEM ADMINISTRATOR AND THE ROLE OF THE CNPD

The Act on the Protection of Personal Data (LPD, 1991), regarding to automatic processing of personal data, covers personal information held by government agencies or private parties. Sensitive information relating to political, philosophical, union, or religious beliefs, racial origin, criminal convictions, health status, marriage, and finances cannot be processed without permission. For other information, individuals have the right of access. The holders or the system administrator have the duty to ensure accuracy and only use the information for the purpose for which it is stored. The Act is enforced by the National Commission for the Protection of Automated Personal Data (hereinafter CNPD). CNPD (Comissão Nacional de Proteção de Dados) is an independent parliament agency that registers, authorizes and controls databases, issues directives, and oversees the Schengen information system, briefly, is the Portuguese Data Protection Authority. This agency has powers of authority throughout national territory, is endowed with the power to supervise and monitor compliance with the laws and regulations in the area of personal data protection, with strict respect for human rights and fundamental freedoms and guarantees enshrined in the Constitution and the law.

The CNPD (2013) exerts investigative powers accessing to data under processing, and it also exerts powers of authority, particularly ordering the blocking, erasure or destruction of data, or imposing a temporary or permanent ban on the processing of personal data. It can act to warn or publicly censure the data controller for failure to comply with legal provisions on data protection and to engage in legal proceedings, in case of violation of the Data Protection Act, reporting to the Public Prosecution Office any criminal offences arising out of its functions, and to take the necessary and urgent measures to provide evidences. In particular, it can authorize or register, as applicable, the process of personal data; it also can authorize in exceptional cases the use of personal data for purposes not giving rise to its collection; or authorise the data interconnection provided for in article 9 of the DP Act, the transfer of personal data in the cases provided in article 20 of the DP Act, establishing the data storage period according to its purpose, ensuring the right of access and the exercise of the right of rectification and updating.

At national level, about protecting privacy, secrecy of communications and data protection the Portuguese Constitution has an extensive framework of protective provisions: articles 26°, 34° and 35° (CRP, 2013). The article 26 states, "(1) Everyone's right to his or her personal identity, civil capacity, citizenship, good name and reputation, image, the right to speak out, and the right to the protection of the intimacy of his or her private and family life is recognized. (2) The law establishes effective safeguards against the abusive use, or any use that is contrary to human dignity, of information concerning persons and families. (3) A person may be deprived of citizenship or subjected to restrictions on his or her civil capacity only in cases and under conditions laid down by law, and never on political grounds." Article 34

states, "(1) the individual's home and the privacy of his correspondence and other means of private communication are inviolable. (2) A citizen's home may not be entered against his will, except by order of the competent judicial authority and in the cases and according to the forms laid down by law. (3) No one may enter the home of any person at night without his consent. (4) Any interference by public authority with correspondence or tele-communications, apart from the cases laid down by law in connection with criminal procedure, is prohibited." Finally Article 35 states, "(1) Without prejudice to the provisions of the law on State secrecy and justice secrecy, all citizens have the right of access to the data contained in automated data records and files concerning them as well as the right to be informed of the use for which they are intended; they are entitled to request that the contents thereof be corrected and brought up to date. (2) Access to personal data records or files are forbidden for purposes of getting information relating to third parties as well as for the interconnection of these files, save in exceptional cases as provided for in the law and in Article 18°. (3) Data processing may not be used in regard to information concerning a person's philosophical or political convictions, party or trade union affiliations, religious beliefs, or private life, except in the case of non-identifiable data for statistical purposes. (4) The law defines the concept of personal data for the purposes of data storage as well as the conditions for establishing data banks and data basis by public or private entities and the conditions of utilization and access. (5) Citizens may not be issued all-purpose national identification numbers. (6) The law defines the provisions applicable to trans-border data flow establishing adequate norms of protection of personal data and of any other data in which the national interest is justified."

The CNPD has an important regulatory and monitoring role, deliberating on the application of fines; promoting the drawing up of codes of conduct and assessing them; promoting the disclosure and clarification of rights relating to data protection, because CNPD can also act on an application made by any person or by an association representing that person concerning the protection of his rights and freedoms in regard to data protection and informing them of the outcome, checking the lawfulness of data processing at the request of any person whenever such processing is subject to restricted access or information, and informing the person that a check has taken place and assessing the claims, complaints or applications of private individuals (article 17, 21, and 22 of the Act DP).

About the case in analyse, the Portuguese system of "E-Invoice" presents some flaws raising some issues of security breach and this is why the CNPD had officially confirmed an "investigation into leak of confidential information through the computer system that connects companies to the Treasury allegations of various merchants because of the new electronic billing system" (Guerra, 2013). The question raised is about the existence of certain inefficiencies of the "E-Invoice" system. The revelation of secret information configures a breach of trust, a grave infraction of the law. This failure is related with the skills of the administrator system, or with another failure aspect of the electronic system of information, because the leak of information at this level represents a crime against the privacy rights, the most basic civil right.

The fundamental question is about how data subjects' interests or rights, freedoms and guarantees are protected or granted by the data controller and what is the role of the system administrator that manage the information.

Explaining the system administrator duties, the question is to realize up to where it interfere in the functioning of the system, understanding if it has the responsibility of a guardian or a keeper. The "system administrator," knew by the "IT systems administrator," "systems administrator," or "sysadmin" (ITS, 2012) is a person employed to maintain and operate a computer system and/or network. In many organizations, in small companies or schools, for example, the system administrator is an Information Services (IS) department (in Portugal CI) within a computer support or even a single person, with several functions. He is a sort of Database Administrator (DBA), who maintains a database system, and is responsible for the integrity of the data and the efficiency and performance of the system. The system administrator is like a network administrator, a security administrator and a Web administrator. As a network administrator, he maintains network infrastructure, such as switches and routers, and diagnoses problems with the behavior of network-attached computers. As a security administrator he is a specialist in computer and network security, including the administration of security devices such as firewalls, as well as consulting on general security measures. The system administrator manages the flow of information safely, using various tools without anyone having to worry about technical issues therefore controls all the functions required for data management and procedures of the site, email general accounts, and all the information contained in the databases. The data update, data delete, data changes are functions of the system administrator of an enterprise/organization. Such tasks usually require physical presence in the room with the computer; and while less skilled than the administrator tasks require a similar level of trust, since the operator has access to possibly sensitive data. A postmaster is the administrator of a mail server.

The responsibilities of a system administrator belong to a vast domain, his tasks can include removing, or updating user account information, resetting passwords, responsibility for security, responsibility for documenting the configuration of the system. Ensuring that the network infrastructure is up and running....so the question of security of personal data is essential. In larger organizations, some tasks listed above may be divided among different system administrators or members of different organizational groups. For example, a dedicated individual(s) may apply all system upgrades, a Quality Assurance (QA) team may perform testing and validation, and one or more technical writers may be responsible for all technical documentation written for a company.

Ever since the adoption of the Interoperability Decision 6 of the European Council and the European Parliament in July 1999, the European Commission has focused on the pan-European dimension of E-Government and on the interoperability requirements for its implementation (EC, 1999). In other hand the proposal from the Commission for a Decision on Interoperable Delivery of pan-European E-Government Services to Public Administrations, Businesses and Citizens (IDABC) has been adopted by the Council and by the European Parliament on 21 April 2004 (EC, 2004). Following on from the IDA Program, IDABC is continuing to work on improving cooperation between public administrations and on supporting the delivery of pan-European E-Government services to citizens and businesses, thus contributing to greater efficiency in both the public and the private sectors. Interoperability, and in particular the European Interoperability Framework, are key elements of the program to support the development of pan-European E-Government services.

A key theme in Government is that all departments need to collaborate to improve citizen service delivery. National and local government departments are increasingly required to reach across portfolio boundaries to find collaborative, networked and multi-channel approaches to delivering information and services to business and to citizens. The development of an Interoperability Framework underpins the provision of integrated services by articulating a set of agreed policies, principles and standards to facilitate the electronic flow of information and transactions seamlessly across government to all its stakeholders. Improving the capability of departments to confidently manage, transfer and exchange information and services is critical to achieving the benefits of 'connected' government.

This Interoperability Framework identifies those components that support an environment where business services and information generated and held by Government will be valued and managed as a strategic, national asset. The framework provides principles, guidelines, and standards that underpin sound management, and establishes concepts, practices and tools that will drive the successful sharing of services across government boundaries. An interoperability framework may focus on several interoperability layers, which may be broadly categorized as follows: the business process layer; the information management layer; and the technical interoperability layer. This document focuses on interoperability at the technical level to enable the exchange of data and harmonization of business transactions across government. The framework covers common methods and shared services for the communication, storage, processing and presentation of data. Information systems have the potential to transform Government and the services it provides to the public. However, without consistent policies, principles and standards to underpin these systems, it is not possible to deliver collaborative services.

The Minimum Interoperability Standards (MIOS) are fundamental in supporting the E-Government policy and comprises the exchange of data and information access government and citizens, or government and employee, and government and external entities. Government includes National and Local Government Departments and their agencies, and the wider public sector, i.e. organs of state and state-owned enterprises. The MIOS comprises the technical principles and standards required to achieve interoperability. These are the minimum set necessary to support the range of transactions and services provided by Government and to integrate information systems within Government. The policies and standards in the MIOS cover three key areas of technical policy which are essential for interoperability. These are Interconnectivity, Data Interoperability, and Information Access. Government information systems are designed to provide protection against security risks of connection to the Internet, including the ability to protect against the vulnerability of downloading executable content code that is not authenticated.

THE SECURITY POLICY OF THE E-GOVERNMENT AND THE E-INVOICE

The security policy at pan-European level of the E-government seems to be based on a reliable exchange of information with sufficient guarantees of secret and confidentiality (OJL, 2001a). In particular, for document classification at EU level and for related security measures, the Council's security regulation applies (OJL, 2001b).

The pan-European E-Government services need to ensure uniform levels of personal data protection, including measures in which individuals have the right to choose whether their data may be used for purposes other than those for which they originally supplied the data in question (EIF, 2004).

The Portuguese E-Invoice has some gaps about the security policy because from the user perspective, functions associated with security (identification, authentication, confidentiality) cannot prevent from the misuse of information by the other users. At a market level that proximity or promiscuity can mean considerable losses. As the confidential information of a company is a valuable asset, the value of the loss is increasing with the lake of consistency, reliability and confidentiality in the treatment of the information by the online portal at the E-Invoice.

Following best practices in information security market is an imperative, in order to reduce the cost and risk of data loss and improve protection of confidential information, and at the level of personal data treatment including invoices matter this question is even more accurate. Having an amount of invoice about the same company or enterprise it is possible design anyone consumer profile drawing new coordinates and discovering new ways of marketing and consumer policies.

This way of processing and using information for consumer or political marketing or other purposes activities and this misuse of sensible information should be stopped and the concerned individuals protected. Full compliance with the existing European and national data protection legislation should be ensured (EIF, 2004).

The E-Invoice of the government represents a kind of work on interoperability and should be coordinated with the mechanisms already in place following the Directive 95/46/EC (EC, 1995).

The design of E-Government applications should comply with the existing legal data protection requirements and, where available, should make use of technologies that are privacy compliant and privacy-enhancing. The changes in privacy legislation may impose requirements to the provision of some E-Services to ensure information security by preventing unauthorized access to systems and, in the case of highly confidential information, securing each record (or even each component) individually.

CONCLUSION

The Portuguese system of E-Invoice presents some flaws that raise some issues of security breach and this is why the CNPD had officially confirmed an "investigation into leak of confidential information through the computer system that connects to companies to the Treasury allegations of various merchants because of the new electronic billing system." The question raised is about the existence of certain inefficiencies of the E-Invoice system. The revelation of secret information configures a breach of trust, a grave infraction of the law. Even though that the system administrator is has major responsibilities to ensure the data security, CNPD may waive the existence of certain security measures, subject to guaranteeing respect for the fundamental rights, freedoms and guarantees of the data subjects, because the systems must assure logical separation between data relating to health and sex life, including genetic data, and other personal data. The Portuguese system of E-Invoice was implemented by the government without express security warranties, due to the urgency of taking measures to fight tax fraud and tax evasion, in attempt of reducing the deficit. The information system exchange at E-Invoice must to (re)consider the security policy about the treatment of personal data at the national level by conducting appropriate risk assessment activities prior of setting-up services with security measures. The role of CNPD is fundamental to enforce the DP act about this security issue. This question is not only about the emergent responsibilities of the system administrator, because any person acting under the authority of the controller or the processor, including the processor himself, has access to personal data that must not to be processed, except under instructions from the controller or if required to do so by law. Controllers and persons who obtain knowledge of the personal data processed in carrying out their functions has to be bound by professional secrecy, even after their functions have ended, according article 17°.

The Act DP, at article 3, (d) states the "controller" shall mean the natural or legal person, public authority, agency or any other body which alone or jointly with others determines the purposes and means of the processing of personal data; where the purposes and means of processing are determined by laws or regulations, the controller

shall be designated in the Act establishing the organization and functioning or in the statutes of the legal or statutory body competent to process the personal data concerned; (e) "processor" shall mean a natural or legal person, public authority, agency or any other body which processes personal data on behalf of the controller.

According to the Article 4, the Scope of the act DP, (a) in the context of the activities of an establishment of the controller on Portuguese territory; (b) outside national territory, but in a place where Portuguese law applies by virtue of international public law; (c) by a controller who is not established on European Union territory and who for purposes of processing personal data makes use of equipment, automated or otherwise, situated on Portuguese territory, unless such equipment is used only for purposes of transit through the territory of the European Union.

This Act (CNPD, 2013) shall apply to the processing of personal data regarding public safety, national defense and State security, without prejudice to special rules in instruments of international law to which Portugal is bound and specific laws pertinent to the respective sectors.

About Security and confidentiality of processing Article 14, 1) The controller must implement appropriate technical and organizational measures to protect personal data against accidental or unlawful destruction or accidental loss, alteration, unauthorized disclosure or access, in particular where the processing involves the transmission of data over a network, and against all other unlawful forms of processing. Having regard to the state of the art and the cost of their implementation, such measures shall ensure a level of security appropriate to the risks represented by the processing and the nature of the data to be protected. 2) Where processing is carried out on his behalf, the controller must choose a processor providing sufficient guarantees in respect of the technical security measures and organizational measures governing the processing to be carried out, and must ensure compliance with those measures. 3) The carrying out of processing by way of a processor must be governed by a contract or legal act binding the processor to the controller and stipulating in particular that the processor shall act only on instructions from the controller and that the obligations referred to in 1 shall also be incumbent on the processor.

The article 15 states that the controllers of the data shall take appropriate special security measures to: prevent unauthorized persons from entering the premises used for processing such data (control of entry to the premises); prevent data media from being read, copied, altered or removed by unauthorized persons (control of data media); prevent unauthorized input and unauthorized obtaining of knowledge, alteration or elimination of personal data input (control of input); prevent automatic data processing systems from being used by unauthorized persons by means of data transmission premises (control of use); guarantee that authorized persons may only access data covered by the authorization (control of access); guarantee the checking of the bodies to whom personal data may be transmitted by means of data transmission premises (control of transmission); guarantee that it is possible to check *a posteriori*, in a period appropriate to the nature of the processing, the establishment in the regulations applicable to each sector of which personal data are input, when and by whom (control of input); in transmitting personal data and in transporting the respective media, prevent unauthorized reading, copying, alteration or elimination of data (control of transport) according the article 15° of the act DP.

Article 6(e) of Law 67/98 obliges the CNPD, in every specific case, to establish whether or not "data subjects' interests or rights, freedoms and guarantees" prevail over the legitimate interest cited by the data controller. This procedure lends itself best to application of the principle of proportionality and, therefore, processing should be abandoned when it is proved to be groundless and excessive, or when—because it is unreliable—it compromises the ends which determine the grounds for the processing. The principle of proportionality is also a decisive criterion which underpins the data protection authorities' decisions on the processing of data, but this is a case about mortgaging the future of freedom of choice and keeping the possibility to decide about "consume or not a product." Companies with information about consumers can design a "tax profile" and a "consumer profile" without any respect for privacy right. Data circulation over a network may jeopardize the fundamental rights, freedoms and guarantees of their data subjects.

REFERENCES

AMCAT. (2013). *Remote infrastructure management*. Retrieved from https://www.myamcat.com/aspiration/featured_sector/featured_sector_remote_infrastructure_management.php

CNPD. (2013). *National commission of data protection*. Retrieved from http://www.cnpd.pt/english/index_en.htm

CRP. (2013). *Constituição da República Portuguesa*. Retrieved from http://dre.pt/comum/html/legis/crp.html

DL. (2008). *Decree law 143-A / 2008, of July 25*. Retrieved from http://www.wipo.int/wipolex/en/details.jsp?id=5461

DL. (2012). *Decree-law No. 197/2012 of August 24*. Retrieved from http://dre.pt/pdf1s-dip/2012/08/16400/0465604666.pdf

EC. (1995). *Directive 95/46/EC of the European parliament and of the council of 24 October 1995 on the protection of individuals with regard to the processing of personal data and on the free movement of such data*. Retrieved from http://ec.europa.eu/justice/policies/privacy/docs/95-46-ce/dir1995-46_part1_en.pdf

EC. (1999). *Decision 1999/1720/EC of the European parliament and of the council of 12 July 1999 to adopt a series of actions and measures in order to ensure interoperability of, and access to, trans-European networks for the electronic interchange of data between administrations (IDA).* Retrieved from http://www.etsi.org/about/our-role-in-europe/public-policy/ec-decisions

EC. (2004). *Decision 2004/387/EC "decision of the European parliament and of the council on interoperable delivery of pan-European services to public administrations, businesses and citizens (IDABC).* Retrieved from http://www.etsi.org/about/our-role-in-europe/public-policy/ec-decisions

EC. (2006). *The council directive 2006/112/EC of 28 November 2006 on the common system of value added tax.* Retrieved from http://eur-lex.europa.eu/LexUriServ/LexUriServ.do?uri=OJ:L:2006:347:0001:0118:en:PDF

EC. (2008). *Status report from the expert group on e-invoicing.* Retrieved from http://ec.europa.eu/enterprise/sectors/ict/documents/e-invoicing/index_en.htm

EC. (2010). The council of the European Union, council directive 2010/45/EU of 13 July 2010 amending directive 2006/112/EC on the common system of value added tax as regards the rules on invoicing. Official Journal of the European Union, 189(1).

EIF. (2004). *European interoperability framework for pan-European e-government service.* Retrieved from http://ec.europa.eu/idabc/en/document/3761/5845.html

Guerra, C. (2013). *A spokesman for the national commission on data protection, Clara Guerra, confirms the Antena 1 that several complaints have been received and that the commission is already on the ground to investigate.* Portugal: Antena 1.

ITS. (2012). *IT systems administrator," " systems administrator," or "sysadmin".* Retrieved from http://www.standalone-sysadmin.com/blog/2012/01/it_system_admin.htm

Kumar, A. (2010). *Network security administrator responsibilities.* Retrieved from http://www.brighthub.com/computing/smb-security/articles/71358.aspx?cid=parsely_rec

LPD. (1991). *Lei no 10/91 da lei da proteção de dados pessoais face à informática.* Retrieved from http://www.cnpdpi.pt/Leis/lei_1091.htm

OJL. (2001a). *101/1 - Council decision of 19 March 2001 adopting the council's security regulations (2001/264/EC).* Retrieved from http://www.etsi.org/about/our-role-in-europe/public-policy/ec-decisions

OJL. (2001b). 137/1 - Commission decision of 29 November 2001 amending its internal RULES OF PROCEDURE (notified under document number C (2001) 3031) (2001/844/EC, ECSC, Euratom).

TSU. (2012). *Bits & bytes.* Retrieved from http://www.cis.txstate.edu/Resources/Newsletters/May2012.html

VIT. (2013). *System administration.* Retrieved from http://venturait.com/system-administration

Section 3
Privacy and Security

Chapter 8
Role of Cloud Systems as Enabler of Global Competitive Advantages

Fawzy Soliman
University of Technology Sydney, Australia

ABSTRACT

The goal of cloud systems is to provide easy, scalable access to computing resources and IT services. However, the ability of the cloud system to transfer knowledge to assist the innovator should also be a key objective of cloud system deployment. This chapter presents an approach for assessment of cloud systems for innovation on the basis of the system's abilities to differentiate between the various types of knowledge. In this regard, the chapter also proposes a number of success factors for deployment of cloud systems for innovation in a global setting.

INTRODUCTION

The intensity of growing competition fuelled by the strength of the rising globalization is presenting firms with further challenge and renewed pressure to innovate. Innovation could be pursued at one or all of the three innovation levels; namely: a) product innovation including creation of new products and/or modification to existing products; b) innovation in providing service to customers and c) innovation in the managerial aspects of the firm including changes of the firm's structure, policies and or procedures (Soliman, 2012a).

Innovation is partly based on learning which in turn is dependent on knowledge and as such there are five stages of the innovation knowledge transfer process (Soliman, 2011b), these are:

DOI: 10.4018/978-1-4666-4526-4.ch008

- **Knowledge Transfer:** Identifying and transferring the necessary knowledge for the innovation (from external and internal sources of knowledge).
- **Scanning:** Scanning the transferred knowledge to exclude knowledge that is not directly relevant for the innovation.
- **Decision:** Regarding what to do with the scanned knowledge. That is to decide whether to adopt or reject the transferred knowledge with the view of weighing the advantages and the disadvantages of using that knowledge in its current form.
- **Implementation:** Employing the transferred knowledge depending on the situation and the usefulness of the knowledge for the innovation.
- **Confirmation:** Finalizing the decision to continue using the knowledge perhaps in its fullest potential. In this case, the knowledge may be referred to as innovation knowledge.

Knowledge may be defined as what makes personal, organizational, and societal intelligent behaviour possible (Spaeth, et al., 2010). Knowledge could be found in a number of different types and forms of artefacts that exist in the form of documents, files, papers, conversations, pictures, thoughts, software, databases, e-mail messages, and in any other form that are used to represent meaning and understanding of that knowledge (Haefliger, et al., 2008). In other words, knowledge artefacts flow throughout and between organisations and individuals in what is known as knowledge flows (Newman, 2004). Knowledge flows must be managed effectively to ensure that the basic objectives of organizations and individuals are attained to the greatest extent possible (Nonaka, et al., 2006). In this context, knowledge in modern organizations should be considered from the following five interrelated perspectives:

1. **Business Perspective:** In business perspective knowledge is required for the development of strategies, products and services, alliances, acquisitions, and creating new products or services. Therefore better knowledge is necessary for the benefit of the business. That is knowledge should be suitable, creditable and fit for the purpose.
2. **Management Perspective:** In management perspective knowledge is used in determining, organizing, directing, planning and controlling and staffing the organisational activities required achieving the desired business strategies and objectives. Therefore better knowledge is necessary for creating policies and practices needed to determine required knowledge related activities.
3. **Operational Perspective:** In management perspective knowledge is employed to determine the available knowledge needed to recruit, train and build Human Resources (HR) further. This also requires better and suitable knowledge for operational purposes.
4. **Learning Perspectives:** In learning perspective knowledge is the basis ingredient that is necessary for organisational learning (Soliman, 2011a). The concept of Learning Organisation originally purposed by Senge (1990) and widely used and recognised as a necessary competitive advantage for organisation (Soliman, 2011a, 2011b, 2011c) require knowledge to facilitate the learning organisation activities proposed by (Garvin, 1993) such as problem solving, experimentation, learning from past experience, learning from others and for transferring knowledge to and from the learning organisation. Accordingly, knowledge for learning must also be suitable and must add value to learning for the organisation and for the individuals involved in the learning organisation activities (Al-Qawabah, 2012).

5. **Innovation Perspectives:** In innovation perspective knowledge is the basic ingredient that is necessary for building the innovative firm resources further. Pedler et al. (1991) and Damanpour (1991) identified different types of innovation within organizations, as to include technical innovation and administrative innovation. Knowledge is needed to conduct better training, better research and development and establish a better pool of knowledge and systems that are necessary for the innovative firm (Davenport et al, 2000; Von Krogh et al., 1999; Bontis et.al., 2003).

It should be noted that the perception that knowledge is also a belief has led to evaluation of knowledge on the basis of the correctness of answers only. According to Hunt (2003) such methods of knowledge measurement usually result in false or unpredictable levels of uncertainty. Hunt (2003) further added that "uncertainty, could adversely impact on the qualities of the correctness and justification". Furthermore uncertainty could lead failure to formulate precise questions about acquiring, retaining and managing knowledge to perform certain tasks safely, effectively with a high quality level (Sveiby, 1997, Von Krogh and Von Hippel, 2006).

In addition, O'Dell and Grayson (1998, p. 3) pointed out that people do not explicitly recognize the importance of knowledge because knowledge is in fact a concept that may be invisible, intangible and cannot be directly observed by people and/or organizations. Further, Sveiby (1997) suggests that knowledge is invisible because it lacks "a generally accepted definition and a measurement standard". However, there is a considerable literature that attempts to define knowledge based innovation suggesting that the process of innovation itself relies heavily on innovation knowledge that is usually created and transferred or disseminated within a company, between companies, between companies and innovators (Nonaka and Von Krogh, 2009).

Furthermore, the continuous and rapid evolution of information and communication technology has raised the ranks of knowledge to become an essential ingredient for the success of innovation. While many attempts to identify knowledge as one of core elements of innovation management have rapidly growing, the paramount concern over knowledge is still due to the fact that knowledge is a remarkable substance.

It is important to mention that Soliman and Youssef (2003) pointed out that the purpose of the critical information for knowledge management is to: "create efficient operations; provide control; measure performance, compare results with the standards and take corrective action if necessary". In other words, firms may need to enhance their efficiency and effectiveness with the aid of good knowledge management tools such as cloud systems that creates opportunities to reduce and eliminate non-value-adding work.

Notwithstanding the type of innovation, many firms may want to purse the innovation in order to gain higher competitive advantages. However, the inherent complexity of managing innovation becomes a serious challenge even for the most experienced innovation leaders (Soliman, 2011a). This is because getting the right knowledge in the right form for the right innovation process at the right time will be challenging (Soliman, 2011a). These challenges may have encouraged some organisations to look for alternatives to the highly complex and expensive IT infrastructures. Those alternatives need to satisfy the firm's immediate needs for managing the innovation, but at the same time it should also offer additional value added to the firm's resources including intangible resources such as knowledge. In this regards, cloud system implementation appears to be a viable option due to the following reasons:

1. Knowledge need to be transferred though sophisticated software applications.
2. Intelligent software applications that are useful for the innovation process could be acquired either by (purchasing) or (hiring) from providers of Software-as-a-Service (SaaS).
3. In addition to other functions, SaaS, provides integration with Enterprise Resource Planning (ERP) systems.
4. SaaS consists of many different sub-components such as, Customer Relationship Management (CRM), Human Capital Management (HCM) and eProcurement. These components are fast becoming necessary for many modern supply chain entities.

The recent steep growth in the SaaS market means many enterprises would be turning to cloud systems for speed and lower costs (Bartoletti and Reichman, 2012). However, firms would be deploying cloud systems for the additional benefits of efficient and effective knowledge transfer.

KNOWLEDGE TRANSFER AND THE INNOVATION CHAIN

Soliman (2011b) has shown that the evolution of the innovation chains could occur in three critical and sequential stages namely, knowledge based stage, learning organisation stage and the innovation stage. Furthermore, knowledge transfer has been shown to be a common critical function throughout all the three stages (Senge, 1990 and 2006; Pedler et al., 1991; Garvin, 1993; Soliman, 2011b). However, the biggest challenge facing the innovation firm is therefore the selection of which cloud system that supports the innovation needs of the organisation, including knowledge transfer and yet satisfy other organisational requirements of the system. Furthermore, innovation firms' key concerns is also knowledge integrity and security as well as ensuring proper management

of the innovation key processes. The difficulty in managing the knowledge integrity may lie in the lack of universally accepted set of knowledge characteristics.

CHARACTERISTICS AND INTEGRITY OF INNOVATION KNOWLEDGE

Soliman (2012b) argues that they integrity of knowledge must be based on sound knowledge characteristics and that there could be at least nine essential knowledge characteristics. Those nine generic characteristics may be considered general in nature as they apply to any type of knowledge. However, literature search reveals that no published works on knowledge characteristics that apply only to innovation activities. Accordingly, the Soliman (2012b) knowledge nine characteristics could be used for innovation as follows:

1. **Accuracy of Innovation Knowledge:** Accuracy is the degree of veracity and could refer to reliability, truthfulness, and correctness of the innovation knowledge content.
2. **Timeliness and Currency of Innovation knowledge:** Timeliness of innovation knowledge is necessary to avoid making decisions that are out of date and hence harm the organisation's progress.
3. **Relevance of Innovation Knowledge:** The innovation knowledge relevance could be evaluated in terms of ease-of-use, functionality, reliability, flexibility, portability, integration, and importance.
4. **Authority of Innovation Knowledge Source:** the authority of innovation knowledge relates to the degree of believability of the knowledge.
5. **Purpose of Innovation Knowledge:** The purpose of the innovation knowledge usage or acquisition or transmission or sharing is necessary to be established.

6. **Importance of Innovation Knowledge:** Importance of innovation knowledge encompasses whether the characteristic of knowledge under consideration can be controlled within the organization, whether it focuses on a key management issue, whether it addresses a real-world problem, and whether it is timely.

7. **Accessibility of Innovation Knowledge:** Accessibility of innovation knowledge encompasses whether the knowledge is understandable.

8. **Applicability of Innovation Knowledge:** Applicability of innovation knowledge encompasses whether the knowledge is complete, whether it provides guidance and/ or direction.

9. **Suitability of Innovation Knowledge:** Suitability of innovation knowledge encompasses whether the knowledge deemed to be important to the organisation and suitable for meeting its needs, can be further elaborated to assist the organisation achieving its strategic objectives.

Soliman (2012d) pointed out that during the development phase of a cloud system implementation strategy, it would be necessary that the integrity of the cloud system be designed and embedded in the implementation strategy to ensure an appropriate level of internal control. Furthermore, such system's integrity components must be focused on establishing robust environments in which the innovation processes would operate. In addition, the development of the integrity environments should mitigate the organisational risks of the innovation, and should also ensure that the controls implemented in the system do not encumber the business processes. Accordingly, the integrity component should address the following seven cloud system attributes:

1. Effectiveness of cloud system deployment.
2. Efficiency in using the cloud system.

3. Confidentiality of data, information and knowledge transferred through the cold system.
4. Relevance of the cloud system to the innovation effort.
5. Availability of the cloud system to transfer knowledge.
6. Compliance of the cloud system with pre-established metrics and operational standards.
7. Reliability of the cloud system to transfer knowledge as required.

Although many authors agree that the challenge is how to ensure that the cloud system is focused on serving the innovation efforts as well as satisfying other organisational needs that are not directly related to the innovation?, there is little work (if any) that identifies those challenge and how to overcome them. However, Soliman (2012d) argue that some of these challenge may be meet by appropriately by addressing the following factors:

1. Security issues when transferring and storing knowledge using the cloud system.
2. Authenticating users and governing access rights to the cloud system.
3. Checking and verifying knowledge transactions throughout the cloud system.
4. Reporting of cloud system usage and knowledge transfer metrics.
5. Cloud system response times to deliver a knowledge query transaction.
6. Frequency, timeliness and detail of performance reporting of the cloud system.
7. Cloud system integration capabilities with internal and external knowledge providers.

In addition, the growing confidence in using could systems could be associated with a growing concerns that the cloud system may not meet the organization's standards especially in the following three important performance criterions:

1. **Compliance:** Although many firms may already have standards in place for the security and integrity of their data, there is still a need for baseline requirement for the cloud system performance in relation to the integrity of data.
2. **Availability:** The availability of the knowledge transfer function through the cloud system should be also considered for the cloud system performance.
3. **Adaptability:** The ability of the cloud system to adapt to changing business should be also considered as indicative of the cloud system performance.

BENEFITS OBTAINABLE FROM DEPLOYMENT OF CLOUD SYSTEMS

Firms may require significant changes in processes and in the way people are managed in order to solve the problems that arise from re-engineering work. That is why many firms find it is necessary to employ proven methods and sophisticated systems such as cloud systems. However, after the deployment of the cloud system, organisations would have in place systems that enable them to be more focused on enhancing their customer-service offerings, expanding into new industries, and entering into mergers and acquisitions that often cross state and national borders.

In current business climate, firms may need a highly adaptable information infrastructure to be able to change or expand their systems quickly and efficiently, in response to new business demands. Thus there would be a need for IT solutions that can work in conjunction with other organisations' IT systems in the supply chain. These systems must be able to grow with the organisation and in the same time facilitate a high level of integration among data sources, (internal and external) and business applications.

In general, the cost of in-house developing of such systems could be beyond the means of one single organisation. That is why there is a growing tendency to move away from developing in-house systems in favour of purchase the processing capacity the organisations needs from a provider of cloud system service provider.

However, most organisations are more concerned with the wider issues of acquiring leading edge cloud system which are versatile and inexpensive and the same time can handle the enterprise business processes and functions. In most cases, companies that implemented cloud system did so after extensive and successful business process re-engineering effort. This raises the question of the firm's readiness for such transformation.

READINESS OF THE INNOVATIVE FIRM FOR CLOUD SYSTEM DEPLOYMENT

Research has found that many enterprises are not ready for adaption of cloud systems unless the cloud system under consideration enjoys the following features (Soliman, 2012d):

- Availability of integrated analytics and flexible reporting options.
- Ability of the cloud system to extend the application in order to suit the firm's needs.
- Fast and easier configurable setting that allows for setup in relatively short period of time.
- Existence of automate routine activities and tasks built in the system.
- Built-in services and support that simplifies the cloud systems operation.

In addition, firms would be searching for a system that integrates all of their key business functions such as HR, CRM, and procurement through to cross-functional business processes. These functions would be needed in order to enable innovation knowledge to flow uninterrupted across the innovation process.

Soliman (2012d) proposes that the integrated analytics and reporting options could ensure that the firm could take advantage of timely and accurate knowledge delivered in the correct context to the concerned user. The integrated analytics could also be used to make better, well informed business decisions - as well as increasing productivity and effectiveness.

CLOUD SYSTEMS AS ENABLER OF GLOBAL COMPETITIVE ADVANTAGES

The surge in global business activities has impacted upon many businesses and has led to significant changes to business environments (Soliman, 2013). Soliman (2013) argues that the competitive frame work originally developed by Hamel and Prahalad (1985) has led to higher levels of intense competition due to the steep rise of globalization activities. It is important to note that the surge in the intensity of competition could also be due an increase in the number of organizations that have realized that it is not enough that firms improve organizational efficiencies, but they should also explore the role of innovation as a driver of sustainable competitive advantages. In doing so, many firms have considered deployment of cloud systems for a number of reasons including enhancing their abilities to transfer knowledge for innovation and to gain and sustain competitive advantages.

In addition, the work by Soliman (2011a, 2011b) points to innovation as a driver of competition and as such is an enabler to competitive advantages. It should be remembered that that innovation and competitive advantages may be linked to some influencing factors drawn from known definitions of competitive advantages

(Das and Joshi, 2007). Das and Joshi (2007) also observed that the capacity of a company to innovate might lead to a competitive advantage and that innovation may require resources for transforming an organization into an innovative firm. These resources (tangibles and intangibles such as knowledge) could be best managed through ERP SaaS systems.

Since knowledge is regarded as the crux of sustainable competitive advantage and is an essential component of the innovation chain (Soliman, 2011b), then the tools that transfer knowledge such as cloud system need to be analysed for their strengths, weaknesses and operationalization. In other words, this analysis must be conducted along the three important dimensions of the tools used for transferring knowledge; namely Organizational, Legal and Technological Dimensions.

Although academics and practitioners have proposed a number of definitions of the above three dimensions, there is still no agreement on acceptable standards that could be used to define the common characteristic of cloud systems along these three dimensions. Furthermore, the lack of acceptable methods or benchmarks for analysing cloud systems along these three dimensions, drives the interest for researching in this filed. Accordingly, the relevant issues of could systems' deployment should be studied and analysed from the following three perspectives:

ORGANIZATIONAL PERSPECTIVES OF CLOUD SYSTEMS

Given that cloud systems are considered key components for managing knowledge, the interrelationships between knowledge management tools and organizational factors should be carefully studied from organisational perspectives. In this regards Robertson and O'Malley Hammersley (2000) noted that success of any knowledge management initiative is likely to be critically dependent on having competent and stable organization that is equipped with the appropriate tools. Furthermore, competency and stability are dependent on the ability of the organization to use these tools effectively and efficiently to manage its important five core organizational elements (Hislop, 2003). Hislop (2003) identified those five core elements as: organizational culture, organizational structure, business processes, Human Resources Management and Leadership.

While the literature is full of published work on issues relevant to all the above five core organizational elements, there is a little (if any) published work in relation to cloud systems. Furthermore, it is widely accepted that for the success of the innovation require the right innovation leadership for the right innovation project (Soliman, 2011a, 2011c). Although the works of Soliman (2011a, 2012a, 2012b, 2012c) and Al-Qawabah (2012) provides a three stage innovation leadership model to suit the innovation chain i.e. from knowledge to learning to innovation, further work is need to relate these models to cloud systems' deployments.

From the above discussion, it is arguable that firms should be focusing on developing effective knowledge transfer culture through the use of sophisticated knowledge transfer tools such as cloud systems. By developing such knowledge transfer culture, firm's ability to achieve some of the objectives of the innovation effort (Soliman, 2012b). However, the need to maximize the efficiency and effectiveness of knowledge transfer may propel these organisations to deploy tools such as cloud systems. This means a knowledge transfer strategy should be developed and used effectively to support the innovative firm in managing their own knowledge.

The knowledge transfer should focus on the characteristics of the innovation knowledge, as it relates to the innovation processes. In this regards, the focus of the knowledge transfer tools should be on value creation and extraction through innovation.

Clearly strategies for deployment of cloud systems must be carefully developed and discussed before a significant investment is made. It is essential to be clear about what the benefits would be for the organisation and what impact is expected from its strategies. The management should decide on the appropriateness of the cloud system for transferring knowledge to ensure the success of the innovation effort as explained below:

Appropriateness of Cloud System for Knowledge Transfer

Many analysts believe that the emergence of cloud technologies could assist in the implementation of knowledge transfer programs. However, there is also a view that these technologies may actually be "anti" knowledge management. For example, without active oversight, technology may just add to the information glut in the organisation. Other technologies already employed by the enterprise could go at least part of the way towards employing the knowledge transfer approach. The commercial emergence of cloud systems represents a tremendous opportunity to enhance the practice of managing organisational knowledge. Unfortunately, much of the potential of knowledge-based systems to leverage expertise and promote organisational learning remains unrealised because of poor management of organisational resources and piecemeal adoption of the technology.

Clark and Soliman (1997) have shown that managing the introduction of knowledge-based systems is a difficult task, which requires team effort and support throughout the enterprise. For instance, in the knowledge management chain a number of decisions need to be made. These decisions are required in each stage in the knowledge management chain, namely the creation, capture, storage, access to and use of knowledge (Soliman, 2012b). Each time a decision is made, input from various teams and groups across the enterprise would be required. In general, the complexity and nature of the input could warrant the use of knowledge-based systems and in turn cloud systems. However, an appropriate cloud system's leadership might be necessary.

Creating the Cloud System Deployment Leadership

The implementation of a cloud system may present the organisation with the challenge of creating a leadership role to develop and drive the process. Many firms have used a cross-functional team to develop cloud system implementation strategy, while others have created separate role and promoted that as a leading role. Therefore, the characteristics and challenges of the cloud system's leadership should include (Jamoo, 2008):

1. Interpersonal/communication skills.
2. Passionate visionary leadership.
3. Business acumen.
4. Strategic thinking skills.
5. Championship of change and the ability to stand ambiguity and uncertainty.
6. Collaborative skills (this is a rare skill and is the ability to pull together people from different parts of the organisation to work as one team).
7. Familiarity with emerging technologies such as cloud systems.

While it could be useful to have a focal point (e.g. a knowledge manager or cloud system manager) to "lead the charge," it is not essential, and the need for this position may be transitory once the knowledge management discipline is embedded in the firm's culture and processes. Regardless of how the responsibility for knowledge transfer is shared, the cloud system is considered a critical tool for selecting and implementing the knowledge transfer for innovation.

Innovation Knowledge as Competitive Advantage

An increasing number of enterprises are now viewing the innovation knowledge as a key competitive advantage from which innovation can emerge, and are encouraging, supporting and rewarding collaboration between people. Moreover, while decentralised enterprises may know where the bulk of their information resides, the problem becomes the dissemination of that innovation knowledge to the people who need it. Using cloud system as knowledge management tools can confer competitive advantage which may result in higher revenue and increased market share, especially in markets where time to market and high quality make a difference (Jamoo, 2008). It should be noted that, implementing knowledge transfer systems such as cloud systems within an organisation can be very costly, especially during the start-up phase. Therefore, a set of strategies for implementing cloud systems need to be developed as discussed below:

Developing and Cloud Systems Implementation Strategies

A recent study suggests that in order to harness and amplify the know-how, experience and expertise of employees, companies should implement a strategy which utilizes the deployment of sophisticated technologies such as cloud systems (Price Waterhouse Coopers, 1999), firms should:

1. Focus only on what the business needs to know; i.e. become knowledge-focused.
2. Make important knowledge visible i.e. become knowledge visible (e.g. create or make explicit pathways to the experts and important wisdom within the company).
3. Pay attention to the vocabulary of knowledge; i.e. become knowledge-defined (e.g. customers' needs versus customers' feedback).

4. Go beyond the company to tap knowledge from customers, suppliers and competitors; i.e. become a knowledge seeker.

5. Make it clear to employees that knowledge sharing is a core value for the company; i.e. become a knowledge culture.

6. Measure the results of the implementation of the knowledge management program; i.e. become a knowledge assessor.

7. Reward top management for sharing expertise and intelligence; so that the firm could become become knowledge-exemplified.

The above strategy could also assist as a checklist to ensure that the knowledge transfer covers all key elements of the innovation process. The role of the cloud system in harnessing innovation knowledge is therefore central to the success of this strategy.

From the above discussion, it can be noticed that the firm should develop its knowledge transfer strategy that is aligned with the objective of the organisation.

LEGAL PERSPECTIVES OF CLOUD SYSTEMS

In general, most firms would acquire and accumulate internally (*in-house*) all the necessary knowledge skills, practices and competencies, for the innovation project. However, specific projects may require additional knowledge or skills, that the firm may seek to acquire from different external sources to the firm. In these cases the firm could be exposed to some legal implications associated with the legal aspects of handling or transferring the innovation knowledge. The main four areas of concern would be centred on: a) Intellectual Property Rights, b) Security of data, c) Culture of knowledge ownership and d) Appropriation of the innovation knowledge.

Arguments about what would be the required minimum criterions for protection against Intellectual Property Rights violations are still being debated. In this regards, the World Trade Organisation WTO has established an Agreement on Trade Related Aspects of Intellectual Property Rights (TRIPs Agreement). Although the TRIPs Agreement does not directly address unauthorised acquisition of knowledge and in particular innovation knowledge, the implications for acquiring or transferring the innovation knowledge without consent(s) could be very significant. Although, the TRIPs Agreement requires member countries to make information for innovative products or processes available in all fields of, there is no effective safeguard for the protection for against unauthorised acquisition of knowledge especially in the three areas:

Intellectual Property Rights

Since the TRIPs Agreement allows members to grant patents, and innovation knowledge artefacts in different forms, a strong incentive for research that could lead to rewards, has emerged and has become an important element of the success of modern innovations projects. Given the significance of the issues involved in the intellectual copy right laws, it is important that any method for assessing the innovation knowledge such as knowledge audits should take the intellectual property rights factors into account.

Security of Data

Many organisations believe security of cloud systems, should be built-in function to prevent unauthorised access to company's innovation knowledge. Security capabilities should be built into the fabric of the cloud system and that cloud administrators have limited rudimentary security techniques. Accordingly, it is necessary to consider who should have access and what level of access each individual should have when implementing and using the cloud data (Ferrarini 2002). In other words, it is imperative that organisations are aware of potential points for breach when implementing a cloud system. Reliable security solutions highlighting these vulnerabilities are necessary to manage security risks created by cloud system implementation. The identification of these risks is useful tools for containing security breaches and to ensure end-users cannot cross between specified cloud storage areas (Radding 1992).

Culture of Innovation Knowledge Ownership

It should be noted that the opponents of the protection laws have argued that such protection will ultimately undermine the processes by which the knowledge and innovation and creativity because historically knowledge has been acquired, preserved and used for the benefit of the community. There is a sizable segment of the community that believe the individual profit resulting from exclusive knowledge ownership could erode confidence in the arrested development of the knowledge base. Given the significance of the issues involved in the ownership of innovation knowledge, it is important that any proposed innovation knowledge audits should take the ownership issues into account.

Appropriation of Innovation Knowledge

The enforcement of TRIPs Agreement may face some difficulties in deciding the appropriate appropriation of innovation knowledge. That is, what is the portion of knowledge that has been created by the researchers? And what is the portion of knowledge obtained from other scholars and institutions from outside the innovative firm. And whether any consent from the relevant bodies has been obtained?

Even when access to the knowledge has been authorized, the critical issue of whether the source of that knowledge has been compensated adequately and whether the levels of compensation were fair. This issue is best illustrated by the recent law suit involving the current CEO of Facebook and the two twins who claimed that the Facebook concept is their own idea. As it appears, there is a doubt about the fairness of the compensation awarded because the awarded compensation did not match the substantial gains obtained from the idea. Therefore, there is a risk that the primary source of the innovation knowledge may not be adequately been compensated when the gains from the idea is taken into account. This implies that issues involved in the appropriation of innovation knowledge, is so important thus is any proposed innovation knowledge audits should take the appropriation of innovation knowledge issues into account. It should be remembered that the knowledge audit should provide an evidence based assessment of the knowledge assets within the innovative firm using a standard way of measuring the innovation knowledge through a better understanding of innovation and knowledge assets that could be captured from the innovation knowledge audit.

TECHNOLOGICAL PERSPECTIVES OF CLOUD SYSTEMS

Soliman and Spooner (2000) addressed the technological issues associated with knowledge transfer and related the defective knowledge (knowledge gaps) to unsatisfactory outcome of organisational strategies. Given that knowledge is essential element of organisational strategies, therefore that defective knowledge could be the sources of (strategic gaps). Furthermore they related the two i.e. knowledge gaps and strategic gaps to each other through a process of knowledge mapping. However there could be a risk of mapping the inappropriate knowledge or even not finding knowledge gaps while the resulting strategies for transferring innovation knowledge are unsatisfactory. Therefore, it is necessary to identify the attributes of both innovation and knowledge, to ensure that the cloud system used for transferring knowledge is being appropriately selected. However, the compatibility and complexity of the cloud system may need to be examined.

Compatibility is the degree to which the system is perceived as being consistent with the existing systems, past experiences, and needs of potential adopters. Many authors believe that a new system reconfigures the traditional system to be compatible with existing values and beliefs, previously introduced ideas and potential adopters' needs. Thus compatibility will have a positive effect on attitude towards use.

Complexity is the degree to which the cloud system is perceived as being difficult to operate and use (Rogers, 1995). Chun-Wang Tsou (2012) added that the inherent difficulty of using a new system is a major concern when deciding to adopt that technology. The argument here is not the complexity of the underlying software but rather the complexity of the use of the cloud system.

It is clear from the above that cloud systems play a significant role in driving knowledge transfer to innovation. However, organisations face the difficult task of ensuring that knowledge is not misdirected. For example it has been shown that many problems could be avoided through appropriate selection of cloud systems. In addition categorising and organising knowledge could be a core competence for future organisations (Davenport, 1999). Therefore, cloud systems could contribute to:

1. Deciding what knowledge is important.
2. Developing a knowledge vocabulary, including a thesaurus.
3. Prolifically creating indices and search tools.
4. Constantly refining knowledge categories.

The need to manage the cloud data at unprecedented speeds is a major strategic value that technologies such as cloud systems already enjoy. However, the following are basic characteristics that cloud systems must have to achieve these strategic values:

- **Availability:** The ability to continually serve customers and internal personnel regardless of how many there are and how much data there is (i.e. the ability to overcome/avoid congestion);
- **Scalability:** The ability to upgrade requirements without interrupting service operations;
- **Security:** Protection from all threats including, viruses, unauthorised access and the corruption of data;
- **Manageability:** The ability to monitor all operations and applications that are used in the business cycle and to act in a way that is just as easy.

CLOUD SYSTEM IMPLEMENTATION CRITICAL SUCCESS FACTORS

Rockart (1979b, p. 3) defined CSFs as "for any business, the limited number of areas in which results, if they are satisfactory, will ensure successful competitive performance for the organisation". They are the few key areas where "things must go right for the business to flourish". According to Rockart (1979b, p. 10), "Critical success factors are the factors that constitute the critical or fundamental components of the system". They are the key areas where things must go right; in other words, if these components fail, the system fails.

Identifying CSFs as a basis for determining the information needs of managers was proposed by Daniel (1961) but popularised by Rockart (1979a, 1979b). This means in any organisation certain factors will be critical to the success of that organisation, in the sense that if objectives associated with the factors are not achieved, the organisation will fail - perhaps catastrophically so. Rockart (1979a, p. 85), by referring to Daniel (1961), provides the following definition of CSFs "new product development, good distribution, and effective advertising for the food processing industry - factors that remain relevant today for many firms" (Bergeron and Begin, 1989; Boynton and Zmud, 1984; Goldsmith, 1991; Leidecker and Bruno, 1984; Pollalis and Frieze, 1993).

Further work by Croteau and Li (2003) addressed the critical success factors of CRM technological initiatives. The work of Soliman et al. (2001) on critical success factors of implementation of CAD/CAM in ERP environments enhances the argument about using CSF. The work by Nelson and Somers (2001) is considered as one of the most extensive reviews of critical success factor in ERP implementations.

RESEARCH MODEL

The use of the proposed research model is justified since there has been little (if any) research in the literature regarding the use of CSF study for cloud systems' implementation.

Papers on CSFs study which were consulted are Rockart (1982a, 1982b), Martin (1982, 1987), McCredie and Updegrove (1999), Kuang et al. (2001), Nelson and Somers (2001), and Jamoo (2008).

In this study, seven sets of hypotheses that are likely to impact on success or otherwise of cloud system implementation are identified. The independent variables were selected from various related literature. The hypothesised factors are as follows:

1. Selection of the cloud system (hardware, software and network).
2. Organisation's technical support to cloud system's implementation.
3. Management commitment and support to cloud system's implementation.
4. Communication and training on cloud system implementation.
5. Cloud system's implementation's effectiveness.
6. Cloud system users' appreciation.
7. Technological competence of staff using the cloud system.

The conceptual research model used consists of seven hypotheses for this research is as formulated below:

- **H^1:** The selection of the cloud system for implementation is positively related to the cloud system's success.
- **H^{1a}:** The appropriateness of the cloud system is positively related to the cloud system's implementation success.
- **H^2:** An organisation's technical support for the implementation of the cloud system is positively related to the success of cloud system's implementation.
- **H^3:** Commitment and support from management are related to cloud system's implementation success.
- **H^4:** Users' training is positively related to the cloud system's implementation success.
- **H^5:** The implementation's effectiveness is positively related to the cloud system's implementation success.
- **H^6:** Users' appreciation is positively related to cloud system's implementation success.
- **H^7:** The organisation's technological competence for implementing the cloud system is positively related to cloud system's implementation success.

Table 1 (after Jamoo, 2008) lists all seven critical Eigen values for cloud system's implementation activities.

Table 1. All seven critical Eigen values (after Jamoo, 2008)

Component	Initial Eigenvalues		
	Total	% of Variance	Cumulative %
1	16.848	35.847	35.847
2	5.668	12.059	47.906
3	5.505	11.714	59.620
4	4.237	9.014	68.634
5	3.240	6.894	75.528
6	2.552	5.429	80.958
7	1.679	3.573	84.530

The resulting Scree Plot for the Conceptual Research Model and Hypotheses is shown in Figure 1 based on Table 1 (after Jamoo, 2008).

Next, the mapping of the seven original research hypotheses and the extracted Composite Factors (CSFs) from factor analysis show that the seven hypotheses have been significantly supported. Correlation from canonical analysis also supported the seven original research hypotheses.

This research project was intended to provide both theoretical and practical new insights into the implementation of a cloud system as a strategic knowledge management tool. A cloud system's implementation is complex and involves a vast

Figure 1. Resulting scree plot for the conceptual research model and hypotheses

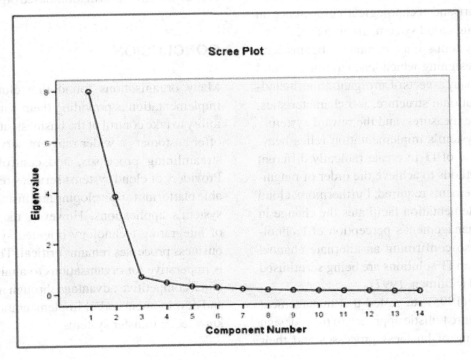

number of different hardware, hardware vendors, software and infrastructure setup. This research found number of factors that can all contribute to the success of a cloud system implementation as a strategic knowledge management tool in organisations. It is hoped that the framework presented in this research and the findings presented could form a base fundamental theory that can aid the further development of cloud systems.

Of the overall goodness of fit measures, it can estimate the observed variance-covariance matrix in the dataset but no more than that (Hair et al., 1998).

The current study delivers valuable insights into the CSFs of cloud system as a strategic innovation management tool in medium to large organisations. Organizations that are considering the implementation of a cloud system strategy can utilise these results to become better acquainted with cloud system's implementation. Results indicate that cloud system's implementation is successful when adequate management commitment and support, supported by a suitable selection of cloud system (hardware, software, and network) IT infrastructure measured by organisations technical support and technological competence in implementing cloud system, are in place.

Cloud system's implementation begins with process redesigning which leads to fundamental changes in many aspects of an organisation, including organisational structure, job characteristics, performance measures, and the reward system.

Cloud system's implementation relies heavily on the use of IT to create radically different working methods to achieve the order of magnitude improvements required. Furthermore, cloud system implementation facilitates the change in corporate management's perception of technology. It is also confirming an alternate channel through which IT solutions are being scrutinised and selected (Soliman, 1997).

Jih et al. (1995) suggested that management is taking a more holistic approach to the redesign and packaging of business processes and their relation with Information Technology. This is fundamentally different from previous approaches where incremental improvements were sought. The reason for this is the belief that radical improvements in performance are both necessary and attainable. This belief is a driver for the cloud system's implementation effort.

Implementing cloud system's applications is traditionally aimed at automating the pre-existing processes in an organisation. Information Technology cannot elevate productivity drastically unless management processes, including the very organisational structure, are changed to accommodate and maximise the benefits of the current advances in Information Technology environment.

The creative use of IT plays an important role in shaping and restructuring the organisation. Previously, IT essentially implemented existing business rules and structures, thus playing the role of passively amplifying the given business structures. In cloud system implementation, IT is used as an active agent of change. After the cloud system implementation, work is completed, organisations should look very similar to Drucker's (1992) notion of information-based organisations.

CONCLUSION

Many organisations found that cloud system implementation is providing them with the flexibility to take control of the business situation and offer customers a wider range of services while streamlining processes, and controlling cost. Providers of cloud systems services require suitable platforms for developing and installing cloud system's applications. However, the challenge of integrating technology-oriented system with business processes remains critical. Therefore, it is imperative for organisations to attain and sustain a competitive advantage through acquisition and development and/or implementation of good knowledge transfer systems.

In order to assess the performance of the nine attributes of knowledge mentioned in this chapter, it is important that assessment of performance should be conducted at the level of the knowledge artefacts rather than at the process or the people levels. This is because the goodness of knowledge could be affected by the performance of either the processes and/or the people who work on the knowledge management processes (Soliman, 2009). According to Evans, and Lindsay (2011), "the performance measures are a quantification of how well the activities achieve a specified goal". Therefore, the performance measures for assessment of innovation knowledge must be developed around assessment of the knowledge itself and not about the performance of processes. Soliman and Youssef (2003) have shown that the performance measures must link to the company's strategies, resources including tangible and intangible resources (such as knowledge). However, in the case of knowledge performance measures, it is necessary to evaluate the outcome of the innovation knowledge artefacts. For example, poor outcome that is entirely due to lack of timeliness of innovation knowledge could be interpreted as a poor performance of knowledge. Similarly, other innovation knowledge attributes could also be assessed on the basis of their outcomes.

The literature search reveals that there is a little attention to the assessment of knowledge. Instead a number of articles that deal with measurement of knowledge management have focused on measuring the outcome of the knowledge management programs.

This chapter argues that measuring innovation knowledge should be based on the value driven from management of innovation. Furthermore, the success of innovative firms today is often a result of good knowledge. This suggests that to improve innovation, then a method for assessment and evaluation of knowledge is required so that management can focus on achieving the innovation objectives. The chapter proposes that good innovation strategies are always based on good knowledge and that in order to differentiate between which knowledge is good and which useful or applicable for innovation, then innovation knowledge must be evaluated or assessed using an appropriate assessment method.

From the above discussion, it is possible to suggest that if firms wishing to maintain a competitive position for a long period of time, then they understand the various life cycles of information and ultimately knowledge particularly along the three important perspectives; namely, the Organizational Dimension, the Legal dimension, and the Technological perspectives.

REFERENCES

Al-Qawabah, M. (2012). *Assessing transformational leadership components as drivers in learning organisations.* (Doctor of Philosophy Dissertation). University of Technology, Sydney, Australia.

Amidon, D. (1997). Dialogue with customers: Secret to innovation strategy. *International Journal of Innovation Management, 1*(1), 73–87. doi:10.1142/S136391969700005X.

Bartoletti, D., & Reichman, A. (2012). *How will you save money in the cloud: Understanding the true cost of cloud computing.* Retrieved from http://www.forrester.com/Will+You+Save+Money+In+The+Cloud+Understanding+The+True+Cost+Of+Cloud+Computing/-/E-WEB11443?objectid=WEB11443&cmpid=mkt:ema:forrWebinaralert

Bergeron, F., & Begin, C. (1989). The use of critical success factors on evaluation of information systems: A case study. *Journal of MIS, 5*(4), 111–124.

Bontis, N., Dragonetti, N., Jacobsen, J., & Roos, G. (2003). The knowledge toolbox: A review of the tools available to measure and manage intangible resources. *European Management Journal, 17*(4), 1–23.

Boynton, A. C., & Zmud, R. W. (1984). An assessment of critical success factors. *Sloan Management Review, 25*(4), 17–27.

Clark, J., & Soliman, F. (1997). Application of scoring method for measuring the value of knowledge based systems to key employees. *Journal of Systems and Information Technology, 2*, 23–40.

Croteau, A.-M., & Li, P. (2003). Critical success factors for CRM technological initiatives. *Canadian Journal of Administrative Sciences, 20*(1), 21–34. doi:10.1111/j.1936-4490.2003.tb00303.x.

Damanpour, F. (1991). Organizational innovation: A meta-analysis of effects of determinants and moderators. *Academy of Management Journal, 34*(3), 555–590. doi:10.2307/256406.

Daniel, D. R. (1961). Management information crises. *Harvard Business Review, 39*(5), 111.

Das, S. R., & Joshi, M. P. (2007). Process innovativeness in technology services organizations: Roles of differentiation strategy, operational autonomy, and risk-taking propensity. *Journal of Operations Management, 25*(3), 643–660. doi:10.1016/j.jom.2006.05.011.

Davenport, T., & Prusak, L. (2000). *Working knowledge: How organizations manage what they know* (p. 240). Cambridge, MA: Harvard Business School Press. doi:10.1145/347634.348775.

Davenport, T. H. (1999). *Think tank: Making the most of an information-rich environment: The future of knowledge management*. Retrieved from http://www.it-consultancy.com/extern/articles/futurekm.html

Drucker, P. F. (1992). *Managing for the future: The 1990s and beyond*. New York: Truman Talley Books.

Evans, R., & Lindsay, W. M. (2011). *The management and control of quality* (8th ed.). Cincinnati, OH: Thomson, South-Western.

Ferrarini, E. (2002). *Want to control network storage space? Put a policy in place and SRM it*. Retrieved 10 April 2002 from http://www.101com.com/solutions/storage

Garvin, D. A. (1993). Building a learning organization. *Harvard Business Review, 71*, 78. PMID:10127041.

Goldsmith, N. (1991). Linking IT planning to business strategy. *Long Range Planning, 24*(6), 67–77. doi:10.1016/0024-6301(91)90045-P.

Haefliger, S., Von Krogh, G., & Spaeth, S. (2008). Code reuse in open source software. *Management Science, 54*(1), 180–193. doi:10.1287/mnsc.1070.0748.

Hair, J. F., Anderson, R. E., Tatham, R. L., & Black, W. C. (1998). *Multivariate analysis* (5th ed.). Englewood Cliffs, NJ: Prentice-Hall International.

Hamel, G., & Prahalad, C. K. (1985). Do you really have a global strategy? *Harvard Business Review, 63*(4), 139–148.

Hislop, D. (2003). The complex relations between communities of practice and the implementation of technological innovations. *International Journal of Innovation Management, 7*(2), 163–188. doi:10.1142/S1363919603000775.

Hunt, D. P. (2003). Hunt the concept of knowledge and how to measure it. *Journal of Intellectual Capital, 4*(1), 100–113. doi:10.1108/14691930310455414.

Jamoo, G. (2008). *Operational implementation of storage area networks as strategic knowledge management tools.* (PhD Dissertation). University of Technology, Sydney, Australia.

Jih, W.-J. K., & Owings, P. (1995). From in search of excellence to business process re-engineering: The role of information technology. *Information Strategy, 11*, 6–19.

Keil, M. (1995). Pulling the plug: Software project management and the problem of project escalation. *Management Information Systems Quarterly, 19*(4), 421–447. doi:10.2307/249627.

Leidecker, J. K., & Bruno, A. V. (1984). Identifying and using critical success factors. *Long Range Planning, 17*(1), 23–32. doi:10.1016/0024-6301(84)90163-8.

Martin, E. W. (1982). Critical success factors of chief MIS/DP executives. *Management Information Systems Quarterly, 6*(2), 1–19. doi:10.2307/249279.

McCredie, J., & Updegrove, D. (1999). Enterprise systems implementation: Lessons from the trenches. *Cause/Effect, 22*(4), 1-10.

Nelson, K., & Somers, T. (2001). The impact of critical success factors across the stages of enterprise resource planning implementations. In *Proceedings of the 34th Annual Hawaii International Conference on System Sciences.* IEEE.

Newman, M. E. J. (2004). Who is the best connected scientist? A study of scientific co-authorship networks. In Ben-Naim, E., Frauenfelder, H., & Toroczkai, Z. (Eds.), *Complex networks* (pp. 337–370). Berlin: Springer. doi:10.1007/978-3-540-44485-5_16.

Nonaka, I., & Von Krogh, G. (2009). Tacit knowledge and knowledge conversion: Controversy and advancement in organizational knowledge creation theory. *Organization Science, 20*(3), 635–652. doi:10.1287/orsc.1080.0412.

Nonaka, I., Von Krogh, G., & Von Hippel, S. (2006). Organizational knowledge creation theory: Evolutionary paths and future advances. *Organization Studies, 27*(8), 1179–1208. doi:10.1177/0170840606066312.

O'Dell, C., & Grayson, C. J. (1998). *If only we knew what we know.* New York: The Free Press.

Pedler, M., Burgoyne, J., & Boydell, T. (1991). *The learning company: A strategy for sustainable growth.* Maidenhead, UK: McGraw-Hill.

Pollalis, Y. A., & Frieze, I. H. (1993). A new look at critical success factors. *Information Strategy*, 24-34.

Porter, M. E. (1980). *Competitive strategy.* New York: The Free Press.

Price Waterhouse Coopers. (1999). *Inside the mind of the CEO: The 1999 global CEO survey.* Paper presented at the World Economic Forum 1999 Annual General Meeting. Davos, Switzerland.

Radding, A. (1992). Dirty downsizing. *Computerworld, 26*(29), 65–68.

Robertson, M., & O'Malley Hammersley, G. (2000). Knowledge management practices within a knowledge-intensive firm: The significance of the people management dimension. *Journal of European Industrial Training, 24*(2/3/4), 241-253.

Rockart, J. F. (1979a). Chief executives define their own data needs. *Harvard Business Review, 57*(2), 81–93. PMID:10297607.

Rockart, J. F. (1979b). The changing role of the information systems executive: A critical success factors prospective. *Sloan Management Review, 23*(1), 3–13.

Rogers, E. (1995). *Diffusion of innovations* (4th ed.). New York, NY: The Free Press. Retrieved from http://www.personal.psu.edu/users/w/x/wxh139/Rogers.htm

Senge, P. M. (1990). *The fifth discipline: The art and practice of the learning organization.* New York: Doubleday.

Senge, P. M. (2006). *The fifth discipline: The art and practice of the learning organization.* Currency.

Soliman, F. (1997). Role of information technology in business process re-engineering. In *Proceeding of Australasia on Conference Technology for Manufacturing.* IEEE.

Soliman, F. (2009). Modelling the appraisal of quality management programs. *The Employment Relations Record, 9*(2), 73–83.

Soliman, F. (2011a). Could one transformational leader convert the organisation from knowledge based into learning organisation, then into innovation? *Journal of Modern Accounting and Auditing, 7*(12), 1352–1361.

Soliman, F. (2011b). Modelling the role of HRM in the innovation chain. *The Employment Relations Record, 11*(2), 1–20.

Soliman, F. (2012a). Business excellence and business innovation: Should HRM play different roles? *The Employment Relations Record, 12*(2), 55–68.

Soliman, F. (2012b). How good is your organisational knowledge? *Academy of Taiwan Business Management Review, 8*(3), 28–35.

Soliman, F. (2012c). Could innovation be driven by globalization? *Journal of Modern Accounting and Auditing, 8*(12), 1848–1860.

Soliman, F. (2012d). Modeling the appraisal of cloud systems' implementation. *Journal of Modern Accounting and Auditing, 8*(12), 1888–1897.

Soliman, F. (2013). Does innovation drive sustainable competitive advantages? *Journal of Modern Accounting and Auditing, 9*(1), 131–144.

Soliman, F., & Spooner, K. (2000). Strategies for implementing knowledge management: Role of human resources management. *Journal of Knowledge Management, 4*(4), 337–345. doi:10.1108/13673270010379894.

Soliman, F., & Youssef, M. (2003). The role of critical information in enterprise knowledge management. *Industrial Management & Data Systems, 103*(7), 484–490. doi:10.1108/02635570310489188.

Somers, T. M., & Nelson, K. (2001). The impact of critical success factors across the stages of enterprise resource planning implementation. In *Proceedings of the 34th Hawaii International Conference on Systems Sciences* (HICSS-34). Maui, HI: IEEE.

Spaeth, S., Stuermer, M., & Von Krogh, G. (2010). Enabling knowledge creation through outsiders: Towards a push model of open innovation. *International Journal of Technology Management, 52*(3/4), 411–431. doi:10.1504/IJTM.2010.035983.

Sveiby, K. E. (1997). *The new organizational wealth: Man-aging and measuring knowledge based assets.* San Francisco, CA: Barrett-Kohler Publishers Inc..

Tsou, C.-W. (2012). Consumer acceptance of windows 7 and office 2010 – The moderating effect of personal innovativeness. *Journal of Research and Practice in Information Technology, 44*(1).

Von Krogh, G., Roos, J., & Kleine, D. (Eds.). (1999). *Knowing in firms: Understanding, managing, and measuring knowledge.* Altamira Press.

Von Krogh, G., & Von Hippel, E. (2006). The promise of research on open source software. *Management Science, 52*(7), 975–983. doi:10.1287/mnsc.1060.0560.

Chapter 9
Cloud Computing:
IT Governance, Legal, and Public Policy Aspects

Carlos Juiz
University of the Balearic Islands, Spain

Victor Alexander de Pous
International Federation for Information Processing (IFIP), The Netherlands

ABSTRACT

Cloud computing evolved as a key delivery model for Information Technology (IT) and data provision for both the private and public sectors. Addressing its governance, legal, and public policy aspects is a condition sine qua non for successful deployment, whether done by the in-house IT department or outsourced. Stakeholders ask for new applications that consumerization is providing. Therefore, IT governance should be adapted to consider this new business pressure. However, the law plays a double role in respect to cloud computing; it functions as a legal framework set by mandatory regulations and as a contractual instrument to manage the cloud technology and information provisioning in an effective way, based on the strategic objectives of any organization. This chapter is devoted to where IT governance frameworks should consider the decisions about specific cloud computing compliance, how to measure them through several indicators, and which are their general legal and public policy aspects.

INTRODUCTION

Several colloquialisms of the IT world converge on cloud computing. Cloud computing takes place in the 'global village,' 'at the speed of light,' and founded on the famous sentence credited to John Gage at Sun Microsystems, that 'the network is the compute,' which enables other more recent phrases like 'information at your fingertips, everywhere, every time.' But, it seems that, for the first time in data processing history, these one-liners have the potential to become a consolidated reality. Place and time independent ways of living our lives, perform work, do business and administer

DOI: 10.4018/978-1-4666-4526-4.ch009

public sector tasks, are facilitated in optima forma by the deployment of cloud computing as the premier and captive delivery model for Information Technology (IT) resources.

This is without doubt an exciting and attractive outlook for any organization, which needs to do more with less, raise the quality of service and aims to innovate—all at the same time. The recent standardization of IT Governance tries to implement frameworks in which IT assets are governed as other corporate ones like: human, physical, intellectual, financial and relationship assets. These governance frameworks should also be implemented at government and public enterprises.

Nevertheless, the often unthinkingly advocated transition to cloud computing does not mean that every government information system or all public sector data should be moved to the Cloud in the first place. The future of Information Technology will be of mixed natures: On-premise and in the Cloud; delivered by the internal IT department and by cloud service providers; using private, public and hybrid clouds. Therefore, the preferred way to assess and manage risks, optimize digital technology assets, and reform public administrations is by deploying sound and well-founded cloud policies at IT governance framework implementations.

Cloud Computing

What constitutes cloud computing? A computer scientist draws computers and software services and connects them to the Internet. Thus 'the Cloud' was born, as a metaphor. Search engines Lycos and Yahoo (1994) and the e-mail service Hotmail (1996) were examples avant la lettre, but the first airline reservation system around 1960 already used a cloud model. Exemplary today, Amazon Web Services, Salesforce, Google Docs and Microsoft Office packages Office365 and the immensely popular social networks Facebook and YouTube—not to mention the literally countless apps for smart phones, tablets and more.

Cloud computing takes place largely invisible, but it shows itself to end-users as Web-based software and information that is stored on servers in data centers elsewhere and no longer on their computers or information systems of the organization they work for. The actual processing is done virtualized—the computer programs and information are disconnected from the physical hardware and infrastructure. Consequently, the nature of data (processing) changes in non-permanent and dynamic, and becomes almost 'liquid.'

Cloud computing developed and keeps developing in an evolutionary way. Technologically speaking, the turning point lies behind us, because essential information technologies, including virtualization and broadband Internet, are now widely available and accessible. Cloud computing may be a service provided by the internal IT department, but cloud computing will more likely involve an outsourcing relationship.

According to the internationally broad-accepted definition, the National Institute of Standards and Technology (NIST) and the Cloud Security Alliance (Mell, 2011) describes 'how cloud computing is a model for enabling ubiquitous, convenient, on-demand network access to a shared pool of configurable computing resources (e.g., networks, servers, storage, applications, and services) that can be rapidly provisioned and released with minimal management effort or service provider interaction.' The cloud matrix comprises public (open and standardized), private (closed and any desired length), community (targeting a particular community) and hybrid (public/private) application models and distinct in the service model (SaaS) software, platforms (PaaS), and infrastructure (IaaS).

IT Governance

IT governance may be defined as specifying the decision rights and accountability framework to encourage desirable behavior in the use of IT. In addition, the IT governance has been identified as the responsibility of executives and senior management that consists to ensure that IT assets are supporting and extending the company objectives and strategies of the organization (Weill, 2004). There are other IT governance definitions, but all converge in the rights and decisions framework about IT at an organization.

Thus, this definition of IT governance aims to consider several important terms: decisions, behavior and accountability framework. In relation to decisions, governance is who decides and what to decide. When we look at behavior in the broader sense of governing information technology use, we are referring to the way that the organization and the individuals act when dealing with situations that require something to be done, or a decision to be made. If action is not taken, or the wrong action is taken, we would consider this bad behavior. Conversely, when the right action is taken in a timely manner, the behavior is good (Toomey, 2009). The same goes for decisions – avoiding them, or intentionally making the wrong choice is bad behavior, while addressing them head-on and seeking the right choice is obviously good behavior. Additionally, behavior also refers as the set of norms, rules, laws and policies that frame these relationships and their compliance. This last set is crucial for the use of cloud solution in public enterprises.

Implementing good IT governance requires a framework based on three major elements (Weill, 2004):

- **Structures:** Who makes the decisions? What structural organizations will be created, who will take part in these organizations, and what responsibilities will they assume?
- **Alignment Processes:** How are IT decisions made? What are the decision-making processes for proposing, principles, architecture, infrastructure, business applications and approving investments, and prioritizing investments?

- **Communication:** How will the results of these processes and decisions be monitored, measured, and communicated? What mechanisms will be used to communicate IT investment decisions to the board, executive management, business management, IT management, employees, and customers and other stakeholders?

An IT framework is straightforward model for helping organizations implement an IT governance standard. In the next section, we relate the compliance of legal assets in IT governance standards and particularly the public policy for cloud computing.

Thus, the objectives of this chapter are:

- To introduce IT governance frameworks and in particular how they have to include several parts about conformance and compliance for legal and policy aspects.
- To show an example of IT governance framework at one public organization.
- To point out how important sections of the IT governance frameworks should be slightly modified to consider cloud computing solutions. Thus, we are going to explain where are the connections between cloud computing and IT governance framework implementations and how to measure its progress at the organization.
- To enunciate which are essential legal and public policy aspects of cloud computing to consider by CIO and boards in public enterprises.

BACKGROUND

IT Governance Frameworks: Principles and Types of Decisions

Even there are industrial de facto standards and several national standards for IT governance; we may conclude that there is only one international standard for IT governance corresponding to the ISO/IEC 38500 (ISO/IEC, 2008). ISO/IEC 38500 is the first international standard that provides guidelines for governance of IT (Toomey, 2009). Different organizations will adopt different approaches to ISO/IEC 38500 conformance – and the systems for governance of IT will differ in their design from one organization to another. However, with recognition that the governance system includes the management system, and understanding that both governance and management systems involve people, process, structure and technology, it should be clear that established frameworks should greatly assist in establishing the corresponding systems (ISO/IEC, 2008). Recommendations around compliance and conformance go directly to specification of the processes and controls in the system of governance, and the policies that communicate the structures intent for all who are involved in making decisions.

The ISO/IEC 38500 standard guides decision making for executive board directors around 6 principles: responsibility, strategy, acquisition, performance, conformance, and human behavior. The model for governance of IT provided in ISO/IEC 38500 also defines that the fundamental governance tasks are evaluate, direct and monitor, which are applied to the proposals for use of IT, the projects (the IT project portfolio selection and execution) that implement use of IT and the operations (that constitutes the IT service catalog) that are dependent on IT.

In addition to the IT governance framework of ISO/IEC 38500, according to (Weill, 2004), the five types of decisions to be taken by the layer corresponding to the governance of IT are as follows: IT principles, IT architecture, IT infrastructure, Need for business applications and Priorization of Investment of IT. These five decision types are not explicitly shown in ISO/IEC 38500 model. However other governance frameworks (Juiz, 2011) may include these five decisions. Additionally, no cloud computing instruments are especially devoted for IT

Governance frameworks, yet. However, there are conformance and compliance sections in the framework. Thus, we are going to introduce how to link IT Governance frameworks based on current standard, cloud computing solutions and conformance legal and policy aspects for public enterprises.

An Example of IT Governance Framework: The dFogIT® Model

The dFogIT® (detailed Framework of governance for Information Technologies) is a governance framework constructor, all rights reserved by the University of the Balearic Islands (Universitat de les Illes Balears or UIB). This framework constructor not only includes in its core the ISO/IEC 38500 standard (ISO/IEC, 2008), and the Thorp's (Thorp, 2005) essential key aspects for management responsibility, but also it considers how communicate to the board (and the rest of the organization) that the value of the IT assets could be extracted from even from the day-to-day operation (Hunter, 2009).

dFogIT® is based on the ISO/IEC 38500 standard, since two of four layers of the model, in particular, the IT Governance and the IT Management ones, are equivalent to the international standard with slightly modifications (see Figure 1). The ISO/IEC 38500 model was extended with two additional layers: the upper Corporate Governance layer, which represents the strategic view of the enterprise; and the lower IT Operation layer, which represents the tangible IT assets. Every layer in the model represents essential actions performed by their main stakeholders.

Therefore, the dFogIT® governance framework model consists of four layers of abstraction of the IT at any enterprise, from bottom to top:

- The layer of IT Line Operation, including IT personnel, assets (real or virtual) and commodities (buildings, computers, networks, cooling, etc.).

Figure 1. dFogIT® governance framework

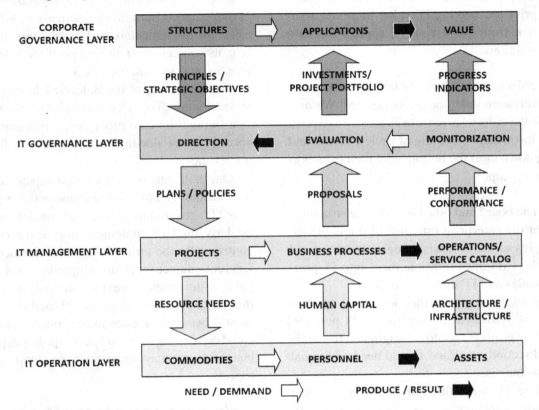

- The layer of IT Management, which corresponds to the transformation of IT projects, which are made to improve business processes, to daily operations. These operations include maintenance and the corresponding implementation of IT services.
- The layer of IT Governance, which corresponds to the direction and planning, based on the evaluation of project proposals, and monitoring the operations and services. The IT Management and IT Governance layers are almost identical to the standards ISO/IEC 38500 (Juiz, 2011).
- The layer of Corporate Strategy, which aims to get value from IT in terms of applications that are requested from governing structures in order to harvest the value of IT.

Thus, each layer of dFogIT® contains a transformation function, from needs/demands to products/results (see white/black arrows in Figure 1), so we have:

- Commodities are transformed in IT assets through IT staff knowledge, training and education in the Line Operation layer.
- IT Projects are transformed into IT Operations contributing to IT Services, when business processes are implemented at the layer of IT Management. This transformation is exactly shown as in ISO/IEC 38500 standard.
- Operation trends and quality of Services are monitored in order to be evaluated transforming the observation into new directions at IT Governance layer. This is also similar to the ISO/IEC 38500 framework.

- Corporate Governance structures at enterprise are seeking IT value by transformation from the use of IT applications and solutions.

In order to interconnect the four layers different IT governance instruments are defined. We may follow the colored arrows in Figure 1 to explain these instruments, starting at up left corner and going down until the bottom, and then from bottom to the top:

- The board and other governance structures at the enterprise establish business principles and high-level strategic objectives and the CIO must translate them into IT principles and IT strategic goals.
- These goals are further developed into tactical goals in detailed plans and IT policies.
- The projects should be originated from this direction plans and should need additional resources.
- The IT staff, through their training and education, understands the business processes and catch the requirements of business units to fill out standard project forms.
- These standard forms are evaluated and some of them will constitute the project portfolio and the investments will be rolled out to be applications that the board visualizes.
- IT infrastructure and IT architecture hold the operations and services.
- These operations and services are monitored providing IT Management indicators and metrics providing progress and advance, giving alignment with the business and its corresponding value.

The IT governance instruments connect the layers of the model and serve communicate the necessary information to deploy a particular implementation of IT governance. Thus, once dFogIT®

is adopted by the enterprise or organization as IT governance framework constructor, it has to select the implementation of its own instruments (e.g. its strategic plan, project portfolio selection process, services catalog, etc.).

The University of the Balearic Islands (UIB) is developing dFogIT® a particular implementation through its own processes, procedures and corresponding documents (UIB, 2013) for IT governance.

One of the main questions this chapter pursues it is whether IT governance frameworks, e.g. the dFogIT® governance framework model or particularly, the UIB implementation, also serves to contribute to the principles of conformance and legal compliance for cloud computing solutions at public enterprises. In next section will show that there are numerous links, explicitly and implicitly shown, between IT governance frameworks and cloud computing legal and public policy aspects, but before we may understand the cloud matrix aspects.

Understanding the Cloud Matrix

The most talked, written, and probably hyped IT topic may easily create a Babylonian confusion of tongues, while misconceptions encourage unfounded speculations. Cloud computing, moreover, comes in fact in shapes and sizes. It consists of an array of IT services. Eventually, just about everything—information technology and data—may be provided over the Internet as an automated service on demand. Indeed, the Cloud may drive all IT activities; from data collecting and processing, to data storage and archiving.

What constitutes cloud computing? A computer scientist draws computers and software services and connects to the Internet. In this way 'the Cloud' was most likely born as a metaphor. The search engines Lycos and Yahoo (1994) and the e-mail service Hotmail (1996) were examples avant la lettre, but an airline reservation system developed around 1960 used already a cloud-alike model. Exemplary today are Amazon Web Services (infrastructure), Salesforce (enterprise), Google Docs and Microsoft Office365 (productivity software) and the immensely popular social network Facebook—not to mention the countless mobile apps (Mobile Apps 2013) for smart phones and tablets (Sabre 2012).

Cloud computing takes place largely invisible. Yet it shows itself to end-users as Web-based software and data, which is not on their computer or recorded within the organization, but on information systems in data centers, literally elsewhere. The actual processing takes place virtualized, that is to say, that computer programs and data are 'separated' from the physical hardware and infrastructure. Then data changes its nature and becomes non-continuous and dynamic, almost 'liquid.' Cloud computing is not a (new) technology, but concerns a method of IT and data delivery as an on-demand and automated-scalable service over the Internet, based on supply chain automation in offshore data centers. In Figure 1, we may observe that Operation and Services are based on IT Architecture and IT Infrastructure. Services, Platforms and Infrastructures can be delivered as cloud solutions.

Evolution

The delivery method developed evolutionary and will most likely continue doing so. Technology speaking, the turning point lies behind us because essential information technologies, including virtualization and broadband Internet, are now widely available and accessible. The Cloud is a chain of IT services, developed and compiled from various building blocks and by different manufacturers and services providers. Based on this mix, the cloud service is ultimately delivered to an organization and/or individual users. The internal IT department may provide the service, but cloud computing will more likely involve an outsourcing relationship. On the conference (CloudGov 2012), the Department of Homeland Security of the US asked rhetorically 'Are we in the data center business or do we need IT functions?'

According to the broadly accepted and extensive definition of the National Institute for Standards and Technology (NIST), cloud computing is 'a model for enabling ubiquitous, convenient, on-demand network access to a shared pool of configurable computing resources (e.g., networks, servers, storage, applications and services) that can be rapidly provisioned and released with minimal management effort or service provider interaction' (NIST 2011). The NIST definition lists five essential characteristics of cloud computing: on-demand self-service, broad network access, resource pooling, rapid elasticity or expansion, and measured service. It also lists three service models (software, platform and infrastructure), and four deployment models (private, community, public and hybrid) that together categorize ways to deliver cloud services.[1]

In the end, cloud computing means—at least for the greater part—the industrialization and automation of IT, that is comparable with the electrification of a century ago. We are seeing IT as an out-of-the-wall available power—as a utility—according to certain standards, in Western Europe an alternating current at 50 Hertz/220 Volt.

Advantages and Disadvantages

It is safe to say that probably every public sector organization already deploys some kind of cloud service when personal make use of their own laptop, tablet, and/or smart phone for work—incidentally or in a more structured way. Indeed, adoption of cloud computing emerged at end-user side (consumer, citizen, and employee) and progresses in this market segment extensively. Facebook today, for example, has approximately one billion registered users. The adoption speed stands out also.[2] After the business world (Domino 2012) and educational institutions (World e.gov 2011), it is now the turn for public sector organizations.

Cloud computing arouses a business-wise interest because of efficiency improvements, especially when sharing and outsourcing prevail. Payment for use replaces investments (CAPEX becomes OPEX), while cloud services are remotely, on-demand, and in this respect above all automated provisioned. IT user organizations not only share computing resources like networks, servers, storage, applications, and services—on closer inspection also the often tight and expensive expertise of IT staff.[3] Also public sector organizations can take full advantage of the economies of scale and skills.

We deduct more points that are important. In technical staff shortage regions like Western Europe, this will limit the basic conflict of interest that IT departments face as they migrate to outsourced cloud services. However, the key benefit delivery model touches the center information provision. The concept of 'information at your fingertips'[4] matures finally in such a way that unprecedented opportunities emerge. Cloud computing enables and facilitates organizational and societal change: from new ways of work to the creation of smart cities.[5]

Also interesting and underexposed as well, is the situation that, when cloud service providers have their legal act together, end-user organizations, including the public sector, will no longer commit software piracy. The delivery model prohibits this.

Concerns

Critics form a minority, but they do stir. Free software creator Richard Stallman swiped the floor with cloud computing. He warned users that Web-based software, such as Google's Gmail, a trap. 'It's stupidity. It's worse than stupidity: it's a marketing hype campaign.'[6] Stallman sees an unprecedented vendor lock-in situation. The General Intelligence and Investigation Service AIVD of the Netherlands designates in its Vulnerability Analysis Espionage negative aspects of cloud computing seen from a different perspective—information security (AIVD 2013).

CISCO CEO John Chambers once referred to the Cloud as a 'security nightmare' (Computerworld 2009). On July 1, the Article 29 Data Protection Working Party—the independent EU Advisory Body on Data Protection and Privacy—adopted an opinion. Despite the acknowledged economic and societal benefits of cloud computing, 'the wide scale deployment of cloud computing services can trigger a number of data protection risks.' The Working Party refers mainly to a lack of control over personal data, and insufficient information with regard to how, where and by whom the data is being processed/sub-processed (EU 2012). Of exceptional importance for the progress of our society is that we debate on rational grounds and weigh cloud characteristics and models carefully on their merits.

For example, not all (public sector) information processed in the Cloud is legally speaking personal data and risk analyses must be the effective first step before adopting cloud services. According to the European Commission, there is no doubt that concerns matter, but the administration is very determined to overcome them with legal (laws, model agreements, international cooperation) and other measures, including security, standardization, best practices, and public procurement.

We encounter the same attitude in the US, where the government cloud train has left the station and is not returning. Existing laws and regulations continue to apply to the Cloud[7] but the United States Government uses new independently audited certification programs to ensure information security for federal clouds (GSA 2013). Figure 1 shows that compliance and conformance of services should be continuously monitored by the layer of IT Governance and reported to the board through progress indicators.

Disruptive

Finally yet importantly—and we can file the circumstances either on threat or chance—cloud computing manifests itself, just as the world wide Web of the Internet twenty years ago, slowly but surely as a disruptive cluster: both in and outside the IT industry. This means that innovations create new markets and eventually go on disruption existing markets, displacing earlier technologies, including delivery and business models. A telling example is the online encyclopedia Wikipedia (disrupting the traditional encyclopedia market) or the advent of online travel agents (disrupting the travel market for travel agencies and airline ticket offices around the corner, (CIO 2009)).

Adjoining, the question arises whether cloud computing—compare the discussion on personal computing in the eighties—is a 'job killer' or in contrary generates employment. A market researcher knows the answer. A recent IDC study shows that cloud spending in the period 2011 to 2015 create nearly 14 million jobs worldwide, half of which originates in China and India. Not only are these large countries, their markets having less trouble with 'the law of the retarding advantage.' They start indeed to automate their business processes often directly based on cloud computing, overleaping earlier models of electronic data processing (Kroes 2012). Nevertheless, do not forget the effects in the Western world. 'In a country like Germany, some estimate that over five years, Cloud computing could generate over €200 billion in economic benefits, and 800,000 jobs. That's around €500 per German citizen per year,' says EU Vice-President and Commissioner Neelie Kroes.

U.S. Government Position

The U.S. Government makes significant steps and rather rapidly. Starting September 2009, the White House formulates extraordinarily energetic, radical reform policies for its information provision (De Pous 2012). Change is required in order to become more efficient, more effective, and cheaper. Stop the waste. At the center we find cloud computing. The new federal policies may count on wide support, although there are question marks. The Federal Cloud Computing Initiative (FCCI, September 2009), developed by the first Federal CIO, Vivek Kundra, contains the rudiments of a new policy for federal automation and includes an Info.Apps.gov Website (apps and cloud services), budgeting, and policy planning and architecture (CNET 2009).

In February 2010, the Office of Management and Budget (OMB) established the Federal Data Center Consolidation Initiative (FDCCI). This government-wide initiative focuses on reducing the total number of federal data centers from 2000 to 1200; a 40 percent closure. FDCCI addresses costs and energy footprint in the light of increasing efficiency, strengthening the overall government security posture, and promoting Green IT. Meanwhile, the targets further tightened. Not 800 but 962 data centers to the end of 2015 have closed their doors. The consolidation provides an estimated savings of 3 to 5 billion dollars (DT Knowledge 2012).

As part of a continued effort to enact the IT reform, Mr. Kundra published in December 2010 a 25 point implementation plan to reform federal information technology management that included the shift to a cloud first policy. Federal agencies are required to evaluate their technology sourcing strategies so that cloud-computing options are fully considered. cloud first, however, aims at accelerating the adoption speed. Each agency will identify three 'must move' services within three months, and move one of those services to the Cloud within 12 months and the remaining two within 18 months.

The U.S. government ranks as the world-largest IT buyer.[8] The government sees cloud computing as the very means of addressing the fragmentation of information systems, poor IT project management and modernizing legacy systems.

Our children go with more technology to school than their parents use at work, President Obama must have said. The ultimate goal focuses on improving productivity and performance of federal government organizations. The ranks close both on cloud computing as the preferred method of delivery of government automation as the need for data center consolidation. We hear nevertheless criticism. Federal IT managers criticized the cloud first strategy last year for short time lines, insufficient funding, and conflicting mandates (IT Knowledge Exchange 2011). Meanwhile, development and implementation of policies proceed assiduously.

In November 2011, Vivek Kundra's successor, Mr. Steven Van Roekel, made a further step and launched future first, which involves a set of additional principles under development—such as xml first, Web services first and virtualization first—that determine in which way federal government arranges its information technology. Also new is shared first. This policy initiative aims at 'opportunities to shift to commodity IT, leverage technology, procurement, and best practices across the whole of government, and build on existing investments rather than re-inventing the wheel' (Van Roekel 2011). At the end of 2011, the OMB introduced the federal risk and authorization management program (FedRAMP 2013). This mandatory government-wide program provides a standardized approach to security assessment, authorization, and continuous monitoring for cloud products and services, through a 'do once, use many times' framework. An important part of the program is the independent, third-party certification for cloud products and services. After its preparatory stage, FedRAMP is now rolling out.

European Union Position

At the 2011 world economic forum in Davos, Switzerland—circa one-and-a-half year after the start of the cloud reforms in the United States—Vice-Premier and Commissioner Neelie Kroes (Digital Agenda) announced the commencement of an EU-wide cloud computing strategy. 'This goes beyond a policy framework. I want to make Europe not just 'cloud-friendly' but 'cloud-active.' (Kroes 2011) 'Fixed and wired networks are already in place, roaming costs are regulated continuously, and a comprehensive report on cloud security was just released (ENISA 2011). Based on the Cloud Computing Strategy, Europe today must become 'cloud-friendly' (barrier-free by law) and 'cloud-active' (wide adoption through standards, public procurement, and stimulation). The Cloud holds the promise of scalable and secure services for greater efficiency and flexibility, at lower cost. This applies also to public sector organizations.

The very soon to be published integrated cloud computing strategy for the European Union has its fundaments most likely based on three key pillars.

1. **The Law:** Data protection is central (privacy law), but reforms concern additional domains that have relevance to the deployment of cloud computing, such as cloud data distribution (copyright law) and the clarification of the liability limitation for cloud service providers who merely host, cache or transmit third-party information (e-commerce law). Moreover, the development of template contracts and service level agreements is foreseen (contract law).

2. **Standardization, Public Procurement, and Stimulation:** The second pillar concerns promoting public standards, e.g. for security and availability of cloud services. Next to that, a newly founded European Cloud Partnership will include advanced public procurement principles. Finally, the EU will facilitate research and development in the cloud computing area.

3. **Global Governance for Cloud Computing:** The EU will actively contribute to international efforts in regards with safe and seamless cross-border use of cloud services.

IT governance should consider these three pillars at EU public enterprises. Our example should include these pillars as principles coming down from the IT Corporate Strategy to the other three layers (see Figure 1).

Data protection Law under Development

A major part of the legislative component of the cloud computing strategy for the European Union exists in the long-awaited uniformed harmonization of the 1995 EU Data Protection Directive (95/46/EC 1995). The comprehensive reform—drafts published on January 25—shows a dual approach (EU Justice 2012). Firstly, the legal protection of citizens in relation to their online privacy will be enhanced. They get more control and rights, also in the respect of cloud-processed personal data. The other main object lies in promoting the digital economy through relieve of administrative burdens for businesses up to savings of around 2.3 billion euro per year.

The underlying rationale does not surprise. The way data is collected, accessed, and used has changed dramatically by technological advancements and globalization. Moreover, the 27 EU Member States implemented the present Directive differently, leading to differences in laws and enforcement. Revision was ultimately inevitable. According to the EU Charter of Fundamental Rights, everyone and everywhere is in principle entitled to protection of personal data.

The proposals are marked as a 'forward-looking' update. In addition to a policy statement on the objectives of the Commission, there are two bills published. A Regulation setting out a general EU framework for data protection (has a direct effect) and a Directive on protecting personal data processed for the purposes of prevention, detection, investigation or prosecution of criminal offences and related judicial activities (requires a legislative national implementation process). Key goals and changes include the following.[9]

- **Harmonization and Consumer Confidence:** One single set of data protection rules applicable throughout the EU, leaving no room for national divergence. The initiative aims at helping reinforce consumer/citizen confidence in online services—including cloud services—by strengthening their legal position, increasing responsibility and account-ability for those processing personal data, increasing competition, and high fines.

- **Obligation to Notify:** Companies and (public sector) organizations having serious data breaches must notify as soon as possible—within 24 hours when feasible—their national data protection authority.

- **One Supervisor:** Companies and (public sector) organizations with cross-border business will only have to deal with the regulator in the EU country where they have their principal place. The national data protection authority is also the contact for citizens, even if an out-of-EU company processes their data.

- **Right of Consent:** Wherever consent is required for personal data to be processed, it must be given expressly, and not be presumed to have been tacitly given (strengthening of the existing right of consent).

- **Access Right:** Citizens will have easier access to their personal data, to be executed online and for free (strengthening of the existing access right).

- **Data Portability Right:** Moreover, citizens are able to transfer personal data from one service provider to another more easily—this concerns a new privacy right.

- **Right to be Forgotten:** A new privacy right will help people better manage data protection risks online. They will be able to delete their data if there are no legitimate grounds for retaining it (a new privacy right).

- **Jurisdiction:** The new rules must apply if personal data is handled abroad by companies and (public sector) organizations that are active in the EU market and offer their services to EU citizens.

IT GOVERNANCE FRAMEWORKS: LEGAL, PUBLIC POLICIES, AND THE CLOUD

The IT governance frameworks, in general, are the main focuses when considering the use of cloud computing. As companies provide IT services in the cloud that have been traditionally managed internally, they will ensure, firstly, that they continue to meet performance objectives, which their technology provisioning and business are strategically aligned, and risks are managed (Toomey, 2009). Ensuring that IT is aligned with the business, IT services are secure, and risk is managed is challenging in cloud computing as complex third-party relationship. Typical governance activities such as goal setting, policy development, defining responsibilities, managing IT business proposals and monitoring performance and conformance must include special considerations when dealing with cloud technology ("Guiding Principles for Cloud Computing", 2012). This chapter is devoted to this last issue, the conformance and compliance of cloud solutions at public enterprises. More precisely, this chapter is introduces where IT governance frameworks should consider the decisions about specific cloud computing compliance, how to measure them through several indicators and which are their general legal and public policy aspects.

IT Governance Frameworks and Cloud Computing (*Where*)

Firstly, considering IT governance frameworks (Juiz, 2011), we are going to overview where cloud computing paradigm is related with the IT governance implementation, i.e. alignment, communication and structures (Weill, 2004) through the dFogIT®.

Following our example of the UIB IT governance implementation, there are several parts where cloud computing technology should be especially considered, the instruments of governance and the layers involved. In Figure 2, we can see the areas where it can be seen explicitly most influential paradigm of cloud computing and IT governance framework.

The zones are numbered from 0 to 9, to locate them in the framework. Thus we find the following:

1. The cloud matrix comprises public (open and standardized), private (closed and any desired length), community (targeting a particular community) and hybrid (public/private) application models and distinct in the service model (SaaS) software, platforms (PaaS) and infrastructure (IaaS). In any case, the infrastructure and the architecture organized the cloud assets for an unique vision for the governance. Organizations can focus on their core business, rather than continuously worried about their infrastructure (which may arrive to be 55% of IT global expenditure) (Hunter, 2009). Solving peak business demands for IT performance can be readily met by using cloud computing.

2. Costs, ROI and value of services. Cloud services (SaaS, PaaS or IaaS) should be priced and monitored in order to establish a clear SLA (Service Level Agreement) and QoS (Quality of Service) expected.

3. Applications demand and Expected Value. As investment, cloud computing requires analysis around its ROI. Because ROI is calculated using return and investment cost, it is important to quantify the value of the return as much as possible and identify all potential costs (expected and unexpected) when weighing a decision whether to proceed

Figure 2. dFogIT® governance framework and cloud computing

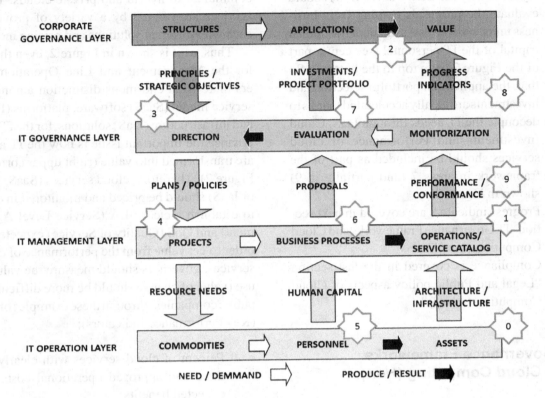

with a cloud solution. Thus, value offered by the cloud include: cost containment, immediacy, availability, scalability, efficiency, resiliency, among others.

4. IT governance should consider all the previous benefits and risks in order to make plans and policies and communicate them to the rest of the enterprise, to embark everyone in this crucial decision.

5. In Figure 2, we observe that the principles and board objectives coming from the Corporate Strategy layer should be transformed by the CIO into plans and policies to be managed through projects (see left side of Figure 1 from top to bottom). These projects may need some cloud resources.

6. IT personnel should facilitate and manage the cloud computing services as part of the IT architecture avoiding the disaggregation of

the one of the most important stakeholders, i.e. the business units. On the other hand, IT staff should be well trained and motivated in order to accept new initiatives from business units related with cloud solutions.

7. Business processes including data processing, development and information retrieval are clearly change areas due to the adoption of cloud computing. The same should be applied to IT processes where the information is stored, archived and backed up. One of the most controversial organizational change issues are that business units personnel, who previously were forced to go through IT, can now bypass IT and receive services directly from the cloud.

8. In Figure 2, we may see that the layer of Corporate Strategy demands applications to produce value, so that the Governance

layer (usually the Office of the CIO) should evaluate the proposals coming from business units with the assessment of the human capital of the IT personnel (see center part of the Figure 2 from top to the bottom). So that, the application portfolio selection and investments are ideally accelerated thanks to decouple the IT needs through IaaS. Cloud Investments and Performance of cloud services should be included as part of the framework in areas 7 (and partially in 9) shown in Figure 2.

9. Progress indicators are covered in next section "IT Governance Frameworks and Cloud Computing (*how*)"

10. Compliance is covered in the last section "Legal and Public policy aspects of Cloud Computing (*which*)"

IT Governance Frameworks and Cloud Computing (*How*)

In order to get value from the performance of cloud services, governors should measure the value of use (value of change should be more difficult for public companies) through KPI (Key Performance Indicators). We may find some good implementation of KPI for processes in ("COBIT 5 Enabling Processes", 2012) but we adapt them for specific cloud solutions in next paragraphs. These progress indicators correspond to the area number 8 at Figure 2.

Costs, ROI, and Value

Services in the cloud may be described as utilities, in pay-per-use business model. However, cloud solutions include many elements beyond the infrastructure costs. Basically, there are three types of costs: start-up, operational and termination costs. To add to the complexity, cloud computing encompasses a variety of service delivery and deployment models, ranging from public and

community to hybrid and private clouds. These services are offered by a variety of providers, each with different solutions and pricing models.

Thus, as it is shown in Figure 2, even though for the Management and Line Operation layers there is an enormous distinction among the service model (SaaS) software, platforms (PaaS) and infrastructure (IaaS) solutions, for the IT governance the important issue is how the IT assets are transformed into value (right upper corner in Figure 2). Therefore, cloud services (SaaS, PaaS or IaaS) should be priced and monitored in order to establish a clear SLA (Service Level Agreement) and QoS (Quality of Service) expected. In order to get value from the performance of cloud services, governors should measure the value of use (value of change should be more difficult for public companies) through these examples of KPI (Key Performance Indicators):

- Percent of cloud services with clearly defined and approved operational costs and expected benefits.
- Number of business disruptions due to cloud service incidents.
- Percent of business stakeholders satisfied that cloud service delivery meets agreed-on SLA.
- Percent of users satisfied with the quality of cloud service delivery.
- Level of stakeholder satisfaction with the enterprise's ability to obtain value from cloud-enabled initiatives.
- Number of critical business processes supported by up-to-date SaaS and IaaS.
- Satisfaction levels of business and IT executives with cloud-related costs and capabilities.

Solving peak business demands for IT performance can be readily met by using cloud computing. Thus, value offered by the cloud include: cost containment, immediacy, availability, scalability, efficiency, resiliency, among others ("Calculating

Cloud ROI", 2012). These advantages should be pointed out as progress indicators, i.e. in area 8 of Figure 2.

Applications Demand and Expected Value

CIOs should examine cloud computing as a real option for their IT resource needs. By offering enterprises the opportunity to decouple their IT needs and their infrastructure, cloud computing accelerates innovation and time-to-market opportunities for the business units. By moving IT services to the cloud, enterprises can take advantage of using services in an on-demand model (Hunter, 2009).

Thus, the application portfolio selection and investments are ideally accelerated thanks to decouple the IT needs through IaaS. Several examples of how to measure the progress through cloud solutions may be:

- Level of stakeholder satisfaction with scope of the planned portfolio of application programs developed through cloud solutions (partially or totally).
- Percent of cloud value drivers mapped to business value drivers.
- Percent of cloud-enabled investments where claimed benefits are met or exceeded.
- Level of business executive awareness and understanding of IT innovation possibilities through cloud solutions.
- Level of stakeholder satisfaction with levels of IT innovation expertise through cloud technologies.
- Level of executive management satisfaction with IT's value delivery and cost through cloud applications.
- Number of approved initiatives resulting from innovative IT ideas based on cloud.
- Level of satisfaction of business executives with IT's responsiveness to new requirements through cloud solutions (partially or totally).

- Percent of projects with appropriate cloud resource allocations.
- Percent of investment business cases with clearly defined and approved expected IT-related costs and benefits due to the cloud implementation.

Defining Principles, Objectives, Plans, and Policies

IT governance should consider all the cloud possibilities in order to make plans and policies and communicate them to the rest of the organization. Thus, CIO plans and policies are implemented through projects (see left side of Figure 2 from top to bottom). These projects may need some cloud resources. Therefore, some additional indicators should be considered in order to monitor the implementation of the strategy:

- Percent of enterprise strategic goals and requirements supported by cloud solutions.
- Frequency of IT strategy (executive) committee meetings related to cloud.
- Actual vs. target cycle time for key decisions related to cloud implementations.
- Level of stakeholder satisfaction (measured through surveys) for cloud solutions.
- Degree by which agreed-on governance principles for IT are evidenced in processes and practices (percentage of processes and practices with clear traceability to principles) where cloud is involved.
- Level of stakeholder satisfaction with progress towards identified goals, with value delivery based on cloud solutions.
- Average time to turn strategic IT objectives into an agreed-on and approved initiative.
- Number of times cloud services are on the board agenda in a proactive manner.

Organizational Changes: Business Processes, Business Units, and IT Personnel

Important indicators about the business processes and their relation IT staff to consider by IT Governance frameworks should be:

- Percent of business stakeholders satisfied that cloud service delivery meets agreed-on service levels.
- Percent of users satisfied with the quality of cloud service delivery.
- Number of approved initiatives resulting from innovative IT ideas based on cloud solutions.
- Level of satisfaction of business executives with IT's responsiveness to new requirements.
- Percent of staff whose IT-related skills are sufficient for the competency required for cloud solutions.
- Percent of staff satisfied with their IT-related roles.
- Number of learning/training hours per staff member about cloud technologies.

Risks: Performance, Conformance, and Compliance

Cloud computing increases the dependency on third-party providers even supplying flexible, available, resilient and efficient IT services. This type of risk in-house changes, moving from hardware and software providers to service providers, shall handle the new processes by governance structures.

Another new challenge introduced by cloud computing is the abstraction of the physical infrastructure where the data is being stored and processed. Data owners have no direct control of the infrastructure affecting the data in cloud. Most of the cloud computing risks for the enterprise that need to be managed

include are legal and assurance issues: sustainability, confidentiality, compliance, business continuity, SLA controversy, among others. There are several indicators to consider about IT risks, we may reshape them to consider in cloud solutions:

- Percent of critical business processes, cloud services and cloud-enabled business programs covered by risk assessment.
- Number of significant cloud-related incidents that were not identified in risk assessment.
- Percent of enterprise risk assessments including IT-related risk.
- Number of security incidents causing financial loss, business disruption or public embarrassment due to cloud incidents.
- Number of IT services with outstanding security requirements.
- Time to grant, change and remove access privileges, compared to SLA.
- Frequency of security assessment against latest standards and guidelines.
- Number of incidents related to non-compliance to policy.
- Percent of stakeholders who understand policies.
- Percent of policies supported by effective standards and working practices.
- Frequency of policies review and update.

We are going to develop these legal and public policies risks and challenges for cloud solutions taking inspiration several sources in next section.

LEGAL AND PUBLIC POLICY ASPECTS OF CLOUD COMPUTING (*WHICH*)

We know now that cloud computing is not a (new) technology, but relates to a different method of IT delivery as an on-demand and automated-scalable service over the Internet, based on supply chain automation in data centers—evolutionary caused by virtualization, Web-based data processing and the generic and accessible availability of broadband Internet. Cloud computing also holds the promise of scalable and secure services for greater efficiency and flexibility, at lower cost.. Cloud computing is a key and unavoidable IT delivery model. Public sector organizations, enterprises, and even small and medium-size companies cannot avoid using cloud services. The procurement process starts with making cloud policies. In this respect, the law plays a double role. It functions as a legal framework created and compiled by diverse mandatory laws and regulations, and as a contractual instrument to manage this new style technology and information provisioning in an effective and sustainable way, based on the strategic goals of the individual organization.

Some of the key assurance issues that will need to be addressed are: transparency, privacy, compliance, trans-border information flow, certification among others.

Major legal Reference Points

That cloud computing is both technologically and commercially something fundamentally different, does not mean in advance that the legal aspects differ. However, let us first take the definition of NIST into account (see Figure 3).

In first instance, two factual aspects have a deviant legal impact. Cloud computing experiences difficulties with existing legal rules, which are a) not only by tradition defined geographi-

cally, but also b) established during a time-period when corporate and government information had a static character. We could literally pinpoint where the data was located. Cross-border data processing and international data flows where often an exception, at least for public sector organizations and the average company as well.

Also enclosed in the cloud delivery model are all kinds of technical, organizational, and societal aspects, together with the consequence that horizontal (applicable to all organizations), vertical (additional for regulated industries), and specific IT-related legal rules apply to cloud computing. That leads to legal concurrence. Furthermore, we note various developments, such as new insights, best practices, and initiatives for the certification of cloud services. Next to those, new privacy regulation for personal data is on its way for the 27 European Union member states, which strengthens and harmonizes the existing 1995 legislation in this domain ("E.C. Justice", 2012).

Yet we must not make the legal aspects of cloud computing more difficult than what they are, and always evaluate the characteristics of a cloud service in a particular case. A number of marks provide guidance and direction for legal analysis, policy development, and drafting agreements.

Take for example the case that a governmental department or municipality wants to open its data for reasons of transparency or re-use by entrepreneurs. Because of its practical characteristics, a public cloud service comes into view immediately: Web-based with flexible scalability, open, and for anyone remotely accessible via Internet. All self-provision. Concerns about information security

Figure 3. Cloud computing according to NIST

5 characteristics	On-demand self-service, broad network access, resource pooling, rapid elasticity or expansion, and measured service.
4 deployment models	Private, community, public and hybrid.
3 service models	Software, platform and infrastructure.

and adverse effects of the reach of foreign jurisdictions no longer exist, because the processed information is not confidential and does not affect personal information.

Innovative Cloud Procurement Design

Another component of the cloud computing strategy for the European Union relates to the public sector as a customer of cloud products and services, offered by market players. The newly founded market place named European Cloud Partnership will function as a hinge between governmental organizations and the cloud industry. The partnership defragments the buying power through more harmonization and integration—even cross-border, thus allowing, for example, municipalities in Denmark and the Netherlands bundle their requests for proposal for a cloud service.

The EU has high expectations that 'the Cloud sector will listen and adapt, creating benefits for Cloud adoption throughout' the European economy through more standardized services, new and better offers, cheaper prices. In the words of Mrs. Neelie Kroes: '(…) it is a true win-win: the Cloud market will grow, bringing opportunities for existing suppliers and new entrants. And Cloud buyers, including the public sector, will buy more with less and become more efficient.' The partnership has a dual goal. To solve problems caused by fragmentation of markets and legislation in Europe for cloud computing, and to publish public sector requirements for clouds across Member States, regions or application areas (such as e-health, taxation, social benefit payments). In terms of benefits, the European Commission has the eye on a better quality of demand and supply, while active cloud service providers can address market with harmonized requirements with an assured user community. Three phases are foreseen.

1. Requirements. In the first phase, the partnership will come up with common requirements for public procurement of cloud service, such as standards, information security, and competition (as opposite of lock-in circumstances).

2. Proof of concept solutions. In the second phase, the partnership will deliver proof of concept solutions for the common requirements.

3. Reference implementations. In the third phase, reference implementations will be built.

The Commission launched the innovative partnership with an initial investment of EURO 10 million. The first results are expected next year. Although the designing the European Cloud Partnership remains in full progress and many questions unanswered, we register signs that 'precommercial procurement' (PCP) will be used as a policy instrument for cloud products and services (CORDIS 2013).

Open Public Sector Information is the Rule

Additional (information society) policies touch government clouds. We note that an increasing number of countries—finally—arrive at more transparency and greater freedom of information. The first freedom of information law (FOIA 1967) dates from almost four decades ago. Over the last ten years this policy trend evolved from merely a passive, statutory access right for citizens to limited government information, to a concept called 'Open Government.' This includes open 'government data' (US) or open 'public sector information' (PSI—EU). At the center, we find the general principle that all public sector information should be made available in an active way, unless severe (legal) grounds prohibit this. A very recent example originates in South America. Brazil introduced in May both a freedom of information law (AIP 2011) and a new open data portal.

The Digital Britain Report (DBR 2009) describes data as 'an innovation currency' and 'the lifeblood of the knowledge economy.' Based on its re-use rights, governments consider open data of the public sector as a valuable resource for innovation for businesses because the provision lowers the investment threshold for new products and services.

Transparency and Fair Competition

One step back. The EU adopted in 2003 the Directive (EURLex 2003) on the re-use of public sector information (2003/98/EC), which introduced a common legislative framework regulating how public sector bodies should make their information available for re-use in order to remove barriers such as discriminatory practices, monopoly markets and a lack of transparency. The PSI Directive is built around two key pillars of the internal market: transparency and fair competition, and focuses on the economic aspects of information rather than the access of citizens to information. Encouragement of public sector organization is often the policy measure used to date.

Now we see the advent of a mandatory approach. At the end of 2011, the European Commission presented its comprehensive threefold Open Data Package that includes

1. A communication on open data.
2. A proposal for a reform of the PSI Directive.
3. New rules of the European Commission on re-use of its own information.

Around this present time, EU Commissioner Kroes expects to have a portal operational that provides free access to all the Commission's own data sources. In addition, a broader, pan-European portal is planned in 2013 through which eventually all re-usable information from public organizations in the EU Member States will made available. The EU data portal will federate existing national and regional data portals, and develop such data capabilities where they do not currently exist across the union.

Open Data Licenses

The legal circumstances that government data and data sets are 'free re-useable'—probably often against the payment of a small fee—does not mean in principle that this public sector information is without intellectual property, including copyright or (in Europe) database rights. Vice versa, open data or open content licenses do not claim rights that are not there. If intellectual property rights are applicable, the licensor simply renounces is rights. When public sector organizations open their data, the question remains: under what legal regime? Administrative law and/or contract law may be applicable.

The government of a continental European country may consider open data licenses not as general terms and conditions under their Civil Law Code (De Pous 2011). Also relevant is the comparison with open source software licenses.

Legal Pointers for Cloud Computing

We know that the cloud delivery model encloses various kinds of technical, organizational, and societal aspects, together with the consequence that horizontal (applicable to all organizations), vertical (additional for regulated industries and the public sector), and specific IT-related legal rules may apply to cloud computing. One and the other lead to 'legal concurrence.' Concurrence relates to a legal problem where the question arises of which legal domain takes precedence or is the best choice between the applicable rules or rule systems. For instance a legal case involving competition law, intellectual property, and contract law. Alternatively, privacy rights and freedom of expression. Et cetera. Add to that the developments in full speed, such as new insights, best practices, and initiatives for the certification of cloud services and model agreements; in particular for the public sector.

The European Commission placed its 'cloud-friendly' legal framework high on the legislative agenda. This means new privacy regulations for personal data processed in the Cloud and data content regulation measures, primarily based on but not limited to copyright law. Moreover, we expect for reasons of legal certainty an uniformed clarification of the application of the liability exemption of the ecommerce Directive (2000/31/EC) for intermediaries that only host, cache or transmit information provided by a third party (EURLex 2000). The named liability exemption—just as the current Data Protection Directive—is enacted differently in the 27 Member States and created divergent case law.

Example

The non-exhaustive legal issues listed above each are relevant and, additionally, partly in reform or otherwise under development. Yet one must not make Cloud Computing Law more difficult than what it is, and always identify and evaluate the characteristics, deployment and service model, and other factual aspects of a particular cloud service first. Consequently, guidance and direction for legal analysis and public policy development emerge.

Look at the situation when a governmental agency or municipality is obliged by law to open public sector information for reasons of transparency or re-use by entrepreneurs. Concerns about information security, data breaches, and possible effects of foreign government access to 'national' data no longer exist—the processed information is non-confidential and does not included personal data within the meaning of the law. Because of its practical characteristics, a third-party public cloud,

SaaS comes into view: Web-based with flexible scalability and for anyone remotely accessible over the Internet. All self-provision.

When working on legal cloud computing policies in general (not only for public sector organizations), the following six point may offer a solid starting point.

Reference Point #1 Self-Provisioning or Outsourcing?

A central legal theme for cloud computing relates to the question whether or not an outsourcing relationship exists. When any organization outsources an IT service to an external cloud service provider, it loses in principle control over the electronic data processing process, unless other contractual arrangements are made. Further, there is a strong situation of dependency towards both supplier and the used technology, partly because in particular software and information are in the hands of this supplier and sub its suppliers.

Outsourcing means at least a shift in technical responsibilities from, in this case, a public sector organization to a cloud service provider, while the public sector organization still keeps its own legal responsibilities (accountabilities).

Reference Point #2 Product or Service?

Factual aspects of the cloud delivery model often have legal implications indeed. Cloud computing is not a product but a service and the law makes a distinction between them in many places, for instance in contract law. More in particular we note that when software is delivered as a service (SaaS), the end-user usually receives no physical copy of the program he uses remotely. Consequently, the licensee loses his statutory right to error correction that only is available to the 'lawful acquirer of a copy of' the program as codified in Dutch copyright law (IVIR 2013).

Furthermore, cloud computing has effects on software licensing. We note that, due to virtualization, the one-to-one relationship with hardware and operating system no longer exists. A license agreement must allow virtualization. The same applies in respect to running third-party computer programs. As cloud service providers deliver or even bundle third-party software as a service to their customers, the software license agreement must grant this right to the cloud service provider in the first place.

Reference Point #3 Technology or Information?

Digital technology concerns the notorious bits and bytes, and brings us eventually back to the ones and zeros. There is, however, an important distinction. What do they form: a computer program or data? The answer plays a central role seen from the technological viewpoint and as well as the legal (statutory) framework. Both sharply divide between software code and electronic information. Providers and customers of cloud services have to deal with this boundary.

Within the European Union for example, strong codified protection rights for software code exist and they knowingly benefit the owner of the program (EURLex 2009). Basic right exceptions for software users (licensees) are in place but cloud customers should be aware that the above mentioned 'immaterial' provisioning character of a computer program by way of SaaS (no physical copy of the software) may limit them. Anyhow, an entirely different and varied body of law governs information (in electronic format) its transfer, and more.

Reference Point #4 Type of Data?

Another relevant pointer for determining the legal framework and analyzing rights and obligations in regards to a cloud service may be found in the major distinction between personal data—of citizens, consumers, patients, employees—and other information held and processed by organizations. The nature of the data determines the applicable legal framework, which in turn may influence the choice of a particular IT delivery model. For a start and explained above, migration of open government data to a (private, public, and/or hybrid) outsourced cloud environment, will highly unlikely encounter legal problems.

Reference Point #5 Cross-Border Data Processing?

Fundamentally, current laws and regulations govern international data transfers, leaving no room for discussion based on the presumption of a legal full vacuum. But legal uncertainties may occur. One can say that the cross-border aspect of data processing matters. Not only based on all kinds of administrative burdens for cloud service providers, but also because it raises questions in connection with applicable laws and competent courts. And dealing with multiple jurisdictions is never considered an easy task. National laws may limit public sector data processing and personal data processing geographically. When governments choose for encrypting the Cloud processed data, restrictions based on data protection and privacy laws will probably reduce significantly.

Reference Point #6 Foreign Governments Access?

Foreign government access to data processed in the Cloud is a much-debated topic. But at the same time, it reflects most likely the global status quo of the law. Many countries vest namely authority in their governments to require customer data of cloud service providers, even when stored outside its national borders. A new comparative analysis of ten international jurisdictions reveals that access of cloud data by governments is a fait accompli (Maxwell 2012). Therefore, this doctrine should be addressed in the right perspective.

Also public sector organizations should take many foreign jurisdictions into account—not just the United States with its often referred to Patriot Act—and include Mutual Legal Assistance Treaties. Therefore, 'safe jurisdictions' are probably non-existing, although some countries consider the introduction of a national brand as a unique selling point for their home cloud industry (e.g. 'Cloud Computing Made in Germany'). The European Union will harmonize its privacy and data protection laws in a mandatory uniform way – leaving no room for national deviation of a single Member State. 'Cloud Computing Made in Europe' cloud be an option. Anyone who wants to prevent access to his corporate data by a foreign country would primarily be well advised not using IT outsourcing and secondary be willing to risk imprisonment, when not complying with an information access request based on a formal and lawfully legal demand or otherwise, through its own government.

But is outsourcing of IT functions—such as Web-based e-mail or using (third-party) social media like LinkedIn, Facebook and Twitter and the countless apps for tablets and smart phones—really avoidably in the line of today's duties?

Fifteen Analyses

1. There is not just one cloud. Cloud computing has various appearances, each with—completely or partly—unique marks and corresponding legal aspects, advantages and disadvantages. This diversity requires insight and nuance. It remains at the same time, however, that both the generic pro and con debates as the discussions in a specific case be conducted on rational grounds. Only than pragmatic public policy and individual decision making come within reach.

2. Doing nothing is explicitly no option at all. Even a public sector organization focusing exclusively on cost reduction or Green IT, cannot avoid cloud computing. (The same is valid when civil servants use their own devices and apps for work.) Politics and public administrations, however, must above doubt look further. This departure point translates technologically—in line, for example, with the prevailing vision of the Dutch Court of Audit—that 'strategic government goals should determine the use of ICT.' The audit in question was directed towards open source software. 'Deciding which software to use solely on the basis of cost savings is too restrictive an approach.' (COURT 2011)

3. Digital technology plays a key role in numerous transformations. Thanks to cloud computing organizational (new ways of living our lives, perform work, do business, and administer public tasks and services) and societal changes (towards a 'better' society) occur, and often fast. While cloud computing is the result of a logical and evolutionary development, its effects may be revolutionary, including, for example, in relation to wearable technology and smart cities.

4. Although a full transition to cloud services is possible, the IT practice in government organizations will almost certainly show a mixed delivery environment. The need to process State Secrets per se in the Cloud is missing. This means IT on-premise and in the Cloud; delivered by the internal IT department and by cloud service providers; using private and public clouds (and hybrid forms). But we see also possibilities for entirely new, innovative public/private partnerships, where IT sourcing moves towards or is transformed in business process outsourcing.

5. In still rare occasions, national governments act themselves as a cloud service provider to public sector organizations of other countries. Governments, however, should not enter the commercial marketplace and compete with IT vendors.

6. The current government data policy in many single countries states that every public sector organization must offer the widest possible access to public sector information for its citizens and businesses and make that data and data sets actively available for re-use. This so-called 'open data, unless' policy rule creates a substantial boost for outsourced public sector clouds.

7. In particular, cloud services as a means of outsourcing raise high expectations. In the words of the European Commission: scalable and secure services for greater efficiency and flexibility, lower costs without large investments. Moreover, we see the advantage of economies of scale and the economy of skills. From a legal viewpoint, software as a service (SaaS) means, among others, the end of software piracy at the end-user side.

8. The benefits of a public sector cloud customer do not remove concerns about information security and legal uncertainties. Nevertheless, there are various means available—such as data classification, standardizing and certification, open data formats, the legal framework and specific statutory rights (e.g. for software interoperability), security arrangements, negotiating cloud agreements—that strengthen the legal position of cloud customers and make risks manageable.

9. Technology standards often intensify the policy debate. The starting point is that the numerous existing IT standards find their way in the cloud environment as we speak. Both the U.S. federal government (OMB 1998) and the European Commission (ISA 2010) pursue a pragmatic policy based on RAND—reasonable and non-discriminatory terms.

10. Although there is little doubt that open technology standards are also important in respect of cloud computing, seen from the public sector organizations' need—for continuity of business processes, digital sustainability for archiving and retrieving purposes, and regulatory compliance—open data formats are key.

11. Not every public sector organization and cloud service provider is aware of the statutory right to interoperability under European Union Law (Software Directive 2009/24/EC). Each licensee of a computer program has the right to decompile the code for unlocking hidden specifications of the program's interfaces, in order to make a connection with other software.

12. Information security is a major concern. So far, however, there is no real technical vacuum or absence of standards as such, because existing standards remain in force at the deployment of cloud computing. ISO/IEC 27000 is a good example (ISO/IEC 2005).

13. The supervising regulatory framework that many countries have in place for the financial sector, might offer excellent (pre)conditions for the procurement of cloud services by a public sector organization. The bottom-line reads that outsourcing may not cause prejudice to supervision.

14. 'Bring Your Own Device' (BYOD)—the circumstances that directors and employees (of a public sector organization) use their own laptop, tablet and smart phone for work—raises perhaps an odd question about computer hardware, such as counterfeit chips. The foremost concerns focus on the legal issues around software, apps, and government data *in the Cloud*. Deployment of BYOD unavoidable leads to 'use your own app' (for example chat programs and Facebook for communication purposes) and 'use your own storage' such as Dropbox, iCloud of Skydrive for personal external data storage.

15. Since many countries vest authority in their governments to require cloud service providers customer data—also when stored outside its borders—foreign government access to cloud data reflects the global status quo of the law. It would be rather unfortunate for the advancement of a country when its public sector uses this acknowledgement as an unnecessary red flag for outsourced public sector clouds.

FUTURE RESEARCH DIRECTIONS

Most of the open problems for research are how to make a minimal regulation of cloud computing services and solutions for private and public enterprises. In the last case, how public investment coming from taxes there are harder requirements from public stakeholders for increasing savings using IT. Thus, cloud solutions seem to produce these savings but the problems we arise on this chapter should be considered for future research directions in IT Governance frameworks and legal issues for cloud computing.

CONCLUSION

The use of governance and legal frameworks will help businesses gain assurance around their cloud computing supplier's controls (ISO/IEC, 2008). From our knowledge, there are no publicly available governance and legal standards specific to the cloud computing paradigm, even there are new efforts in management concerns. However, existing governance standards should be consulted to address the legal and policy should look to adjust their existing frameworks. Cloud computing represents a technical opportunity to for a better business. Many businesses will no doubt grab this opportunity to improve both governance and legal issues and not only their IT portfolio (Juiz, 2012). After roughly sixty years of deploy-

ment of commercial electronic data processing, modern information society develops today with unprecedented pace. Without IT, society comes to a standstill. Without cloud computing, we no longer advance. Citizens, with their state-of-the-art devices such as smarts phones and tablets, already embraced the new delivery model with great enthusiasm.

In this chapter we tried to clear where IT governance frameworks should consider the decisions about specific cloud computing performance and compliance, how to measure them through several indicators and moreover which are their general legal and public policy aspects to consider. In order to locate the three main questions we have used an IT governance framework constructor called dFogIT® from the University of the Balearic Islands, as an extension of the ISO/IEC 38500 standard. Public sector organizations simply cannot afford to pass up on the next logical step in information technology and therefore must become truly 'cloud-active.' In the words of EU Commissioner Neelie Kroes: 'at a time when we need growth, we need jobs, and we need more efficient public services, the Cloud is something we should be getting excited about.' This calls for new pragmatic policies in which strategic objectives should lead the way. Of exceptional importance for the progress of our society remains that we debate on rational grounds and weigh cloud characteristics and models carefully on their merits. The law fulfills in this respect a crucial double role: it functions as a borderline for cloud computing set by mandatory laws and regulations; and the law functions as an instrument to manage the 'new style' technology and information provisioning in an effective and sustainable way.

REFERENCES

AIP. (2011). Retrieved July 4, 2013 from http://www.cgu.gov.br/acessoainformacao/acesso-informacao-brasil/index.asp

AIVD. (2013). Retrieved July 4, 2013 from https://www.aivd.nl/english/publications-press/@1587/three-publications/

CIO. (2009). Retrieved July 4, 2013 from http://www.cio.com.au/article/296892/nick_carr_ways_cloud_computing_will_disrupt_it/

CloudGov. (2012). Retrieved from http://www.siia.net

CNET. (2009). Retrieved July 4, 2013 from http://news.cnet.com/8301-13772_3-10353479-52.html

Computerwold. (2009). Retrieved July 4, 2013 from http://www.computerworld.com/s/article/9131998/Cloud_computing_a_security_nightmare_says_Cisco_CEO

CORDIS. (2013). Retrieved July 6, 2013 from http://cordis.europa.eu/fp7/ict/pcp/home_en.html

COURT. (2011). Retrieved July 6, 2013 from http://www.courtofaudit.nl/english/Publications/Audits/Introductions/2011/03/Open_standards_and_open_source_software_in_central_government

DBR. (2009). Retrieved July 6, 2013 from http://www.official-documents.gov.uk/document/cm76/7650/7650.pdf

De Pous, V. (2011). *Open source computing and public sector policy*. Retrieved July 6, 2013 from http://www.depous.nl/DEPOUS-OPEN-SOURCE-COMPUTING-AND-PUBLIC-SECTOR-POLICY.pdf

De Pous, V. (2012). *Cloud computing en het nieuwe Amerikaanse overheidsbeleid (executive update)*. Retrieved July 4, 2013 from http://www.forumstandaardisatie.nl/english/

Domino. (2012). Retrieved July 4, 2013, from http://www.itworld.com/cloud-computing/251214/dominos-pizza-finishes-last-piece-cloud-computing-move

DT Knowledge. (2012). Retrieved July 4, 2013, from http://www.datacenterknowledge.com/archives/2012/01/04/feds-now-plan-to-close-1200-data-centers/

ENISA. (2011). Retrieved July 4, 2013, from http://www.enisa.europa.eu/activities/risk-management/emerging-and-future-risk/deliverables/security-and-resilience-in-governmental-clouds

EU. (2012). *European commission, justice*. Retrieved October 30, 2012, from http://ec.europa.eu/justice/newsroom/data-protection/news/120125_en.htm

EU Justice. (2012). Retrieved July 4, 2013, from http://ec.europa.eu/justice/newsroom/data-protection/news/120125_en.htm

EURLex. (1995). Retrieved October 30, 2012, from http://eur-lex.europa.eu/LexUriServ/LexUriServ.do?uri=CELEX:31995L0046:en:HTML

EURLex. (2000). Retrieved October 30, 2012, from http://eur-lex.europa.eu/LexUriServ/LexUriServ.do?uri=CELEX:32000L0031:En:HTML

EURLex. (2003). Retrieved October 30, 2012, from http://eur-lex.europa.eu/LexUriServ/LexUriServ.do?uri=CELEX:32003L0098:EN:NOT

EURLex. (2009). Retrieved October 30, 2012, from http://eur-lex.europa.eu/LexUriServ/LexUriServ.do?uri=OJ:L:2009:111:0016:01:EN:HTML

FedRAMP. (2013). Retrieved July 4, 2013, from http://www.gsa.gov/portal/category/102371

FOIA. (1967). Retrieved July 4, 2013, from http://en.wikipedia.org/wiki/Freedom_of_Information_Act_(United_States)

GSA. (2013). Retrieved October 30, 2012, from http://www.gsa.gov/portal/category/102371

Hunter, R., & Westerman, G. (2009). *The real business of IT: How CIOs create and communicate value*. Boston: Harvard Business School Press.

ISA. (2010). Retrieved July 4, 2013, from http://ec.europa.eu/isa/documents/isa_annex_ii_eif_en.pdf

ISACA. (2012a). *Calculating cloud ROI: From the customer perspective*. Cloud Computing Vision Series, White Paper. ISACA.

ISACA. (2012b). *Guiding principles for cloud computing adoption and use*. Cloud Computing Vision Series, White Paper. ISACA.

ISACA. (2012c). *COBIT 5: Enabling processes*. ISACA.

ISACA. (2012d). *COBIT 5: A business framework for the governance and management of enterprise IT*. ISACA.

ISO/IEC. (2005). *ISO/IEC 27000, information technology -- Security techniques -- Information security management systems -- Overview and vocabulary*. Retrieved October 30, 2012, from http://www.iso.org/iso/catalogue_detail?csnumber=56891 ISO/IEC. (2008). *ISO/IEC 38500: IT governance standard*. Retrieved October 30, 2012, from http://www.38500.org

IT Knowledge Exchange. (2011). Retrieved October 30, 2012, from http://itknowledgeexchange.techtarget.com/cloud-computing/ex-fed-cio-vivek-kundra%E2%80%99s-cloud-first-policy-trashed/

IVIR. (2013). Retrieved October 30, 2012, from http://www.ivir.nl/legislation/nl/copyrightact.html

Juiz, C. (2011). New engagement model of IT governance and IT management for the communication of the IT value at enterprises. []. Berlin: Springer.]. *Proceedings of Digital Enterprise and Information Systems*, *194*, 129–194. doi:10.1007/978-3-642-22603-8_13.

Juiz, C., Gómez, M., & Barceló, M. I. (2012). Business/IT projects alignment through the project portfolio approval process as IT governance instrument. In *Proceedings of ICIBSoS 2012*, (vol. 65, pp. 70-75). Amsterdam: Springer.

Kroes. (2011). Retrieved October 30, 2012, from http://europa.eu/rapid/pressReleasesAction.do?reference=SPEECH/11/50&format=HTML&aged=0&language=EN&guiLanguage=en

Kroes. (2012). Retrieved October 30, 2012, from http://europa.eu/rapid/pressReleasesAction.do?reference=SPEECH/12/490&format=HTML&aged=0&language=EN&guiLanguage=en

Maxwell, W., et al. (2012). *A global reality: Government access to data in the cloud*. A Hogan Lovells White Paper, 23 May 2012. Retrieved October 30, 2012, from http://computer3.org/a/a-global-reality-governmental-access-to-data-in-the-cloud-e157-book.pdf.html

Mell, P., & Grance, T. (2011). *The NIST definition of cloud computing: Recommendations of the national institute of standards and technology*. Retrieved October 30, 2012, from http://csrc.nist.gov/publications/nistpubs/800-145/SP800-145.pdf

Mobile Applications. (2013). *Final version definition published*. Retrieved July 4, 2013 from http://en.wikipedia.org/wiki/Mobile_apps

NIST. (2011). *Final version of NIST cloud computing definition published*. Retrieved July 4, 2013, from http://www.nist.gov/itl/csd/cloud-102511.cfm

OMB. (1998). Retrieved July 4, 2013, from http://www.whitehouse.gov/omb/circulars_a119/

Sabre Computer System. (2012). *Final version definition published*. Retrieved July 4, 2013, from http://en.wikipedia.org/wiki/Sabre_(computer_system)

Thorp, J. (2005). *Rethinking IT governance - Beyond alignment to integration.* The Thorp Network.

Toomey, M. (2009). *Waltzing with the elephant: A comprehensive guide to directing and controlling information technology.* Infonomics Pty Ltd..

UIB. (2013). Retrieved February 28, 2013, from http://governti.uib.es

Van Roekel. (2011). Retrieved July 4, 2013, from http://www.whitehouse.gov/sites/default/files/svr_parc_speech_final_0.pdf

Weill, P., & Ross, J. W. (2004). *IT governance: How top performers manage IT decision rights for superior results.* Boston: Harvard Business School Press.

World e.gov. (2011). Retrieved July 4, 2013, from http://wegf.org/en/2011/02/uk-universities-to-adopt-cloud-shared-services/

KEY TERMS AND DEFINITIONS

Cloud Computing: Model for enabling ubiquitous, convenient, on-demand network access to a shared pool of configurable computing resources (e.g., networks, servers, storage, applications, and services) that can be rapidly provisioned and released with minimal management effort or service provider interaction (NIST).

Governance Framework: A framework is a basic conceptual structure used to solve or address complex issues; an enabler of governance; a set of concepts, assumptions and practices that define how something can be approached or understood, the relationships amongst the entities involved, the roles of those involved, and the boundaries (what is and is not included in the governance system) (COBIT 5).

Governance: The action or manner of directing and controlling (ISO/IEC 38500). Governance ensures that stakeholder needs, conditions and options are evaluated to determine balanced, agreed-on enterprise objectives to be achieved; setting direction through prioritization and decision making; and monitoring performance and compliance against agreed-on direction and objectives (COBIT 5).

Information Technology (IT): Resources required to acquire, process, store, and disseminate information (ISO/IEC 38500).

IT Governance: The system through which the current and future use of IT is directed and controlled (ISO/IEC 38500). A governance view that ensures that information and related technology support and enable the enterprise strategy and the achievement of enterprise objectives. It also includes the functional governance of IT, i.e., ensuring that IT capabilities are provided efficiently and effectively (COBIT 5).

IT Service: The day-to-day provision to customers of IT infrastructure and applications and support for their use. Examples include service desk, equipment supply and moves, and security authorisations (COBIT 5).

Legal Compliance: Conforming to laws, regulations, standards, and other requirements, including internal business rules and for example licensing agreements.

Policy: Clear and measurable statements of preferred direction and behavior to condition the decisions made within an organization (ISO/IEC 38500).

Public Policy: Overall intention and direction as formally expressed by public governance.

Stakeholders: Those people or entities who may affect, be affected by, or perceive themselves to be affected by, a decision or activity

ENDNOTES

[1] 'The definition is intended to serve as a means for broad comparisons of cloud services and deployment strategies, and to provide a baseline for discussion from what is cloud computing to how to best use cloud computing.'

2   In a three-month time period Apple signed on one million users for its cloud storage service iCloud.

3   Especially Western Europe has to deal with a structural shortage of software developers, system and network managers and more.

4   A 1970s motto of the Information Industry Association (of the US) was 'Putting Information at Your Fingertips.' However, it became famous through Bill Gates in 1995. 'At the center of this will be the idea of digital convergence. That is, taking all the information – books, catalogs, shopping approaches, professional advice, art, movies – and taking those things in their digital form, ones and zeroes, and being able to provide them on demand on a device looking like a TV, a small device you carry around, or what the PC will evolve into.'

5   'A city can be defined as 'smart' when investments in human and social capital and traditional (transport) and modern (ICT) communication infrastructure fuel sustainable economic development and a high quality of life, with a wise management of natural resources, through participatory governance.'

6   *The Guardian*, 29 September 2008.

7   In US perspective for example the Federal Information Security Act (FISMA).

8   76 to 80 billion dollar per year for more than 10.000 information systems, including 19 billion dollar on IT infrastructure.

9   The Commission's proposals are passed on to the European Parliament and EU Member States (meeting in the Council of Ministers) for discussion. They will take effect two years after they have been adopted.

Chapter 10
Information Security and Information Assurance:
Discussion about the Meaning, Scope, and Goals

Yulia Cherdantseva
Cardiff University, UK

Jeremy Hilton
Cranfield University, UK

ABSTRACT

Despite great interest of researchers and professionals in Information Security (InfoSec) and Information Assurance (IA), there is still no commonly agreed understanding of the disciplines. This chapter clarifies the meaning, scope, and goals of InfoSec and IA as well as the relationship between the disciplines. Clarity of the scope and goals of InfoSec and IA is important because this knowledge serves as a foundation for the definition of (1) curricula for the InfoSec and IA education programs, (2) responsibilities of practitioners, and (3) organisations' InfoSec strategy and policies. The study analyses US and European InfoSec- and IA-related official publications and standards and discusses the perception of the disciplines in academic and industry works. The study highlights the importance of clear and precise definitions of InfoSec and IA and a need for the definitions to promote open-mindedness among practitioners and researchers. Since the existing definitions of InfoSec and IA do not fully reflect the complexity and the evolving nature of the disciplines, the contemporary adapted definitions of InfoSec and IA are elaborated in the chapter.

DOI: 10.4018/978-1-4666-4526-4.ch010

1. INTRODUCTION

The beginning of wisdom is the definition of terms. - Socrates

Information Security (InfoSec) and Information Assurance (IA) have become increasingly important in an era in which information is recognised as a key asset by many organisations. The rapid advancement of Information and Communication Technology (ICT), and the growing dependence of organisations on IT infrastructure continuously intensify the interest in these two disciplines. Organisations pay increasing attention to information protection also because the impact of security breaches today has a more tangible, often devastating effect on business (Dlamini et al., 2009).

The number and severity of security breaches grows. In 2007, the TJX Company lost, according to different sources, from 36.2 to 94 million customers' credit and debit cards records (Shaw, 2010). In 2011, Sony reported a data breach that had resulted in the loss of personal details of 77 million customers (Sony, 2011). According to the *Information Security Breaches Survey 2010* (PwC, 2010), the number of large companies in the UK that suffered a security incident during 2010 increased up to 92%, in comparison to 72% in 2008. The average cost of the worst security incident in large UK companies increased from £170,000 to £690,000. In the US, the number of security breaches detected by law enforcement increased up to 33% in 2011, against 7% in 2010 (Trustwave, 2012). The spending on InfoSec worldwide stayed stable in 2011 (ISC, 2011), even despite the economic downturn. In 2012, security budgets received higher priority worldwide compared with 2011 (Gartner, 2012). Gartner predicts a stable (at the annual rate of 9%) growth of security market until 2016. As a result, the spending on security is expected to grow from $55 billion in 2011 to $86 billion in 2016 (Gartner, 2012).

In response to the growing interest, a significant amount of research has been conducted over the past two decades to cover various perspectives of InfoSec and IA: the technical side (Anderson, 2001a); the human factor (Lacey, 2009); the business and economic perspectives (Pipkin, 2000; Anderson, 2001b; Sherwood et al., 2005); and the governance (SANS, 2004; FRC, 2004; Sherwood et al., 2005). Despite great interest in InfoSec and IA, there is still no commonly agreed understanding of the disciplines. Every author makes a unique interpretation of InfoSec and IA by identifying the divergent scopes and goals of the disciplines. The approaches to InfoSec and IA vary, depending on the background of the author and on the nature of the author's occupation. InfoSec and IA remain open to diverse interpretations, partly due to the fact that both disciplines are inevitably evolving. Many studies highlight the continual changes of InfoSec (Parker, 1998; Pipkin, 2000; Anderson, 2001a; Lacey, 2009; ISACA, 2009). Therefore, a revision of the meaning, scope and goals of the disciplines has to be conducted periodically to reflect this fluctuating environment.

The motivation of this study stems largely from the lack of a consistent, clear approach to InfoSec and IA, and, furthermore, from the existing misinterpretations of the terms. Despite the fact that both, InfoSec and IA, have been intensively discussed, there are still no commonly accepted definitions of the terms. The relationship between InfoSec and IA remain disputable. This study also originates from the necessity to resolve the controversy within InfoSec and IA concerning the overall goals and scope of the disciplines. This paper analyses different approaches to InfoSec and IA in order to draw a state-of-the-art picture of the disciplines in the permanently changing landscape.

The main objectives of this study are, first, to outline the up-to-date and precise realms of InfoSec and IA and, second, to develop a refined definition of each discipline in light of these findings. The paper aims to answer the following questions:

- What is Information Security: its meaning, scope and main goals?
- What is Information Assurance: its meaning, scope and main goals?
- What are the differences, similarities and relationship between the disciplines?

The clarity and unambiguity of the scope and goals of InfoSec and IA are important because this knowledge serves as a foundation for the definition of (1) curricula for the InfoSec and IA education programs, (2) responsibilities of practitioners, and (3) organisations' InfoSec strategy and policies. Hence, the discussion may also be seen as answering the question about what an InfoSec or IA expert should be taught and what s/he should be responsible for in an organisation.

The conventions used in the study are explained below. The members of the classic InfoSec triad -confidentiality, integrity and availability (also referred to as the CIA-triad) - are interchangeably referred to in the literature as security attributes, properties (CSIA, 2007; CNSS, 2010), goals (NIST, 2002), fundamental aspects (Pipkin, 2000), information criteria (ITGI, 2007), critical information characteristics (McCumber, 1991) and basic building blocks (Pipkin, 2000). In order to highlight the fact that these are the *desirable* properties of information (or *desirable* abilities of information systems, where appropriate), in this paper the term *security goal* will be applied to refer to confidentiality, integrity, availability, non-repudiation, accountability, privacy and the like. In this study we will also distinguish between a security goal and a *security mechanism*, which is defined as an established process by which certain security goals are achieved. This work does not aim to provide a detailed analysis of security goals. Security goals are discussed to the extent required to answer the research questions.

The rest of the paper is structured as follows. Sections 2 and 3 provide a detailed overview of InfoSec and IA respectively. In order to draw a clear image of the present state of the disciplines, for each discipline (1) a general perception of the term is discussed, (2) the interpretations of the term in the official standards and publications are analysed, and (3) the understanding of the term in related academic and industry publications is overviewed. Section 4 outlines the comparison of InfoSec and IA and formalises the relationship between the disciplines. In Section 5, we present the adapted definitions of InfoSec and IA. Section 6 draws some conclusions and illustrates the benefits of the study.

2. INFORMATION SECURITY

This section contains a detailed analysis of the term InfoSec. First, an analysis of the term based on common English is conducted. Second, the definitions of the term as suggested in the official standards are discussed. Third, the understanding of InfoSec in academic and industry publications is researched, and the latest trends in InfoSec are distilled. Finally, an adapted contemporary definition of InfoSec is presented and discussed.

2.1 The Definition of Information Security Based on Common English

Formal or academic definitions are often distinct from the common comprehension of terms (Neumann, 1995; Parker, 1998). In order to understand the common perception of the term InfoSec we start from the definitions of isolated words "information" and "security" in the Collins English Dictionary (2012) (the definitions are abridged):

- Information n.
  - Knowledge acquired through experience or study.
  - Computing

- ▪ The meaning given to data by the way in which it is interpreted.
- ▪ Another word for data.
- • Security n.
  - ◦ The state of being secure.
  - ◦ Precautions taken to ensure against theft, espionage, etc.

Secure is defined as "free from danger, damage, etc; not likely to fail; able to be relied on" (Collins English Dictionary, 2012). Precaution is defined as "an action taken in advance to prevent an undesirable event" (Collins English Dictionary, 2012). The Oxford English Dictionary (2012), in turn, defines security as "the state of being free from danger or threat". Based on the above, a general definition of InfoSec could be derived:

Information Security is a discipline, the main aim of which is to keep the knowledge, data and its meaning free from undesirable events, such as theft, espionage, damage, threat and other danger. Information Security includes all actions, taken in advance, to prevent undesirable events happening to the knowledge, data and its meaning so that the knowledge, data and its meaning could be relied on.

In the general definition of InfoSec five points should be highlighted. First, there are no restrictions on the information type. In the broad sense, InfoSec is concerned with information of any form or type (e.g. electronic, paper, verbal, visual). Second, InfoSec includes all actions to protect information. Thus, InfoSec is concerned not only with technical actions, but deals with the full diversity of protecting actions required during information processing, storage or transmission. Third, the list of undesirable events is broad and open. The definition explicitly lists theft, espionage and damage of the information, but is not restricted to them. Thus, InfoSec deals with the protection of information from *all* undesirable events. Fourth, the general definition of InfoSec does not state any

security goals such as confidentiality, integrity, availability or any other. Therefore, in line with the third point, the main aim of the discipline is the overall protection of information, and not just the achievement of several pre-defined security goals. Fifth, InfoSec includes actions taken in advance. Therefore, InfoSec should be concerned not only with an analysis of undesirable events, which have already taken place, but also with the anticipation of such events and an assessment of the their likelihood.

2.2. Information Security as Defined in the Official Documents

There is a plethora of standards covering the various aspects of InfoSec published by international organisations (ISO, IEC, ITU), national standards bodies (BSI, NIST, SAA, SNZ, JISC), non-profit organisations (ISACA, ANSI, IEEE, OMG, OASIS, ETSI) and international communities (IETF, W3C, EEMA, Wi-Fi Alliance, ISF).

In this section the definitions of InfoSec provided in the vocabulary of the ISO/IEC 27000 series (ISO27000, 2009) and in the National Information Assurance Glossary (CNSS, 2010) are analysed, and compared to the definition suggested by ISACA (ISACA, 2008).

The ISO/IEC 27000 series of standards is an internationally recognised and widely adopted InfoSec standard. The series was developed by a joint committee of the International Organisation for Standardisation (ISO) and the International Electronic Commissions (IEC) and covers InfoSec management, InfoSec risk management, implementation of InfoSec Management Systems (ISMS), measurements and metrics of ISMS. In 2000, the ISO adopted BS7799, the standards published by the British Standard Institute in 1995, under the name ISO/IEC 17799. BS7799 was based on the Code of Practice for Information Security Management, which was developed by the Department of Trade and Industry in close rapport with leading UK organisations.

In 2007, ISO/IEC 17799 was incorporated in the ISO/IEC 27000 series as ISO/IEC 27002.

The National Information Assurance Glossary, published by the Committee on National Security Systems (CNSS), is also known as the CNSS Instruction 4009 (CNSSI) (CNSS, 2010). The glossary was created to resolve the differences between the definitions of terms used by the U.S. Department of Defense (DoD), Intelligence Community and National Institute of Standards and Technology Glossary (NIST). NIST develops U.S. Federal Information Processing Standards publications (FIPS PUB). The standards are primarily oriented on the government systems, but are also useful for industry.

ISACA is a non-profit, global association of over 95,000 members worldwide. It develops practices for information systems. ISACA is an originator of the globally accepted Control Objectives for Information and related Technology (COBIT) framework.

The definitions of InfoSec suggested in the three documents mentioned above are summarised in Table 1, along with the definitions of integrity, which are discussed later in this section.

The official definitions of InfoSec presented in Table 1 differ from the general definition (Section 2.1) and are inconsistent with each other. For example, the CNSSI definition includes in the scope of InfoSec protection of information systems, as well as information. An information system according to the CNSSI is defined as "a discrete set of information resources organized for the collection, processing, maintenance, use, sharing, dissemination, or disposition of information". Thus, information resources are in the scope of InfoSec according to the CNSSI definition, but this is explicitly captured neither in the general definition of InfoSec, nor in the definition suggested by the ISO/IEC.

Both the CNSSI and ISO/IEC 27000 define InfoSec based on a set of security goals to be achieved. Thus, the essential discrepancy between the general comprehension of InfoSec and the definitions provided in the standards is that the general definition implies that information is secure if it is protected from all threats, whereas the standards imply that the information is secure if it complies with the certain security goals. This refers back to the fourth point stated in Section 2.1.

According to the definitions in Table 1, the scope of InfoSec defined by the ISO/IEC is wider than the scope defined by the CNSS. Apart from confidentiality, integrity and availability, the ISO/IEC also includes reliability, accountability, authenticity and non-repudiation in the realm of InfoSec, while the CNSS does not. For example, the breach of non-repudiation does not relate to

Table 1. Definitions of information security and integrity

Term Standard	Information Security	Integrity
ISO27000 (2009)	Preservation of confidentiality, integrity and availability of information. Note: In addition, other properties, such as authenticity, accountability, non-repudiation and reliability can also be involved.	The property of protecting the accuracy and completeness of assets.
CNSS (2010)	The protection of information and information systems from unauthorized access, use, disclosure, disruption, modification, or destruction in order to provide confidentiality, integrity, and availability.	The property whereby an entity has not been modified in an unauthorized manner.
ISACA (2008)	Ensures that only authorized users (confidentiality) have access to accurate and complete information (integrity) when required (availability).	The accuracy, completeness and validity of information.

any of the undesirable events stated in the CNSS definition. It is not mentioned in the CNSS definition of InfoSec as a security goal either.

Although the set of security goals associated with InfoSec in the CNSSI and ISO/IEC 27000 standards vary, they agree that the three fundamental goals of InfoSec are confidentiality, integrity and availability. ISACA clearly reflects this concept in its definition of InfoSec (Table 1). Consequently, the COBIT framework restricts the sphere of InfoSec to issues related to confidentiality, integrity and availability.

Since the standards correlate InfoSec with a certain set of security goals, then the origins of the goals and their interpretation becomes extremely important. The straightforward logical consequence of the steps to define an absolute list of security goals should be as follows: 1) identify all possible threats to information; 2) categorise the threats; 3) define a security goal for each category of threats. Due to the constant change in the environment, new threats constantly emerge and information received at the first step quickly becomes obsolete. Thus, security goals are only valid for the environment at a certain stage. This highlights the inadequacy of defining InfoSec purely through security goals, because any set of goals becomes incomplete in a transforming landscape and some threats stay out of the realm of InfoSec.

The definitions provided in the standards are used to define an organisation's InfoSec program, strategy and policies. The limitation of InfoSec in this context leads to undesirable consequences that stem from overlooking essential threats and critical vulnerabilities that stay below the radar of InfoSec (Parker, 1998).

Defining the scope of InfoSec through certain security goals gives rise to two problems. First problem is the differing interpretations of the goals. The ISO/IEC 27000 standard and CNSSI definitions of availability and confidentiality correspond with each other, but the approaches to integrity

in these two standards differ . The comparison of the definitions of integrity in Table 1 shows that the CNSS is concerned with the authenticity of data, while the ISO/IEC concentrates on the state of data, characterised by completeness and accuracy. Second problem: the CNSSI definition of InfoSec includes in its scope both information and information systems and, therefore, considering integrity in the definition of InfoSec, it is not clear whether it is integrity of information, or integrity of an information system, or both. If it is integrity of an information system, then to which part of the system it refers to: hardware, software, personnel or procedures.

In comparison to the general definition of InfoSec, the definitions suggested in the documents discussed narrow down the scope of the discipline because they define confidentiality, integrity and availability as the fundamental goals of InfoSec, rather than an overall protection of information. In the foreword to the first edition of Anderson's Security Engineering Schneier, wrote: "You have to consider all the ways your system can fail. You have to look at everything backwards, upside down, and sideways" (Anderson, 2001a, Foreword). It is obvious now that the ways a system can fail could not necessarily be characterised by a breach of confidentiality, integrity or availability. A definition of InfoSec which is restricted to a certain set of security goals prevents security specialists from having a necessarily broad view of InfoSec. Therefore, the focus on the achievement of several pre-defined security goals, rather than on the achievement of adequate security is a flawed and dangerous approach, since it may lead to an oversight of some threats.

In Section 2.3, we discuss how academics and practitioners overcome the narrowing down of InfoSec to the CIA-triad. An overview of the comprehension of InfoSec in the academic and industry publications of the last twenty years is presented, and the recent trends in the evolution of InfoSec are distilled.

2.3. The Perception of Information Security in Academic and Industry Publications

Significant research has been conducted over the last twenty years in order to establish the scope and to clarify the goals of InfoSec. Nevertheless, there is still no single commonly agreed definition of InfoSec. The challenge of defining the scope and goals of InfoSec stems, firstly, from the complexity of the discipline, secondly, from a variety of approaches to the discipline and, thirdly, from the evolving nature of the discipline.

Traditionally, InfoSec is defined via a set of security goals. Since the late 1970s, InfoSec has been rigorously associated with the CIA-triad (Whitman and Mattord, 2012). The major problem that arises from Defining InfoSec via security goals is that the definition becomes obsolete as soon as new threats, not addressed by any of the existing security goals, evolve.

In recent years, there is a pronounced tendency to extend the scope of InfoSec beyond the CIA-triad since the latter is found to be no longer adequate (Parker, 1998; Whitman and Mattord, 2012) for a complex interconnected environment. A plethora of security goals is considered to be relevant to InfoSec and intensively discussed in the literature. Table 2 lists security goals associated with the discipline in the security-related publications. The publications are listed on the vertical axis in the chronological order. The horizontal axis lists the security goals.

The analysis demonstrates the lack of an agreement about security goals and, consequently, about the scope of InfoSec. The variety of security goals discussed in the literature leaves the scope of InfoSec ambiguous. Moreover, the

Table 2. Analysis of the literature in terms of goals associated with information security

Reference	Confidentiality	Integrity	Availability	Accountability	Assurance	Authentication	Non-repudiation	Authenticity	Reliability	Effectiveness	Efficiency	Compliance	Utility	Possession/Control	Authorisation	Awareness	Access	Identification	Accuracy	Administration	Information Classification	Anonymity	Audit	Safety	Other (not specified)
(Clark and Wilson, 1987)	X	X	X																						
(NCSC, 1991)	X	X	X																						
(McCumber, 1991)	X	X	X																						
(Parker, 1998)	X	X	X					X					X	X											
(Pipkin, 2000)	X		X	X											X	X	X	X	X	X					
(Schneier, 2000)		X				X																X	X	X	
(NIST, 2002)	X	X	X	X	X																				
(Gordon and Loeb, 2002)	X	X	X			X	X																		
(Avizienis et al., 2004)	X	X	X						X															X	
(ISO13335, 2004)	X	X	X	X		X	X	X																	
(ITGI, 2007)	X	X	X						X	X	X	X													
(JF, 2007)	X	X	X	X		X									X				X						
(ISACA, 2008)	X	X	X																						
(ISO15408, 2009)	X	X	X																						
(ISO27000, 2009)	X	X	X	X		X	X	X																	
(CC, 2009)	X	X	X																						X
(CNSS, 2010)	X	X	X			X	X																		
(Tiller, 2010)	X	X	X																						
(Dubois et al., 2010)	X	X	X	X		X																			
(HMG, 2011)	X	X	X																						
(Whitman and Mattord, 2012)	X	X	X					X					X	X					X						

problem with varying definitions of the same security goals is also present in the academic publications, similar to the official documents, as discussed in Section 2.2.

The lack of clear InfoSec terminology gives rise to another problem: security goals are not clearly distinguished from security mechanisms. A clear distinction between a security goal and a security mechanism is required, as well as the association of a security mechanism with a certain security goal.

This may enable the easier choice of an appropriate mechanism to pursue a certain security goal. This calls for a comprehensive model of InfoSec that helps to resolve these issues.

Going deeper into the discussion of security goals associated with InfoSec, it is important to highlight a substantial contribution to the clarification of InfoSec done by Parker (1998). Parker criticises the InfoSec definitions of being limited to the CIA-triad and claims they are dangerously incorrect. Parker introduces a new model of InfoSec that consists of six foundation elements: confidentiality, integrity, availability, possession or control, authenticity and utility. (Later, Kabay suggested the term Parkerian Hexad for the model, as a sign of respect to Parker.)

Possession or control is defined by Parker as "the holding, control, and ability to use information". Consideration of possession as an additional security goal gains particular importance at the time of cloud computing. Utility is defined as "usefulness of information for purpose". The definition of authenticity suggested by Parker, is much wider than the definitions of the same term provided in CNSS (2010) and ISO27000 (2009). A comparison of the definitions is presented in Table 3.

The definitions in the ISO/IEC 27000 standards and CNSSI correlate authenticity with the ability to verify the identity of the author. According to Parker, authenticity reflects "the conformance to reality" and "extrinsic value or meaning of the

Table 3. Definitions of authenticity

Standard/ Term	Authenticity
ISO27000 (2009)	Property that an entity is what it claims to be.
CNSS (2010)	The property of being genuine and being able to be verified and trusted; confidence in the validity of a transmission, a message, or message originator.
Parker (1998)	Validity, conformance, and genuineness of information.

information with respect to external sources". Parker states that even information provided by an authorised user, whose identity has been verified, may not necessarily comply with authenticity. That, for example, may happen in the case when an authorised user misrepresents information.

Parker (1998) argues that his model replaces the incomplete description of InfoSec limited to the CIA-triad. Albeit the model of InfoSec, suggested by Parker (1998), is not widely accepted, the research undertaken is fruitful because it addresses three issues, essential for the clarification of InfoSec:

1. The focus of the discipline is set on protection of information, rather than on protection of an information system. Parker consistently includes in his model properties of information and does not mix them with security mechanisms.

2. The importance of a complete and accurate definition of the discipline and, consequently, of the discipline's goals is highlighted and justified.

3. An attempt to extend the model of InfoSec and to address the limitations of the CIA-triad is undertaken. The overstepping of the CIA-triad leads to the switch of InfoSec from the technical to the multidimensional discipline.

In agreement with Parker, Anderson (2001a) confirms that InfoSec is more than the CIA-triad. Anderson proclaims a multidimensional approach to InfoSec and sets forth that people, institutional and economic factors are no less important than the technical ones. Describing a security specialist, Anderson propones the requirement for such a specialist today to be familiar with business, management and accountancy, in addition to technology, in order to be able to communicate effectively with the top management as well as with the technical staff.

Anderson also is a pioneer of security economics. The economic perspective of security has been intensively discussed since the turn of the 21st century. Anderson (2001b) conducted an analysis of economic incentives behind some InfoSec failures and concluded that a purely technical approach to InfoSec is ineffective . Further, Anderson states that collaboration between managers, economists and lawyers is required in order to solve problems related to InfoSec. While Anderson (2001b) provides the general inside view on the economic incentives behind InfoSec, Gordon and Loeb (2002) look at the economics of investments into InfoSec. In 2002, they proposed the economic model that helps to determine the optimal amount of investment in InfoSec. In their work, Gordon and Loeb associate InfoSec with such goals as confidentiality, availability, authenticity, non-repudiation and integrity of

information (Gordon and Loeb, 2002, p. 439). The importance of economic motives is also recounted by Schneier (2008), who states that the number of vulnerabilities may only be reduced "when the entities that have the capability to reduce those vulnerabilities have the economic incentive to do so". In addition to economics, Schneier reveals a consideration of physiology and management to be essential for InfoSec (Schneier, 2000, 2008). In line with Anderson, Schneier confirms the multidimensional nature of InfoSec.

Schneier (2000) describes InfoSec as a process that includes: understanding of threats, design of polices and building of countermeasures to address the threats and, further, states that all the components of the process must fit together in order to achieve a best state of the overall process. He distinguishes the following goals of InfoSec: privacy, information classification (referred to as multilevel security), anonymity, authentication, integrity and audit (Schneier, 2000). Schneier lists among security goals not only properties of information (as it was consistently done by Parker [1998]), but also security mechanisms or abilities of information systems (e.g. authentication).

In line with Schneier, Pipkin (2000) defines InfoSec as a process, in this case as "the process of protecting the intellectual property of an organisation". Pipkin includes in the scope of InfoSec, and discusses in detail, ten security goals: awareness, access, identification, authentication, authorisation, availability, accuracy, confidentiality, accountability and administration. This is another confirmation of a wide trend in InfoSec to combine security goals and security mechanisms as a result of considering information and information systems simultaneously to be subjects of protection in InfoSec.

Importantly, Pipkin (2000) takes InfoSec outside the hard perimeter of an organisation by Defining that information should be protected "in all its locations". In the present complex collaborative environment, information often intentionally leaves the safe boundaries of an organisation, but still requires protection. Pipkin (2000) also highlights a necessity of InfoSec flexibility in a constantly evolving environment.

Pipkin explores InfoSec from a business standpoint and argues the need for InfoSec to become a business enabler and an integral part of a business. A similar approach to InfoSec is presented by Sherwood et al. (2005) who states that at present InfoSec, unfortunately, is often understood as a business preventer rather than a business enabler. According to Sherwood et al. (2005), InfoSec may help to raise the trust in an organisation by customers and partners, and to allow an organisation to use effectively newly emerging technologies for a greater commercial success. InfoSec enables business by increasing its competitiveness. Delving deeper into the business approach to InfoSec, it should be understood that security of information is required not for its own sake, but for the advantages it gives to business (e.g. improved efficiency due to the exploitation of new technologies, increased trust from partners and customers). Sherwood et al. (2005) adopt a multidimensional and enterprise-wide approach to InfoSec and include in the scope of InfoSec, for example, such aspects of business as marketing and customer service. The authors declare protection of business assets and assistance with the achievement of business goals to be the main aim of InfoSec. Sherwood et al. (2005), in greater detail than Pipkin (2000), address the change of InfoSec approach related to the erosion of the hard perimeter of an organisation caused by active collaboration, operation in a distributed environment, and outsourcing of IT and other services. Pipkin (2000) and Sherwood et al. (2005), by the adoption of a business-oriented approach, support the tendency to extend the realm of the discipline. Thus, InfoSec is no longer considered purely from a technical perspective, but also from a managerial, system architect's and designer's points of view.

In line with others, Von Solms (2001) confirms the transition of InfoSec from purely technical to the multidimensional discipline and identifies thirteen closely interdependent dimensions of InfoSec:

1. The Strategic/Corporate Governance Dimension.
2. The Governance/Organisational Dimension.
3. The Policy Dimension.
4. The Best Practice Dimension.
5. The Ethical Dimension.
6. The Certification Dimension.
7. The Legal Dimension.
8. The Insurance Dimension.
9. The Personnel/Human Dimension.
10. The Awareness Dimension.
11. The Technical Dimension.
12. The Measurement/Metrics (Compliance monitoring/Real time IT audit) Dimension.
13. The Audit Dimension.

According to Von Solms (2001), the dynamic nature of InfoSec does not allow one to create a complete list of InfoSec dimensions at any given time. Despite the constant change of dimensions of the discipline, the identification of different dimensions is desired because it will lead to the structuring of InfoSec complexity. Furthermore, only through addressing all InfoSec dimensions in a holistic manner could an organisation develop a secure environment. The list of the InfoSec dimensions proposed by Von Solms (2001) may be extended with the following dimensions derived from the comparative analysis of (Anttila et al., 2004; Shoemaker et al., 2004):

1. The Physical Security Dimension.
2. The System Development Dimension which ensures that the security is built into the development process.
3. The Security Architecture Dimension.
4. The Business Continuity Dimension.
5. The Privacy Dimension.

Blakley et al. (2002) refers to InfoSec as a management of risks associated with information and claims that the ultimate task of InfoSec is the determination of the effectiveness of security mechanisms. This attitude to InfoSec was later captured in the term IA (see Section 3 for the detailed discussion.)

Blakley et al. (2002) points out two reasons of the majority of security failures: (1) limited focus of the discipline (InfoSec is generally concerned with technical and logical security mechanisms), and (2) ineffectiveness of security mechanisms. The first reason clearly testifies for a need in diversified solutions for security problems.

The shift of InfoSec from the technical to the broad, multidimensional discipline is also supported by Lacey (2009), who recounts that InfoSec "draws on a range of different disciplines: computer science, communications, criminology, law, marketing, mathematics and more." Lacey (2009) confirms the importance of technologies for protection of information, but emphasises the even greater importance of the human factor which is based on the fact that all technologies are designed, implemented and operated by people. In addition to the human factor, Lacey also considers how organisational culture and politics affect InfoSec. Addressing the growing interconnectivity, Lacey (2009) gives an account of a recent Internet Age phenomenon - de-perimeterisation. De-perimeterisation refers to the erosion of the hard perimeter of an organisation in order to leverage achievement of business goals. Lacey (2009) points out an important switch in InfoSec from the protection of isolated enterprise systems to the protection of systems with open corporate boundaries.

De-perimeterisation is also intensively discussed by the Jerico Forum (JF), the international IT security association, that aims to develop solutions for secure business IT operations. According to the JF, de-perimeterisation is a result of "a huge explosion in business collaboration and commerce on the Web" (JF, 2011). The JF Commandments state that de-perimeterisation "has happened, is happening, and is inevitable" (JF, 2007) and provide a set of principles to be used for achievement of a "good security" in a collaborative, networked world. Although the JF follows a business-oriented approach, it still has a very technical standpoint and concentrates primarily on technical solutions of the issues related to de-perimeterisation (e.g. authentication and authorisation) (JF, 2007). Albeit de-perimeterisation is a recent phenomenon, significant research already exists about the technical solutions that may be used for information protection in the de-perimeterised environment. Nevertheless, for the dimensions of InfoSec other than technical one, the effect of de-perimeterisation is not thoroughly investigated (Cherdantseva et al., 2011).

At the time of massive interconnection and collaborative information sharing, InfoSec becomes more challenging since information now needs protection not only within the safe organisation's perimeter, but also outside it. This important change within the InfoSec domain is outlined in (Pipkin, 2000; Sherwood et al., 2005; Lacey, 2009; JF, 2007, 2011; Cherdantseva et al., 2011).

The multidimensional nature and the broadening scope of InfoSec is also supported by Dlamini et al. (2009) who state that in the first decade of the 21st century three areas became important for InfoSec: legal and regulatory compliance, risk management and information security management. As a consequence, the number of people involved in InfoSec is increasing. If previously there were only technical experts involved in InfoSec, now managers, legal personnel, compliance regulators, human resources specialists are also involved in InfoSec.

In agreement with other authors, Tiller (2010) states the omnipresent nature of InfoSec and, most importantly, proclaims that in addition to a comprehensive approach, InfoSec is required to be agile and adaptable to meet the requirements of continuously evolving business needs. The adaptable nature of InfoSec, shown by many authors (Pipkin, 2000; Von Solms, 2001; Tiller, 2010), should be seen as a need to revise the approach to InfoSec as well its definition and its scope on the regular basis.

At the end of the 20th and in the beginning of the 21st century a number of documents emerged escalating the importance of corporate governance: the Turnbull Guidance "Internal Control: Guidance for Directors on the Combined Code," the American Institute of Certified Public Accountants (AICIPA) standards, the King report on Corporate Governance, the Organisation for Economic Co-operation and Development (OECD) Principles of Corporate Governance, the 8th audit directive of the European Union and the Sarbanes-Oxley Act. These documents attracted the attention of senior management to InfoSec problems that were previously deemed to be low-level activities and the responsibility of technical personnel. The growing dependence of business on IT systems led to the importance of InfoSec being recognised at the managerial level. This is depicted in many academic publications where InfoSec, among other dimensions, includes the governance, administration or management dimensions (Anderson, 2001a; Von Solms, 2001; Sherwood et al., 2005; Dlamini et al., 2009).

Analysis of the literature shows that there is a paradigm shift in InfoSec towards a coherent approach to information protection. Previously, the basic assumption was that the technology could provide "absolute security." Nowadays, it is clear that the technology alone is insufficient for solving complex tasks of the discipline. Business needs, the human factor, economic incentives, cultural and organisational aspects should be taken into account in order to achieve an adequate protection of information. At present, a comprehensive, multidimensional approach to the protection of information is required. At the end of this section, in order to summarise the review of the related literature and in order to portray the present state of InfoSec, we list the recent discernible trends within the discipline:

1. InfoSec moves from a low-level technical activity and responsibility of computer specialists to a top priority activity dealt with at the strategic managerial level (Dlamini et al., 2009).

2. InfoSec becomes a multidimensional discipline. Aspects related to management (Pipkin, 2000; Sherwood et al., 2005; Tiller, 2010), marketing (Sherwood et al., 2005), economics (Anderson, 2001b; Schneier, 2008), physiology (Schneier, 2008; Lacey, 2009), law (Von Solms, 2001; Lacey, 2009), sociology (Theoharidou et al., 2005), criminology (Theoharidou et al., 2005; Lacey, 2009), mathematics Anderson, 2001a; Lacey, 2009) and other disciplines are now in the scope of InfoSec.

3. InfoSec shifts from the protection of closed IT systems to the protection of open systems operating in a collaborative interconnected environment (Pipkin, 2000; Sherwood et al., 2005; ISACA, 2009).

4. As a result of the above, the CIA-triad is considered to be obsolete and not reflecting the complete scope of InfoSec (Parker, 1998; Anderson, 2001a). A plethora of security goals and security mechanisms is deemed to be relevant to InfoSec in addition to the CIA-triad (Table 2).

3. INFORMATION ASSURANCE

Information Assurance (IA) is quite a new discipline, perhaps the most striking feature of which is that everyone seems to have different opinion about what it actually is. In order to identify the scope and to understand the meaning of IA, in this section we follow the procedure similar to the one used to analyse InfoSec. First, the understanding of the term based on common English is examined. Then, we present the analysis of the definitions of IA provided by the official organisations, followed by the analysis of the comprehension of the discipline in the academic and industry publications. Finally, an adapted definition of IA is presented.

3.1. The Definition of Information Assurance Based on Common English

For the purpose of working out the general definition of IA, we begin with the definition of the word assurance in the Oxford English Dictionary (2012):

- Assurance n.
  - A positive declaration intended to give confidence; a promise;
  - Confidence or certainty in one's own abilities.

Confidence is defined as "the feeling or belief that one can have faith in or rely on someone or something" (Oxford English Dictionary, 2012). Based on the "distilled knowledge and wisdom embodied in the dictionary definitions" (Sherwood et al., 2005) we coin a general definition of IA:

Information Assurance is a discipline the main aim of which is to give confidence or certainty in information; to give belief that one can rely on data, knowledge, facts, and its meaning.

One important assumption that comes out of the above definition is that confidence in information must be based on confidence in all entities involved in the processes of information processing, storage and transmission. An entity, in this context, may mean a technical tool or system, a process, an individual or an organisation.

Similarly to the general definition of InfoSec, the definition of IA identifies a broad scope of the discipline. In this case, the general definition leaves a plethora of questions for discussion, for example:

- What are the properties that information should have in order for one to be able to rely on it?

- What actions should be undertaken in order to give confidence in information?
- What evidence is required to ensure confidence in information?

In order to find the answers for the above questions, in Section 3.2 we analyse the definitions of IA suggested in the official sources.

3.2. Information Assurance as Defined in the Official US and UK Documents

The term IA was coined by the US Joint Staff in 1998 and for the first time appears in Joint Doctrine for Information Operations (Joint Pub, 1998). This document provided the classical definition of IA that for the first time declared five security goals, also known as the Five Pillars of IA: availability, integrity, authentication, confidentiality and non-repudiation.

In 2000, the term IA was included into the US National Information Systems Security Glossary, published by The National Security Telecommunications and Information Systems Security Committee (NSTISSC), which in 2001 was given a new name the Committee on National Security Systems (CNSS). Over the decade, the definition has changed so that the latest definition refers to measures, rather than information operations as in the original definition. Below is the definition of IA extracted from the CNSSI (CNSS, 2010):

Information Assurance - Measures that protect and defend information and information systems by ensuring their availability, integrity, authentication, confidentiality, and non-repudiation. These measures include providing for restoration of information systems by incorporating protection, detection, and reaction capabilities.

For the purposes of this definition, the following meanings also apply:

- **Availability:** The property of being accessible and useable upon demand by an authorized entity.
- **Integrity:** The property whereby an entity has not been modified in an unauthorized manner.
- **Authentication:** The process of verifying the identity or other attributes claimed by or assumed of an entity (user, process, or device), or to verify the source and integrity of data.
- **Confidentiality:** The property that information is not disclosed to system entities (users, processes, devices) unless they have been authorized to access the information.
- **Non-Repudiation:** Assurance that the sender of information is provided with proof of delivery and the recipient is provided with proof of the sender's identity, so neither can later deny having processed the information.

This original CNSS definition, based on the Five Pillars, remains the only rigorous definition of IA until now and, therefore, is highly cited. The analysis of the CNSS definition of IA is presented below. First, according to the CNSSI the scope of IA, in terms of security goals, is wider than the scope of InfoSec defined in the same document. In addition to the three security goals of InfoSec—confidentiality, integrity and availability—IA also aims to achieve authentication and non-repudiation. Second, the definition includes in the scope of IA not only information, but also explicitly states an information system as an object for control. The second sentence of the definition is particularly oriented on information systems and gives a technical sense to IA. Third, the Five Pillars of IA present an amalgamation of security goals and security mechanisms. Whereas, non-repudiation is another security

goal that aims to achieve a state where none of the entities may deny participation in the transaction, authentication is a security mechanism that helps to achieve such security goals as confidentiality, integrity and non-repudiation through the identity verification. The fact that security mechanisms are mixed in the definition with security goals is confusing. Adding to the confusion is the concentration on a certain security mechanism—authentication—and ignorance of other non-less important security mechanisms, e.g. authorisation and cryptography.

The CNSS definition of IA declares security goals, but does not define any methods to be used to achieve them. The clarification on that regard is found in (JS, 2000; DOD, 2002) which explain that IA may be achieved "through a defense-in-depth approach that integrates the capabilities of personnel, operations, and technology, and supports the evolution to network centric warfare." The defense-in-depth concept was adopted by the US DoD from the Information Assurance Technical Framework (IATF) and is based on the long-existing military principle of multilayered protection of fortifications (Boyce and Jennings, 2002, p. 39). As a result of the adoption of the defense-in-depth concept, IA includes into its realm such aspects as (JS, 2000):

- Risk management.
- Training, education and professionalism of the staff.
- Program, issue-specific and system-specific policies.
- Monitoring, management and administration.
- Assessment and audit.

In order to understand the concept of IA accepted by the UK government, we examined A National Information Assurance Strategy that was published by the Cabinet Office in 2007 and related documents. The glossary of A National Information Assurance Strategy (CSIA, 2007) defines IA as follows:

Information Assurance is the confidence that information systems will protect the information they carry and will function as they need to, when they need to, under the control of legitimate users.

According to this definition, IA has a very narrow scope and concerned only with the security of information systems. HMG Security Policy Framework (HMG, 2011), published by the Cabinet Office, also follows a similarly narrow approach to IA, and concentrates on the risks associated with confidentiality, integrity and availability of information within an information system. IA here has a purely technical interpretation. A detailed analysis of A National Information Assurance Strategy shows that this document, in defining IA, puts a strong emphasis on the management of risks to information. That is derived from a definition of IA given in (CSIA, 2007, Foreword): "Information Assurance is the term given to management of risk to information. Effective IA ensures that the opportunities provided by new technology can be exploited to maximum benefit." Further in the text CSIA (2007) inconsistently refers to the Five Pillars (rather than to the CIA-triad that is stated in the definition of IA provided in the glossary of the same document) and includes information in the scope of IA as well as information systems: "The term 'information assurance' (IA) is used to describe confidence in the processes of information risk management. Effective IA should ensure appropriate levels of availability, integrity, confidentiality, non-repudiation and authentication of information and information systems."

In fact, industry response to the IA strategy indicated that the key priorities of the strategy are not obvious and "clouded by inconsistencies in delivery, belief or understanding" (IACG, 2007).

In contrast with (CSIA, 2007; HMG, 2011), the HMG Information Assurance Maturity Model and Assessment Framework (HMG, 2010) proclaims a broader viewpoint on IA. It considers IA as a systematic, business enabling and dynamic approach to InfoSec which is not limited purely to information systems. According to (HMG, 2010), the IA scope is much wider than the scope defined in (CSIA, 2007) and comprise a diverse range of aspects including: leadership and governance; training, education and awareness; information risk management; through-life IA measures; assured information sharing; and compliance.

Albeit the uncertainty with the interpretation of IA in the UK official sources, it is clear that the perception of IA has a pronounced tendency towards technologies and information systems, and is focused on the management of risks to information, primarily associated with information systems.

This is clearly declared in the vision of the UK National IA strategy for 2011 (CSIA, 2007): "A UK environment where citizens, businesses and government use and enjoy the full benefits of information systems with confidence."

Finally, according to the official sources, IA is concerned with a coherent multilayered protection of information. It is worth noting that the documents concentrate on protection of information in electronic form circulating within computer systems and networks. The aspects such as risk assessment, monitoring and management are included in the scope of IA as a way of achieving a fair balance between security controls in the three layers of protection.

3.3. The Perception of Information Assurance in Academic and industry Publications

Since 1998, when the term IA was coined by the US military agencies, researchers and industry have been showing constant interest in IA. Although IA has existed for more than ten years, there is still no commonly agreed understanding of it in the literature. In 2002, Kovacich stated:

"Information Assurance is one of the newly refined processes of information protection that has evolved from computer security and information system security. Is it InfoSec by another name, a subset, or just the other way around? There is some argument about that." (Boyce and Jennings, 2002, Foreword). This argument is still valid today. In this section, delving deeper into the meaning of IA, we examine the perception of IA in academic and industry publications.

At the time when IA emerged, the environment was changing in two directions simultaneously: first, the world was getting more interconnected and, second, the importance of InfoSec was recognised at the managerial level (Section 2.3). Consequently, IA, which was deemed to address the change of the environment, received several interpretations, and, as a result, the focus and goals of the new discipline are noticeably inconsistent in various sources. Analysis of the related publications has identified three divergent interpretations of IA:

1. IA as a discipline dealing with the technical network-related security issues.
2. IA as a process of establishing confidence in information and information systems.
3. IA as a comprehensive management of InfoSec.

The third interpretation is the broadest one and is widely inclusive. It includes the technical aspect of IA, dominating in the first approach, and the establishment of confidence in information and information systems, dominating in the second approach. In some publications, an amalgamation of the approaches could be found. Nevertheless, in most cases the publication places a clear emphasis in its approach to IA which allows us to ascribed the work precisely to one of the three approaches. The approaches to IA listed above are outlined in detail in the following three sections.

3.3.1. Information Assurance as a Discipline Dealing with the Technical Network-Related Security Issues

This interpretation is reflecting the change of the environment in terms of the growing interconnectivity and is solidly based on the original definition of IA, proposed by the US military agencies. IA here is considered as a subset of InfoSec, focusing on network security. The Five Pillars (confidentiality, integrity, availability, authentication and non-repudiation) are the goals of the discipline. This approach was prevalent in the late 1990s and the early 2000s. It was and still is mainly supported by technical security specialists and government agencies.

The technical orientation implies that the discipline focuses on the security of information systems and information within information systems. Consequently, security goals here describe the desirable properties of information systems, rather than properties of information. This, possibly, explains the fact that authentication, which is, in fact, a security mechanism, is included in the list of security goals.

In 2001, Maconachy et al. (2001) presented a model of IA. IA according to Maconachy is the next step of the InfoSec evolution, and the model is an extension of the InfoSec model, originally proposed by McCumber (1991), where the CIA-triad is replaced with the Five Pillars. Maconachy et al. (2001) adopts a comprehensive and multidimensional approach to IA which stems from the defense-in-depth concept, but the goals of the discipline in this work are still limited to Five Pillars.

In 2002, McKnight (2002) defined IA from a purely technical viewpoint. Importantly, McKnight (2002) acknowledges that none individual viewpoint (including the technical one) would allow the creation of a correct picture of the discipline. Thus, the author recognises that IA extends beyond the technical domain. McKnight (2002) further states that in a broad sense IA incorporates the product, procedures, and policies that allow the timely transfer of information in an accurate and secure way among involved parties. McKnight (2002) claims that InfoSec is not the same discipline as IA, but does not discuss the distinction between the disciplines. The author claims that technology and policies may change over time, whereas security goals will remain persistent. This claim is only partially true: although previously defined security goals (confidentiality, integrity, availability) stay consistent, the new security goals constantly evolve to reflect new threats. This issue is discussed in more detail in Section 2.

3.3.2. Information Assurance as a Process of Establishing Confidence in Information and Information Systems

This approach is based on a common understanding of the term assurance and correlates with the general definition of IA derived in Section 3.1. Here, IA is not an independent discipline, but an InfoSec subset which deals with (1) the classification of information by the level of confidence one may have in it or by correctness of information (Pipkin, 2000) and (2) the evaluation of the system's level of security (Anderson, 2001a).

In order to establish confidence in an information system, one needs to have an up-to-date model of evaluation criteria, as well as unambiguous security metrics and an agreed evaluation procedure. The Common Criteria has been serving as a model of evaluation criteria for a long time. This approach is clearly focused on the evaluation and demonstration of the security level in order to gain the trust of internal and external parties (stakeholders, users, authorities, partners, customers, etc.)

3.3.3. Information Assurance as a Comprehensive Management of Information Security

This interpretation reflects the recognition of the importance of InfoSec for business success and a need to address it at the managerial level. A certain element of fashion plays its role in the use of the term IA in this context. This approach to IA emerged in the early years of the 21st century and is widely adopted by the commercial world. The origins of this approach are rooted in the defense-in-depth concept. Here, IA is interpreted as comprehensive and systematic InfoSec management. The main aim of IA is not the achievement of pre-defined security goals, but the successful business operation and the overall protection of information (IAAC, 2002). This approach may be considered as an extension to the original concept of IA proposed by the DoD where IA is taken from the technical level, considering protection of information in the networked computerised systems, to the managerial level, concerned with the protection of business in the interconnected world.

This approach more than any other correlates with the general definition developed in Section 3.1, because only the comprehensive and systematic management of information and information systems may provide a sought for confidence in information. In this approach technology is not the primary focus of the successful information protection. Here, InfoSec is deemed to be either a subset of IA or a concomitant discipline.

In 2002, the Information Assurance Advisory Council (IAAC), a UK-based not-for-profit research organisation, in association with Microsoft published "Benchmarking Information Assurance" (IAAC, 2002). This document most prominently illustrates the approach to IA discussed in this subsection. This document presents public and industry point of view on IA, and supports the argument about the small amount of agreement on the concept and terminology related to IA. The IAAC states that the terms InfoSec and IT security over-emphasise the importance of confidentiality and miss out other problems such as accessibility or reliability, whereas IA overcomes these issues. Furthermore, the emphasis put on IT, also means that the risk to information is seen as a low-level activity, which is outside of the interests of senior management (IAAC, 2002). The survey conducted by the IAAC demonstrated that IA attracts more and more attention of top managers across multiple sectors, but an integrated approach to information protection is more rapidly accepted by smaller organisations.

The IAAC considers IA to be an activity dealt with at a higher level than InfoSec. InfoSec is the responsibility of computer specialists, whereas IA is the responsibility of senior management. IA is the systematic management of InfoSec, based on a holistic strategy. This is also confirmed by the fact that BS7799 Information security management. Code of practice for information security management systems is considered to be the foundation of IA (IAAC, 2002). Interestingly, neither BS7799, nor the ISO/IEC 27000 series use the term IA or provide a definition of it. Nevertheless, other works (e.g. IAAC, 2002) refer to BS7799 and the ISO/IEC 27000 series as the IA standards, confirming the understanding of IA as a management of InfoSec.

Boyce and Jennings (2002) explain the concept of IA as it may be applied in the private and public sectors. The authors define IA as "the process for protecting and defending information by ensuring its confidentiality, integrity, and availability. At its most fundamental level, IA involves protecting the rights of people and organisations." Boyce and Jennings discern two main functions provided by IA: (1) the protection of an organisation's own rights (rights to survive, coexist and grow) and (2) the protection of other parties that interact with

an organisation. The approach to IA presented in (Boyce and Jennings, 2002) spreads through both technical and managerial perspectives. The authors point out that at present, when technology is at the very core of any business, IA becomes an indispensable component of overall business performance. In terms of the goals of the discipline Boyce and Jennings, in addition to the CIA-triad also discuss in detail auditability (the ability to verify the activity of a security control), accountability (holding of individuals liable for certain activities), access control, risk management, cost effectiveness, comprehensive and integrated approach, life-cycle managements, training and awareness, and continual reassessment. Although the authors still consider in detail the technical side of IA, they place the main emphasis on the importance of addressing information protection in the networked environment at the managerial level. Boyce and Jennings (2002) highlight that IA, by protecting information, a "critical and strategic business resource", supports the mission of an organisation.

Tawileh and McIntosh (2007) also perceive IA as a separate discipline and the next step of the evolution of InfoSec, which in the process of its development and expansion, includes new aspects. The shift from InfoSec towards IA stems from "the changes in the organisational environments and the information systems developed to serve these organisations" (Tawileh and McIntosh, 2007) when in addition to the technological solutions, human and organisational aspects began to be taken into account.

Analysis of the literature shows that the commercial sector eagerly adopted the defense-indepth concept which serves as the kernel of IA. The commercial world, rather than to concentrate on the technical side of network protection and on the Five Pillars of IA, preferred to focus on the essence of IA – the comprehensive and systematic management of InfoSec based on the utilisation of a reasonable combination of the capabilities of people, operations and technology.

In 2011, a survey was conducted among one hundred InfoSec and IA professionals. One of the aims of the survey was to identify the most commonly accepted perception of IA. The survey showed that the largest group of respondents (45 out of 100) is inclined to understand IA as a holistic, multidisciplinary and systematic approach to InfoSec. This approach corresponds with the interpretation of IA as a comprehensive management of InfoSec as outlined in this subsection. The full results of the survey are presented in (Cherdantseva and Hilton, 2013).

4. INFORMATION SECURITY VS. INFORMATION ASSURANCE: THE DISCUSSION

In Sections 2 and 3, we have thoroughly studied the terms InfoSec and IA. In Section 5, the adapted definitions of InfoSec and IA are presented. In this section, we conduct a comparison of the disciplines and attempt to describe the relationship between them. We also compare the disciplines with Computer Security (CS), a predecessor of InfoSec. The demonstration of the differences and similarities between the disciplines helps in the clarification of the scope and the specifics of each discipline. In this section, we endeavour to get beyond arguments about the definitions and into the understanding of the nature of InfoSec and IA.

Table 4 presents a comparison of CS, InfoSec and IA. In the horizontal axes, the table outlines the following characteristics for each discipline:

1. **Dates:** specifies the approximate date since the discipline has existed.
2. **Subject of Protection:** describes what the discipline aims to protect.
3. **Goals:** outlines the important goals of the discipline.
4. **Type of Information:** references the type of information to be protected.

5. **Approach:** outlines the approach to information protection adopted within the discipline as well as the aspects of protection included in the approach.
6. **Security Mechanisms:** describes security mechanisms that are exploited within the discipline in order to protect information.
7. **Role within a Business:** describes the role which the discipline plays within a business.
8. **Responsible Employees:** list the roles of employees, whose primary responsibility is protection of information. By the dedicated staff we refer to the employees who deals with information protection as their primary duty (e.g. Chief Information Security Officer (CISO) and employees under his/her management).
9. **Involved Employees:** lists employees who are involved in information protection.
10. **Drivers:** describes the drivers behind security decisions.
11. **Flow of Security Decisions:** describes how security decisions are taken within an organisation.

As described in Section 3, IA has three distinct interpretations. For the purpose of the comparison in this section, we adopt the perception of IA as a comprehensive and systematic management of InfoSec. There is no such thing as "absolute security", but there is adequate security which is sufficient to address an organisation's risk appetite within the existing technical, cultural, legal and organisational constraints. IA aims to identify the level of adequate security and the best ways to achieve it, whereas InfoSec deals with the achievement itself.

In parallel with the formation of IA, InfoSec has been changing and growing in terms of the scope and goals. As a result, many characteristics that are outlined in Table 4 for IA are often attributed to InfoSec as well. This makes the border between InfoSec and IA very vague. It is hard to conduct a comparison of these disciplines due to

Table 4. Comparison of computer security, information security, and information assurance

Discipline Characteristics	Computer Security	Information Security	Information Assurance
Dates (approx.)	Since the early 1960s	Since the 1980s	Since 1998
Subject of protection	Computers	Information and information systems	Business as a whole
Goals	Reliability	Confidentiality, Integrity, Availability, and in addition Authenticity & Trustworthiness, Auditability, Accountability, Non-repudiation and Privacy	Overall business protection
Type of information	Electronic	Primarily electronic	All types (electronic, paper and verbal)
Approach	Strictly technical	Domination of the technical approach, initial attempts to consider soft aspects (e.g. human factor, administration)	All-encompassing multidisciplinary systematic approach
Security Mechanisms	Technical	Primary focus is on technical security mechanisms; initial consideration of organisational and human-oriented mechanisms	All available (technical, organisational, human-oriented, legal)
Role within a business	Supporting system	Supporting system, often inducing some restrictions on business	An integral aspect of business, business enabler
Responsible employees	Technical staff	Dedicated staff and technical staff (often in addition to the other duties)	Senior management and dedicated staff
Involved employees	Technical staff	Senior management, dedicated and technical staff	All employees with an organisation
Drivers	Technical-needs driven	Security-needs driven	Business-needs driven
Flow of security decisions	Bottom-Top (senior management is not concerned with technical aspects of security)	Bottom - Top (security measures are initiated by technical specialists, based on their experience and passed to senior management for approval)	Top - Bottom (security measures are initiated by senior management based on risk analysis and implemented by relevant departments)

their natural changeability. Nevertheless, in this section we attempt to do the comparison by fixing the understanding of InfoSec according to the official definitions discussed in Section 2.2. CS is included in the comparison in order to demonstrate the evolution of attitude to information protection over the longer period and to draw the prominent change in this attitude.

Table 4 shows that whereas CS is concerned with the protection of computers, InfoSec is concerned with the protection of information and information systems. IA, in its turn, deals with the protection of a business as a whole. Consequently, the goals of the disciplines are differing. CS aims to achieve reliability of hardware and software. The main goals of InfoSec are confidentiality,

integrity and availability of information, along them a wide range of goals is attributed to InfoSec including authenticity, accountability, non-repudiation etc. IA addresses protection of all aspects of the business.

If the sphere of responsibilities of InfoSec specialists is confined to protection from expected threats, e.g. unauthorised access (confidentiality), unauthorised modification (integrity) and unauthorised denial-of-use (availability), IA specialists are accountable for the organisation's resistance not only to known, but also to unknown and unexpected threats. Thus, the cornerstone principle of the contemporary approach to information protection may be summarised in the phrase "Expect the Unexpected!" (Neumann, 1995).

"Information exists both inside and outside the computer and has to be protected wherever it travels" (Pipkin, 2000, p.13). Hence, information protection should not be restricted to considering information within computer systems only. Whereas CS and InfoSec concentrate on the protection of electronic information, from the IA perspective information of any type (electronic, paper, verbal etc.) requires adequate protection.

The approach to information protection adopted within InfoSec is primarily focused on technical solutions to security issues. The protection of information systems and networks is certainly important, but represents only one facet of the problem. In order to achieve adequate security the full spectrum

of issues related to information protection should be addressed. In response to this call, IA adopts an all-encompassing, multidisciplinary and systematic approach to information protection. As a result, the security mechanisms exploited by the disciplines vary from solely technical mechanisms within CS to all available security mechanisms within IA.

CS, as well as InfoSec, plays the role of a supporting system within a business. InfoSec is also often deemed to be a business preventer (Sherwood et al., 2005). The transformation of InfoSec from a business preventer into a business enabler and an integral part of a business is clearly depicted within the IA concept. For IA, security is not a self-contained goal; security contributes to the achievement of business objectives and security measures address the real business risks (Parker, 1998, p.30). Moreover, IA looks for a subtle compromise between productivity and security.

In terms of responsibility for information protection, IA promotes the organisation-wide culture of InfoSec. All employees and not only dedicated staff should recognise the importance of InfoSec and their personal responsibility for information protection. Senior management and such departments as IT, legal, marketing, human resources, compliance, accounting, risk manage-

ment, quality control, business continuity and physical security, are often engaged in the implementation of some parts of InfoSec strategy and policies without explicitly acknowledging that. IA integrates InfoSec-related activities under an overarching administration. The interrelationships between the activities of the various departments are approached in a structured manner which helps to improve the InfoSec posture of an organisation and to reduce security costs by the elimination of duplicated activities.

The flow of security decisions within CS is described as bottom-top since technical security decisions are generally out of the scope of the senior management and are deemed to be a low-level activity. InfoSec has changed the situation slightly: the senior management began to be involved in security decisions, but still the decisions are mostly originated at the bottom by technical staff, and passed to the senior management for financial approval. IA promotes the opposite flow of security decisions: security decisions are taken by senior management based on a thorough risk assessment and business needs analysis and then passed to the relevant departments for implementation. Security decisions within the IA concept are business-needs-driven, whereas InfoSec solutions are often based on the security needs and ignore or even contradict business needs.

Finally, the importance of the comparison and understanding of the differences between the disciplines is explained. A widely-known saying declares that the right diagnosis is a half of the treatment. Therefore, at an initial stage it is important to describe carefully the problem of information protection, as well as to identify available means that could be exploited for the solution. The evolution of the approaches to information protection, presented via a comparison of CS, InfoSec and IA helps one to become familiar with the state-of-the-art in information protection. An appreciation of the differences between InfoSec and IA assists in the judgment about whether the organisation's approach to information protection is up-to-date with the latest trends. It also helps to clarify the sphere of responsibility and interests of InfoSec and IA practitioners and researchers.

The usage of the term IA to refer to a comprehensive and systematic management of InfoSec is debatable. The term InfoSec may be used under the assumption that it reflects the broad scope including management as well. Nevertheless, the use of the term IA in the context described is more desirable, since it demonstrates, without additional explanations, that there are differences between the approaches to information protection. The distinction between InfoSec and IA comes down to the distinction between the actions taken to protect information and the management of those actions. First, this notion brings the understanding of the need to the management in general, and second, it outlines the variety of security mechanisms and actions that could be used for information protection. IA helps to overstep the limitation to the technical perception of InfoSec problems and takes them to the higher managerial level. The use of the right term will lead to a better understanding of the underlying problem and to the optimal choice of the preventive measures.

The principal question of the interrelation between InfoSec and IA is quite difficult. For example (Whitman and Mattord, 2012), see InfoSec management (IA as we refer to it) to be one of the components of InfoSec along with computer & data security and network security (Figure 1).

The survey of InfoSec and IA professionals (introduced in Section 3.3) invited participants to describe the relationship between InfoSec and IA. The summary of responses concerning the relationship between the disciplines is depicted in Figure 2. The data presented in Figure 2 are open to two different interpretations. The opinions of the respondents were spread fairly evenly between the three statements describing the relationship between disciplines (options C, D and E). This clearly indicates that there is no single widely accepted understanding of how these two disciplines relate to each other.

Figure 1. Components of information security (Whitman & Mattord, 2012, p. 9)

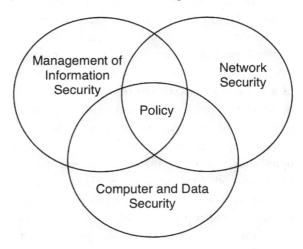

The problem of the mutual relationship between InfoSec and IA is debatable and deserves discussion. Contrary to the most popular perception of the relationship between the disciplines, as identified in the survey, it is our opinion that IA is a discipline of a wider scope which includes InfoSec (Figure 3a). The fact that the management of actions designed to address information protection would include the actions themselves and that both activities have a common goal supports this approach. We see IA as an umbrella term. On the other hand, InfoSec and IA may be deemed to be different disciplines that have a significant overlap in their interests (Figure 3b). The argument to support the second approach is that both disciplines consider certain issues that are out of the scope of another discipline. For example, (1) the technical details of the firewall technology are out of the scope of IA, while in the scope of InfoSec and (2) the calculation of the optimal investments in security is out of the scope of InfoSec, while in the sphere of the IA interests. The authors of the paper are more inclined to the second approach, although the second approach gives rise to another question about how the joint area of InfoSec and IA should be referred to.

Figure 2. The results of the survey of InfoSec and IA professionals. How would you describe the relationship between information security and information assurance (Cherdantseva & Hilton, 2013)?

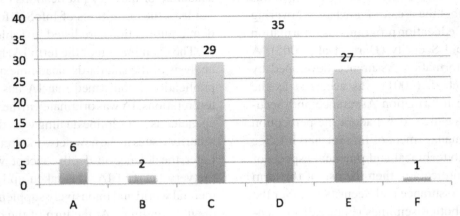

A) Information Security and Information Assurance are the same
B) Information Security and Information Assurance do not overlap
C) Information Security is a part of Information Assurance
D) Information Assurance is a part of Information Security
E) Information Security and Information Assurance are different
    disciplines, but they have some common areas
F) Other

In 2001, a group of representatives of fifteen U.S. undergraduate Information Technology programs, IEEE, ACM and ABET began work to formalise Information Technology as an accredited academic discipline (Dark et al., 2005). One of the challenges was to define the area of knowledge referred to as security. Since the term security was deemed too restrictive and not reflecting the broad range of concepts included in the discipline, the group turned its attention to the term

Figure 3. The relationship between information security (InfoSec) and information assurance (IA)

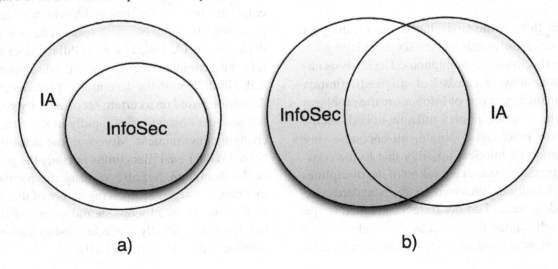

a)   b)

Information Assurance, which was at that time used by U.S. NSA and CNSS. In 2005, it was decided to label the area of knowledge, covering security in IT education programs, as Information Assurance and Security (Dark et al., 2005). A model of Information Assurance developed by Maconachy et al. (2001) was accepted as the model of the Information Assurance and Security knowledge area. If we adopt the perception of IA as the management of InfoSec and InfoSec as referring to technical and practical aspects of information protection, then the use of the term Information Assurance and Security to cover the joint area of both disciplines (Figure 3b) is sensible.

The authors are not aware of other sources that attempt to clarify the interrelationship between InfoSec and IA and draw a border between them. This section presents only the authors' opinion on the subject. It does not pretend to be the absolute truth and is open to discussion. The main aim of this discussion is to attract the attention of InfoSec and IA experts to the important question of the scope of InfoSec and IA, their interrelationship and the border between the disciplines.

5. THE ADAPTED DEFINITIONS OF INFORMATION SECURITY AND INFORMATION ASSURANCE

Albeit that, at the first glance, the meaning of InfoSec is fairly intuitive, the scope and the goals of the discipline are ambiguous. The analysis undertaken shows that the lack of an agreed definition and an unclear scope of InfoSec are the problems troubling the discipline. Until now, nobody seems to have produced a single, all-encompassing definition of InfoSec, possibly due to the complexity and persistent alteration of the discipline. The definitions provided in the standards are not adequate and do not reflect the broad scope of the discipline described by the academic and professionals (Section 2.2). We have not found a

clear rigorous definition of InfoSec in either the academic or industry publications (Section 2.3). Some of the definitions of InfoSec found in academic publications are listed in Table 5.

The examination of the term IA, based on the analysis of the standards, academic and industry publications, confirmed that IA has various interpretations. IA was originated in the US military agencies as a discipline dealing with the technical security issues in the new networked environment. Later, the defence-in-depth concept, which lies at the very heart of IA, was taken up by the commercial world and intensively supplemented with the new findings. At the turn of the century, the commercial sector recognised a need for a comprehensive and systematic approach to managing InfoSec. IA, which was coined at the same time, was deemed to be a modern response to that growing need. As a result, IA transformed from a discipline dealing with the exploitation of people, operations and technology capabilities in order to protect information in the networks to the discipline of a comprehensive and systematic management of InfoSec needed in order to improve overall business security and productivity. Thus, over the last decade IA evolved from the technical discipline dealing with the network security issues into the broad discipline which now includes soft aspects like administration, training and education.

Further, research has showed that, at present, there is no definition of IA which reflects the discipline in its broadest sense. The original definition of IA, based on Five Pillars, does not reflect the complexity and scope of the discipline in full. Similarly with the definitions of InfoSec, the definition based on a certain set of security goals has become obsolete very rapidly in the current changing environment. Moreover, the definition based on the Five Pillars limits not only the goals of the discipline, but also security mechanisms that may be used. The evolving nature of the discipline and its broad scope should be captured in the definition. Ideally, the relationship between InfoSec and IA should be clarified.

Table 5. The existing definitions of information security

Source	Definition of Information Security
Pipkin (2000)	Information Security is the process of protecting the intellectual property of an organisation.
Blakley et al. (2002)	...information security is a risk management discipline, whose job is to manage the cost of information risk to the business.
Anderson J. (2003)	A well-informed sense of assurance that information risks and controls are in balance.
Venter and Eloff (2003)	Information security is the protection of information and minimises the risk of exposing information to unauthorised parties.
Shoemaker et al. (2004)	Rather than being a separate study, information security draws from a number of other academic domains. These include: computer science, computer architecture, forensics, cryptography, knowledge and information theory, business, mathematics, military science, law and ethics, software engineering, statistics and all things having to do with the Internet.
Sherwood et al. (2005)	Information security is the enabling technology of electronic business [p.5]. Information systems security is only a small part of information security, which in turn is but one part of a wider topic: business assurance [p.24].
Dlamini et al. (2009)	Information security has evolved from addressing minor and harmless security breaches to managing those with a huge impact on organisations' economic growth. ... Does this mean information security is a new field or just another "fad"? No, information security is neither new nor a "fad". What is new is its broader focus and wider appeal.
Chahino and Marchant (2010)	Information Security is a discipline governing the framework for the continuous cycle of safeguarding information and ensuring related regulatory compliance.
Kazemi et al. (2012)	Information security is not just a technical issue, but a very important management issue, its main purpose is to create a secure information environment.
Whitman and Mattord (2012)	Information Security, to protect the confidentiality, integrity and availability of information assets, whether in storage, processing, or transmission. It is achieved via the application of policy, education, training and awareness, and technology. [p.8]

In order to summarise the enhanced understanding of the burgeoning areas of InfoSec and IA, and to address the drawbacks of the existing definition, we endeavour to develop the adapted contemporary definitions of the disciplines. The definitions, by no means, attempt to introduce new knowledge or concepts. They only attempt to synthesise and express in a concise form the outcomes of a thorough analysis of the security-related literature presented in the previous sections. Below we present a two-part adapted definition of InfoSec and an adapted definition of IA:

- **Information Security:** Is a multidisciplinary area of study and professional activity which is concerned with the development and implementation of security mechanisms of all available types (technical, organisational, human-oriented and legal) in order to keep information in all its locations (within and outside the organisation's perimeter) and, consequently, information systems, where information is created, processed, stored, transmitted and destructed, free from threats. Threats to information and information systems may be categorised and a corresponding security goal may be defined for each category of threats. A set of security goals, identified as a result of a threat analysis, should be revised periodically to ensure its adequacy and conformance with the evolving environment. The currently relevant set of security goals may include: confidentiality, integrity, availability, privacy, authenticity & trustworthiness, non-repudiation, accountability and auditability.

- **Information Assurance:** Is a multidisciplinary area of study and professional activity which aims to protect business by reducing risks associated with information and information systems by means of a comprehensive and systematic management of security countermeasures, which is driven by risk analysis and cost-effectiveness.

We conclude this section by reviewing the advantages of the elaborated definitions. The advantages of the proposed two-part definition of InfoSec:

- The definitions explicitly reflects the multidisciplinary nature and the diverse scope of InfoSec in its current reincarnation (1) by declaring a wide range of security mechanism that could be exploited for information protection and (2) by outlining an extensive list of security goals. The set of security goals is adopted from Cherdantseva and Hilton (2012).
- The definition puts the correct emphasis among the priorities of InfoSec by stating the protection of information from threats as a primary goal of InfoSec and protection of information systems as a consequent goal.
- The definition clearly distinguishes security goals from security mechanisms which may be exploited in order to achieve security goals.
- The definition distinguishes four types of security mechanisms:
  - Technical (e.g. biometrics, firewalls, PKI, digital signature, malicious code, virus and intrusions detection systems, etc.)
  - Organisational (e.g. strategy, policies, processes, audit, physical security, recovery plans, etc.)

  - Human-oriented (e.g. training, education, motivation, ethics, culture, etc.)
  - Legal (e.g. legislation, Job contracts, non-disclosure agreements, service-level agreements, etc.)
  - (The lists of security mechanisms within each type are by no means exhaustive and only intended to give an idea of a variety of security mechanisms available.)
- Following the traditional approach to Defining InfoSec, the proposed definition refers to security goals. (Anderson, 2003) states that the definition of InfoSec should provide more guidance about the objectives of InfoSec programs. In addition to naming security goals, the second part of the definition explains the origins of security goals. This information is essential for understanding, particularly, for newcomers to the field, but omitted in all known to us definitions of InfoSec.
- Although the definition outlines the currently relevant set of security goals, it does not limit the scope of InfoSec to the listed goals. The refined definition leaves the space for the natural changeability of the discipline and for open-mindedness among security experts by declaring a need of a regular revision of security goals.
- The definition reflects the growing trend in InfoSec towards the open, de-perimeterised environment by pointing out the need to protect information outside an organisation's perimeter as well as inside it.

The advantages of the proposed definition of IA:

- Importantly, the definition of IA declares the protection of a business as the ultimate goal. Although the security goals of InfoSec are inherited by IA, since IA has a wider scope and incorporates InfoSec (see Section 4 for the explanation), it is important to outline in the definition of IA that the reason behind all IA activities is the overall protection of business.

- The definition declares a need in a comprehensive and systematic management of security countermeasures. Comprehensive management means that security mechanisms of all available types should be exploited, the scope should not be limited to technical mechanisms. Systematic management refers to the fact that information protection should be addressed consistently at every stage of the system life-cycle.

- The definition declares two main drivers behind security decisions:
  - **Risk Analysis:** IA does not attempt to eliminate all risks, the risks should be prioritised, according to the organisation's specifics, and reduced to an acceptable level;
  - **Cost-Effectiveness:** IA does not attempt to achieve security at any price, but in a most efficient and cost-effective way.

- The suggested definition clarifies the relationship between InfoSec and IA. If InfoSec is concerned with the development and implementation of security mechanisms, IA is concerned with the design of a sensible and effective combination of security mechanisms. In short words, it is possible to say that IA is a comprehensive and systematic management of InfoSec. Thus, the adapted definition fully supports the approach to IA exposed in Section 3.3.3.

6. CONCLUSION

The problem with Defining terms may seem to be far from the real world and has no practical value. We would argue with that. Looking in depth, the paper tries to tackle a vital problem – that a restricted vision or misunderstanding of such important domains as InfoSec and IA will lead to different perceptions and behaviours that will introduce vulnerabilities into our world of interconnected systems. How could an organisation trust, for example, security strategy and policy creation or implementation to an employee who does not recognise the complexity of the security domain? In support of our argument, Anderson (2003) in the paper "Why we need a new definition of information security" declares that the absence of a clear definition of InfoSec which identifies what InfoSec professionals are in charge of and on what organisations spend significant funds is causing confusion and problems. Furthermore, according to (Anderson J., 2003), the lack of a generally accepted definition of InfoSec is one of the reasons for difficulties with measurement of InfoSec outcomes.

Although both disciplines—InfoSec and IA— have existed for some time the interrelationship between them is not obvious and not easy to trace in the literature. The numerous informal discussions on the Internet, that aim to find the meaning of InfoSec and IA, the differences between them and the goals of the disciplines, confirm that the answers to these questions are important for individuals interested in information protection, but are not straightforward. Although experts in the field, who benefit from years of learning and experience, may see no need in the discussion like this, for the newcomers this discussion provides a valuable insight into InfoSec and IA.

As stated in the introduction, the aim of this work is to clarify the existing misinterpretations of the terms InfoSec and IA and to present a clear, contemporary picture of both disciplines, by identifying the scope and goals, and by formulating an adapted definition of each discipline. In order to answer the research question, a thorough analysis of InfoSec and IA, based on common English, was conducted. We analysed US, UK and European InfoSec and IA related official publications and standards, and discussed the perception of the disciplines in the related academic and industry works, published over the last twenty years.

The analysis has shown that the existing definitions of InfoSec and IA do not fully reflect the complex subject of the disciplines and, therefore, dangerously restrict the scope of the disciplines. The analysis has also allowed us to achieve the main research goal – to elaborate the contemporary adapted definitions of InfoSec and IA (Section 5). This chapter contributes to the fields of InfoSec and IA by providing an analysis of the related literature and by giving an account of the state-of-the-art in both disciplines. This research ventures beyond previous works by distinguishing and describing three approaches to IA.

We hold firmly to the belief that the business and academic domains may benefit from the overview of the latest trends in InfoSec and IA, and from the definitions of the disciplines presented in the paper. The paper may further the understanding of security professionals and young academics in the disciplines. The research, generally, promotes the culture of InfoSec and IA by increasing awareness about the disciplines. Furthermore, the adoption of an integral and consistent viewpoint of information protection described in

the paper may increase the ability of business to foresee and, consequently, to avoid many threats to information in a continuously changing environment.

Business requires a growing number of highly educated InfoSec and IA specialists with knowledge of new technologies and negotiation skills (PwC, 2010). The need for training in a diverse range of subjects (e.g. information risk management, forensics, end-user awareness etc.) also increases. Therefore, InfoSec and IA higher education programs, in order to meet the expectations of prospective students and employers, should be kept up-to-date with the recent trends of the disciplines. The perception of InfoSec and IA should be agreed between business and academia in order to assist graduates to comply with industry requirements.

The discussion presented in this paper contributes to the more precise interpretation of InfoSec and IA and clarifies the scope, goals and approach of each discipline. We hope that this paper will catalyse a fruitful discussion and development of the InfoSec and IA education programs, which cover the entire body of knowledge associated with the disciplines and not only some parts of it. Having an agreed area for research, teaching and practice raises the status of the disciplines and enhances their further development.

Security is always context-specific, therefore some may argue that the definition of InfoSec will always be organisation specific and is a matter of a lexicon. This argument may be valid only in a "closed" environment, when an information system of an organisation is completely isolated from the rest of the world. For a collaborative de-perimeterised environment, where organisations share information, integrate information systems and business processes, a harmonised understanding of InfoSec expressed in a mutually agreed definition is essential.

For example, Company A believes that the scope of InfoSec is limited to the CIA-triad, Company B, who exchange sensitive information with Company A, expects that authenticity, non-repudiation and accountability are also covered by security policies. Customers of both companies expect that their privacy is protected. This sort of dissimilar expectation about InfoSec exists. We do not claim that an agreed definition on its own would solve all the problems, but it is good to start a discussion and is a solid stepping stone on the way towards a synchronised approach to information protection.

In order to summarise the outcomes of the study, we draw attention to two important conclusions. First, this research highlights the importance of clear and precise definitions of such crucial disciplines as InfoSec and IA. Incomplete definitions may lead to a perilous circumscription of the discipline (Section 2.3). As alluded to in the previous sections, the definitions of InfoSec and

IA tend to set a list of security goals in order to define a realm of the fields. The reason is obvious: security specialists must be provided with a rigorous framework of responsibilities. The drawback of this approach is that some threats and vulnerabilities, in particular newly emerging ones, may be overlooked and omitted because they stray out of the boundary of InfoSec and IA.

This leads us to the second essential conclusion: since InfoSec and IA are inherently open and evolving arenas, any definition, although providing a scrupulous framework and stating security goals, has to promote open-mindedness among experts dealing with InfoSec. The ultimate aim of both disciplines is to protect the life-blood of an organisation its strategic information – by the exploitation of all available security mechanisms.

As a direction for further research, we see a call for an up-to-date conceptual model of InfoSec and IA, which will depict the complexity and multidimensional nature of the disciplines in an increasingly interconnected environment. A model allowing the structuring of the existing body of knowledge of the disciplines discussed here will be a significant contribution to the art and science of information protection.

REFERENCES

Anderson, J. M. (2003). Why we need a new definition of information security. *Computers & Security*, 22(4), 308–313. doi:10.1016/S0167-4048(03)00407-3.

Anderson, R. (2001a). *Security engineering: A guide to building dependable distributed systems*. New York: Wiley Publishing.

Anderson, R. (2001b). Why information security is hard? An economic perspective. In *Proceedings of the Computer Security Applications Conference, 2001*, (pp. 358-365). ACSAC.

Anttila, J., Kajava, J., & Varonen, R. (2004). Balanced integration of information security into business management. In *Proceedings of the 30th EUROMICRO Conference*, (pp. 558–564). EUROMICRO.

Avizienis, A., Laprie, J.-C., Randell, B., & Landwehr, C. E. (2004). Basic concepts and taxonomy of dependable and secure computing. *IEEE Transactions on Dependable and Secure Computing*, 1(1), 11–33. doi:10.1109/TDSC.2004.2.

Blakley, B., McDermott, E., & Geer, D. (2001). Information security is information risk management. In *Proceedings of the 2001 Workshop on New Security Paradigms NSPW '01*, (pp. 97–104). ACM. doi:10.1145/508171.508187

Boyce, J., & Jennings, D. (2002). *Information assurance: Managing organizational IT security risks*. London: Butterworth-Heinemann.

Chahino, M., & Marchant, J. (2010). *CIS conference presentation*. Paper presented at the CIS Conference. Washington, DC.

Cherdantseva, Y., & Hilton, J. (2012). *The evolution of information security goals*. Retrieved from http://users.cs.cf.ac.uk/Y.V.Cherdantseva/publications.html

Cherdantseva, Y., & Hilton, J. (2013). The survey of information security and information assurance professionals 2011. In Almeida, F., & Portela, I. (Eds.), *Organizational, Legal, and Technological Dimensions of Information System Administrator*. Hershey, PA: IGI Global.

Cherdantseva, Y., Rana, O., & Hilton, J. (2011). Security architecture in a collaborative de-perimeterised environment: Factors of success. In *Proceedings of the ISSE Securing Electronic Business Processes*, (pp. 201-213). ISSE.

Clark, D., & Wilson, D. (1987). A comparison of commercial and military computer security policies. In *Proceedings of the IEEE Symposium on Security and Privacy*, (pp. 184-195). IEEE.

Collins English Dictionary Online. (2012). Retrieved from http://www.collinsdictionary.com

CSIA. (2007). *A national information assurance strategy*. New York: Crown.

Dark, M., Ekstrom, J., & Lunt, B. (2005). Integration of information assurance and security into the IT2005 model curriculum. In *Proceedings of the 6th Conference on Information Technology Education*. ACM.

Dlamini, M. T., Eloff, J. H. P., & Eloff, M. M. (2009). Information security: The moving target. *Computers & Security*, *28*(3-4), 189–198. doi:10.1016/j.cose.2008.11.007.

Dubois, E., Heymans, P., Mayer, N., & Matulevicius, R. (2010). A systematic approach to define the domain of information system security risk management. In *Intentional Perspectives on Information Systems Engineering* (pp. 289–306). London: Springer. doi:10.1007/978-3-642-12544-7_16.

FRC. (2004). *The Turnbull guidance as an evaluation framework for the purposes of Section 404(a) of the Sarbanes-Oxley Act*. Retrieved from http://www.frc.org.uk/documents/pagemanager/frc/draftguide.pdf

Gartner, Inc. (2012). *Forecast overview: Security infrastructure, worldwide, 2010-2016, 2q12 update*. Washington, DC: Gartner, Inc..

Gordon, L., & Loeb, M. (2002). The economics of information security investment. *ACM Transactions on Information and System Security*, *5*(4), 438–457. doi:10.1145/581271.581274.

HMG. (2010). *HMG information assurance maturity model and assessment framework*. New York: Crown.

HMG. (2011). *HMG security policy framework*. Boston: Crown Copyright.

Information Assurance Advisory Council (IAAC) & Microsoft. (2002). Benchmarking information assurance. Washington, DC: Information Assurance Advisory Council (IAAC) & Microsoft.

Information Assurance Collaboration Group (IACG). (2007). *Industry response to the HMG information assurance strategy and delivery plan*. IACG Working Group On The Role Of Industry In Delivering The National IA Strategy (IWI009).

ISACA. (2008). *Glossary of terms, 2008*. Retrieved from http://www.isaca.org/Knowledge-Center/Documents/Glossary/glossary.pdf

ISACA. (2009). *An introduction to the business model for information security*. ISACA. (ISC)². (2011). *The 2011 (ISC)² global information security workforce study*. (ISC)².

ISO/IEC 13335-1:2004. (2004). *Information technology - Security techniques - Management of information and communications technology security: Concepts and models for information and communications technology security management*. ISO/IEC.

ISO/IEC 15408-1:2009. (2009). *Information technology-Security techniques: Evaluation criteria for IT security: Introduction and general model*. ISO/IEC.

ISO/IEC 27000:2009 (E). (2009). *Information technology - Security techniques - Information security management systems - Overview and vocabulary*. ISO/IEC.

IT Governance Institute (ITGI). (2007). *COBIT 4.1: Excerpt*. ITGI.

Jericho Forum (JF). (2007). *Jericho forum commandments*. Retrieved from https://collaboration.opengroup.org/jericho/commandments v1.2.pdf

Jerico Forum (JF). (2011). *The what and why of de-perimeterization*. Retrieved from http://www.opengroup.org/jericho/deperim.htm

Joint Pub 3-13. (1998). *Joint doctrine for information operations*. USA.

Kazemi, M., Khajouei, H., & Nasrabadi, H. (2012). Evaluation of information security management system success factors: Case study of Municipal organization. *African Journal of Business Management*, 6(14), 4982–4989.

Lacey, D. (2009). *Managing the human factor in information security*. New York: J. Wiley and Sons Ltd..

Maconachy, W., Schou, C., Ragsdale, D., & Welch, D. (2001). A model for information assurance: An integrated approach. In *Proceedings of the 2001 IEEE Workshop on Information Assurance and Security*. West Point, NY: IEEE.

McCumber, J. (1991). Information systems security: A comprehensive model. In *Proceedings of the 14th National Computer Security Conference*. Baltimore, MD: NIST.

McKnight, W. (2002). What is information assurance? CrossTalk. *The Journal of Defense Software Engineering*, 4-6.

National Computer Security Center (NCSC). (1991). *Integrity in automated information systems*. C Technical Report 79-91 Library No. S-237, 254 (IDA PAPER P-2316). NCSC.

Neumann, P. (1995). *Computer-related risks*. New York: ACM Press/Addison Wesley.

NIST. (2002). *Risk management guide for information technology systems (Special Publication 800-30)*. NIST.

Oxford Dictionaries Online. (n.d.). Retrieved from http://oxforddictionaries.com

Parker, D. (1998). *Fighting computer crime*. New York, NY: John Wiley and Sons.

Pipkin, D. (2000). *Information security: Protecting the global enterprise*. New York: Hewlett-Packard Company.

PwC. (2010). *Information security breaches survey 2010* (Technical report). PwC.

SANS Institute. (2004). *An overview of Sarbanes-Oxley for the information security professional*. Retrieved from http://www.cs.jhu.edu/rubin/courses/sp06/Reading/soxForInfoSec.pdf

Schneier, B. (2000). *Secrets and lies*. New York: John Wiley and Sons.

Schneier, B. (2008). *Schneier on security*. New York: Wiley Publishing.

Shaw, A. (2010). Data breach: From notification to prevention using PCI DSS. *Columbia Journal of Law and Social Problems*, 43(4), 517–562.

Sherwood, J., Clark, A., & Lynas, D. (2005). *Enterprise security architecture: A business-driven approach*. New York: CMP Books.

Shoemaker, D., Bawol, J., Drommi, A., & Schymik, G. (2004). A delivery model for an information security curriculum. In *Proceedings of the Third Security Conference*. Las Vegas, NV: Information Institute.

Sony Computer Entertainment America. (2011). *Letter to the subcommittee on commerce, manufacturing, and trade of the U.S. House of Representatives*. New York: Sony Computer Entertainment America.

Tawileh, A., & McIntosh, S. (2007). Understanding information assurance: A soft systems approach. In *Proceedings of the United Kingdom Systems Society 11th International Conference*. Oxford, UK: Oxford University.

The U.S. Joint Staff (JS). (2000). *Information assurance through defense in depth*. US Joint Staff.

Theoharidou, M., Kokolakis, S., Karyda, M., & Kiountouzis, E. (2005). The insider threat to information systems and the effectiveness of ISO17799. *Computers & Security*, 24, 472–484. doi:10.1016/j.cose.2005.05.002.

Tiller, J. S. (2010). *Adaptive security management architecture*. Boston: Auerbach Publications.

Trustwave Holdings, Inc. (2012). *The trustwave 2012 global security report*. Trustwave Holdings, Inc..

U.S. Department of Defense (DOD). (2007). *Directive number 8500.01E October 24, 2002: Certified current as of April 23, 2007*. Washington, DC: DOD.

Venter, H. S., & Eloff, J. H. P. (2003). A taxonomy for information security technologies. *Computers & Security*, 22(4), 299–307. doi:10.1016/S0167-4048(03)00406-1.

Von Solms, B. (2001). Information security - A multidimentional discipline. *Computers & Security*, 20(6), 504–508. doi:10.1016/S0167-4048(01)00608-3.

Whitman, M. E., & Mattord, H. J. (2012). *Principles of information security* (4th ed.). Course Technology, Cengage Learning.

KEY TERMS AND DEFINITIONS

Accountability: An ability of a system to hold users responsible for their actions (e.g. misuse of information).

Auditability: An ability of a system to perform persistent, non-bypassable monitoring of all actions performed by humans or machines within the system.

Authenticity and Trustworthiness: An ability of a system to verify identity and establish trust in a third party and in information it provides.

Availability: A system should ensure that all system's components are available and operational when they are required by authorised users.

Confidentiality: A system should ensure that only authorised users access information.

Information Assurance: Is a multidisciplinary area of study and professional activity which aims to protect business by reducing risks associated with information and information systems by means of a comprehensive and systematic management of security countermeasures, which is driven by risk analysis and cost-effectiveness.

Information Security: Is a multidisciplinary area of study and professional activity which is concerned with the development and implementation of security mechanisms of all available types (technical, organisational, human-oriented, and legal) in order to keep information in all its locations (within and outside the organisation's perimeter) and, consequently, information systems, where information is created, processed, stored, transmitted and destructed, free from threats.

Integrity: A system should ensure completeness, accuracy and absence of unauthorized modifications in all its components.

Non-Repudiation: An ability of a system to prove (with legal validity) occurrence/non-occurrence of an event or participation/non-participation of a party in an event.

Privacy: A system should obey privacy legislation and enable individuals to control (where feasible) their private information (user-involvement). Threats to information and information systems may be categorised and a corresponding security goal may be defined for each category of threats. A set of security goals, identified as a result of a threat analysis, should be revised periodically to ensure its adequacy and conformance with the evolving environment. The currently relevant set of security goals may include: confidentiality, integrity, availability, privacy, authenticity & trustworthiness, non-repudiation, accountability and auditability.

Chapter 11
A Conceptual Framework for Big Data Analysis

Fernando Almeida
University of Porto, Portugal

Mário Santos
University of Aveiro, Portugal

ABSTRACT

Big data is a term that has risen to prominence describing data that exceeds the processing capacity of conventional database systems. Big data is a disruptive force that will affect organizations across industries, sectors, and economies. Hidden in the immense volume, variety, and velocity of data that is produced today is new information, facts, relationships, indicators, and pointers that either could not be practically discovered in the past, or simply did not exist before. This new information, effectively captured, managed, and analyzed, has the power to enhance profoundly the effectiveness of government. This chapter looks to the main challenges and issues that will have to be addressed to capture the full potential of big data. Additionally, the authors present a conceptual framework for big data analysis structured in there layers: (a) data capture and preprocessing, (b) data processing and interaction, and (c) auxiliary tools. Each has a different role to play in capturing, processing, accessing, and analyzing big data.

INTRODUCTION

The term "big data" has recently grown in prominence as a way of describing the phenomenon of growth in data volume, complexity and disparity. The definition of big data is not totally consensual in literature and there may be some confusion around what it really means. Big data is not just an environment in which accumulated data has reached very large proportions. The word "big" does not just refer to size. If it was just a capacity issue the solution would be relatively simple.

DOI: 10.4018/978-1-4666-4526-4.ch011

Instead, big data refers to environment in which data sets have grown too large to be handled, managed, stored and retrieved in an acceptable timeframe (Slack, 2012).

Big Data can be often characterized by three fundamental factors: volume, velocity, and variety. According to Wilson and Kerber (2011) only fifteen percent of the information today is structured information, or information that is easily stored in relational databases of spreadsheets, with their ordinary columns and rows. However, unstructured information, such as email, video, blogs, call center conversations, and social media, makes up about 85% of data generated today and presents challenges in deriving meaning with conventional business intelligence tools. Information-producing devices, such as sensors, tablets, and mobile phones continue to multiply. Social networking is also growing at an accelerated pace as the world becomes more connected. Such information sharing options represents a fundamental shift in the way people, government and businesses interact with each other.

The characteristics of Big Data will shape the way government organizations ingest, analyze, manage, store, and distribute data across the enterprise and across the ecosystem. Table 1 illustrates the characteristics of Big Data and highlights the difference of "Big Data" from the historical perspective of "normal" data.

Many citizens around the world regard this collection of information with deep suspicion, seeing the data flood as nothing more than an intrusion of their privacy. But there is strong evidence that big data can play a significant economic role to the benefit not only of private commerce but also of national economies and their citizens. In fact, the data can create significant value for the world economy, enhancing the productivity and competitiveness of companies and the public sector and creating substantial economic surplus for consumers (Lehdonvirta & Ernkvist, 2011). Manyika et al. (2011) estimate that government administration in Europe could save more than €100 billion in operational efficiency improvements alone by using big data.

Table 1. Characteristics of big data (Wilson & Kerber, 2011)

Characteristic	Description	Attribute	Driver
Volume	The sheer amount of data generated or data intensity that must be ingested, analyzed, and managed to make decisions based on complete data analysis.	The digital universe is generating a high volume of data, which is expected to increase with exponential growth.	Increase in data sources, higher resolution sensors.
Velocity	How fast data is being produced, changed and the speed with which data must be received, understood and processed.	Metrics used can be defined in the segments of accessibility, applicable and time value.	Increase in data sources, improve throughput connectivity and enhanced computing power of data generating devices.
Variety	The rise of information coming from new sources both inside and outside the walls of the enterprise or organization creates integration, management, governance, and architectural pressures in IT.	The data can be divided in the following segments: structured, unstructured, semistructured, and complexity.	Mobile, social media, videos, chat, genomics, and sensors.
Veracity	The quality and provenance of received data.	The quality of Bid Data may be good, bad, or undefined due to data inconsistency, incompleteness, ambiguities, latency, deception, and model approximations.	Data-based decisions require traceability and justification.

Furthermore, this estimate does not include big data levers that could reduce fraud, errors, and tax gaps (i.e., the gap between potential and actual tax revenue).

Digital data is currently in every economic sector, organization and user of digital technology. Big data can be used in a lot of different fields for the following purposes:

- **Retail:** CRM applications, supply chain optimization, and fraud detection/prevention.
- **Financial Services:** Algorithmic trading, risk analysis, and portfolio analysis.
- **Manufacturing:** Product research, engineering analysis, process and quality analysis, and distribution optimization.
- **Government:** Market governance, econometrics, and counter-terrorism.
- **Advertising and Public Relations:** Demand signaling, ad targeting, sentiment analysis and customer acquisition.
- **Media and Telecommunications:** Network optimization, churn prevention and fraud detection;
- **Healthcare and Life Sciences:** Bio-informatics, pharmaceutical research, and clinical outcomes research.

According to IDC (2009), it is expected a 2500 exabytes of new information until the end of 2012 with digital content as the primary driver. Moreover, digital universe grew by 62% in 2011. This scenario is illustrated in Figure 1.

In the early 2012, the Big Data market stands at just over $5 billion based on related software, hardware, and services revenue (Kelly et al., 2012). Currently, the services component represents almost half of the total revenue. Increased interest in and awareness of the power of Big Data and related analytic capabilities to gain competitive advantage and to improve operational efficiencies, coupled with developments in the technologies and services, will result in a super-charged CAGR of 58% until 2017 (Kelly et al., 2012).

The ability to store, aggregate, and combine data and then use the results to perform deep analysis has become ever more accessible as trends such as Moore's Law in computing, its equivalent in digital storage, and cloud computing continue to lower costs and other technology barriers (Brill, 2007). Further, the ability to generate, communicate, share, and access data has been revolutionized by the increasing number of people, devices, and sensors that are now connected by digital networks. According to Manyika et al. (2011), more than

Figure 1. Data growth and expansion (IDC, 2009)

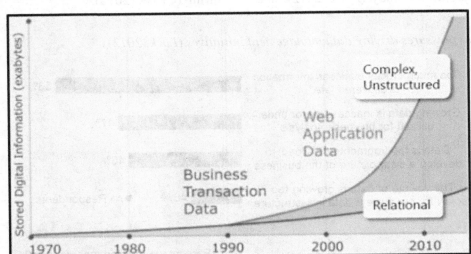

4 billion of people in 2010 were using mobile phones, and about 12 percent of those people had smartphones, whose penetration is growing at more than 20 percent a year. At the same time, more than 30 million networked sensor nodes are present in the transportation, automotive, industrial, utilities, and retail sectors. The number of these sensors is increasing at a rate of more than 30 percent a year (Manyika et al., 2011).

Aberdeen's research demonstrates that companies are seeing an average year growth of 38% in data volume (Lock, 2012). The average company confronts 2.5 times more data than it did three years ago, which is an increase that might seem particularly small for particularly data-driven companies. However, data is growing in complexity and variety as well as volume. Between data warehouses, data marts, enterprise applications, spreadsheets and external unstructured or social data, companies are drawing on an increasing number of unique data sources to drive their business analysis.

However, the influx of data presents many barriers to effective analytics, and to the creation of business insight for most decision makers (Adhikari, 2012). Whether their data is inaccessible, fragmented, or simply unwieldy from a volume perspective, companies are seeking formalized data management strategies in response. According to the Aberdeen's study (Lock, 2012), late delivery of information is the top pressure driving to develop their data management initiatives. This situation is depicted in Figure 2.

There are many ways that big data can be used to create value across sectors of the global economy. Many pioneering companies are already using big data to create value, and others need to explore how they can do the same if they are to compete. Governments also have a significant opportunity to boost their efficiency and the value for money they offer citizens at a time when public finances are strongly constrained. According to Smith (2012), big data contributed an estimated £25.1 billion to the UK economy in 2011 but, as the adoption of analytics increases, it is forecasted to reach £40.7 billion by 2017. Smith (2012) study suggests that at the same time big data analytics adoption will raise from 34 percent in 2011 to 54 percent by 2017, which is equivalent to 22 percent of the UK net debt (c. £1 trillion) or more than the 2011/12 defense, healthcare and education budgets combined. The emergence of big data is expected to benefit economies is terms of business creation, efficiency gains and innovation. Additionally, the Centre for Economics and Business Research (CEBR) in UK predicts that the most beneficial sectors from big data analysis will be the financial services, public sector, retail and manufacturing (CEBR, 2012).

Figure 2. Top pressures driving data management initiatives (Lock, 2012)

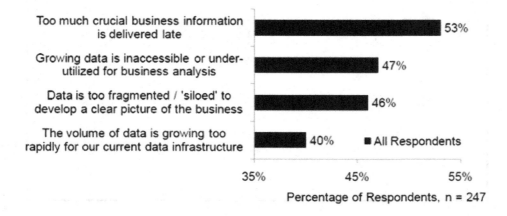

PHASES IN BIG DATA PROCESSING

Big data does not arise instantaneously, but it is recorded from some data generating sources, typically OLTP systems, spreadsheets, text files and Web content. Much of this data is of no interest, and it can be filtered and compressed by orders of magnitude. However, relevant data must be collected and loaded in a target data warehouse and business intelligence system. One challenge in this process is to define these filters in such a way that they do not discard useful information. The second big challenge is to automatically generate the right metadata to describe what data is recorded and how it is recoded and measured. Finally, another important issue here is data provenance. It is important to mention that, for instance, recording information about the data at its birth is not useful unless this information can be interpreted and carried along through the data analysis pipeline.

Data warehouse operational processes normally compose a labor intensive workflow and constitute an integral part of the back-stage of data warehouse architectures, where the collection, extraction, cleaning, transformation, and transport of data takes place, in order to populate the warehouse. To deal with this workflow, and in order to facilitate and manage the data warehouse operational processes, specialized tools are already available in the market, under the general title Extraction-Transformation-Loading (ETL) tools.

ETL tools represent an important part of data warehousing, as they represent the mean in which data actually gets loaded into the warehouse. The Figure 3 illustrates each individual stage in the process.

Data is extracted from the data sources using a data extraction tool via whatever data connectivity is available. It is then transformed using a series of transformation routines. This transformation process is largely dictated by the data format of the output. Data quality and integrity checking is performed as part of the transformation process, and corrective actions are built into the process. Transformation and integrity checking are performed in the data staging area. Finally, once the data is in the target format, it is then loaded into the data warehouse ready for presentation.

The process is often designed from the end backwards, in that the required output is designed first. In so doing, this informs exactly what data is required from the source. The routines designed and developed to implement the process are written specifically for the purpose of achieving the desired output, and only the data required for the output is included in the extraction process. In addition, the output design must incorporate all facts and dimensions required to present both the aggregation levels required by the business intelligence solution and any possible future requirements.

Figure 3. ETL process (Golfarelli & Rizzi, 2009)

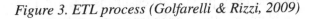

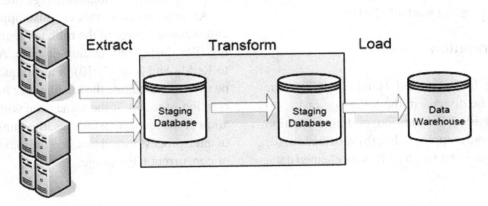

Business rules that define how aggregations are achieved and the relationships between the various entities in both the source and target, are designed and therefore coded into the routines that implement the ETL process. This process leads to tight dependencies in the routines at each stage of the process.

In all phases of an ETL process, individual issues can arise, making data warehouse refreshment a very troublesome task. In next sections, we briefly describe the most common issues, problems, and constraints that turn up in each phase separately.

Extraction

During the ETL process, one of the very first tasks that must be performed is the extraction of the relevant information that has to be further propagated to the warehouse. In order to minimize the overall processing time, this involves only a fraction of the source data that has changed since the previous execution of the ETL process, mainly concerning the newly inserted and possibly updated records. Usually, change detection is physically performed by the comparison of two snapshots (one corresponding to the previous extraction and the other to the current one). Efficient algorithms exist for this task, like the snapshot differential algorithms presented by Labio and Garcia-Molina (1996). Another popular technique is log sniffing, which consists in the scanning of the log file in order to reconstruct the changes performed since the last scan (Jorg & Dessloch, 2010).

Transformation

According to Rahm and Hai Do (2000), this phase can be divided in the following tasks: (a) data analysis; (b) definition of transformation workflow and mapping rules; (c) verification; (d) transformation; and (e) backflow of cleaned data.

In terms of transformation tasks, Lenzerini (2002) distinguishes two main classes of problems: (a) conflicts and problems at the schema level (e.g., naming and structural conflicts) and (b) data level transformations (i.e., at the instance level). According to Vassiliadis et al. (2005), the main problems with respect to the schema level are in terms of naming conflicts, where the same name is used for different objects (homonyms) or different names are used for the same object (synonyms). Furthermore, structural conflicts can also appear where one must deal with different representations of the same object in different sources.

The integration and transformation programs perform a wide variety of functions, such as reformatting, recalculating, modifying key structures, adding an element of time, identifying default values, supplying logic to choose between multiple sources, summarizing, merging data from multiple sources, etc.

Loading

The final phase of the ETL process has also its own technical challenges. A major problem is the ability to discriminate between new and existing data at loading time. This problem arises when a set of records has to be classified to the new rows that need to be appended to the warehouse, and rows that already exist in the data warehouse, but their value has changed and must be updated (Castellanos et al., 2009). Currently modern ETL tools already provide mechanisms towards this problem, mostly through language predicates.

An extra problem that can also appear is the simultaneous usage of the rollback segments and log files during the loading process. According to Reddy and Jena (2010), a technique that can be used that facilitate the loading task involve the creation of tables at the same time with the creation of the respective indexes, the minimization of inter-process wait states, and the maximization of concurrent CPU usage.

CHALLENGES IN BIG DATA ANALYSIS

Applying big data analytics faces several challenges related with the characteristics of data, analysis process and social concerns.

The first challenge appears in terms of privacy. The privacy is the most sensitive issue, with conceptual, legal, and technological implications. This concern increases its importance in the context of big data. In its narrow sense, privacy is defined by the International Telecommunications Union (Gordon, 2005) as the "right of individuals to control or influence what information related to them may be disclosed". Privacy can also be understood in a broader sense as encompassing that of companies wishing to protect their competitiveness and consumers and stages eager to preserve their sovereignty and citizens. In both these interpretations, privacy is an overarching concern that has a wide range of implications for anyone wishing to explore the use of big data for development in terms of data acquisition, storage, retention, use and presentation.

Another challenge, indirectly related with the previous, is the access and sharing of information. It is common to expect reluctance of private companies and other institutions to share data about their clients and users, as well as about their own operations. Obstacles may include legal or reputational considerations, a need to protect their competitiveness, a culture of secrecy, and more broadly, the absence of the right incentive and information structures. There are also institutional and technical challenges, when data is stored in places and ways that make it difficult to be accessed and transferred.

Another very important direction is to rethink security for information sharing in big data use cases. Many online services today require us to share private information (i.e., Facebook, LinkedIn, etc), but beyond record-level access control we do not understand what it means to share data, how the shared data can be linked, and how to give users fine-grained control over this sharing.

The size of big data structures is also a crucial point that cans constraint the performance of the system. Managing large and rapidly increasing volumes of data has been a challenging issue for many decades. In the past, this challenge was mitigated by processors getting faster, which provide us with the resources needed to cope with increasing volumes of data. But there is a fundamental shift underway now considering that data volume is scaling faster than computer resources.

Considering the size issue, we also know that the larger the data set to be processed, the longer it will take to analyze. The design of a system that effectively deals with size is likely also to result in a system that can process a given size of data set faster. However, it is not just this speed that is usually meant when we refer to speed in the context of big data. Rather, there is an acquisition rate challenge in the ETL process. Typically, given a large data set, it is often necessary to find elements in it that meet a specific criterion which likely occurs repeatedly. Scanning the entire data set to find suitable elements is obviously impractical. Rather, index structures are created in advance to permit finding qualifying elements quickly.

Finally, working with new data sources brings a significant number of analytical challenges. The relevance and harshness of those challenges will vary depending on the type of analysis being conducted, and on the type of decisions that the data might eventually inform. The big core challenge is to analyze what the data is really telling us in a fully transparent manner. The challenges are intertwined and difficult to consider in isolation, but according to King & Powell (2008), they can be split into three categories: (a) getting the picture right (i.e., summarizing the data), (b) interpreting or making sense of the data through inferences, and (c) defining and detecting anomalies.

IMPLEMENTATION FRAMEWORK

There are many different options that can be selected for a big data analysis program. Options include vendor tool types and tool features, users' techniques and methodologies, and team or organizational structures. When we look to the conceptually organization of a big data analysis, we can organize these tools in the following three components:

- **Data Capture and Preprocessing:** Includes the ETL process, API methods, crawlers and messaging systems.
- **Data Processing and Interaction:** Adopts three domains: NoSQL systems, NewSQL systems and search engines.
- **Auxiliary Tools:** Includes complementary tools for virtualization, deep correlation analysis, business intelligence and visualization tools.

Data Capture and Preprocessing

Traditionally the data in the real world is dirty. The main issues arise from incomplete information, errors and inconsistent levels. As a consequence, if there is no quality data, then no quality mining results could be obtained. It is crucial that quality decision must be based on quality data and, for that, data warehouses need consistent integration of quality data.

ETL Tools

ETL (Extract, Transform and Load) tools are used to map and move large volumes of data from one system to another. They are most frequently used as data integration aids, particularly to consolidate data from multiple databases into a central data warehousing through bulk data transfers.

The times of increasing data-dependence forced a lot of companies to invest in complicated data warehousing systems. Their differentiation and incompatibility led to an uncontrolled growth of costs and time needed to coordinate all the processes. The ETL (extract, transform, load) tools were created to simplify the data management with simultaneous reduction of absorbed effort.

Depending on the needs of customers there are several types of tools. One of them perform and supervise only selected stages of the ETL process like data migration tools and data transformation tools. Another are complete ETL Tools, which have many functions that are intended for processing large amounts of data or more complicated ETL projects.

Some of them like server engine tools execute many ETL steps at the same time from more than one developer, while other like client engine tools are simpler and execute ETL routines on the same machine as they are developed. There are two more types. First called code base tools is a family of programming tools which allow you to work with many operating systems and programming languages. The second one called GUI base tools remove the coding layer and allow you to work without any knowledge (in theory) about coding languages.

The ETL process brings important benefits in the big data toolbox. Firstly, it simplifies the process of migrating data with a standardization method of data migration. Secondly, when we follow an ETL approach, all the data transformation logic/rules is stored as metadata. At last, it enables users, managers and architects to understand, review and modify the various interfaces. Additionally, it reduces significantly costs and efforts associated with building interfaces.

A common mistake is to write custom programs to perform the extraction, transformation, and load functions. Writing an ETL program by hand may seem to be a viable option because the program does not appear to be too complex and programmers are available. However, there are serious problems with hand-coded ETL programs.

Unlike OLTP applications, the functions to be supported by individual data marts cannot be predicted in advance. In a typical data mart, over 50% of the required functionality is defined by end users after the data mart goes into production. To keep up with the high volume of changes initiated by end users, hand-written ETL programs have to be constantly modified and in many cases rewritten. The effort required to maintain these programs often becomes a major burden for the project.

Metadata is not generated automatically by hand-generated ETL programs. Metadata is the key to integrating data marts across business units. If metadata is not available, it is difficult to avoid the development of "stovepipe" data marts that satisfy the needs of individual business units, but cannot be integrated across the enterprise. Hand-coded ETL programs are likely to have a slower speed of execution, compared with directly executable code generated by off-the-shelf ETL tools. Hand generated programs are typically single-threaded, while modern ETL tools generate multi-threaded, directly executable code that can run on parallel, high-speed engines.

A good solution is the adoption of Off-the-shelf ETL tools, which are increasingly being used to extract, cleanse, transform, and load data into target databases. An important function of these tools is to generate and maintain centralized metadata. The ETL tool provides coordinated access to multiple data sources. Functions supported by ETL tools include extraction of data from multiple source environments, data cleansing, reorganization, transformation, aggregation, calculation, automatic loading of data into the target database, and automatic generation of executable code to perform parallel processing of transformations on multiple engines. These tools are used to generate and maintain a central metadata repository. The metadata repository provides a "single version of the truth" that can be used to define enterprise-wide source data definitions, data models for target

databases, and transformation rules that convert source data into target data. A metadata exchange architecture is used to synchronize central business rules with local business rules, maintained as local metadata by end-user BI tools.

The ETL tool also addresses the dirty data problem. Data from source files can be cleansed and inconsistencies in the data resolved as part of the extraction and transformation process, using procedural data cleansing techniques. Name and address correction, de-duping, and house-holding functions require use of an external data cleansing tool. Analysts define source-to-target mappings, data cleansing rules, and data transformation rules using a graphical point-and-click interface provided by the ETL tool. When all mappings and transformations have been specified, the ETL tool automatically generates the data extract/transformation/load programs, which typically run in batch mode.

In Big Data environments, the extract process can sometimes place an unacceptable burden on source systems, and the transform stage can be a bottleneck if the data is minimally structured or very raw (most ETL platforms require an external or add-on module to handle unstructured data). The load process can also be quite slow even when the code is optimized for large volumes. This is why ETL transfers, which are widely used to feed data warehouses, tend to be executed during off-hours (usually overnigh) resulting in unacceptable data latency in some situations.

APIs

An Application Programming Interface (API) is a software interface that allows two different applications to communicate, or interface, with each other. An API is used to enhance features and add functionality to one or both applications. APIs are implemented by writing function calls in the program, which provide the linkage to the required subroutine for execution. Thus, an API implies that some program module is available in the computer to perform the operation or that it must be linked into the existing program to perform the tasks. APIs typically employ standard programming languages and protocols to facilitate exchanges (e.g., HTTP/REST, Java, XML). Specific instances of packaged APIs on system are often referred to as "connectors" and may be general in nature, like the Java Database Connectivity (JDBC) API for connecting to most common DBMS.

With Big Data loads, APIs can cause bottle necks due to poor design or insufficient computing or network resources, but they have generally proven to be flexible and capable tools for exchanging large-volume data and services. In fact, it is common to achieve better performance with an embedded ETL tool than an API. Furthermore, APIs are generally not the best choice for collecting data from the Web. This happens because only a tiny percentage of online data sources are currently accessible via an API. Besides that, formats and access methods can often change at any time.

Crawlers

A crawler is a software program that connects to a data source, methodically extracts the metadata and content it contains, and sends the extracted content back to a host system for indexation. The features of crawlers include:

- **Robustness:** Ability to handle spider-traps (cycles, dynamic Web pages, etc.).
- **Distribution:** Crawling should be distributed within several machines.
- **Scalability:** Crawling should be extensible by adding machines, extending bandwidth, etc.
- **Efficiency:** Clever use of the processor, memory, bandwidth (e.g., as few idle processes as possible).
- **Freshness:** Should continuously crawl the Web (visiting frequency of a page should be close to its modification frequency).

One type of crawler is a file system crawler. This kind of crawler works its way recursively through computer directories, subdirectories and files to gather file content and metadata (e.g., file path, name, size, and last modified date). File system crawlers are used to collect unstructured content like text documents, semi-structured content like logs, and structured content like XML files. Another type of crawler is a Web (HTTP/HTTPS) crawler. This type of crawler accesses a Website, captures and transmits the page content it contains along with available metadata (page titles, content labels, etc.), then follows links (or a set visitation list to proceed to the next site.

The crawler working process can be divided in four steps: (a) the crawler begins with a seed set of URLs to fetch; (b) the crawler fetches and parses the corresponding Webpages, and extract both text and links; (c) the text is fed to a text indexer, the links (URL) are added to a URL frontier (e.g., crawling agenda); and (d) already fetched URLs are appended to the URL frontier for later re-processing. There are, of course, some potential issues within these steps. Some links encountered during parsing may be relative paths that need normalizations. Additionally, pages of a given Web site may contain several duplicated links and some of these links may point to robot-free areas. The basic architecture of a standard Web crawler is given in Figure 4.

As with other data collection tools, one needs to configure crawls so as not to place an undue load on the source system. The quality of the crawler determines the extent to which loads can be properly managed. It should also be kept in mind that crawlers recognize only a limited number of document formats (e.g., HTML, XML, text, PDF, etc.). If there is the need to use a crawler to gather non-supported document formats, then we need to convert data into an ingestible format using tools like API connectors (standard with most commercial search engines), source-system export tools, ETL platforms or messaging systems.

Figure 4. Basic architecture of a standard web crawler (Wilber, 2012)

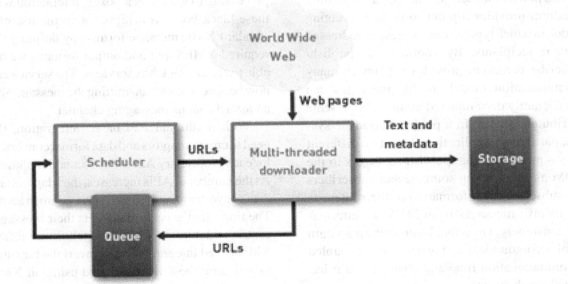

There are some special challenges associated with Web crawling, which are particularly relevant in a Big Data scenario:

- **Missed Content:** Valuable data on the Web exists in unstructured, semi-structured and structured form, including deep Web content that is dynamically generated as a result of form input and/or database querying. In fact, not all engines are capable of accessing this data and capturing its full semantic logic;

- **Low Quality Content:** While crawlers are designed to cast a wide net, with back-end search engines (or other DMS) being responsible for separating the wheat from the chaff, overall quality can nevertheless be improved if a crawler can be configured to do some preliminary qualitative filtering, for example, excluding certain document types, treating the content of a site as a single page to avoid crowding out other relevant sources (Website collapsing), detecting and applying special rules for duplicate and near duplicate content, etc.;

- **Performance Problems:** Load management is especially important in Web crawling. If it is not possible to properly regulate the breadth and depth of a crawl according to the business needs and resources, then easily performance problems can be found. On the same way, encounter performance issues can be found if a refined update strategy is not employed.

Messaging Systems

While traditional point-to-point and synchronous communication models are popular in rigid and static applications, Message-Oriented Middleware (MOM), provides a versatile middleware system to loosely integrate distributed systems (Ashraf & Helal, 2012). As the name suggests, a Message-Oriented Middleware system enables distributed applications to communicate by routing their messages through the middleware system. In this system, the client application sends messages to the MOM and the MOM is responsible for delivering the message to remote receivers. There are two broad categories of message- oriented middleware: message queuing and publish/subscribe. The message queuing paradigm provides a point-to-point messaging model, in which typically messages are addressed to their recipients. By contrast, the publish/subscribe paradigm provides a many-to-many communication model so that messages can be efficiently disseminated across a large scale distributed system. In a publish/subscribe system, participant applications have two different roles – publishers that publish messages to the MOM as information sources, and subscribers that subscribe the information of their interests and receive messages from MOM as information consumers. The publish/subscribe paradigm enables communicating parties to be decoupled in communication time and channel and it has gained much attention in last several years.

A fundamental problem in a publish/subscribe system is how to match the interests of subscribers with the available messages from publishers. The publish/subscribe systems can be classified in two categories: topic-based or content-based. In a topic-based system, each message is classified as belonging to one of a fixed set of topics, also referred as groups, channels, or subjects. A publisher labels each message it produces with a particular topic.

MOM platforms may be standalone applications or they may be bundled within broader SOA suites. They are often used to manage the asynchronous exchange of event-driven, small-packet data (like barcode scans, stock quotes, weather data, session logs and meter readings) between diverse systems. In some instances, a Complex Event Processing (CEP) engine may be deployed to analyze this data in real time, applying complex trend detection, pattern matching and causality modeling to streaming information and taking action as prescribed by business rules.

Through the combination of these technologies, we are able to create Service-Oriented Architectures (SOA). The fundamental design concept behind these architectures is to reduce application processing to logic black boxes. Interaction with these black boxes is achieved with the use of a standard XML message format; by defining the required XML input and output formats, we are able to create black box services. The service can now be accessed by transmitting the message over an asynchronous messaging channel.

With traditional API-based integration, the need to create adaptors and data format converters for each proprietary API is not a scalable solution. As the number of APIs increases, the adaptors and data converters required will scale geometrically. The important aspect of SOAs is their message-centric structure. Where message formats differ, XML-based integration can convert the message to and from the format required using an XML transformation pipeline.

In this approach, data transformation can be seen as just another assembly line problem, allowing services to be true black box components with the use of an XML-in and XML-out contract (Ashraf & Helal, 2012). Users of the services simply need to transform their data to the services contract XML format. Integration via SOA is significantly cheaper than integration via APIs, with transformations taking place outside of the applications. In this deployment, the system has been created by interconnecting six subsystems and integrating them, each of the subsystems is built using a different technology for their primary implementation.

Message systems were specifically designed to meet the high volume, high velocity data needs of industries like finance, banking and telecommunications. Bi g data volumes can nonetheless overload some MOM systems, particularly if the MOM is performing extensive data processing, which includes filtering, aggregation, transformation, etc. This data processing is performed at the bus level. In such situations, performance can be improved by offloading processing tasks to either source or destination systems.

Data Processing and Interaction

Nowadays, classic DBMS platforms are complemented by a rich set of alternative DMS specifically designed to handle the high volume, variety, velocity and variability of Big Data collections (the so-called "4Vs" of Big Data). These DMS include NoSQL, NewSQL and Search-based systems. All can ingest data supplied by any of the capture and preprocessing tools discusses in the previous sections.

NoSQL

NoSQL, for "Not Only SQL", refers to an eclectic and increasingly familiar group of non-relational data management systems (e.g., Hadoop, Cassandra, and BerkeleyDB). NoSQL systems generally have six key features:

1. The ability to horizontally scale throughput over many servers.
2. The ability to replicate and to distribute (partition) data over many servers.
3. A simples call level interface or protocol (in contrast to a SQL binding).
4. A weaker concurrency model than the ACID transactions of most relational (SQL) database systems.
5. Efficient use of distributed indexes and RAM for data storage.
6. The ability to dynamically add new attributes to data records.

Another key feature of NoSQL systems is the horizontal scaling, which consists in replicating and portioning data over many servers. This allows them to support a large number of simple read/write operations per second. This simple operation load is traditionally called OLTP (online transaction processing), but it is also common in modern Web applications.

The NoSQL systems generally do not provide ACID (Atomicity, Consistency, Isolation, and Durability) transactional properties: updates are eventually propagated, but there are limited guarantees on the consistency of reads. Therefore, NoSQL follows the BASE (Basically Available, Soft state, Eventually consistent) paradigm. The idea is that by giving up ACID constraints, one can achieve much higher performance and scalability. As a consequence, NoSQL systems generally give up of the consistency attribute.

The idea behind NoSQL systems is to use it when we need speed and availability but, at the same time, we must accept some level of inconsistency, including lost transactions. There are two important concepts regarding consistence maintenance. The strict consistency approach defends that all read operations must return data from the latest completed write operation, regardless of which replica the operation went to. This implies that either read and write operations for a given dataset have to be executed on the same node or that strict consistency is assured by a distributed transaction protocol (like two-phase-commit). On the other side, eventually consistency approach advocates that system will eventually return the last written value. Clients, therefore, may face an inconsistent state of data as updates are in progress. For instance, in a replicated database updates may go to one node which replicates the latest version to all other nodes that contain a replica of the modified dataset so that the replica nodes eventually will have the latest version.

Assuming that data in large scale systems exceeds the capacity of a large machine and should also be replicated to ensure reliability and allow scaling measures such as load-balancing, ways of portioning the data of such a system have to be thought about. Strauch (2011) states that depending on the size of the system and the other factors like dynamism there are different approaches to address the portioning issue:

- **Memory Caches:** In-memory databases as they replicate most frequently requested parts of a database to main memory, can rapidly deliver this data to clients and therefore disburden database servers significantly. The memory cache consists of an array of processes with an assigned amount of memory that can be launched on several machines in a network and are made known to an application via configuration.
- **Clustering:** It is another approach to partition data which strives for transparency towards clients who should not notice talking to a cluster of database server instead of a single server. While this approach can help to scale the persistence layer of a system to a certain degree many criticize that clustering features have only been added on top of DBMS that were not originally designed for distribution;
- **Separating Reads from Writes:** Means to specify one or more dedicated servers, write-operations for all or parts of the data are routed to masters, as well as a number of replica-servers satisfying read-requests slaves. If the master replicated to its clients asynchronously there are no write lags but if the master crashes before completing replication to at least one client the write-operation is lost; if the master replicates write synchronously to one slave lags the update does not get lost, but read cannot go to any slave if strict consistency is required and furthermore write lags cannot be avoided.
- **Sharding:** It means to partition the data in such a way that data typically requested and updated together resides on the same node and that load and storage volume is roughly even distributed among the servers (i.e., in relation to their storage volume and processing power). Data shards may also be replicated for reasons of reliability and load-balancing and it may be either al-

lowed to write to a dedicated replica only or to all replicas maintaining a partition of the data. To allow such a sharding scenario there has to be a mapping between data partitions (shards) and storage nodes that are responsible for these shards.

Table 2 summarizes the pros and cons of a NoSQL system.

NoSQL systems offer affordable and highly scalable solutions for meeting particular large-volume data storage, processing and analysis needs. However, the following common constraints should be kept in mind in evaluating NoSQL solutions:

- **Inconsistent Maturity Level:** Many are open source solutions with the normal level of volatility inherent in that development methodology, and they vary widely in the degree of support, standardization and packing offering. Therefore, what one saves in licensing can sometimes be eaten up in professional services.
- **Lack of Expertise:** There is limited talent pool of engineers who can deploy and manage these systems. There are likewise relatively few developers or end users who are well-versed in the query languages and tools they use.
- **Inaccessibility:** NoSQL systems generally do not provide native full-text indexing, full text searching, and most do not provide automatic categorization and clustering. A separate search engine would need to be deployed to provide these functions.
- **Weak Security:** In terms of access rights, many have weak to non-existent native security, leaving security to be enforced in the application layer. In terms of physical security, most compromise on data recoverability in order to boost performance, though most also allow the user to manage this trade-off.

Table 2. Pros and cons of NoSQL systems

Pros	Cons
Scalability	Not ACID
Fast	No security (authentication and authorization)
Availability	No SQL (no ad-hoc support)
Suitable for Big Data	Data independence missing

NewSQL

Like their NoSQL counterparts, these new SQL-based DBMS achieve Big Data scalability through the use of distributed architectures (e.g., MPP), in-memory processing, the use of solid state drive (SDD) technology and by incorporating some NoSQL-inspired flexibility into their data models. Others employ in-database analytics, which is a strategy that combines data warehousing and analytical functions in a single system to reduce latency and avoid the overhead of moving data back and forth between the database and a separate analytics platform.

Those achieving their primary gains through in-memory and SSD technologies tend to be ACID-compliant solutions focused on OLTP. Those gaining on a primary advantage through in-database and MPP technologies (like inventive parallelization techniques) are generally intended for data analytics and often relax consistency-related ACID constraints in boos performance. Unlike NoSQL solutions, NewSQL systems tend to be commercial rather than open source (though they may incorporate open source components), with their MPP capacity usually achieved through symmetric processing across a large number of processors embedded within a single high-end computer (usually proprietary), or a small cluster of such computer.

NewSQL solutions offer also a number of specific technical characteristics. In a first instance, SQL is established as the primary mechanism for application interaction and offers ACID support

for transactions. Additionaly, NewSQL paradigm offer a non-locking concurrency control mechanism so real-time reads will not conflict with write, and thus cause them to stall. Besides that, NewSQL supports a scale-out, shared-nothing architecture, capable of running on a large number of nodes without suffering bottlenecks (Venkatesh & Nirmala, 2012).

The NewSQL paradigm represents a new breed of relational database products retaining SQL and ACID properties. Like NoSQL, the NewSQL is designed to meet scalability requirements of distributed architectures. Therefore, the performance is improved, so horizontal scalability is no longer a necessity.

When we look to the commercial implementation of NewSQL systems we verify that these solutions are expensive particularly for SME segment. In addition to licensing and developing costs, they either need to run on expensive high-end servers, or they are high-ticket integrated hardware/software applicances, sometimes requiring a full replacing of an existing system, making scaling costly, and restricting business agility through vendor lock-in.

These systems are also expressly engineered for transaction processing or deep analytics. For ACID-compliant transaction processing or complex analytics at Big Data scale, such constraints may represent worthwhile compromises. However, discrete NoSQL and search-based solutions based in Cloud environments are likely to better fit the company needs, particularly in terms of complex exploratory analytics without structured data integration (NoSQL), low latency, and enrichment of an existing database with unstructured content.

Search Platforms

Modern enterprise search platforms are built to combine the ability to extract value from the scale, the information and user inconsistency of the Internet, and the information richness and strategic importance in enterprises. A key word in a Data Warehousing is performance. The use of complex ad-hoc queries traditionally necessitated the creation of separate data marts to shield the data warehouse from loads that can impact performance. AIW changes this by consistently delivering sub-second query response to a broad range of SQL queries that represent typical use in a BI environment. This is true regardless of data model, and without prior optimization of either queries or schema. Users and enterprises demand these systems to handle terabytes of data, hundreds of data updates per second, thousands of queries per second, while maintaining sub-second query response, all at the same time. And they demand high speed analysis across all of these parameters, therefore ad-hoc query performance is a unique differentiator and makes possible all the following search-enabled differentiators (Sutija et al., 2007).

Object Association and Dynamic Profiling: Extracting and analyzing classes of variables in each data source, such as names, addresses and transactional metadata, ranging to hundreds of attributes typically stored in CRM system and data marts, allows the creation of new associated objects for the purposes of dynamic relationship discovery. Profiled dimensions are discovered on the fly for each result set, and regardless of their cardinality their component elements are numerically displayed to the user. These allow the user to properly create complex queries through intuitive contextual navigation. This provides BI developers with a short time to information distribution, because it removes the need to tag and classify the data. The time that traditional BI systems need to build new information cubes is one of the major pain points for information freshness and accessibility. Easy access and a complete view of supporting data provides business users with the tools to unearth new levels of associated information that support better decisions as well as the means to detect trends and relationships that were previously never known or explored.

Combining structured and unstructured information, data warehousing solutions leverages the advancement of XML technologies, a de facto standard document structuring framework that allows authors to define their own sets of meta data. Retrieval systems dealing with a large number of sources need the same flexibility, so they must be "schema independent." Contextual search engines provide this independence by replacing predefined index layouts with a nested structure that has scopes and tags. With this, new types of precise queries can be asked that combine structure and content, imposing contextual constraints on the content. Scalability and consistency of the system are the very foundation for heavy data crunching behind the scenes, seamlessly filtering and improving structured, unstructured and rich media content, queries and results, with no performance penalty for the users. Once again, this power depends on simultaneous scalability in several dimensions: data volume, query traffic, data and query complexity, fault tolerance, real time capabilities, etc.

Currently search platforms are already mature, highly usable solutions for aggregating, accessing and analyzing large volume multi-format, multi-source data. They are also suitable for quickly developing secure, successful business applications built upon such data. However, they are not the best for archival data storage, OLTP or complex or historical OLAP due to performance issues.

It is essential to keep in mind that not all search engines are not created equal. In addition to the process of formal checking compatibility issues, it is helpful to use a checklist like the one presented in Table 3, to ensure a product can support a wide range of information consolidation, access, discovery and analysis needs in Big Data environments.

Auxiliary Tools

Auxiliary tools are not integrally part of the big data analysis solution but can have an important impact in its adoption level and maturity. In fact, they have the role to facilitate the integrated analysis or improve its performance

Table 3. Key questions for the choice of search platforms

Question	Criticality Level
Collect and process unstructured, structured and semistructured data?	High
Feature an open, standards-based API and connector framework?	Medium
Use semantic technologies to effectively analyze and enrich source data?	Low
Automatically categorize and cluster content to support faceted search, navigation and reporting?	Low
Offer a distributed architecture with parallel processing to ensure satisfactory performance and scalability?	Medium

and robustness. It is expected that these system will have an increased impact and evolution in next year's.

Cloud Environment

Cloud computing refers to both the applications delivered as services over the Internet and the hardware and systems software in the data centers that provide those services. Cloud computing is related to the term "grid computing" from the high-performance computing community, suggests protocols to offer shared computation and storage over long distances, but those protocols did not lead to a software environment that grew beyond its community.

Cloud computing solutions offers up several common characteristics:

- **On-Demand Self-Service:** The ability for an end user to sign up and receive services without the long delays that have characterized traditional IT.
- **Broad Network Access:** Ability to access the service via standard platforms, such as desktop, laptop, mobile, etc.
- **Resource Pooling:** Resources are pooled across multiple customers.

- **Rapid Elasticity:** Capacity can scale to cope with demand peaks.
- **Measured Service:** Billing is metered and delivered as a utility service.

Cloud computing can be seen in three categories: SaaS, PaaS and IaaS. The SaaS are designed for end-users, delivered over the Web; PaaS is the set of tools and services designed to make coding and deploying those applications quick and efficient; IaaS is the hardware and software that powers it all, which include servers, storage, networks, operating systems, etc. Figure 5 provides a more detailed overview of those models.

The data center hardware and software is what we call a "cloud". When a cloud is made available in a pay-as-you-go manner to the general public, we call it a public cloud; the service being sold is utility computing. We use the term private cloud to refer to internal data centers of a business or other organization, not made available to the general public, when they are large enough to benefit from the advantages of cloud computing that we discuss here. Thus, cloud computing is the sum of SaaS and utility computing, but does not include small or medium-sized data centers, even if these rely on virtualization for management.

From a hardware provisioning and pricing point of view, three aspects are new in cloud computing:

- The appearance of infinite computing resources available on demand, quickly enough to follow load surges, thereby eliminating the need for cloud computing users to plan far ahead for provisioning.
- The elimination of an up-front commitment by cloud users, thereby allowing companies to start small and increase hardware resources only when there is an increase in their needs.
- The ability to pay for use of computing resources on a short-term basis as needed (for example, processors by the hour and

Figure 5. Service models of cloud computing (GSA, 2012)

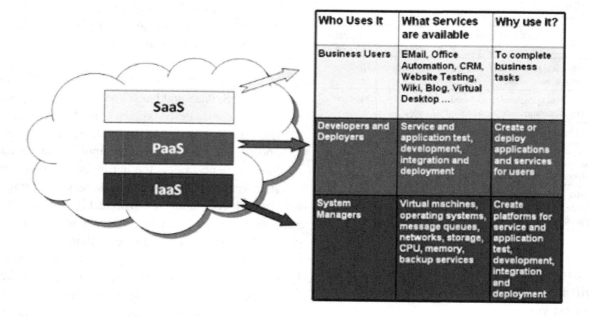

Who Uses It	What Services are available	Why use it?
Business Users	EMail, Office Automation, CRM, Website Testing, Wiki, Blog, Virtual Desktop ...	To complete business tasks
Developers and Deployers	Service and application test, development, integration and deployment	Create or deploy applications and services for users
System Managers	Virtual machines, operating systems, message queues, networks, storage, CPU, memory, backup services	Create platforms for service and application test, development, integration and deployment

storage by the day) and release them as needed, thereby rewarding conservation by letting machines and storage go when they are no longer useful.

Literature in the field of cloud computing identifies five main reasons for its adoption: scalability, cost savings, business agility, built-in disaster recovery and location independence.

Scalability is a key aspect in cloud computing. The ability of the platform to expand and contract automatically based on capacity needs (sometimes referred as "elasticity"), and the charging model associated with this, are key elements that distinguish cloud computing from other forms of hosting. Cloud computing provides resources on-demand for many of the typical scaling points that an organization needs including servers, storage and networking. The on-demand nature of cloud computing means that as the business demands grow, the company can more easily match the capacity (and costs) to the demand. There is no need to over-provision for the peaks. On the other

side, at the software level, cloud computing allows developers and IT operations to develop, deploy and run applications that can easily grow capacity, work fast and never, or at least rarely, fail, all without any concern as to the nature and location of the underlying infrastructure.

One of the most cited benefits of the Cloud Computing migration is the economy of scale. Costs savings are particularly important in the actual scenario of economic recession. With the introduction of a Cloud Computing solution, costs savings may be generated:

- By lowering the opportunity cost of running technology.
- By allowing for a shift from capital expenditure to operating expenditure.
- By lowering the Total Cost of Ownership (TCO) of technology.
- By giving organizations the ability to add business value by renewed focus on core activities.

Another advantage of cloud computing is that it enables an organization to be more agile. The speed at which new computing capacity can be requisitioned is a vital element of cloud computing. Adding additional storage, network bandwidth, memory, and computing power can be done rapidly and often instantaneously. At the same time, cloud computing allows organizations to react more quickly to market conditions and to scale up and down as needed. New applications can be quickly released with lower up-front costs. The flexibility offered by cloud computing enables innovative ideas to be rapidly tried and tested without the need to divert existing IT staff from their daily routine.

With cloud computing, the burden of managing technology is placed on the technology provider. It is their responsibility to provide built-in data protection, fault tolerance, self-healing and disaster recovery. Typical disaster recovery costs are estimated at twice the cost of the infrastructure. With a cloud-based model, true disaster recovery is estimated to cost little more than one times the costs, a significant saving. Additionally, because cloud service providers replicate their data, even the loss of one or two data centers will not result in lost data. Furthermore, cloud computing provides a high level of redundancy at a price point traditional managed solutions cannot match.

Cloud computing is already enabling greater device independence, greater portability, and greater opportunities for interconnection and collaboration. With applications and data located in the cloud it becomes much easier to enable users to access systems regardless of their location or what device they are using. However, the introduction of a corporate cloud computing also brings some additional issues that should be properly managed and analyzed. Among them we highlight security, data location and privacy, Internet dependency, performance, availability, and migration issues.

The information housed on the cloud is often seen as valuable to individuals with malicious intent. There is a lot of personal information and potentially secure data that people store on their computers, and this information is now being transferred to the cloud. This makes it critical for a company to understand the security measures that your cloud provider has in place, and it is equally important to take personal precautions to secure your data. Therefore, the first thing the company must look into is the security measures that the cloud provider already has in place. These vary from provider to provider and among the various types of clouds, but they are three key questions: What encryption methods do the providers have in place? What methods of protection do they have in place for the actual hardware that your data will be stored on?

Another concern for many organizations is that cloud computing relies on the availability, quality and performance of their Internet connection. Moving an existing in-house application to the cloud will almost certainly have some trade-offs in terms of performance. Most existing enterprise applications will not have been designed with the cloud in mind. On the other side, data in cloud computing environment has to exist on physical servers somewhere in the world and the physical location of those servers is important under many nations' laws. This is especially important for companies that do business across national boundaries, as different privacy and data management laws apply in different countries.

One of the most common concerns regarding cloud computing is the potential for down-time if the system is not available for use. This is a critical issue for line-of-business apps, since every minute of downtime is a minute that some important business function cannot be performed. Every minute of downtime cannot only affect revenue but can also cause reputation damage. As a result, many companies think of adoption cloud computing will look to the Service-Level Agreements (SLAs) to give them some comfort about availability.

Moving an existing application to a cloud platform is not as easy as it might first appear. Different cloud providers impose different application architectures which are invariably dissimilar to architectures of enterprise applications. So, for a complex multitier application that depends on internal databases and that serves thousands of users with ever-changing access right it is not going to be an easy switch-over to a cloud platform.

In addition to addressing concerns common to the Cloud model in general (like privacy, efficiency, vendor lock-in, availability, etc.), one needs in particular to be carefully weigh the unique challenges of working remotely with very large data sets. Such sets are expensive and slow to move around, and can tax even the best network capabilities.

Visualization Tools

Data visualization can be seen as a set of techniques used to turn a set of data into visual insight. It aims to give the data a meaningful representation by exploring the powerful discerning capabilities of the human eye.

Data warehouses and Online Analysis Processing (OLAP) have been recognized and effective solutions for helping in the decision-making process. Online analysis, thanks to operators, make it possible do display data in a multi-dimensional manner. Four views regarding the design of a data warehouse must be considered:

- **Top-Down View:** Allows selection of the relevant information necessary for the data warehouse.
- **Data Source View:** Exposes the information being captured, stored, and managed by operational systems.
- **Data Warehouse View:** Consists of fact tables and dimension tables.
- **Business Query View:** Sees the perspectives of data in the warehouse from the view of end-user.

OLAP supports the following basic operators presented in Table 4.

Table 4. Main OLAP operators

Operator	Description
Roll up	Summarize data by climbing hierarchy by dimension reduction
Drill down	Reverse of roll-up from higher level summary or lower level summary or detailed data, or introducing new dimensions
Slice and dice	Project and select
Pivot	Reorient the cube, visualization, 3D to series of 2D planes
Drill through	Through the bottom level of the cube to its backend relational tables (using SQL)

The OLAP technology is well-suited when data are simple and when the facts are analyzed with numeric measures and qualitative descriptors in dimensions. However, the advent of complex data and the increased demand of big data analysis have questioned this process of data warehousing and online analysis. By this means, new approaches to extending OLAP capabilities to complex have been suggested. The idea is the use Visual Data Mining technology for visually and interactively exploring OLAP cubes. This process combines data mining and online analysis. Two approaches are suggested: CPM model (Cube Presentation Model) and VoCoDa (Visualization Operator for Complex Data). The former is an extended model for OLAP data which is composed of two parts: (a) a logic layer, which involves the formulation of cubes and (b) a presentational layer that involves the presentation of these cubes (normally, on a 2D screen) (Maniatis et al., 2005). The latter is an approach to online analysis for complex objects, which displays complex objects naturally in the outline analysis taking into account the semantic content of complex objects (Loudcher & Boussaid, 2012).

OLAP Visualization field is still in its preliminary stage. According to Cuzzocrea & Mansmann (2009) a key point for the success of this branch of OLAP research is represented by the relevant range of applicability of Visual OLAP in a plethora of real-life, leading applications such as real-time monitoring of multiple streaming data sources and visualization of results produced by advanced Knowledge Discovery tools including clustering, association rule discovery, frequent item set mining, sub-graph mining etc. Future improvements are particularly needed in terms of integration with data warehouse management systems, improvement of techniques for visualization integrated data-cube/data-warehouse schemes, and visual query languages for multidimensional databases.

CONCLUSION

The effective use of big data has the potential to transform economies, delivering a new wave of productivity growth and consumer surplus. Using big data will become a key basis of competition for existing companies, and will create new competitors who are able to attract employees that have the critical skills for a big data world. Leaders of organizations need to recognize the potential opportunity as well as the strategic threats that big data represent and should assess and then close any gap between their current IT capabilities and their data strategy and what is necessary to capture big data opportunities relevant to their enterprise. In this task, they will need to be creative and proactive in determining which pools of data they can combine to create value and how to gain access to those pools.

However, many technical and organizational challenges described in this chapter must be addressed before this potential can be realized fully. The challenges include not just the obvious issues of scale, but also privacy, security, heterogeneity, integration, lack of structure, data quality and regular feedback. These challenges will require transformative solutions, and will not be addressed naturally simply by the evolution of business intelligence systems. Not only enterprise IT architectures and systems administrators will need to change to accommodate it, but almost every department within a company will undergo adjustments to allow big data to inform and reveal. However, big data analysis does not replace other systems. Rather, it supplements the BI systems, data warehouses, and database systems, which are essential to financial reporting, sales management, production management, and compliance systems. The difference is that these information systems deal with the knowns that must meet high standards for rigor, accuracy, and compliance, while the emerging big data analytics tools help the companies to deal with unknowns that could affect business strategy and its execution.

Achieving and implementing the vast potential of big data analysis can be done with tools accessible to organizations of all sizes and types, without the need of supercomputers or high reliable systems. The proposed conceptual framework introduces a number of capabilities that should be consider in a big data solution, including the data collection, data management, data analysis, integration, information automation and visualization, data exchange and exploitation of cloud computing architectures.

As future research directions, there is a need to analyze deeply issues related with the aggregation of multiple sources data and its impact in data consistency and performance. Because there is limited value that can be obtained from any one source, aggregation of multiple sources is key to unlocking the potential in the enterprise data. However, an unfortunate side effect of the ability to analyze increasing volumes of data using commodity infrastructure and cloud services is the emergence of unstructured and semistructured data, which does not fit well the traditional structured databases and so creates issues around data management.

Another research point is a deeper analysis of the opportunities given by the convergence of big data and cloud environments. It will be interesting to explore possibilities for harmonizing cloud and big data measurement, benchmarking and standards in ways that bring the power of these two approaches together to facilitate innovation. The combination of cloud and big data not only can create useful insights but also can bring incredible value downstream like public safety and economic benefit.

REFERENCES

Adhikari, S. (2012). *Time for a big data diet.* Retrieved August 12, 2012, from http://technologyspectator.com.au/emerging-tech/big-data/need-big-data-speed?

Ashraf, A., & Helal, A. (2012). Measuring the latency of semantic message oriented middleware system. *Contemporary Engineering Sciences, 5*(7), 307–313.

Brill, K. (2007). The invisible crisis in the data center: The economic meltdown of Moore's law. *Uptime Institute White Paper, 7,* 1-8.

Castellanos, M., Simitsis, A., Wilkinson, K., & Dayal, U. (2009). Automating the loading of business process warehouses. In *Proceedings of International Conference on Extending Database Technology (EDBT),* (pp. 612-623). Saint-Petersburg, Russia: EDBT.

CEBR. (2012). Data equity: Unlocking the value of big data. *Centre for Economics and Business Research White Paper, 4,* 7-26.

Cuzzocrea, A., & Mansmann, S. (2009). OLAP visualization: Models, issues and techniques. In Wang, J. (Ed.), *Encyclopedia of Data Warehousing and Mining* (pp. 1439–1446). Academic Press.

Golfarelli, M., & Rizzi, S. (2009). *Data warehouse design: Modern principles and methodologies.* Columbus, OH: McGraw-Hill.

Gordon, A. (2005). *Privacy and ubiquitous network societies.* Paper presented at the Workshop on ITU Ubiquitous Network Societies. Geneva, Switzerland.

GSA. (2012). *What are the services?* Retrieved October 18, 2012, from http://info.apps.gov/content/what-are-services

IDC. (2009). As the economy contracts, the digital universe expands. *IDC White Paper, 5,* 12-18.

Jorg, T., & Dessloch, S. (2010). Near real-time data warehousing using state-of-the-art ETL tools. In Castellanos, M. et al. (Eds.), *Enabling Real-time for Business Intelligence* (pp. 100–117). Heidelberg, Germany: Springer-Verlag. doi:10.1007/978-3-642-14559-9_7.

Kelly, J., Vellante, D., & Floyer, D. (2012). *Big data market size and vendor revenues.* Retrieved October 10, 2012, from http://wikibon.org/wiki/v/Big_Data_Market_Size_and_Vendor_Revenues

King, G., & Powell, E. (2008). *How not to lie without statistics.* Boston: Harvard University. Retrieved August 12, 2012, from http://gking.harvard.edu/gking/files/nolie.pdf

Labio, W., & Garcia-Molina, H. (1996). Efficient snapshot differential algorithms for data warehousing. In *Proceedings of the 22nd International Conference on Very Large Data Bases,* (pp. 63-74). Bombay, India: IEEE.

Lehdonvirta, V., & Ernkvist, M. (2011). Converting the virtual economy into development potential: Knowledge map of the virtual economy. *InfoDev/World Bank White Paper, 1,* 5-17.

Lenzerini, M. (2002). Data integration: A theoretical perspective. In *Proceedings of the 21st Symposium on Principles of Database Systems (PODS),* (pp. 233-246). PODS.

Lock, M. (2012). Data management for BI: Big data, bigger insight, superior performance. *Aberdeen Group White Paper, 1*, 4-20.

Loudcher, S., & Boussaid, O. (2012). OLAP on complex data: Visualization operator based on correspondence analysis. *IS Olympics: Information Systems in a Diverse World, 107*, 172–185. doi:10.1007/978-3-642-29749-6_12.

Maniatis, A., Vassiliadis, P., Skiadopoulos, S., Vassiliou, Y., Mavrogonatos, G., & Michalarias, I. (2005). A presentation model & non-traditional visualization for OLAP. *International Journal of Data Warehousing and Mining, 1*(1), 1–36. doi:10.4018/jdwm.2005010101.

Manyika, J., Chui, M., Brown, B., Bughin, J., Dobbs, R., Roxburgh, C., & Byers, A. (2011). Big data: The next frontier for innovation, competition, and productivity. *McKinsey Global Institute Reports, 5*, 15–36.

Rahm, E., & Hai Do, H. (2000). Data cleaning: Problems and current approaches. *A Quarterly Bulletin of the Computer Society of the IEEE Technical Committee on Data Engineering, 23*(4), 3–13.

Reddy, V., & Jena, S. (2010). Active data warehouse loading by tool based ETL procedure. In *Proceedings of International Conference on Information and Knowledge Engineering (IKE'10)*, (pp. 196-201). Las Vegas, NV: IKE.

Slack, E. (2012). *What is big data?* Retrieved September 23, 2012, from http://www.storage-switzerland.com/Articles/Entries/2012/8/3_What_is_Big_Data.html

Smith, D. (2012). *Big data to add £216 billion to the UK economy and 58,000 new jobs by 2017*. Retrieved August 3, 2012, from http://www.sas.com/offices/europe/uk/press_office/press_releases/BigDataCebr.html

Strauch, C. (2011). *NoSQL databases*. Retrieved March 16, 2013, from http://www.christof-strauch.de/nosqldbs.pdf

Sutija, D., Thorsen, T., Wilson, T., Cammarano, J., & Seres, S. (2007). Business intelligence built on search: The adaptive information warehouse. *Fast White Paper*, 1-9.

Vassiliadis, P., Simitsis, A., Georgantas, P., Terrovitis, M., & Skiadopoulos, S. (2005). A generic and customizable framework for the design of ETL scenarios. *Information Systems, 30*(7), 492–525. doi:10.1016/j.is.2004.11.002.

Venkatesh, P., & Nirmala, S. (2012). *NewSQL – The new way to handle big data*. Retrieved March 16, 2013, from http://www.linuxforu.com/2012/01/newsql-handle-big-data/

Wilber, L. (2012). A practical guide to big data: opportunities, challenges & tools. *Dassault Systems White Papers*, 4-36.

Wilson, C., & Kerber, J. (2011). Demystifying big data: A practical guide to transforming the business of government. *TechAmerica Foundation White Papers*, 6-37.

ADDITIONAL READING

Chung, W., Chen, H., & Jay, F. (2002). *Business intelligence explorer: A knowledge map framework for discovering business intelligence on the web*. Tucson, AZ: The University of Arizona.

Collier, K. (2011). *Agile Analytics: A value-driven approach to business intelligence and data warehousing*. Boston: Addison-Wesley Professional.

Collison, C., & Parcell, G. (2001). Learning to fly. London: Capstone Publishing Limited (A Wiley Company).

Conte, R., Gilbert, N., Bonelli, G., & Helbing, D. (2011). FuturICT and social sciences: Big data, big thinking. *Zeitschrift für Soziologie, 40*, 412–413.

Cusamano, M. (2010). Technology strategy and management cloud computing and SaaS as new computing platforms. *Communications of the ACM, 53*(4), 27–29. doi:10.1145/1721654.1721667.

Gentzsch, W., & Reinefeld, A. (2009). Special section d-grid. *Future Generation Computer Systems, 25*(3), 266–267. doi:10.1016/j.future.2008.09.008.

Greenberg, A., Hamilton, J. R., Jain, N., Kandula, S., Kim, C., & Lahiri, P. et al. (2011). VL2: A scalable and flexible data center network. *Communications of the ACM, 54*(3), 95–104. doi:10.1145/1897852.1897877.

Halevy, A., Norvig, P., & Pereira, F. (2009). The unreasonable effectiveness of data. *IEEE Intelligent Systems, 24*(2), 8–12. doi:10.1109/MIS.2009.36.

Imhoff, C., Galemmo, N., & Geiger, J. G. (2003). *Mastering data warehouse design: Relational and dimensional techniques*. London: John Wiley & Sons.

Kalil, T. (2012). *Fact sheet: Big data across the federal government*. Washington, DC: Office of Science and Technology Policy, Executive Office of the President.

Kimball, R., & Caserta, J. (2004). *The data warehouse ETL toolkit: Practical techniques for extracting, cleaning and transforming*. Hoboken, NJ: Wiley.

Kimball, R., & Ross, M. (2002). *The data warehouse toolkit: The complete guide of dimensional modeling*. Hoboken, NJ: Wiley.

Meng, S., Liu, L., & Wang, T. (2011). State monitoring in cloud datacenters. *IEEE Transactions on Knowledge and Data Engineering, 23*(9), 1328–1344. doi:10.1109/TKDE.2011.70.

Miller, M. (2008). *Cloud computing: Web-based applications that change the way you work and collaborate online*. Indianapolis, IN: Que Publishing.

Ponniah, P. (2010). *Data warehousing fundamentals for IT professionals*. Hoboken, NJ: Wiley. doi:10.1002/9780470604137.

Velte, A. T., Velte, T. J., & Elsenpeter, R. (2010). *Cloud computing: A practical approach*. San Francisco, CA: McGraw-Hill/Osborne.

Vouk, M. (2008). Cloud computing - Issues, research and implementations. In *Proceedings of IEEE Information Technology Interfaces 30th International Conference*, (pp. 31-40). IEEE.

Williams, S., & Williams, N. (2007). *The profit impact of business intelligence*. Boston: Morgan Kaufmann Publishers.

Yoo, C. (2011). Cloud computing: Architectural and policy implications. *Review of Industrial Organization, 38*(4), 405–421. doi:10.1007/s11151-011-9295-7.

KEY TERMS AND DEFINITIONS

Big Data: Term typically used to describe a massive volume of both structured and unstructured data that is so large that it is difficult to process using traditional database and software techniques.

Crawler: A program that automatically fetches Web pages. Crawlers are used to feed pages to search engines. It can also be called a spider because it crawls over the Web.

Data Miner: A software application that monitors and/or analyzes the activities of a computer, and subsequently its user, of the purpose of collecting information that typically will be used for marketing purposes.

ETL: Is short for Extract, Transform and Load. These three database functions are combined into one tool to pull data out of one database and place it into another database. ETL is used to migrate data from one database to another, to form data marts and data warehouses and also to convert databases from one format or type to another.

Metadata: Describes how and when and by whom a particular set of data was collected, and how the data is formatted. Metadata is essential for understanding information stored in data warehouses and has become increasingly important in XML-based Web applications.

OLAP: Is short for Online Analytical Processing. A category of software tool that provides analysis of data stored in a database. OLAP tools enable users to analyze different dimensions of multidimensional data.

OLTP: Is short for On-Line Transaction Processing. In this model the computer responds immediately to user requests. Each request is considered to be a transaction.

Raw Data: Information that has been collected but not formatted or analyzed.

Section 4
Survey and Case Studies

Chapter 12
The Role of Security Culture

Jo Malcolmson
QinetiQ Ltd, UK

ABSTRACT

This chapter provides a discussion of the importance of the wider organisational context that the network administrator needs to deal with by describing how the organisational culture can impact on the degree to which security can be successfully maintained. It starts with an acknowledgement of the general clusters of factors that affect security (technology, processes, organisational, and human), and focuses on the human element within these. The types of risk that arise from humans in the system are described, such as motivation, ability, awareness (and lack of awareness). Errors and purposeful violations are compared, and individual, organisational, and latent risk factors explained. The chapter's key focus is the role of organisational culture. A general description of culture and its application in organisations leads into a discussion of security culture. A comparison is made between safety and security culture. Similarities are listed as the impacts of regulatory influence, reputational damage, having multiple causes, and the fact both are often driven by adverse events. Differences are examined. For example, the victim of a poor safety culture is often the perpetrator, whereas this is less often true in security violations. Intrinsic motivation and the impact of certain systems designs are further differences. Gaps in security culture research are noted as a lack of an accepted practical definition, a lack of an accepted way of measuring security culture that can be used outside narrow domains, research into engendering and enhancing security culture is narrowly focused on specific aspects of culture, and a lack of research relating security culture to organisational performance. A project to address some of these gaps by defining and measuring security culture is described. Qualitative and quantitative research was used to develop a questionnaire consisting of seven scales and fourteen sub-scales, each measuring a reliable and distinct factor. The content of these factors is noted, and a case study of the questionnaire's application to facilitate the development of security culture is outlined. Two key benefits result from the use of the questionnaire: diagnosis of aspects of security culture that may need improvement and benchmarking within (and between) organisations.

DOI: 10.4018/978-1-4666-4526-4.ch012

INTRODUCTION

This chapter begins by defining the risks to security that arises from the human in the system, and describing these in context.

Organisational performance is generally assumed to be a function of its whole system: technology, processes, and people. When designing technology and processes, managers are primarily concerned to ensure that these support the organisation's goals. Put simply, commercial organisations are designed first and foremost to make a profit, by producing goods or services, while public organisations generally provide a service. Therefore, technology and processes created in support of these aims will usually enable easy communications with potential customers / users, capture sales data, and so on.

Whilst the security of the processes and technology can be vital to organisational performance, it is rarely the case that security is of itself a primary aim: instead, security is a supporting driver, and this affects the level of significance that is attributed to it. Elements of the system are expected to provide protection against security breaches without this impacting on performance. In his book *Managing the Risks of Organisational Accidents*, James Reason (1997) describes the relationship between production and protection. He describes a "parity zone" (Reason, 1997, p.3) in which the level of protection matches the hazards of production. Outside this parity zone, it is possible to set the level of protection either too high, or too low, with both having adverse effects on the organisation. While Reason applies these concepts to safety, the conclusions are true for security also. Where protection is too high, a system may be so secure that it prevents or delays communication or some other activity that is essential to production. Where it is too low, it allows a security breach, and associated problems. Organisations are always at some risk of setting the security protection wrongly.

It is assumed that the contribution of technology and processes to security are covered in other chapters in this book, and elsewhere. This chapter focuses on the contribution of people and organisational culture to security. In it, I will argue that just as technology and processes are focused primarily to address other organisational aims, so too are people, and it should therefore be unsurprising that people chosen for their communications skills or ability to produce goods rapidly may not also be naturally focused on security. And just as a process may be set outside the "parity zone", it is also the case that staff (individually and collectively) can have an inappropriate view of the balance between the production and security needs of the organisation, that causes them to behave in a way that negatively impacts on security. These, and other factors that drive human behaviour, will be discussed.

This chapter therefore has a number of objectives. First, it will discuss the types of risk that arise from the human in the system, with a specific focus on organisational culture. Second, the role of culture in affecting organisational outcomes will be set out. Third, the commonalities and differences between security culture and safety culture will be set out. Specific research on security culture has been limited, while safety culture has attracted much interest. Researchers have proposed that there are some parallels between the two: so comparisons are worthy of consideration and an attempt to set out some of the fundamentals of this debate will be made. Fourth, a case study will be described, illustrating some key messages. These include how to define and describe security culture; how to measure it; and a practical example of data analysis and identification of actions needed for improvement.

HUMAN RISKS

The human in the system creates a number of types of risk. Whilst much has been written about outsiders who hack into organisations directly, they are not the focus of this chapter. Instead, I will focus on employees themselves. They may breach security either intentionally, or unintentionally, and knowingly or unknowingly. Both ability and motivational factors are important, and in addition to the impact of individuals, the impact of humans collectively must be considered. The organisational culture influences to what extent individuals deploy their abilities, and in what ways they are willing to do so.

Take, as an example, an employee who should use an encrypted memory stick for data transfer, but fails to do so. Even a simple action such as this may have a number of different causes, and it follows that a number of different interventions may be appropriate to prevent its recurrence. The individual may not know that he should use an encrypted device. He simply does not realize that he is the source of the problem: he is "unconsciously unskilled", and therefore needs to learn about the importance of encryption. He may know that he should encrypt the data, but not know how to: that is, he is "consciously unskilled" (Gordon Training International, 2012). In this case, he may be willing to learn how to secure it in future, and so it would be appropriate to teach him how. Conversely, there may be motivational issues - he may be able to encrypt his data but unwilling to do so, because he does not believe it is important enough, or because the process of doing so is perceived to be time-consuming. Here, security awareness training may be beneficial. In today's rapidly changing technological climate, where the types of attack, such as spear-phishing, from outside the organisation undergo frequent metamorphoses, it seems likely that many employees find it difficult to keep up with current advice about what to do. This in itself can create further ability and motivational difficulties.

The situation is further complicated when the employee has something to gain by purposely breaching security. A literature review revealed that in the financial sector the greatest threat faced in terms of theft and fraud is from inside the company (Malcolmson and Scognamiglio, 2007). Nor is personal gain the only factor that may motivate employees: they may want to damage the organisation's reputation. A review of a number of purposeful insider breaches of security revealed that individuals could be motivated by disaffection, revenge, or perceptions of injustice in the organisation, and in some cases saw the breaching security by "leaking" defamatory information about the organisation as a way of whistle-blowing when they believed the organisation was acting in a way that was unethical (Chapman, Appleyard, Christie, D'Silva, & Glanville, 2008).

What have been described so far are individual human actions in the form of errors and purposeful violations. These are often collectively called "active failures". For many years in the field of safety research accident investigations were focused on this individual factor in accidents. However, a number of conditions have combined to change the way we think about such events:

- In the 1960s and 1970s there was a growing trend to recognise the impact of other social pressures (e.g. peer pressure) on an individual's behaviour. Shortly after the Second World War, experimenters such as Asch (1952) became interested in why groups acted as they did. His work on conformity formed the basis of later work on the impact of social desirability on behaviour, and could be seen as paving the way for research into group phenomenon such as culture.

- The rise of "systems" analysis has also facilitated the recognition that a myriad of factors can impact on outcomes.

- A number of high profile accidents in the 1970s and 1980s that were the subject of significant and detailed investigation revealed that causes were often complex and multiple. In many cases a number of individuals had either collectively made poor decisions or had in sequence failed to recognise one another's errors (e.g. the Piper Alpha disaster, 1988; the Bhopal disaster, 1984).

As Reason says, "it is now recognized that people working in complex systems make errors or violate procedures for reasons that generally go beyond the scope of individual psychology. These reasons are known as latent conditions" (Reason, 1997, p.10). "Latent conditions" are defined by the Health and Safety Executive as "managerial influences and social pressures…. that influence the design of equipment or systems" (Health and Safety Executive 2012). Hence, investigations of major disasters such as Chernobyl have revealed that where things go wrong, there has often been some latent condition such as poor training, overly complex and impracticable procedures, or poor equipment that has been present for some time. It is these, combined with an inappropriate human action, (an active failure), that lead to safety breaches: and parallels have been drawn with the conditions that result in security failures. (For example, following the collapse of Barings Bank in 1995, investigators revealed a number of warning signs that fraud was occurring, that had been ignored by the bank's managers). Further, what is most interesting about latent conditions is that they are frequently the result of decisions taken by managers in the organisation or by other influencers. Often they are a result of focusing technology, processes, or people, on something else that is important—such as communications with customers—without realizing the secondary impact on safety or security. And because once these conditions exist they may become pervasive (e.g. poor processes may exist across a number of functions) they can contribute to a number of different types of security failures. In fact, both because they are designed into the organisation, (albeit inadvertently) and because of their ubiquity, these latent conditions are likely to contribute to the shaping of organisational culture.

THE ROLE OF CULTURE

At this point, it is worth discussing what organisational culture is, and why it might be assumed to be important. Organisational culture as a concept worthy of scientific enquiry has its origins in social anthropology research dating back to the early 1970s, and in social psychology of the 1950s and 1960s, that demonstrated the impact of other people's behaviour on individual actions (e.g. Asch, 1952). During the early 1980s, the study of culture became recognized as being important in the organisational sciences. It was seen as a way to provide possible explanations as to why some organisations were more successful than others, and presented as having the potential to integrate a variety of measures of performance (Zar, Stewart, Tate, Cheyne, & Cox, 2002).

Credible researchers have differing views of how to describe and define culture and, to some extent, this can be explained as being because organisational culture is made up of multiple facets. However, although definitions of culture differ, common themes are apparent. A key theme within definitions is that culture includes a common set of understandings (and beliefs) shared by members of a particular social grouping. Hence culture is essentially a set of common understandings, expressed in language (Becker and Geer, 1970): transmitted patterns of values, ideas and other symbolic systems that shape behaviour (Kroeber and Kluckhoh, 1952); the glue that holds together an organisation through shared patterns of meaning (Martin and Siehl, 1983); or the values, beliefs, and expectations that members come to share (Van Maanen and Schein, 1979).

Two of the most useful and influential definitions of culture are those of Uttal (1983) and of Schein (1986). Uttal's definition is distinctive for his recognition of the importance of non-human factors in creating culture. Notably, he stresses the impact of factors such as technology and processes within the organisation, and states that culture is the shared values and beliefs that interact with an organisation's structures and control systems to produce behavioural norms (Uttal). Schein's seminal model of culture, proposed over 20 years ago, (Schein, 1986) notes a number of indicators of culture, including artefacts, assumptions, values, and behaviours. Schein, and later Rousseau (1990), developed a model of culture as an "onion", with outer layers such as organisational artefacts (e.g. handbooks, operating manuals) and patterns of behaviour being easy to observe, and inner layers such as values and assumptions being more difficult. Both Uttal and Schein's models suggest that there is likely to be a degree of consistency across the elements that make up culture. Hence the behaviours observed and artefacts designed (the structures and control systems) are likely to be in keeping with the values and assumptions that pertain (see Figure 1).

It is generally agreed that the culture of an organisation helps its members to interpret, understand and accept their world, and is expressed in terms of the organisation's collective values, norms and knowledge, and consequently affects the behaviour of employees.

Culture is of interest in a security context if it can be proven to affect security outcomes. Substantial evidence supports the notion that culture impacts on a range of business outcomes, for example Kotter and Heskett (1992) found that culture was a predictor of revenue and workforce growth, while the role of a safety culture in impacting outcomes has been cited in both the nuclear Khripunov, Nikonov, and Katsva, (2004) and airline industries (O'Leary and Chappell, 1996). It is logical to hypothesise that relationships exist between security culture and organisational security metrics (for example security breaches). Hence, understanding and then enhancing the security culture within organisations where security is a critical success factor is likely to lead to those organisations being better able to achieve their primary goals and maintain their reputation.

Figure 1. The "onion" model of organisational culture (adapted from Schein, 1986)

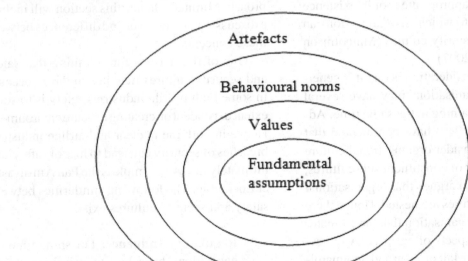

Although research suggests that work on security culture is in its early stages, this potential link between culture and security outcomes is widely accepted. Indeed, following a review of security within the nuclear industry in France, the commissioner at the French Economy, Finance and Industry Ministry was quoted as saying: "Every [security] system is inadequate if there is no security culture shared by the whole staff" (Nuclear Threat Initiative, 2005).

While the topic of safety culture has attracted considerable interest, partly driven by legislation that forces organisations to prioritise safety, the topic of security culture has attracted much less interest. The nature of security culture within organisations, especially within the UK, is a relatively young topic of study. It gained some prominence in part as a result of the terrorist attacks in New York in September 2001, London in July 2005, and Bali, Indonesia in 2002 and 2005. These events drove research into security culture for some time, and much work was instigated in direct response to each. And yet, in 2007 when a wide review of culture measures was undertaken, there was neither a widely agreed definition of what is meant by security culture (within the psychological / sociological literature, or in common usage), nor an appropriate tool in existence to assess the degree to which an organisation can be said to have a security culture (Malcolmson and Scognamiglio, 2007).

An additional consideration is that it is generally agreed that organisations may have several types of culture pertaining at the same time. Adams and Ingersoll (1989) have commented that it is often best to consider organisational culture in terms of a number of constituent sub-cultures, while Pidgeon (1989) argues that organisational cultures and sub-cultures are nested. Hence there may be parts of an organisation that have greater or lesser focus on aspects of security. A review of UK organisations (Malcolmson and Scognamiglio, 2007) showed that the way in which security functions are currently managed within govern- ment and industry organisations often seems to be separate from the main business management and day-to-day business operations. Within security, there has been a reliance on technology and procedures to try to drive behaviours, rather than acknowledging the need to capture hearts and minds. This means that the impact of security on the organisation's overall culture is likely to be limited.

Yet, while specific research on security culture has been limited, it has been suggested that relationships exist between security culture and organisational security metrics (for example security breaches). Understanding and then enhancing the security culture within organisations where security is a critical success factor is likely to lead to those organisations being better able to achieve their primary goals and maintain their reputation.

SAFETY CULTURE AND SECURITY CULTURE

In the absence of a widely accepted definition of security culture, for some time researchers drew parallels between safety and security culture. However, there is good reason to assume this approach is limited – hence this section will include a discussion of crossover and differences between these concepts.

One of the reasons for assuming that safety and security cultures may be similar is because in some high profile industries safety is to some extent dependent on creating a secure environment. Hence in both the nuclear and airline industries breaches of security can lead to loss of safety, and ultimately life. An example is the Pan Am disaster at Lockerbie. The following similarities between safety and security cultures exist:

- **Regulatory Influence:** For some time organisations have had to prioritize safety, due to regulations. Security is subject to similar influences, for example where regulations apply to customer and employee personal data. Research in the transport sector supports the idea that security is highly regulated, in part because of its relationship to safety, especially for aviation (with some aspects such as airport screening now highly regulated).

- **Reputational Damage:** In both cases, the damage caused by a breach may suggest in significant reputational impact. For example, within 2 trading days after the recent Global Payments breach, more than 12% had been wiped from their share price, and Visa had dropped them from their list of vendors. (BBC News, 2012). Following the 1988 Lockerbie terrorist attack on Pan Am flight 103, Pan Am went from being the USA's largest international airline, to bankruptcy in 1991.

- **Causes:** Both safety incidents and security may have several causes, with a number of factors operating simultaneously, leading to defences being breached.

- **Events Driven:** In both cases, improvements are often precipitated by an adverse event.

On the other hand, there are significant differences that mean that organisations need to exercise caution in trying to extrapolate lessons from one context to the other. Key differences are:

- **Victims:** Although not always true, it is often the case that where safety violations occur, the perpetrator and the victim are the same person. This gives people a natural motivation to try to avoid safety breaches. By contrast, security breaches are more likely to impact on others: either customers, or the organisation as a whole.

- **Intrinsic Motivation:** Whereas the literature on safety assumes a universal commitment to safety, the literature on security suggests that, by contrast, employees have no automatic propensity to maintain security. Ruighaver, Maynard, and Chang (2007) examined a number of case studies, and found no evidence in that an organisation's employees were intrinsically motivated to adopt secure practices. Indeed, it is well documented that in certain circumstances individuals may develop a malicious intent against security.

- **System Design:** Khripunov, Nikonov, and Katsva (2004) argue that a safety regime entails building increased redundancy into "at-risk" systems, whereas increased redundancy in security systems may actually make them more vulnerable to malicious attacks.

There are, therefore some dangers in simply assuming that models that operate to maximise safety culture will also facilitate an excellent security culture. One of the most widely accepted models of safety culture is that proposed by James Reason. He argues that a good safety culture has five building blocks. It is an informed culture (information from accidents and near misses is collected, analysed and disseminated); a reporting culture (people are prepared to report incidents); a just culture (errors and violations are treated appropriately, and blame is apportioned only where there is purposeful fault); it is a flexible culture (and can shift from a hierarchical structure to a flatter one, where experts in safety are given greater authority in emergency); and a learning culture (there is a will to learn lessons and implement change when necessary) (Reason, 1997, p. 195). Whilst some of these building blocks might transfer to security culture, it is unlikely that they contribute to security in quite the same way as they do to safety, mainly because of one of the key differences between safety and security: that safety is almost universally accepted as being laudable, while security sometimes has active enemies. It seems unlikely that security managers, for example, would unanimously welcome shared reporting of all breaches or near misses, for fear that such a policy might actually open the organisation up to attempts to penetrate perceived weaknesses. Where there is not complete trust that everyone shares the same goals, the lessons that might be taken from safety research may prove unworkable.

SECURITY CULTURE

As noted, there is a scarcity of scientific literature with regard to security culture. A comprehensive review was undertaken by Malcolmson and Scognamiglio, (2007). While the literature was characterised by an acceptance that security culture is of importance and should be embedded within organisations there are significant gaps. Research revealed that the two sectors where most has been written about security culture are the nuclear and transport sectors. Khripunov et al (2004) attempted a definition of security culture, as follows:

"...a concept that encompasses a set of managerial, organizational and other arrangements. Security culture connotes not only the technical proficiency of the people entrusted with security, but also their willingness and motivation to follow established procedures, comply with regulations and take the initiative when unforeseen circumstances arise" (Khripunov, 2004, p.1).

Whilst this overall definition is a general one, these researchers have developed a model of security culture that is specific to the nuclear industry, with the goal of protecting nuclear materials. Meanwhile in the transport sector, attention has

been paid to elements of culture, such as Security Awareness, and Security processes, rather than to culture per se. For example, within the Transport sector there is much research into baggage screener attitudes and processes.

Gaps

The key research gaps are summarised as follows:

- There is no accepted, practical definition of general security culture.
- There is no accepted way of measuring security culture that can be used outside narrow domains (for example the nuclear industry) to compare organisations.
- Research into how security culture can be engendered and enhanced is narrowly focused on specific aspects of culture.
- There is a lack of research relating security culture to organisational performance.

Until these have been resolved, security practitioners have little that supports them in either emphasising the importance of security culture, developing a security culture, or leveraging resources to do so.

ADDRESSING THE GAPS: A CASE STUDY

In view of the gaps identified above, the need for a measure of security culture was identified by the UK Centre for the Protection of the National Infrastructure. Such a measure would facilitate the acceptance of a definition of security culture, and enable managers to understand their organisations better, and compare themselves to others, such as those deemed to be performing well. The case study that follows describes work whose initial development stage was funded by CPNI. In this section, the development of a measurement tool, the composition of security culture (that is, how its content can be defined using its component parts), and the application of this measure of culture will be outlined. This will include a discussion of results achieved using the tool, and how it might benefit organisations in the future.

Aims

The main aims of the tool are:

- To provide a credible measure of security culture (that has "face validity").
- To provide a comprehensive measure.
- To provide reliable measures of defined aspects of culture.

The achievement of these aims allows organisations to realise two key benefits:

- Benchmarking within (and between) organisations.
- Diagnosis of aspects of security culture that may need improvement.

Development

The development of a psychometric tool measuring culture consists of two main work phases. During the first phase an exploration of what security culture is, and what it means to the members of organisations, was required. Data needed to be gathered that allowed security culture to be defined, and that further allowed the description of security culture to be developed such that the dimensions or indicators of culture can be elucidated. The underlying premise of this approach is that the definition of the term "security culture" needs to be constructed from the meanings attributed by research participants. Since a key feature of definitions of culture is that culture is shared by members of an organisation, it follows that the definition of culture should emerge from them. Qualitative data, therefore, needed to be

generated. ("Qualitative analysis is concerned with describing the constituent properties of an entity") (Smith, 2003), and with understanding and interpreting participants' experiences, in context ("from the point of view of those being studied") (Bryman, 1988). .

The approach taken to eliciting qualitative data is a way of ensuring that the assessment tool has construct validity (i.e. that it measures the concept that it is supposed to) and face validity (i.e. that it seems to end users to be correct). Key to this approach was the participation of appropriate personnel as participants.

A total of eleven focus groups and fourteen interviews were conducted. The main aims of both focus groups and interviews were to: understand people's view, perception, and understanding of culture and security culture; gain views from participants with respect to the indicators of security within an organisation (for example specific behaviours, values, attitudes, etc.) and thereby gain initial information for item generation for the assessment tool; gain feedback on how an assessment tool would be received by staff within organisations; gain an understanding of those aspects of security culture that are generalisable, and those that are specific.

Initial design and development was conducted in consultation with a number of organisations. These included organisations whose security interests were in terms of protecting people (e.g. a company responsible for running rail services); production facilities (e.g. a company supplying water to a sizable portion of the UK population); and assets such as financial and personal information (e.g. a major UK high street bank).

There were a number of criteria that were considered in choosing appropriate techniques for this phase of the work programme. First and foremost, techniques were required that allow the participants to define the construct of interest, with as little intervention from the researcher as possible. Techniques should be scientifically proven and have a high level of acceptance amongst participants. Three techniques were chosen; the Twenty Statements Test; repertory grids, and the critical incidents technique. The Twenty Statements Test (TST) (Kuhn and McPartland, 1954) was developed by Manfred Kuhn. It is an ideographic tool aimed at uncovering the way that individuals construct and perceive themselves and the world around them. Repertory grid analysis, designed by Kelly (1955), is based heavily on Personal Construct Theory and seeks to break down the way in which an individual views the world from their perspective. Like the TST, it allows the participant to define both the topic under consideration (security culture) and the dimensions (constructs) that characterise that topic. Critical incidents technique was developed by Flanagan in (1954). This technique demands that the participants describe meaningful incidents in detail. Critical (decisive or influential) events are chosen by the participants themselves. The underlying premise is that detailed examination of such events will allow those factors that caused the event to be decisive to be extracted.

The data gathered using qualitative techniques confirmed the researchers' expectations about the ways that participants were likely to conceptualise security culture, and led to the use of the following high level definition of security culture: "Security culture is indicated in the assumptions, values, attitudes and beliefs, held by members of an organisation, and behaviours they perform, which could potentially impact on the security of that organisation, and that may, or may not, have an explicit, known, link to that impact. Some aspects of culture have evolved as a logical response to security threats, and are espoused by the management of the organisation. These manifest themselves in the security practices and policies of the organisation, the level of compliance with, and understanding of, those practices and policies, and the acknowledgement and awareness of security threats to the organisation. Others are informally learnt as part of a natural socialisation process that is not controlled, and that leads to

behaviours and attitudes in use[1] that may or may not be approved by the organisation's managers". (Malcolmson and Scognalmiglio, 2007). That is, the data was in keeping with Schein and later Rousseau's, definitions of culture as comprising assumptions, behaviours, artefacts, and so on.

For that reason, the questionnaire includes a mixture of the following, all of them taken from statements that individuals had made in describing what culture meant to them:

- **Procedures/Artefacts:** Tangible indicators: these can be seen or touched. Examples are the physical environment, processes, procedures, documents.
- **Behaviours:** What people say they do, or do not do.
- **Attitudes/Opinions:** Opinions, point of view.
- **Ideals/Values:** Standards, statements of what is "the right thing" to do.
- **Stated Assumptions:** Supposition, hypothesis, postulation as to inherent worth of security.

Having gathered information from participants about their perspectives of culture, the next task was to transform the dimensions of security culture into a tool that could be piloted and validated. The qualitative research phase had allowed participants to list what security culture meant to them. The techniques chosen yielded textual data that could readily be transformed into questionnaire items. For example, the Twenty Statements Test consists of presenting the stem of a sentence, in this case "Security culture in my organisation…" or "Security in my organisation means…," and asking participants to complete the sentence. The underlying premise is that how the participant chooses to complete the sentence reveals his or her understanding of the concept being studied. Hence, participants might state "Security culture in my organisation is critical in ensuring client confidence" or "Security in my organisation means

I must lock my computer away at night". Statements elicited using all the qualitative techniques were used to form items for potential use in the questionnaire. This method resulted in over two hundred potential items: however, these needed to be refined to remove possible duplicates or overlaps. To achieve this, transcripts of interviews and focus groups were analysed to uncover themes within the data. For example, a number of participants had talked about how the physical security of their organisation was maintained (or in some cases breached), and so this was treated as a theme. For each theme, the statements made by participants were listed. The main aim was to ensure that the final tool contained a broad range of items that reflect all the aspects of culture that participants had considered to be important, as so doing would give the questionnaire the best likelihood of being able to identify strengths and weaknesses in an organisation, and ultimately be used in a predictive manner.

An initial pilot study was undertaken, with a number of items trialed in several organisations to assess their readability, and conduct preliminary item statistics (e.g. to remove any items that respondents did not understand, or that attracted universal agreement or disagreement). Finally, to shorten the list to an acceptable number for its first practical administration, items were reviewed by security managers. Where necessary, statements were re-drafted so as to conform with best practice in questionnaire item writing. Responses were based on a five-point scale (strongly agree, to strongly disagree).

Structure of Tool and Composition of Security Culture

A seventy-five item version of the questionnaire was administered over a 4-week period in summer 2012. It was applied in a large, multi-site research company in the UK. The organisation is structured into a number of business units, each with its own Managing Director. The questionnaire was administered on-line. It is worth noting that the tool was open for completion during the summer holiday period, and during the London Olympics, and it is possible this had an adverse effect on completion rates: nonetheless, the rates achieved are high for a survey of this nature.

As noted, key aims were to create a credible, comprehensive, and reliable tool. We were seeking to understand and describe in the simplest way possible what aspects of security culture are important, so that the tool would be user friendly. Ideally, it was hoped that the data could be described in a way that readers would immediately recognise as reflecting their own experience of what security culture is.

Early phases of the questionnaire development suggested that responses tended to cluster into a number of factors. Statistical analysis was now used to test the factorial structure of the data. Principal Components analysis was used to show patterns of responses. For each factor, a scale was created, and (in accordance with normal psychometric practice) tested for reliability using Cronbach's Alpha. The data structure shown is based on these analyses, and contains only scales with Cronbach's Alpha of .7 or above, this being the generally accepted standard for scale reliability.

Seven scales and fourteen sub-scales were revealed, and used from this point forward to analyse and report data. This structure provides a useful definition of what should be included within security culture. Reliability analysis showed that the scales were robust even with fewer items than originally included. Hence the questionnaire could be reduced to fifty items.

This method of identifying and selecting questionnaire items is in keeping with best practice in questionnaire design, and is widely accepted as an appropriate way to develop questions that are valid and reliable (Oppenheim, 1992).

The scales represent two facets of security (information security, and physical security);

three people enablers (staff, line management, and Human Resources activities); and two contextual scales (infrastructure and working context). The people enablers relate to three main groups in the organisation – the staff themselves, line managers and how they try to influence staff, and HR activities, which relates to how people are managed through activities that are not directly the line manager's responsibility, such as such as recruitment and training.

Security Culture Composition

Security culture, then is influenced by the drivers of the organisation (in this case, keeping both physical assets and data secure, which give rise to aspects or facets of security), and by the context within which the organisation works, as well as by what people in the organisation do. This is in keeping with Uttal's ideas about culture being what arises out of the interface between people and processes, and with Cox and Cox's (1996) view that culture is an emergent property of any organization (see Figure 2).

The fourteen sub-scales that make up the questionnaire are described in Table 1.

Application

It is not possible to state detailed results here, for reasons of client confidentiality. However, high level results are noted. In addition, a description of the way in which the data were used to facilitate actions to enhance security culture is provided.

The questionnaire allowed internal benchmarking in two ways:

- Results on each scale were compared to those achieved on other scales, to identify overall areas of strength and areas for improvement in the organization.
- Results were compared across company sites, and business units.

To benchmark results on the fourteen sub-scales, sub-scale averages were calculated. A "traffic light" system was used: hence areas where respondents rated the organisation as performing well (in that they agreed with positive statements about that aspect of the organisation's culture) the overall rating was "green"; where ratings were lowest it was "red", and middle ranked ratings were "amber."

Figure 2. Security culture composition

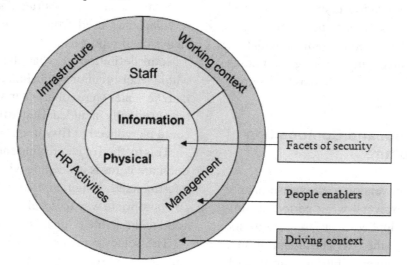

Table 1. Security culture: sub-scales descriptions

	Scale	Subscale	Description: What is Measured (Each sub-scale is measured by 3-4 questionnaire items)
Faces of security	Physical	Visibility of security	Are security staff perceived to be present and visible?
		Secure environment	Does the organisation secure its physical assets?
	Information security	Data protection	Are data secured in the organisation?
		Individual responsibility	Do individual staff members take appropriate steps to secure information and assets containing information?
People enablers	Staff	Understanding and clarity of behaviours	Are staff clear about what they should do?
		Beliefs and consequences	Do staff buy-in to the idea that security is important, and they can affect it?
	Management	Management of communications	Is necessary information about security communicated to staff?
		Management activities	Do managers model good practice?
	HR Activities	Training	Is security training adequate?
Driving context	Infrastructure	Clarity of infrastructure	Are procedures and levels of security clear and consistent?
		Infrastructure testing and resourcing	Is security well-resourced and reviewed?
	Working context	External influences	The extent to which security is seen to impact on client confidence and reputation
		Impact on business	The extent to which security is seen as important to every aspect of the business, including for staff
		Working with others	Are third parties made aware of security procedures?

To benchmark across business units and sites, average scores were compared using analysis of variance (ANOVA). This enabled sound statistical evaluation of whether differences might be due to chance.

The data indicate that there are a number of areas where the organisation's security culture is strong. These include both how the organisation handles data security, and how individuals within it believe they personally deal with the security of assets and information. Security is perceived by staff to be critical to the organisation, and there is buy-in to the idea that client confidence and company reputation depend on security.

However, data also revealed areas for improvement in some areas, notably:

- The training of security.
- The communication of security processes and activities.

- The modelling of security practice by managers.

The areas that could benefit from improvement are consistent: for example, reports of a lack of awareness of processes and activities are in keeping with a lack of training.

Internal benchmarking revealed differences across sites and business units. Some of the discrepancies could be explained by referring to the key business aims of the individual units: however, some differences could not.

Following the data analysis, a discussion was held with a number of security managers in the organisation to conduct action planning. The results were seen as helpful both in revealing new insights to the organisation and confirming some of the managers' expectations about patterns of staff attitudes. Overall, the results were seen as benefiting the organisation by providing an evidence base for the need to take certain actions for improvement, such as enhancing induction training and training on certain types of security. In particular, the use of the questionnaire gave the advantage of being able to target budgets on those areas where spend would have most positive impact. It has been agreed that it will be valuable to repeat the survey in one year, to track progress towards improvement. Andy Hodgson, the Head of Information Security, stated: "The Security Questionnaire is a key input to identifying the security culture of our organisation and provides some hard data to support the anecdotal evidence I have. As we know people are the weakest link in the security of any enterprise, whether it be due to ignorance of the risk and the related counter-measure, or through guilty intent. To combat the former I wanted to identify by business unit, by geographical site, by length of service whether there was differing levels of security awareness in my organisation. Although it is fair to say the response rate to the Security Questionnaire was high and virtually all the respondents had a very positive approach to security it was clear there was a need for more targeted security risk awareness and training. As a result a security campaign has commenced targeted at specific sites and business units... its success will be measured by the now annual Security Questionnaire and whether the organisation wants more or less security awareness and training."

SOLUTIONS AND RECOMMENDATIONS

The extent to which solutions can be offered and recommendations made depends to large degree on whether the gaps in research on security culture that were identified earlier in the chapter have been addressed. These were identified as follows:

- There was no accepted, practical definition of general security culture.
- There was no accepted way of measuring security culture that can be used outside narrow domains (e.g. the nuclear industry) to compare organizations.
- Research into how security culture can be engendered and enhanced was narrowly focused on specific aspects of culture.
- There was a lack of research relating security culture to organisational performance.

Progress has been reported against some of these. In particular, the composition of the model of security culture offered here offers a definition of security culture in terms of its content: the facets of security that are of interest, the people enablers, and the contextual factors. These were derived from data gathered from a number of organisations operating in different sectors, and cross-comparisons suggest that the elements outlined here are generalizable.

The measurement of security culture in an organisation has been achieved and reported. To date, internal benchmarking between sites and business units has been completed. However greater exploitation of this tool is needed in order to be able to develop a deeper understanding of the way in which security culture is operationalized in differing contexts. Benchmarking across sectors would provide a body of information that could be used by security managers and others to help set standards and expectations, and to focus efforts on those aspects of security that are most beneficial and cost-effective. It would reveal trends in security culture, such as the relative level of importance attributed to information security and physical security. It is therefore recommended that the tool be disseminated, in the expectation that if widely adopted useful data comparisons could be made.

To some extent, it remains to be seen how security culture can be engendered and controlled. Data gathered in the early stages of the work to develop a security culture measure suggest that some aspects of culture have evolved as a logical response to security threats, and are espoused by the management of the organisation. These manifest themselves in the security practices and policies of the organisation, the level of compliance with, and understanding of, those practices and policies, and the acknowledgement and awareness of security threats to the organisation. However, as for other types of culture, some aspects are informally learnt as part of a natural socialisation process that is not strictly controlled, and that leads to behaviours and attitudes that may or may not be approved by the organisation's managers. In the case study presented here, there is an opportunity to monitor to what extent progress can be made and measured in one year's time, and this will reflect to what extent certain actions are able to enhance the culture.

As yet, there is still little research that specially relates security culture to outcomes. However, in part, this may be because of a lack of willingness to report internal security breaches widely, and on the fact that there is still a lack of research into security culture generally.

FUTURE RESEARCH DIRECTIONS

This chapter has discussed some research to define and measure security culture. The question now is, where does security culture go from here? What further research is needed, and how can it help?

The work reported here aside, it is interesting that the situation outlined five years ago in 2007 with regard to security culture research has changed little. That is, there has been little published research on security culture in organisations, and what work there is still largely confined to fairly narrow domains. While there have been many high profile security lapses in organisations in the last few years, these seem to be have been eclipsed in their overall impact by the global economic downturn, and as a result attention has been deflected away from such matters.

Further, while the benefits of measuring and benchmarking security cultures may seem obvious, there are also organisational barriers to so doing. In particular, security managers are often reluctant to conduct measurements and in particular to expose the results to scrutiny. As noted earlier, this is likely to be due to a fear of exposing a weakness in the system that could be exploited. Researchers therefore need to be especially careful to build trust within the organisation, and to ensure that data are handled sensitively.

Nonetheless, further work is likely to be beneficial. As has happened in the safety domain, it is likely that the act of measuring security culture would demonstrate to staff and investors that the organisation takes security seriously. Moreover, further work is needed, ideally using a standardised measure across domains, to help to explore the relationships between security facets (e.g. information security, physical security), enablers (such as training, and policies), and contextual drivers (such as perceptions of the operating context). Such work would help to pinpoint exactly how security culture forms and changes, and enable security managers and others to influence this for the better.

The questionnaire used for the case study outlined here may be made available on application. [2]

CONCLUSION

This chapter has provided a discussion of the individual, latent, and organisational factors that lead to errors and violations. It has particularly focused on the role of security culture, drawing on research that has shown a link between culture and organisational outcomes such as accidents and financial metrics such as revenue and workforce growth. It was acknowledged that in the absence of a widely agreed definition of security culture, parallels to safety culture have often been drawn. Similarities (such as the influence of regulations: the impact in terms of reputational damage: the likely causes: and the impact of adverse events) were drawn. These were contrasted with differences (such as the fact that while in safety events the perpetrator and victim are often one and the same, this is not so in security incidents; the idea that there is intrinsic motivation towards safety, but not security; and the differing impacts of systems designs). Gaps in security culture research were outlined, including the lack of a widely accepted practical definition; the lack of a way of measuring security culture; the narrow focus of research thus far into security culture; and the lack of research mapping security culture to outcomes. The development and administration of a security culture tool was described. The composition of security culture was outlined as including seven key aspects: facets of security (information and physical); people enablers (staff, management, and HR activities); and contextual factors (the infrastructure and working context). Fourteen subscales addressing aspects of these seven aspects were described. Future work is recommended to measure and benchmark security culture across organisations, with a view to identifying how organisations can improve, and how they can prioritise limited budgets in a time of increasing threat but financial austerity.

REFERENCES

Adams, G. B., & Ingersoll, V. H. (1989). Painting over old works: The culture of organisations in an age of technical rationality. In Turner, B. A. (Ed.), *Organisational Symbolism*. Berlin: Walther De Gruyter.

Argyris, C. (1976). *Increasing leadership effectiveness*. New York: John Wiley and Sons.

Asch, S. E. (1952). *Social psychology*. Englewood Cliffs, NJ: Prentice-Hall. doi:10.1037/10025-000.

Becker, H. S., & Geer, B. (1970). Participant observation and interviewing: A comparison. In Filstead, W. (Ed.), *Qualitative methodology* (pp. 133–142). Chicago: Rand McNally.

Bryman, A. (1988). *Quantity and quality in social research*. London: Unwin Hyman. doi:10.4324/9780203410028.

Cox, S., & Cox, T. (1996). *Safety systems and people*. Oxford, UK: Buttherworth Heinemann.

Department for Transport. (2004). *Safety culture and work-related road accidents*. Road safety Research Report No. 51. Washington, DC: Department of Transport.

Flanagan, J. C. (1954). The critical incident technique. *Psychological Bulletin, 51*(4), 327–359. doi:10.1037/h0061470 PMID:13177800.

Gordon Training International. (n.d.). Retrieved from http://www.gordontraining.com/free-workplace-articles/learning-a-new-skill-is-easier-said-than-done/

Health and Safety Executive Core Topics. (n.d.). *Core topic 2: HF in accident investigations*. Retrieved from http://www.hse.gov.uk/humanfactors/topics/core2.pdf

Kelly, G. (1955). *Principles of personal construct psychology*. New York: Norton.

Khripunov, I., Nikonov, D., & Katsva, M. (2004). *Nuclear security culture: the case of Russia*. The University of Georgia. Retrieved from http://www.uga.edu/cits/documents/pdf/Security%20Culture%20Report%2020 041118.pdf

Kotter, J. P., & Heskett, J. L. (1992). *Corporate culture and performance*. New York: Free Press.

Kroeber, A. I., & Kluckhohn, C. (1952). *Culture: A critical review of concepts*. Academic Press.

Kuhn, M. H., & McPartland, T. S. (1954). An empirical investigation of self attitudes. *American Sociological Review*, *19*, 68–76. doi:10.2307/2088175.

Martin, J., & Siehi, C. (1983). Organizational culture and counterculture: An uneasy symbiosis. *Organizational Dynamics*, *12*(2), 52–64. doi:10.1016/0090-2616(83)90033-5.

News, B. B. C. (2012, April 3). *Credit card data breach contained, says global payments*. Retrieved from www.bbc.co.uk/news/technology-17596394

Nuclear Threat Initiative. (2005). *Global nuclear security culture needed, experts say*. Retrieved from http://www.nti.org/d_newswire/issues/2005/3/21/18cd7338-c686-42c1-aa46-68b39c511622.htm

O'Leary, M., & Chappell, S. (1996). Confidential incident reporting systems create vital awareness of safety problems. *ICAO Journal*, *1*, 11–13, 27. PMID:11541832.

Oppenheim, A. (1992). *Questionnaire design, interviewing and attitude measurement*. London: Pinter.

Pidgeon, N. F. (1991). Safety culture and risk management in organisations. *Journal of Cross-Cultural Psychology*, *22*, 129–140. doi:10.1177/0022022191221009.

Reason, J. T. (1997). *Managing the risks of organizational accidents*. Aldershot, UK: Ashgate.

Rousseau, D. M. (1990). Assessing organisational culture: The case for multiple methods. In Schneider, B. (Ed.), *Organisational Climate and Culture* (pp. 153–192). San Francisco, CA: Jossey-Bass.

Ruighaver, A. B., Maynard, S. B., & Chang, S. (2007). Organisational security culture: Extending the end-user experience. *Computers & Security*, *26*, 56–62. doi:10.1016/j.cose.2006.10.008.

Schein, E. (1986). What you need to know about organizational culture. *Training and Development Journal*, *40*, 30–35.

Smith, J. (2003). *Qualitative psychology: A practical guide to research methods*. Thousand Oaks, CA: Sage Publications.

Uttal, B. (1983, October 17). The corporate culture vultures. *Fortune*.

Van Maanen, J., & Schein, S. (1979). Toward a theory of organizational socialization. *Research in Organizational Behavior*, *11*, 209–259.

Zar, A., Stewart, K., Tate, L., Cheyne, A., & Cox, S. (2002). *Development and trials of tools to assess safety culture: Final technical report. QinetiQ Report: QinetiQ/CHS/CAP/TR020057*. QinetiQ..

KEY TERMS AND DEFINITIONS

Attitudes/Opinions: Opinions, point of view.

Behaviours: What people do.

Ideals/Values: Standards, statements of what is "the right thing" to do.

Latent Factors: Managerial influences and social pressures that influence the design of equipment, procedures, technology or systems.

Organisational Culture: A pattern of behaviour, attitudes, and norms shared by members of a particular social grouping, and arising from factors including latent conditions.

Procedures/Artefacts: These can be seen or touched. Examples are the physical environment, processes, procedures, documents.

Psychometric Tool: A tool to measure knowledge, ability, or culture that is designed in accordance with certain known measurement and evaluation principles.

Safety Culture: That aspect of culture that relates to safety.

Security Culture: That aspect of culture that relates to security.

Stated Assumptions: Supposition, hypothesis, postulation as to inherent worth.

ENDNOTES

1. The use of the terms 'espoused' and 'in use' is similar to that used in Chris Argyris' *Theories of Action*, (1976), wherein 'espoused' refers to those things people say they should do, while 'in use' refers to what they actually do.

2. For further information about availability of the questionnaire, please contact either the author, jemalcolmson@qinetiq.com Tel. +44 (0)252 393964 or QinetiQ's customer contact team, customercontact@qinetiq.com Tel. +44 (0)843 658 4668 or +44 (0) 8700 100942 Postal address: QinetiQ Customer Contact Team, Cody Technology Park, Ively Road, Farnborough, Hampshire, GU14 0LX, UK.

Chapter 13
The 2011 Survey of Information Security and Information Assurance Professionals:
Findings

Yulia Cherdantseva
Cardiff University, UK

Jeremy Hilton
Cranfield University, UK

ABSTRACT

Information Assurance (IA) is an intensively discussed discipline. Perhaps the most striking feature of IA is that everyone has a different opinion about what it actually is. The literature analysis enables us to distinguish three different approaches to Information Assurance: 1) Technical approach, concentrated on protection of networks; 2) Business approach, where IA is perceived as the comprehensive and systematic management of Information Security (InfoSec); 3) General approach, where IA is considered as a way to establish a level of confidence in information. Interviews with InfoSec practitioners reveal that they interpret the term IA differently and have contradictory views on how IA relates to InfoSec. It was felt that a survey with a greater number of practitioners might help to identify a commonly accepted perception of IA and to clarify the goals of the discipline. In 2011, a survey was conducted among one hundred InfoSec and IA professionals across the world. This chapter presents the results of the survey.

DOI: 10.4018/978-1-4666-4526-4.ch013

INTRODUCTION

Information Assurance (IA) is a highly interesting and intensively discussed discipline. Perhaps the most striking feature of IA is that everyone has different opinion about what it actually is about. A series of interview with Information Security (InfoSec) and IA practitioners revealed that they interpret the term IA differently and they have contradictory views on how IA relates to InfoSec. This perceived misunderstanding fueled a decision to employ the survey with a greater number of people with different backgrounds. It was felt that it might help to identify a commonly accepted perception of IA and to clarify the goals of the discipline.

The results of the survey were expected either to support or to challenge our initial assumptions about the lack of a generally accepted understanding of IA. Thus, the main purpose of the survey was to discover participants' perceptions of the two disciplines under discussion – InfoSec and IA. Participants' views on the relationship between InfoSec and IA and on the goals of each discipline were also surveyed since a comparison between the disciplines was of particular interest for this research.

According to Murrey (2005), "the formation of a questionnaire requires a clear definition of the issues under consideration, and the related concepts involved". The questionnaire was based on the outcomes of an IA literature analysis which is presented in detail in Cherdantseva and Hilton (2013).

The literature analysis enabled us to distinguish three different approaches to IA:

1. **Technical Approach:** Which is concentrated on the protection of networks.
2. **Business Approach:** Where IA perceived as the comprehensive and systematic management of InfoSec.

3. **General Approach:** Where IA is considered as a way to establish a level of confidence in information.

Generally, the survey attempted to establish which of the three approaches to IA, as identified in the literature, has greater support among InfoSec and IA practitioners.

The survey consisted of 10 questions, which were split into two equal parts. In the first part, respondents were asked to:

- Provide personal details: age group, country of the origin and nature of occupation (Questions 1-3).
- Define their level of familiarity with each discipline (Question 4).
- State the sources of their knowledge about the disciplines (Question 5).

In the second part of the questionnaire, the respondents were asked to:

- Describe the relationship between InfoSec and IA *(Question 6)*.
- Choose or provide the best description of IA *(Question 7)*.
- Specify the main aim of IA *(Question 8)*.
- Indicate the goals of both disciplines *(Question 9)*.
- Provide comments (in a free form) that may clarify the respondent's understanding *(Question 10)*.

The survey was conducted in April – November 2011, using functionality provided at http://www.surveymonkey.com. The links to the survey were distributed by email to PhD students and staff of computer science schools and to members of various InfoSec groups in the UK, USA and Europe. The survey was also advertised in a number of InfoSec and IA professional groups on the

LinkedIn Website (http://www.linkedin.com). In addition to the online survey, a series of interviews with InfoSec professionals was conducted at the InfoSecurity Europe 2011 event (19th-21st April 2011). The interviewees answered the survey questions either verbally or by filling in paper-based questionnaires. The responses received at the event were added to the database of online responses. Although the respondents were not individually selected, generally we targeted people who are competent in InfoSec, IA or related areas.

The aim of this chapter is to report and discuss the overall results of the survey.

THE SURVEY RESULTS

Participants' Profile

In total, 100 complete anonymous questionnaires were collected. Table 1 and Table 2 illustrate the age and geographical distribution of respondents respectively. As shown by data in Table 1 participants come from different age groups. Table 2 reveals that more than a half of respondents are based in the UK, a fifth of survey participants come from the USA and the rest come from a variety of countries from all over the world. Table 3 illustrates the type of occupation of the survey participants. 44 respondents indicated that they work in industry, 19 have academic backgrounds and 26 respondents are either students or PhD students. There are 11 respondents in the category *Other, which* mainly specified such fields as Government, Business and Consultancy.

Results Report

In this section, we present the analysis and discussion of the findings on a question-by-question basis. In question 4, respondents were asked, "How familiar are you with Information Security and Information Assurance?" Respondents were invited to answer using the scale: Not familiar, Have some knowledge, Very Familiar (Expert). For each discipline the respondents were able to choose only one answer. Figure 1 shows the level of familiarity of the survey respondents with InfoSec and IA and allows a comparison of the values between the disciplines.

The highest number of respondents (59) indicated that they are very familiar with InfoSec, i.e. experts in the field. 42 respondents positioned themselves as IA experts. 39 and 43 respondents declared that they have some knowledge about InfoSec and IA respectively. Only 2 respondents indicated that they are unfamiliar with InfoSec. In contrast, a significant number (15 out of 100 respondents) stated that they are not familiar with IA.

Table 1. Age distribution of respondents (question 1)

Age group	Number of respondents
Under 18	0
18-24	14
25-34	28
35-44	20
45-54	20
55-64	17
Over 65	1
Total	100

Table 2. Geographical distribution of respondents (question 2)

Respondent's country of origin	Number of respondents
UK	52
USA	20
Portugal	2
Brazil	2
Bulgaria	2
India	2
Turkey	2
Germany	2
Saudi Arabia	2
UAE	2
Poland	2
Australia	2
Greece	1
Ukraine	1
Nigeria	1
Philippines	1
Mexico	1
Spain	1
Canada	1
Egypt	1
Total	100

Table 3. Distribution of respondents by nature of occupation (question 3)

Respondent's Nature of Occupation	Number of respondents
Student or PhD Student	26
Academia	19
Industry	44
Other	11
Total	100

The analysis of data in Figure 1 reveals that among the participants there are substantially more experts in InfoSec than in IA. The participants more willingly positioned themselves as experts in InfoSec, whereas for IA the respondents preferred to state that they have some knowledge in the discipline, but were reluctant to position themselves as experts. The significant difference between the number of experts in InfoSec and the number of experts in IA might be considered as indirect evidence that InfoSec and IA are not considered to be the same discipline.

In question 5, the participants were prompted to specify the sources of their knowledge about

Figure 1. How familiar are you with information security and information assurance? (question 4)

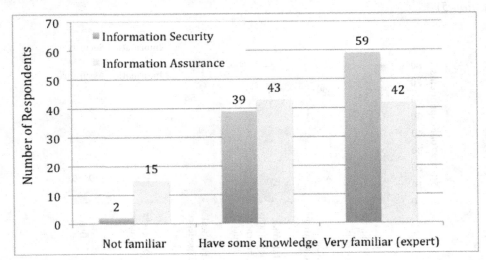

InfoSec and IA. The respondents were allowed to choose as many options out of the six suggested as they believed appropriate. The options suggested were:

1. Official Standards.
2. Academic Publications.
3. Informal Publications, Internet, Media.
4. Practical Experience.
5. My guess only.
6. Other.

As depicted in Figure 2, knowledge in both disciplines is mainly gained from informal publications, the Internet and other media. In fact, informal publications, official standards and practical experience are the most popular sources of knowledge about InfoSec. Almost equal numbers of respondents use the above-mentioned sources. Although, the number of people who use academic publications to build their understanding of InfoSec is less than the number of people using standards or informal publications, it is still quite significant (60 out of 100 respondents).

As can be seen from a comparison of data in Figure 2, the respondents generally use fewer sources of information to gain knowledge about IA. The overall popularity of sources of knowledge for IA is similar to InfoSec: the leading three are informal publications, practical experience and official standards. Finally, whereas there were only 7 people that had no knowledge about Info-Sec and used only guesswork to answer further questions on the survey, there were 16 people who had no other sources of knowledge about IA and had to guess the answers.

These results could partially be explained by the fact that that the number of publications referring to IA is significantly smaller in comparison to a number of publications using the term Info-Sec. First, the term IA was coined later than the term InfoSec (refer to Cherdantseva and Hilton (2013) for the detailed discussion about InfoSec and IA terminology). Second, due to the lack of consensual approach to InfoSec and IA, authors often prefer to use more familiar term InfoSec, even in cases when the use of the term IA seems to be more appropriate.

In light of the results of answers to questions 4 and 5, we can conclude that the survey was successfully directed to people who recognise themselves as experienced and knowledgeable specialists in InfoSec and IA. It is worth pointing out here that this positioning of respondents as

Figure 2. What are the sources of your knowledge about information security and information assurance? (question 5)

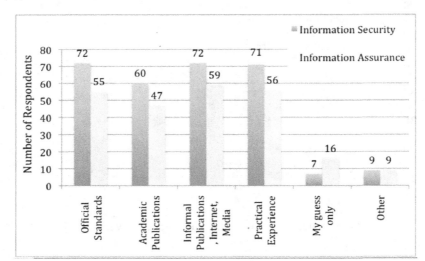

InfoSec/IA experts is based upon self-judgement of the respondents, rather than formal qualification check or knowledge test.

The fact that the significant part of the participants are experts in the disciplines or, at least, have adequate knowledge in the area makes the results of the survey more reliable and valuable for the research.

In question 6, the respondents were invited to describe the relationship between InfoSec and IA. There were 5 statements describing the relationship suggested. There also was the option "Other" available which allowed the respondents to provide an answer in their own words. The list of the suggested statements for question 6 was as follows:

1. Information Security and Information Assurance are the same.
2. Information Security and Information Assurance do not overlap.
3. Information Security is a part of Information Assurance.
4. Information Assurance is a part of Information Security.
5. Information Security and Information Assurance are different disciplines, but they have some common areas.
6. Other (please specify).

The summary of responses concerning the relationship between the disciplines is depicted in Figure 3. The majority of respondents (35) were inclined to perceive IA as a part of InfoSec (statement D). A slightly lower number of people (29) supported the opposite view that InfoSec is a part of IA (statement C). The difference between the numbers of supporters of the two contrary statements is not substantial. The third most popular perception is that InfoSec and IA are different disciplines, but they have some common areas - 27 respondents favored the corresponding statement E. Only 6 participants assumed that InfoSec and IA are the same. Thus, although the terms InfoSec and IA are often used interchangeably in the literature, the survey, on the contrary, shows that the disciplines, in the majority of cases, are not considered to be the same. A minority of participants (2) believes that the disciplines do not over-

Figure 3. How would you describe the relationship between information security and information assurance? (question 6)

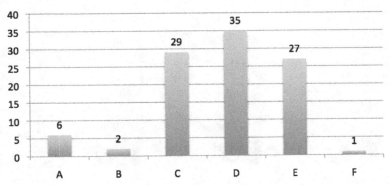

A) Information Security and Information Assurance are the same
B) Information Security and Information Assurance do not overlap
C) Information Security is a part of Information Assurance
D) Information Assurance is a part of Information Security
E) Information Security and Information Assurance are different disciplines, but they have some common areas
F) Other

lap. In the category "Other" only one respondent provided a comment and stated that "IA requires InfoSec". This, in our opinion, may be classified as equivalent to statement C, i.e. InfoSec is a part of IA. As we were unsure whether the respondent meant exactly that, we decided to leave the answer in the category "Other."

At first sight, the data presented in Figure 3 indicates that IA is mainly considered to be a part of InfoSec. This view is based upon the fact that the majority of respondents (35) preferred statement D. However, the fact that the opinions of the respondents were spread fairly evenly between the three contradicting statements describing the relationship between disciplines (approximately one thirds of respondent supported each statement: statements C – 29 respondents; statement D – 35 respondents; and Statement E – 27 respondents) indicates that there is no single widely accepted understanding of how these two disciplines relate to each other.

In question 7, the respondents were presented with the list of four statements and asked to choose which of them better describes IA. The descriptions of IA suggested were as follows:

1. Information Assurance deals with the technical aspects of information security.
2. Information Assurance is a holistic, multidisciplinary and systematic approach to information security.
3. Information Assurance is the practice of assuring confidence in information security.
4. Other.

The suggested descriptions of IA were formulated on the basis of the literature analysis conducted. The detailed discussion of the literature analysis findings and conclusions are presented in the previous section. Here, we only briefly outline the descriptions suggested. Thus, statement A depicts IA as very technically oriented discipline. Statement B refers to the perception of IA as an holistic and systematic approach to InfoSec which could also be referred to as management of InfoSec. Statement C corresponds with the narrow approach to IA, where the scope of the discipline is limited to assuring confidence in information and InfoSec on the basis of some measurements. We would like to highlight the difficulty of expressing

Figure 4. Which of the following better describes information assurance? (question 7)

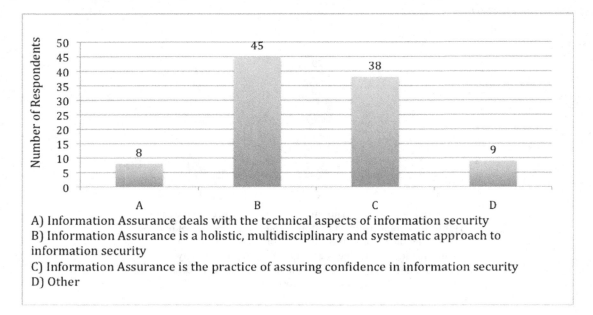

A) Information Assurance deals with the technical aspects of information security
B) Information Assurance is a holistic, multidisciplinary and systematic approach to information security
C) Information Assurance is the practice of assuring confidence in information security
D) Other

concisely the three distinct approaches to IA that were identified in the process of the literature analysis. Question 7 is a cornerstone question of the survey. Nevertheless, in order to avoid misinterpretations of the descriptions suggested in question 7, we added questions 8 and 9 for clarification of the perception of IA. Thus, the results of responses to question 7 should be considered in a conjunction with the results of responses to questions 8 and 9.

Figure 4 demonstrates the summary responses to question 7. Thus, when asked to choose the best definition of IA, 45 people gave preference to the description B in which IA is described as a holistic, multidisciplinary and systematic approach to InfoSec. 38 respondents chose description C, supporting the opinion that IA is responsible for assuring confidence in InfoSec. A minority of people (8) supported technical approach to IA by choosing description A. 9 respondents formulated description of the discipline in their own words. The valuable answers in the category "Other" were:

Respondent 1: IA is responsible for the quality of the information that will be secured later on.

Respondent 2: IA is a method to manage the integrity aspect of information security.

Respondent 3: IA means ensuring the quality, completeness and correctness of information.

Respondent 4: Information Assurance refers to the extent to which you can have confidence in information from a given source, which includes the security of that information in terms of its confidentiality, integrity and availability.

Respondent 5: IA deals with the non-technical part of InfoSec mostly with confidentiality.

Other responses were of less interest for the research.

We assume that the opinions of Respondents 1-4 could be associated with the description C. In all of them IA relates to the confidence in information gained on the basis of certain characteristics of information. This makes the discrepancy between the numbers of supports for options B and C even lower – 45 and 42 respondents respectively. Respondent 5 pointed out to the important aspect in perception of IA as a non-technical part of InfoSec. This viewpoint is contrary to statement A.

In question 8, the participants were invited either to choose from the list or to specify in their own words the main aim of IA. The list of choices suggested in question 8 is below:

1. To prevent threats and vulnerabilities caused by new technologies.
2. To create an organisation-wide framework for information security and to promote a culture of information security.
3. To evaluate a level of confidence in information security.
4. Other.

The analysis of responses regarding the aim of IA is depicted in Figure 5. As alluded above, question 8 was set to avoid misleading results due to misinterpretations of the descriptions of IA suggested in question 7. Thus, the aims suggested in

question 8 correspond with the descriptions of IA provided in question 7. For example, we assume that if one believes that IA is a technologies oriented discipline, then s/he should deem the main aim of the discipline to be a prevention of threats and vulnerabilities caused by new technologies. Thus, if a respondent chose statement A answering question 7, then we expect the respondent to choose corresponding aim A whilst answering question 8.

In general, the analysis of responses to questions 7 and 8 shows the similar trends with some minor disparity. The majority of respondents (52) support aim B which refers to the creation of an organisation-wide framework for information security and promotion of a culture of information security. Although only 45 respondents supported definition B when answering question 7, 52 respondents supported corresponding aim B when answering question 8. The aims A and C in question 8, in contrast, received less support than the corresponding descriptions of IA in question 7. Thus, despite the fact that 8 respondents supported the technical approach to IA in question 7, only 5

Figure 5. What is the main aim of information assurance? (question 8)

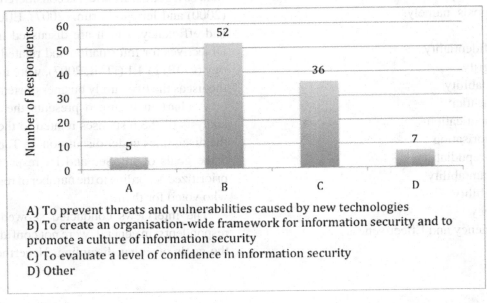

A) To prevent threats and vulnerabilities caused by new technologies
B) To create an organisation-wide framework for information security and to promote a culture of information security
C) To evaluate a level of confidence in information security
D) Other

stated that the main aim of IA is protection from threats caused by new technologies answering question 8.

In the category "Other" the following aims of IA were stated:

Respondent 1: Quality of Information and Availability.

Respondent 2: To ensure that the security policy flow down is applied pragmatically during project life cycles as part of security quality gates.

Respondent 3: To provide a measure of integrity.

Respondent 4: To (justify and) provide an appropriate level of protection to information assets, and of confidence in the integrity of selected business processes.

Respondent 5: To ensure information is of high quality, correct and complete when it is needed.

Respondent 6: To provide the circumstances by which reliable, secure, relevant, accurate information can be made available to intended users.

In question 9, the respondents were invited to indicate the goals that they find relevant to InfoSec and IA. The respondents were presented with the list of 11 goals, namely:

1. Confidentiality
2. Integrity
3. Availability
4. Authenticity
5. Authentication
6. Authorisation
7. Non-repudiation
8. Accountability
9. Reliability
10. Privacy
11. Efficiency and Effectiveness

There also was an option Not Sure suggested, but the respondents were asked not to choose this option where possible. For each discipline, the respondents were allowed to choose as many goals as they believed appropriate.

The list of goals was formed on the basis of the literature analysis conducted and presented in the previous section. Here, we only briefly state the origins of each security goal listed above. The list includes confidentiality, integrity and availability, which are also jointly referred to as the CIA-triad. For more than twenty years, the CIA-triad has been considered a cornerstone of InfoSec. These three goals are mentioned in the majority of security-related standards (e.g. ISO/IEC, CNSSI, COBIT). Properties such as non-repudiation, accountability, reliability and authenticity come from the ISO/IEC 27000:2009 definition of Info-Sec (ISO 27000, 2009). Authentication is stated as one of the goals of IA in the definition of IA provided in the Committee on National Security Systems: National Information Assurance (IA) Glossary (CNSS Instruction No. 4009 dated 26 April 2010). Privacy is discussed in Anderson (2001) and Lacey (2009). A thorough analysis of the privacy concept and its role within InfoSec is presented in Smith and Shao (2007). Authorisation, as a goal of InfoSec, is considered in Pipkin (2000) and Jericho Forum (2007). Effectiveness and efficiency, which are discussed in Control Objectives for Information and related Technology (COBIT) 4.1 (ITGI, 2007), were included in the list as the two purely business-oriented goals.

A chart in Figure 6 presents the summary analysis of the responses related to the goals of the disciplines under discussion. In Tables 4 and 5 the goals of InfoSec and IA respectively are prioritized according to the number of respondents who voted for them.

The interviews conducted showed that the respondents, in general, were not confident about the goals of either discipline. Nevertheless, the

Figure 6. What are the goals of information security and information assurance? (question 9)

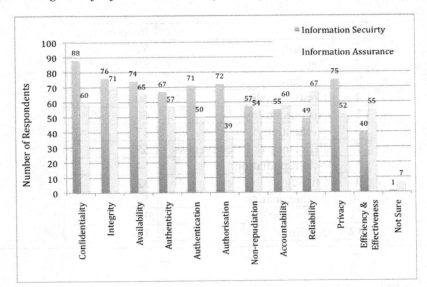

final results, especially for InfoSec, are as expected. The respondents considered confidentiality, integrity, privacy and availability to be important for InfoSec in the stated order. As for the goals of IA, the respondents deemed the goals important in the following order: integrity, reliability, availability and confidentiality. This can be seen from a comparison of Tables 4 and 5. Thus, for both disciplines all three element of the

CIA-triad took their places among the leading goals. Nonetheless, there are clear differences in the goals' priorities. If for InfoSec the main emphasis is placed on confidentiality, then for IA the main emphasis is placed on integrity of information. InfoSec is considered to be concerned with privacy, in addition to the CIA-triad. IA is concerned with reliability, in addition to the CIA-triad. The priority of goals for the IA discipline

Table 4. Analysis of the goals priority for information security

No.	Goal	Respondents
1	Confidentiality	88
2	Integrity	76
3	Privacy	75
4	Availability	74
5	Authorisation	72
6	Authentication	71
7	Authenticity	67
8	Non-repudiation	57
9	Accountability	55
10	Reliability	49
11	Efficiency & Effectiveness	40
12	Not Sure	1

Table 5. Analysis of the goals priority for information assurance

No.	Goal	Respondents
1	Integrity	71
2	Reliability	67
3	Availability	65
4	Confidentiality	60
5	Accountability	60
6	Authenticity	57
7	Efficiency & Effectiveness	55
8	Non-repudiation	54
9	Privacy	52
10	Authentication	50
11	Authorisation	39
12	Not Sure	7

supports the idea of its less-technical nature than InfoSec. This is because goals such as reliability, accountability, efficiency & effectiveness occupy higher places in the IA goals priority list than in the InfoSec list. We can also conclude that IA is deemed to be more business-oriented than Info-Sec as goals such as efficiency & effectiveness occupy 7th place in the IA goals priority list, whereas in the InfoSec priority list these goals took the last place. Finally, 7 people expressed uncertainty about the goals of IA, while only 1 respondent indicated that s/he is not sure about the goals of InfoSec.

The last question of the survey was an open-ended one and gave opportunity to the respondents to express thoughts or comments that were not captured by the other questions of the survey. 10 respondents provided additional comments. The comments, that in our opinion, provided some valuable contribution to the survey results are presented below (some of the responses are abridged, but the essence of the messages are conveyed):

Respondent 1: *In 1986 when I first started to become involved with IT security the general practice was know as Information Security.*

Then in about 2002 we started to hear about IA. Now we have Cyber Security.

Respondent 2: *As I read from some definitions about IA that there are differences between Security and Assurance. However, Information Security covers all topics for assurance. I really don' t understand why we need Information Assurance while we have Information Security.*

Respondent 3: *Information Assurance is largely around systems and technology, while Information Security extends more into the people and process domain*

Respondent 4: *Information Assurance is about risk management.*

Respondent 5: *Information Assurance is whatever it takes (including people/process/technology) to have confidence in the information your business or enterprise is using, that it is available when required and that it is not available to those not authorised to access it.*

Respondent 6: *Information Assurance is something which information providers need to provide to information users, as well as the information. It is associated with value judgment of information.*

Respondent 7: *Information Assurance is the process of dealing with the risks involved within Information Security so as to safely transfer data as well as manage it. It is focused not only on the software but the physical also.*

Thus, respondents 1 and 2 strongly supported the idea about a complete overlap of InfoSec and IA and do not see any distinctions between the disciplines. Respondent 3 supported the idea that was also clearly captured in the comment provided by respondent 5 in question 7 regarding non- or, at least, less-technical nature of IA than it is attributed to InfoSec. Respondents 4 and 7 related IA to risk associated with information and its management. Respondents 5 and 6 supported, according to their comments, an interpretation of IA as a practice related to getting confidence in information relying on certain properties of information.

CONCLUSION

To conclude the report on the survey findings we fulfilled our main task, which was to discover how IA is understood at present. This was achieved in three steps. First, respondents were asked to describe the relationship between InfoSec and IA. Second, the respondents were invited to choose or state in their own words a description of IA and to specify the main aim of the discipline. Third, the participants were asked to indicate the goals that, in their opinion, are relevant to each of the two disciplines under discussion. The results of the survey show that the respondents, in general, are more familiar with InfoSec than with IA and do not perceive InfoSec and IA as the same discipline. However, Figure 3 demonstrates that even the knowledgeable public is uncertain about the relationship between the two disciplines as the votes are divided between the three different options with

only a small discrepancy. The majority of the respondents supported the description of IA as an holistic, multidisciplinary and systematic approach to InfoSec, the main aim of which is to create an organisation-wide framework for information security and to promote a culture of information security. Nevertheless, the overall results of the survey show that the survey participants understand IA in different ways as the leading approach to the discipline overtakes the approach to IA as a practice of assuring confidence in information security only by a small number of respondents. This conclusion supports the initial assumption of the research that there is no single commonly accepted perception of IA and its relation to InfoSec discipline. The outcomes of the survey highlight (1) the necessity to raise awareness about IA, its meaning and goals among InfoSec and IA practitioners and (2), as a consequence, justify timeliness of the research, presented in chapter *, which aims to clarify the meaning, scope and the goals of both InfoSec and IA.

Although, initially, the problem with vaguely defined terminology may seem to be far from the practical problems facing system administrators nowadays, in reality miscommunication in the field of security may result in system security faults. Unambiguous and clear communication with regards to security issues between system administrators, security experts, managers and other stakeholders is vital since it helps to overcome misunderstanding and raises effectiveness of communications.

ACKNOWLEDGMENT

The authors are grateful to all individuals who participated in the survey both in person and online. The authors also thank the anonymous reviewers who provided valuable comments that assisted with better interpretation of the survey results.

REFERENCES

Anderson, R. (2001). *Security engineering: A guide to building dependable distributed systems.* New York: Wiley Publishing.

Cherdantseva, Y., & Hilton, J. (2013). Information security and information assurance: The discussion about the meaning, scope and goals. In Almeida, F., & Portela, I. (Eds.), *Organizational, Legal, and Technological Dimensions of Information System Administrator.* Hershey, PA: IGI Global Publishing.

ISO/IEC 27000:2009 (E). (2009). *Information technology - Security techniques - Information security management systems - Overview and vocabulary.* ISO/IEC.

IT Governance Institute (ITGI). (2007). *COBIT 4.1: Excerpt.* ITGI.

Jericho Forum. (2007). *Jericho forum commandments.* Retrieved April 5, 2012, from https://collaboration.opengroup.org/jericho/commandments_v1.2.pdf

Lacey, D. (2009). *Managing the human factor in information security.* New York: J. Wiley and Sons Ltd..

Murrey, P. (2005). Fundamental issues in questionnaire design. *Accident and Emergency Nursing, 7*(3), 148–153. doi:10.1016/S0965-2302(99)80074-5.

Pipkin, D. (2000). *Information security: Protecting the global enterprise.* New York: Hewlett-Packard Company.

Smith, R., & Shao, J. (2007). Privacy and e-commerce: A consumer-centric perspective. *Electronic Commerce Research, 7*(2), 89–116. doi:10.1007/s10660-007-9002-9.

KEY TERMS AND DEFINITIONS

CIA-Triad or CIA-Triangle: Refers to confidentiality, integrity and availability which together for several decades have been playing a role of a comprehensive model of Information Security.

Information Assurance: A multidisciplinary area of study and professional activity which aims to protect business by reducing risks associated with information and information systems by means of a comprehensive and systematic management of security countermeasures, which is driven by risk analysis and cost-effectiveness.

Information Security: A multidisciplinary area of study and professional activity which is concerned with the development and implementation of security mechanisms of all available types (technical, organisational, human-oriented and legal) in order to keep information in all its locations (within and outside the organisation's perimeter) and, consequently, information systems, where information is created, processed, stored, transmitted and destructed, free from threats. Threats to information and information systems may be categorised and a corresponding security goal may be defined for each category of threats. A set of security goals, identified as a result of a threat analysis, should be revised periodically to ensure its adequacy and conformance with the evolving environment. The currently relevant set of security goals may include: confidentiality, integrity, availability, privacy, authenticity & trustworthiness, non-repudiation, accountability and auditability.

Respondent: A person whose opinion is being investigated by means of asking questions.

Survey: Investigation of the opinions of a number of people by asking them questions.

Terminology: A vocabulary of terms used in a specific area of knowledge or professional activity.

Chapter 14
Mitigation of Security Concerns of VoIP in the Corporate Environment

Fernando Almeida
University of Porto, Portugal

José Cruz
University of Porto, Portugal

ABSTRACT

The convergence of the voice and data worlds is introducing exciting opportunities to companies. As a consequence, Voice over IP (VoIP) technology is attracting increasing attention and interest in the industry. Flexibility and cost efficiency are the key factors luring enterprises to transition to VoIP. However, voice services also introduce a new level of vulnerability to the network. This chapter categorizes and analyzes the most common security threats of a VoIP solution in a corporate environment. Besides that, the authors discuss the most relevant security policies that could have been adopted to mitigate the security vulnerabilities introduced by VoIP. These new policies and practices can have a positive impact on the security of the whole network, not just voice communications.

INTRODUCTION

The business environment has changed dramatically within the last decade. Globalization and market liberalization has altered the way a firm competes within this environment and how the firm interacts both with its customers and suppliers. Currently, both customers and competition have become global. To cut costs and to ensure easy access to customers, production and sourcing have shifted overseas. On the other hand, more firms than ever are using technology for a variety of tasks and several options exist for technology procurement. The technology has become complex and sophisticated and, simultaneously, the use of communication networks is widely available at many parts of the world.

DOI: 10.4018/978-1-4666-4526-4.ch014

To compete during this new economy corporations are considering several strategic choices. Recent IT studies, conducted by Kaufman (2008) and Biggs (2009) agree that corporations, in several activities domains, are exploring the adoption of Voice over Web Protocol (VoIP) as a way to cut prices, to enhance productivity and, consequently, alter the firm's strategic position.

VoIP is a technology that enables voice communication on a high speed Internet interconnection. It includes the software, a hardware and network protocol that enable the delivery of reliable service through the Internet instead of the local phone company. As shown in Figure 1 the communication can be initiated from a computer or a telephone to either a computer or to a phone via Internet. If an analog phone is used, a phone adapter is needed to convert the analog signal into a digital signal for transmission via the Internet. In many instances, the service comes with a special phone, VoIP phone, which does not require an adapter. This technology is cheap compared to the traditional phone service as international calls can be charged as local calls in some service packages.

Unlike Public Switched Telephone Network (PSTN), an IP network is packet switched. In PSTN, when a phone call between two parties is initiated, there exists a physical circuit connecting the two parties. After the call is established, the parties communicated and the circuit is reserved until the parties finish the communication. In contrast, on an IP network, all communication is carried out using IP packets. When a calling party communicated with a called party, the analog signals are digitized, encoded, and packed into an IP packet at the transmitting end and converted back to analog signals at the receiving end (Wallingford, 2005).

With VoIP, widespread acceptance by telecommunication markets of all sizes, advanced features integrated in unified communications solutions, have started emerging (Ransone &

Figure 1. Structure of a VoIP communication schema (Kumar, 2011)

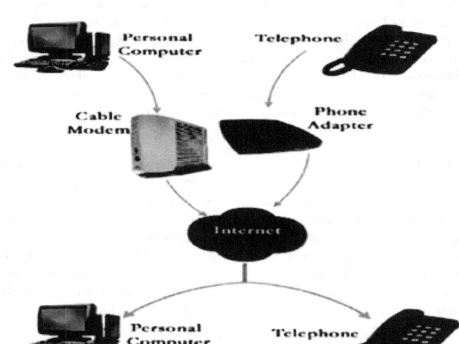

Rittinghouse, 2005). However, the convergence of the voice and data worlds introduces not just opportunities but also security risks. According to Latif (2007), the much lower cost and greater flexibility are key factors attracting enterprises to transition to VoIP. However, VoIP should not be installed without careful consideration of the security problems it can introduce.

This chapter presents the main relevant security policies that could be adopted to mitigate the security vulnerabilities introduced by VoIP. Initially, Section 2 investigates the adoption status of VoIP in corporate environment. Then, Section 3 exposes the main security risks of a VoIP solution. Finally, Section 4 proposes some relevant mitigation strategies to deal with the main security issues, and Section 5 draws conclusions.

THE VOIP IN CORPORATE ENVIRONMENT

The Adoption Status

Today, businesses of all sizes are using VoIP. Not only has VoIP reached critical mass, but the adoption rate is poised to accelerate dramatically, and soon become the dominant mode for business telephony. The VoIP penetration rate differs from country to country, attending to their economical conditions and network infrastructure (Schuk, 2010). According to InStat, the VoIP penetration rate in USA was 42% in the end of 2009 and expects to reach to 79% until the end of 2013 (Viscusi, 2010). When we consider all world, attending to IDC, the penetration rate is lower (23%) and expects to reach 37% by the end of 2013 (Bookman, 2011). When we look only to the SMB market, we can realize a significant increase in terms of VoIP adoption. In 2007, only 15% of SMB companies adopted VoIP, but in the end of 2010 the adoption rate reached 27% (Bookman, 2011).

According to Erica (2013) countries as United States, Japan, France, South Korea, Germany and China have nearly 80% of the reported global VoIP market share. The number of seats for hosted business VoIP and unified communications services is on track to more than double between 2012 and 2016. Additionally, VoIP industry value added (the industry's contribution to the economy) is expected to increase at an annualized rate of 15,3% until 2017 (Erica, 2013).

Benefits from VoIP

The most basic benefit of VoIP is the cost of service. In many VoIP services, the costing is flat with no discrimination between local and international calls. Furthermore, due to the low costs on Internet traffic, minimal overheads are incurred by deploying VoIP services. For enterprises, optimizing network bandwidth by deploying both data and voice communication on the same network could save resources (Kumar, 2011).

Additionally, VoIP offers great flexibility and portability by allowing subscribers to use their phones at any location with Internet connection without network signal and physical limitations associated with wireless and wired telephones respectively.

Finally, VoIP offers the opportunity to consolidate data and voice on the same network with lesser resource duplication. According to Nunn et al. (2010), this enables consolidated network management with potential positive impacts on enterprise bottom-line. Besides, a consolidated system is typically less complicated to manage.

There are many areas where VoIP scores over traditional Plain Old Telephone Service (POTS) and Public Branch Exchange (PBX), and the Table 1 makes that clearer.

Barriers to a VoIP Adoption

Several authors already conducted significant studies in this field. Varshney et al. (2002) consider that the major barriers are in terms of quality, equipment availability, Internetworking with

Table 1. Main advantages of VoIP (Thadani, 2010)

Advantages of VoIP over POTS	Advantages of VoIP over PBX
Considerably cheaper than POTS	Easier to use than a PSTN PBX in companies and business
Very easy and flexible to use due to portability	Allows unlimited number of extensions and voicemail boxes
Additional bundled services free of cost	Allows the ability to record conversations as well
No toll charges for long distance calls	Cost is much lesser, going up to a maximum of $100
Wastage of bandwidth due to multiple parties, and this is paid for you	Allow easy desktop management with the help of a Web browser, rather than PSTN switches

diverse networks, security and hacking threats, and reliability and failure measures. Tobin and Bidoli (2006) agree on the same barriers, but include two more issues: market confusion with large number of suppliers and time to recover of Return on Investment (ROI).

In summer of 2005, INS a provider of IT consulting and software solutions conducted a Web based survey to assess the VoIP market and its growth potential. They concluded that the significant barriers to VoIP implementation are: integration issues (43%), cost of upgrading the network to provide the required quality of service (40%), lack of experienced staff (37%), high cost of products and tools (37%), and justifying the costs and benefits to upper management (35%) (Mathiyalakan, 2006). The same study identified the three most criteria when selecting VoIP solutions, which include: network reliability (91%), voice quality (84%), and security (75%) (Mathiyalakan, 2006).

In 2010, another study conducted by the Yankee Group Research, identified that VoIP and Unified Communications have become linked together providing both cost savings and productivity gains (Kerravala, 2010). However, some barriers to a more widely adoption still remains. These identified barriers are: high up-front costs, integration complexity and security issues. In this chapter, we will focus our study only in the security aspects of a VoIP solution.

Implementation Steps

Planning is the first step in an IT and infrastructure project. A first step includes the verification that the company' existing network is ready for this transition. This requires that the network administrator or CIO assesses any possible negative effects to the applications currently running on the network evaluates the potential performance issues that occur with VoIP traffic after installation or upgrade, and prepares for what happens if the network goes down. According to Ransome and Rittinghouse (2005), it is also wise to explain to the company' users and the management team what they can expect from these changes, along with the benefits they will receive from the new project.

The next stage in the VoIP implementation process is the evaluation and purchase of equipment, software and services. When evaluating products from multiple vendors, it is very important to run consistent and repeatable tests to ensure that we are comparing what we want with what we actually get and to ensure that the metrics match the performance statistics provided by the vendor. Additionally, testing is also vital to verify that each vendor's products will interoperate in the network with the current equipment when we are making purchasing decisions that affects a significant portion of the budget.

Deployment and verification are also a very important process in a VoIP implementation. Deploying multimedia applications will challenge a networking team that is only familiar with transaction-oriented applications. Proactive management will increase users' satisfaction and will be a welcome change to the thankless firefighting resulting from severe mismanagement that is typically common in today's IT environments.

Finally, the maintenance process should not be forgotten. For most companies, network performance is vital to the success of the business. The complexity of today's applications and networks drives the absolute requirement for monitoring and event management to ensure the performance of specific devices, LAN segments, or applications. Service Level Agreements (SLAs) can be used to provide a standard for measuring the performance of the solutions against the expectations of users. Ideally, such performance should exceed, or at a minimum, be equal to the level of service the users are currently receiving. This is critical to proper service-level and contract management. By establishing trends that show network behavior and performance over time, it will be possible to tune the existing infrastructure and plan future investments for future growth.

MAIN SECURITY ISSUES

Traditional voice security problems are simple and well-understood. In the PSTN world, security problems include fraudulent use of service, privacy concerns, and loss of service (Hung & Martin, 2006).

The security problems faced by VoIP are related with the adopted VoIP protocols. Table 2 briefly present the most relevant issues associated with each protocol.

IP Telephony has the same security issues as traditional telephony, including fraudulent use of service, privacy concerns, and loss of service. Even though traditional telephony has faced and solved these very same issues, placing calls and their corresponding signaling onto an IP infrastructure changes the dynamics of how these fundamental security considerations must be addressed. Many groups of technology problems must be successfully identified and addressed during the migration from traditional voice services to an IP Telephony environment.

The main authors are presented bellow and identified the following threat categories:

- Masquerading.
- Denial of service.
- Eavesdropping.
- Abuse of access.
- Social context.

In summary, we briefly present in Table 3 the five common attacks and related threats to security requirements in VoIP applications.

Masquerading

A masquerade is the pretence of an entity to be another entity. Masquerading can lead to charging fraud, breach of privacy, and breach of integrity. This attack can be carried out by hijacking a link after authentication has been performed, or by eavesdropping and subsequent replaying of authentication information (Rossebo & Sijben, 2006).

Using a masquerade attack, an attacker can gain unauthorized access to VoIP services. An attacker can steal the identity of a real user and obtain access by masquerading as the real user. By employing a replay attack, the attacker can capture the authentication credentials of an authorized user and replay the authentication message at a later time to obtain fraudulent access to a service (and in this case the real user may be charged for the calls placed by the masquerading user). In another form of masquerade, an attacker replaying or masquerading as a service may deceive the user, so that the service the user intended to access is then not available.

Table 2. Protocols commonly used in VoIP (Junipter, 2006)

Protocol	Application	Maturity	Risk Level
H.323	Call Signaling, Control Message Formatting, Stream Packetization	Medium-high: high multi-vendor interoperability, but proprietary extensions still used by most vendors	High: uses up to 11 port numbers per session; standard firewall configurations open all potential application ports, rendering networks extremely vulnerable
Internet Protocol (IP)	The network layer protocol in the IP suite, used to communicate data across a packet-switched network	Relatively high: IPv6 improves upon IPv4, the most prevalent version of IP in use worldwide, primarily in the use of 128-bit addresses, rather than 32-bit addresses	High: due to its nature, IP provides only best-effort delivery, and upper-layer protocols must address reliability issues
Media Gateway Control Protocol (MGCP)	Control and call state communications between Softswitch/Media Gateway Controller and Media Gateway	Relatively low: the industry de facto standard is the informational RFC 2705, maintained by PacketCable and the Softswitch Consortium; implementation of subsequent standard MEGACO/H.248 remains sparse	Medium: MGCP supports IPSec for message protection, and allows call agents to provide gateways with session keys for encrypting audio messages, to protect against eavesdropping
Real-time Transport Protocol (RTP)	Streaming Media (e.g., tones, announcements, voice messages)	Medium-High: first defined by ITU-T, later "adopted" by IETF, and now encompasses specific profile for audio and video conferencing and optional Secure RTP	Medium: encryption supported, but typically with compromised performance
Session Initiation Protocol (SIP)	Initiation, Modification, and Termination of interactive multimedia user sessions	Medium: proprietary extensions still used by key system vendors to unable nonstandard features	Medium: SIP supports point-to-point encryption, but management and technical drawbacks persist, and definition is lacking for SIP requests sent to multiple endpoints

Table 3. Most common attacks and threats in VoIP applications

Threats	Confidentiality	Integrity	Availability
Masquerading	X	X	
Denial of service			X
Eavesdropping	X	X	
Abuse of access	X		
Social context	X	X	

Denial of Service

The main goal of Denial of Service (DoS) attacks is not to gain access to networks and computers, but to deny the access to these systems for legitimate users. There are several ways to perform these kind of attacks and there are several reasons for the attackers to carry out DoS attacks. According to Ehlert et al (2010), typical ways to carry out network DoS attacks are either the usage of hand-crafted networks packets aimed at known vulnerabilities, or the generation of large quantities of network traffic to cause overload conditions.

The different basic types of DoS that occur over the IP network can be organized in three categories: implementation flaw DoS, flood DoS and application-level DoS.

The implementation flaw DoS occurs when an attacker sends a carefully crafted packet or sequence of packets that exploit an implementation flaw in a VoIP component, such as an IP PBX. The packet may be very long, syntactically incorrect, or otherwise malformed in a way that causes the target component to fail because it wasn't implemented robustly enough to handle unexpected packets.

The flood DoS occurs when a large number of normal packets are sent to a target VoIP component. With this form of DoS, the target system is so busy processing packets from the attack, that it will not be able to process legitimate packets. Legitimate packets will either be ignored or processes so slowly that the VoIP service is unusable.

The application-level DoS occurs when a feature of the VoIP service is manipulated to cause DoS. For example, hijacking the registration for an IP phone can cause loss of any inbound calls to that phone (Zhang et al, 2009).

A variant of denial of service issue is the media degrading, which is an authorized method in which an attacker manipulates media or media control (e.g., Real-time Control Protocol [RTCP]) packets and reduces the QoS of any communication. Some examples may include (Park, 2009):

1. An attacker intercepts RTCP packets in the middle, and changes (or erases) the statistic values of media traffic (packet loss, delay, and jitter) so that the endpoint devices may not control the media properly.
2. An attacker intercepts RTCP packets in the middle, and changes the sequence number of the packets so that the endpoint device may play the media with wrong sequence, which degrades the quality.

Eavesdropping

Eavesdropping is the unauthorized interception of voice packets and the decoding of the conversations. In fact, it is relatively easy and simple to implement it, if we consider that there are many free network analyzer, sniffers and packet capture tools that convert VoIP traffic to wave files (Jahanirad et al, 2011).

Possible attacks related to eavesdropping include conversation alternation, impersonation and hijacking. Conversation impersonation and hijacking includes various modifications of any voice, video, text and/or imaging data. As in the conversation reconstruction scenario, the first step is VoIP information collection and translation. However, in this case the contents of the conversation could be altered and provide the entities using VoIP services with false and misleading information.

Abuse of Access

Abuse of access is a threat where malicious users/ programs abuse their access to the system. Abuse of access can take all kinds of forms. Typically, it includes the access to the system by a malicious user and access by a malicious program on interfaces exposed by the system.

One common abuse of access form in VoIP happens with click-to-dial services, where companies will call back users via the regular phone system. This service is usually offered through a Webpage where anyone can enter any phone number (Rossebo & Sijben, 2006). Currently, as this is very much open to abuse, many companies have discontinuing this option.

According to Park (2009) another method of QoS abuse is exhausting the limited bandwidth with a malicious tool so that legitimate users cannot use bandwidth for their service. Some VoIP service providers or hosting companies limit the bandwidth for certain groups of hosts to protect the network. An attacker may know the rate limit and generate excessive media traffic through the channel, so voice quality between users may be degraded.

Social Context

A threat against social context is somewhat different from other technical threats against availability, confidentiality, or integrity, particularly in terms of the intention and methodology. It focuses on how to manipulate the social context between communications parties so that an attacker can misrepresent himself as a trusted entity and convey false information to the target user.

The typical threats against social context are as follows:

- **Misrepresentation of Identity, Authority, Rights, and Content:** Typically an attacker presents his identity with false information, such as false caller name, number, domain, organization, email address or presence information. On the other side, authority or rights misrepresentation is the method of presenting false information to an authentication system to obtain the access permit, or bypassing an authentication system by inserting the appearance of authentication when there was none;

- **Spam of Call (Voice), IM, and Presence:** Typically consists in a bulk unsolicited set of session initiation attempts (e.g., invite requests), attempting to establish a voice or video communication session. If the user should answer, the spammer proceeds to relay their message over real-time media. This is often called Spam over IP telephony, or SPIT;

- **Phishing:** The general meaning of phishing is an illegal attempt to obtain somebody's personal information (e.g., ID, password, bank account number, credit card information) by posing as a trsut entity in the communication. In VOIP, phishing is typically happening through voice or IM communication.

TECHNIQUES FOR THE MITIGATION OF SECURITY ISSUES

A first recommendation is the implementation of a network segmentation, making possible the separation of data segments from IP Telephony segments. This strict separation has many benefits. First, it is much easier to enforce filtering and security rule sets on IP Telephony hosts when they comprise a well-defined group. This is advantageous when trying to create and enforce QoS, Security, and Intrusion Detection System (IDC) policies. The second and perhaps biggest benefit to segmenting the network is that it places IP phones in a position where they are no longer subject to direct attacks from neighboring PCs. In a flat design, IP phones might be attacked from neighboring PCs that were either compromised or infected. A flat network also would aid an attacker who might attempt to use a compromised PC to capture voice packets. Keeping networks logically separate makes this activity more difficult for an attacker to perform and hide.

Currently, the majority of IP phones are already capable of providing network access to a PC through a jack on the phone. This allows network operators to deploy only single cabling drops to each user. Fortunately, it is possible to configure the PC to be on a different virtual LAN (VLAN) than the one on which the phone resides. It is also possible to prevent the PC that is connected to the phone from marking datagrams with forged QoS indicators.

Another important step is the building of redundancy into the VoIP network. The ability to combine both the data and voice networks into a single network is a major economic driving force in the rapidly growing move to VoIP. Users have become accustomed to occasional short outages in the data network, but phone service is another issue. When planning the VoIP implementation the company shall consider alternate ways to provide phone service in the event of major network problems. This is especially true for emergency services. Therefore, a company shall plan for schedules network downtimes a policy that guarantees that the hone service can still be maintained.

A typical issue that frequently appears in a network is the bottlenecking at the routers due to the encryption issues (Marcus & Elixmann, 2008). A good way to fix it is to handle encryption/decryption solely at the endpoints in the VoIP network. One consideration with this method is that the endpoints must be computationally powerful enough to handle the encryption mechanism. Ideally encryption shall be maintained at every hop in a VoIP packet's lifetime, which may not be feasible with simple IP phones with little in the way of software o computational power. Therefore, migration for IP phones with increased processing power is recommended. In addition, SRTP and MIKEY are key protocols for media encryption and key management enabling secure interworking between H.323 and SIP based clients.

The adoption of Secure Real Time Protocol (SRTP) is also important in replacement of Real-time Transport Protocol (RTP). The RTP is commonly used for transmission of real-time audio/video data in Internet telephony applications. Without protection RTP is considered insecure, as a telephone conversation over IP can easily be eavesdropped. Additionally, manipulation and replay of RTP data could lead to poor voice quality due to jamming of the audio/video stream. The SRTP is a profile of RTP offering not only confidentiality, but also message authentication, and replay protection for the RTP traffic as well as Real-time Transport Control Protocol (RTCP).

The SRTP provides increased security, achieved by the confidentiality for RTP as well as for RTCP by encryption of the respective pay-loads, and integrity for the entire RTP and RTCP packets, together with replay protection. There is also the possibility to refresh the session keys periodically, which limits the amount of cipher text produced by a fixed key, available for an adversary to cryptanalyze. Additionally, SRTP provides an extensible framework that permits upgrading with new cryptographic algorithms.

Another way to improve simultaneously the security and performance is to consider better scheduling schemes. For that, we can consider the Advanced Encryption Standard (AES) which is a specification for the encryption of electronic data. The incorporation of AES or some other speedy encryption algorithm could help temporarily alleviate the bottleneck, but this is not a scalable solution because it does not address the highest degree cause of the slowdown. Without a new way for the crypto-engine to prioritize packets, the engine will still be susceptible to DoS attacks and starvation from data traffic impeding the time-urgent VoIP traffic. Ideally, the crypto-engine would implement QoS scheduling to favor the voice packets, but this is not a realistic scenario due to speed and compactness constraints on the crypto-engine. One solution implemented in some routers is to schedule the packets with QoS in mind prior to the encryption phase. Although this heuristic solves the problem for all packet poised to enter the crypto-engine at a given time, it does not address the problem of VoIP packets arriving at a crypto-engine queue that is already saturated with previously scheduled data packets. QoS prioritizing can also be done after the encryption process provided that the encryption procedures preserve the ToS bits from the original IP header in the new IPsec header. This functionality is not guaranteed and is dependent on one's network hardware and software, but if it is implemented it allows for QoS scheduling to be used at every hop the encrypted packets encounter.

In all situations, the company must verify if its firewall is VoIP aware. In some cases, an application aware proxy server that can handle dynamic ports and addressing may be needed. However, the company must be ware that by allowing VoIP packets through a firewall a potential security risk is involved. When using NAT and encryption, there are additional difficulties with the SIP protocol because IP addresses appear in the body of protocol.

Table 4 presents a situation where the firewall just allows incoming traffic from external hosts only if the session was initiated from the internal network. Therefore, incoming calls, coming from applications fails to establish connection between the end users.

A typical solution to the problem described above is manually specifying the port numbers to be left open in the firewall. This approach introduces a severe risk because an intruder, with knowledge of these open ports, can create malicious software to take advantage of the fact that the firewall is letting traffic in through the open ports. Leaving ports open defeats the purpose of installing a firewall in the first place. Another problem with opening ports is that manual configuration is required by end-users or network administrators.

To solve the NAT transversal problem, we can consider the inclusion of a Application Level Gateway (ALG), which will act as a protocol-aware firewall that monitors traffic and permits traffics flows for specific applications. Another solution is considering the use of emergent protocols such as Session Transversal Using NAT (STUN) and Interactive Connectivity Establishment (ICE). STUN allows the application to discover the public IP address and port mappings that the applica-

tions can use to communicate with its peer. ICE is a framework that defines how to use the STUN protocol to solve the NAT traversal problem, by choosing the best possible interconnection method between two users.

CONCLUSION

VoIP has become a key enabling technology for multimedia communication on the IP network. Currently, the adoption rate of VoIP has increased significantly, and soon will become the dominant mode for business telephony. VoIP enthusiasts promise many benefits over the traditional PSTN. A great deal of industry excitement has been generated about the potential cost savings, the new calling features, and the reduced infrastructure of converged networks in a VoIP implementation. In addition, the Internet being an open network virtually eliminates geographic limitations for placing phone calls.

However, as VoIP uses the existing IP network and this inherits its vulnerabilities, namely in terms of QoS, equipment availability, internetworking with diverse networks, security and high costs of migration. Today, some of these vulnerabilities still remain, namely in terms of high up-front costs, integration complexity and security. Within the domain of this chapter we analyzed the most relevant concerns related with security. These identified vulnerabilities can be categorized in five groups: masquerading, denial of service eavesdropping, abuse of access and social context.

Finally, we proposed some concrete policies to be adopted by companies to mitigate the identified security vulnerabilities of VoIP. Among them we highlight the need to implement a network segmentation between data and IP Telephony segments, build a redundancy in a VoIP network, encrypt the endpoints in VoIP network, adopt the SRTP protocol, use of better scheduling schemes incorporating AES and verify that the firewall is properly VoIP aware.

Table 4. VoIP call between users behind NAT

Layer	Packet Content
IP	S: 61.27.36.54 ; D: 64.92.38.182
UDP	S: 9238 ; D: 5060
SIP	sip:tux@fe.up.pt ; by: 192.178.32.3:1939
SDP	v=0 ; c=IN IPv4 192.178.32.3 ; m=audio 1940 RTP/AVP

REFERENCES

Biggs, P. (2009). *Voice over the internet protocol: Enemy or ally?* GSR Discussion Paper. Retrieved October 17, 2012, from http://www.itu.int/ITU-D/treg/Events/Seminars/GSR/GSR09/doc/GSR09_VoIP-Trends_Biggs.pdf

Bookman, S. (2011). Going mobile: hosted VoIP extends PBX mobile functionality to the SMB. *Fierce Enterprise Communications*. Retrieved January 17, from http://www.fierceenterprisecommunications.com/special-reports/going-mobile-hosted-voip-extends-pbx-mobile-functionality-smb

Ehlert, S., Geneiatakis, D., & Magedanz, T. (2010). Survey of network security systems to counter SIP-based denial-of-service attacks. *Computers & Security*, *29*(1), 225–243. doi:10.1016/j.cose.2009.09.004.

Erica, D. (2013). *Mobile VoIP users will reach 1 billion by 2017?!* Retrieved January 19, from http://blog.voxox.com/the-future-of-voxox-and-the-global-voip-revolution/8623

Hung, P., & Martin, M. (2006). Security issues in VoIP applications. In *Proceedings of Canadian Conference on Electrical and Computer Engineering*, (pp. 65-71). Ottawa, Canada: IEEE.

Jahanirad, M., Al-Nabhani, Y., & Noor, R. (2011). Security measures for VoIP application: A state of the art review. *Scientific Research and Essays*, *6*(23), 4950–4959.

Junipter. (2006). Enterprise VoIP security best practices. *Junipter Networks*. Retrieved March 18, from http://netscreen.com/solutions/literature/white_papers/

Kaufman, C. (2008). *The benefits of business VoIP*. Teledata White Papers. Retrieved October 17, 2012, from http://www.teledata.com/PDF_Resources/Resources/Not%20ShoreTel%20-%20Why%20VOIP%20makes%20Business%20Sense.pdf

Kerravala, Z. (2010). Demystifying VoIP for business. *Yankee Group Research*. Retrieved January 19, from http://www.windstreambusiness.com/media/1015/voip_Webinar.pdf

Kumar, A. (2011). Security and risk challenges of VoIP over IP telephony. *International Journal of Electronics*, *3*(1), 85–87.

Latif, T. (2007). *Adoption of VoIP*. (Master thesis). Department of Business Administration and Social Sciences, Lulea University, Lulea, Sweden.

Marcus, J., & Elixmann, D. (2008). The future of IP interconnection. *Wik-Consult*. Retrieved January 23, from http://ec.europa.eu/information_society/policy/ecomm/doc/library/ext_studies/future_ip_intercon/ip_intercon_study_final.pdf

Mathiyalakan, S. (2006). VoIP adoption: Issues & concerns. *Communications of the IIMA*, *6*(2), 19–24.

Nunn, L., McGuire, B., & Crowe, B. (2010). VoIP cost efficiencies and the decision to implement. *Review of Business Information Systems*, *14*(1), 1–14.

Park, P. (2009). Voice over IP security: Security best practices derived from deep analysis of the latest VoIP network threats. *CISCO White Paper*, 7-43.

Ransome, J., & Rittinghouse, J. (2005). *VoIP security*. Burlington, UK: Elsevier Digital Press.

Rossebo, J., & Sijben, P. (2006). Security issues in VoIP. *Telektronikk*, *2*, 130–145.

Schuk, C. (2010). The future of consumer VoIP. *Business Insights*. Retrieved January 17, 2013, from http://www.globalbusinessinsights.com/content/rbtc0141t.pdf

Thadani, R. (2010). Advantages of VoIP. *Buzzle.com*. Retrieved January 19, from http://www.buzzle.com/articles/advantages-of-voip.html

Tobin, P., & Bidoli, M. (2006). Factors affecting the adoption of VoIP and other converged IP services in South Africa. *South African Journal of Business Management, 37*(1), 31–40.

Varshney, U., Snow, A., McGiven, M., & Howard, C. (2002). Voice over IP. *Communications of the ACM, 45*(1), 89–95. doi:10.1145/502269.502271.

Viscusi, S. (2010). Business VoIP penetration to grow rapidly. *TMCNet*. Retrieved January 17, 2013, from http://www.tmcnet.com/channels/business-voip/articles/74242-business-voip-penetration-grow-rapidly-report.htm

Wallingford, T. (2005). Switching to VoIP. Sebastopol, CA: O' Reilly Media.

Zhang, R., Wang, X., Farley, R., Yang, X., & Jiang, X. (2009). On the feasibility of launching the man-in-the-middle attacks on VoIP from remote attackers. In *Proceedings of ASIACCS*, (pp. 61-69). Sydney, Australia: ASIACCS.

ADDITIONAL READING

Berger, T. (2006). Analysis of current VPN technologies. *First International Conference on Availability, Reliability, and Security*, 108-115.

Bishop, M. (2003). *Computer security: Art and science*. Reading, MA: Addison-Wesley.

Butcher, D. et al. (2007). Security challenges and defense in VoIP infrastructure. *IEEE Transactions on Systems, Man, and Cybernetics, 37*, 1152–1162. doi:10.1109/TSMCC.2007.905853.

Clayton, B. (2007). *Securing media streams in an asterisk-based environment and evaluating the resulting performance cost*. (Mater thesis). Rhids University, Grahamstown, South Africa.

Cole, E. (2002). *Hackers beware: The ultimate guide to network security*. New York: New Riders Publishing.

Davidson, J. (2000). *Voice over IP fundamentals*. Hoboken, NJ: Cisco Press.

Endler, D., & Collier, M. (2007). *Hacking exposed VoIP: Voice over IP security secrets and solutions*. Osborne, UK: McGraw-Hill.

Junipter (1). (2007). *Centralized security management for large organizations*. Retrieved from http://netscreen.com/solutions/literature/white_papers/200199.pdf

Junipter (2). (2005). *Secure and assured networking with an enterprise intranet*. Retrieved from http://netscreen.com/solutions/literature/white_papers/200144.pdf

Kopsidas, S., Zisiadis, D., & Tassiulas, L. (2007). A secure VoIP conference system: Architecture analysis and design issues. In *Proceedings of the 3rd ACM workshop on QoS and Security for Wireless and Mobile Networks*, (pp. 180-183). ACM.

Kuhn, R., Walsh, T., & Fries, S. (2005). *Security consideration for voice over IP systems*. Washington, DC: National Institute of Standards and Technology Publications.

Marsan, C. (2006). VoIP security services taking hold. *Network World, 23*(26).

Matrawy, A., et al. (2005). Mitigating network denial of service through diversity-based traffic management. In *Proceedings of the 3rd International Conference on Applied Cryptography and Network Security (ACNS)*. New York: ACNS.

Maynor, D. et al. (2006). *Emerging threat analysis: From mischief to malicious*. Boston: Syngree Publishing.

Mirkovic, J., Dietrich, D., & Reither, P. (2004). *Internet denial of service: Attack and defense mechanisms*. New York: Prentice Hall.

Porter, T. (n.d.). *Practical VoIP security*. Boston: Syngress Publishing.

Sicker, D., & Lookabaugh, T. (2004). VoIP security: Not an afterthought. *ACM Queue; Tomorrow's Computing Today*, 2(6), 56–64. doi:10.1145/1028893.1028898.

Thermos, P., & Takanen, A. (2007). *Securing VoIP networks: Threat, vulnerabilities and counter measures*. Boston: Addison Wesley.

KEY TERMS AND DEFINITIONS

Call Control Service: It includes the call establishment, reporting, mid-call service features, and teardown. The Call Control Service is provided by a Call Controller. Multiple Call Controllers may exist within the VoIP Network.

Denial of Service (DoS): An attack on a system that cause loss of service to the users of that system.

Domain Name Service (DNS): A network service used to translate between domain name and IP addresses.

Network Infrastructure: The collection of all of the parts and places of a Network and more specifically all of the devices on a Network including their embedded or downloaded subcomponents.

Network Service: VoIP Service may make use of a number of generic Network Services such as DNS, TFTP, FTP, DHCP, HTTP or Telnet.

Switch: In terms of a networking device, a switch (similarly to a hub), provides interconnection function to multiple network devices at layer 2 of the OSI reference model. But unlike hub, which provides interconnection via a shared channel, a switch provides interconnection by switching frames of data to their destination.

VoIP Gateway: A VoIP gateway is a network device that helps to convert voice and fax calls between an IP network and Public Switched Telephone Network (PSTN) in real time. It is a high performance gateway designed for Voice over IP applications. A VoIP gateway can typically support at least two T1/E1 digital channels. Most VoIP gateways feature at least one Ethernet and telephone port. Various protocols, such as MGCP, SIP or LTP can help to control a gateway. VoIP Gateway benefits VoIP gateway's main advantage is that it connects existing telephone and fax machines through traditional telephone.

VPN Gateway: Virtual Private Netowrks (VPNs) enable users to connect to a remote private network through the InternetInternet. Virtual private networks therefore span the InternetInternet because the user connects over the InternetInternet to the remote VPN server. With a VPN, data is first encrypted and encapsulated before it is sent to the remote VPN server. When the VPN server obtains the data, it decrypts the packet so that it can be interpreted. VPNs are usually implemented to enable remote access users to connect to and access the network.

Chapter 15
Practical Approach for Data Breach Cases in ERP Systems

Pedro Sousa
Higher Polytechnic Institute of Gaya, Portugal

José Costa
Higher Polytechnic Institute of Gaya, Portugal

Vitor Manso
Higher Polytechnic Institute of Gaya, Portugal

ABSTRACT

This chapter is based on a case study scenario where a major data breach happens in one institution of public sector, a municipality, in Portugal. The focus of this chapter is to explain the gap between software development and security specialists because these are two fields of information and technology with specialized staff, but they do not work together. Quality Software may increase if these two fields work together and all specialists work for a good end product. At the other extreme are organizations with security problems because the software is bad in the security field, and these organizations do not have mechanisms that help internal teams in case of security incidents. If security is not a concern when companies are developing software, the security specialists have a lot of problems when trying to audit the system.

INTRODUCTION

From the point of view of the organization's management, computer security is seen as an irrelevant factor in the business concerns. This area is usually a concern for the departments of information and communication technologies. This minimizes the factor and the scope of computer security being reviewed at the local level of the department and not as a general concern. This idea is not true, generating a false sense of security for the organization. This feeling lasts while the organization is not compromised.

DOI: 10.4018/978-1-4666-4526-4.ch015

From the start, that business management platform, known as Enterprise Resource Planning (ERP), is the privileged place for the storage of important information. These are careless in terms of computer security, and investments/measures in security are targeted to the equipment and services of perimeter systems, such as firewalls, intrusion detection systems, proxies and security devices. There is a gap between the development and implementation of ERP and computer security efforts made by organizations, the investment area focused in other areas forgetting ERP systems. On the other hand, software development companies have little focus on the issue of computer security and the development of systems is careless in these themes.

In a society where all are connected to the network and the Internet, information systems security or computer security is not a major concern for organizations in general, in Portugal. This reality has changed in the last few years, but organizations are not fully alerted to this problem and IT (Information and Technology) Departments need a cultural change and the mindset needs to change.

Security problems in the public sector need to be a major concern, because public institutions have information from citizens and are financed by taxing money, the money of every contributor. The reality is very different, normally security issues are the last concern for IT Departments in the public sector, and in this paper we have a case study about a real life situation of how security problems can change one organization.

This paper intends as follows: Section 2 is the literature review – we defined to take a closer look of various fields in computer security or information security and this look takes a tour into technology and formal methodology; Section 3 describes a real world case study based on real security incidents and we take a look at the improvement that can be done in an organization if we have concerns about security; Section 4 is the future research directions chapter where all

key points inside the work is focused and what can be done to improve in the future. The conclusion of this proposal and the next steps to be taken are presented in Section 5.

LITERATURE REVIEW

The security problem of ERP starts before implementing in the organizations, ie, starts in the development phase and in software development companies. Traditionally companies that produce software don't have security concerns, in the initial stages of development, and don't have the human resources with expertise in this field. There are some concerns in terms of users and passwords and the need to create a model for privileges inside the software, but the focus of professional in software development are the features and purpose of the operation of the product, according to customer specifications or market where the software is located. There is a gap between software development and the field of computer security and information security. We found highly specialized human resources in software development and highly specialized human resources in computer security. The problem lies in the lack of cooperation and communication between these two fields in the area of information and technology (van Wyk & McGraw, 2005).

The software development companies wake up to this issue only after the implementation of software to their customers and when security incidents happen. Creating a culture of interdisciplinary work between software development and computer security can lead to the development of a top quality product and avoid many future problems in the implementation of systems. It is not only necessary to implement an interdisciplinary culture between the two fields, it is necessary to create models for the various specialists to communicate and understand the concerns and both parties, because the human resources software development does not dominate the themes of information security and information security specialists are not programmers or developers. You can find security methodologies to software development, the same way we found the UML (Unified Modeling Language) or other languages for communication between the client, analysts and programmers (van Wyk & McGraw, 2005).

Figure 1 describes a model of the key points for a methodology of analysis and implementation of security best practices for the development of computer software. This methodology follows the philosophy identical to the UML to ensure proper communication between the various elements forming part of the production process of software.

This joint effort allows the various specialties to grow, increasing the quality of final products, creating a subset of specialists working the field of software security. The advantage of software security is to be a new and growing area, where the standards are still being defined. The success or failure of implementing a process of joint work between programmers and computer security experts is directly related to the culture of the organization where human resources are inserted along with the interpersonal skills of each human resource (van Wyk & McGraw, 2005).

The safety of an ERP system is a continuous process, according to (Marnewick & Labuschagne, 2006), this process begins with the initial design of ERP implementation and ends with the entry into full operation. However, the safety assess-ment cannot have this vision, as new technologies emerge every day, as well as new threats and the need to keep the information intact, is a constant and daily goal. Moreover, the ERP system is an integral part of this organization and adapts and changes daily, security must accompany all internal and external changes that occur within the purview of the organization.

According to Wolf and Gehrke (2009) the SoD (Segregation of Duties) or segregation of duties is a first step towards creating a framework that allows constant monitoring of the activity and performance of functions, particularly in complex ERP. This method allows us to identify conflicts of privileges of several users on their performance of duties. With this method we can understand:

- The creation of a system of rules under the principle of segregation of duties is fundamental to the success of the process and to a correct understanding of the system.
- The map of business rules to the rules of the control system requires a mature analysis and a thorough knowledge of the system, requiring key and experienced users.
- When the system of privileges, the ERPs, is not based on static rules and has mechanisms, it is necessary to consider specific implementations translation privileges to implement.

Figure 1. Methodology for security best pratices implementation (van Wyk & McGraw, 2005)

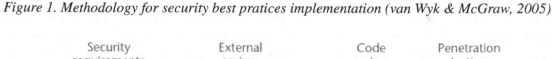
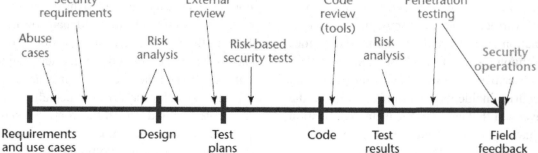

- The restructuring model privileges to meet the SoD model, can lead to denial of access to users. This factor is very important because it can influence the performed work, impairing the normal functioning of the system.

According to Alexander and Ayers (2011), the continuous monitoring and control is the best weapon to approach zero the possibility of a security incident happens. However there is a need for systematic procedures for monitoring and control, in order to implement a framework that will ensure the safety of the ERP system. Risks exist, but generally are not identified and enumerated in order to understand whether they are controlled. The most common risk is fraud, deliberate or unconsciously, causing data corruption and that has the effect of generating false information.

The SIEM (Security Information and Event Management) appear as a mechanism for excellence to support the collection and correlation of security logs, ensuring the traceability of operations, evaluation of the dangers and implementing alerts on activity systems. However, these systems are focused on traditional systems (firewall, servers, authentication, etc.), because the job requires ERPs linked to a technological vision, but also organizational (Lane, 2010).

CASE STUDY: DATA BREACH IN PUBLIC SECTOR

Case Study Scenario

The case study scenario is conducted in the municipality of Portuguese territory, a public sector institution and applies to ERP that supports the organization's business.

Information System Data for Case Study

- **Number of Staff that Works with ERP:** > 200 persons;
- **Database Server Operating System:** Linux CentOS 5.x;
- **Database Server System:** Oracle Database 10G R2;
- **Application Server Operating System:** Windows Server 2003 Standard Edition;
- **Application System:** SAGA System from Medidata;
- **Domain Controller:** Yes, there are 2 domain controllers supported by Linux;
- **Computers are Integrated into the Domain:** All computers are integrated;
- **Audit System:** The ERP has no audit system;
- **Activity Logs:** The ERP has no activity logs;

How the Information System Works

Databases: The system has one instance, called MC, and each application inside the ERP has a specific owner where the tables, views and procedures are stored. For example, the application of construction has an owner called OBP and accounting application has an owner called CTA2011 (or CTA2010, or CTA2012), in this case there is one owner for each year;

Privileges system: The system security privileges are developed by the supplier of ERP and controlled based on tables within the database;

Database connection: The connections to the database are made by ODBC. Users and passwords are stored in a local file, along with the executable for each application. Users used for binding, are the owners of the database tables;

The next steps describe the process of connecting to the ERP:

Step 1: Each user accesses the file server to run the application. This access is guaranteed by a shortcut installed on each computer on the network;

Step 2: The application is loaded with data from the local file, along with the executable, where users are stored and passwords connected.

Step 3: On the computer user is a connection over ODBC (Open Database Connectivity), to Oracle database with data from the local file;

Step 4: The database connection is established with full privileges because the user owns the connection tables;

Step 5: The application is started and you can work; operations are controlled by the security privileges of the application;

In Figure 2, the process flow each user have to do to connect to ERP System.

Security Issues in ERP Systems

In the scenario presented, some computer security issues are raised. These issues are placed at various levels, ability to audit, control, access and logging.

One major issue is the lack of activity records in the database and one audit system for cases where security incidents happen. ERP systems, especially the system with financial functions, should have mechanisms to register the activity performed to enable auditing in the event of an incident. No system is one hundred percent a proof against security incidents, for this reason software development companies need to implement independent mechanisms for activity records. These records allow access to all activities inside database and leave forensic evidence for security auditors.

Another big issue, in this scenario is the access to the database. All users connected to the infrastructure of the municipality have direct access to three key points in the ERP:

Figure 2. Processo diagram for connect to ERP database

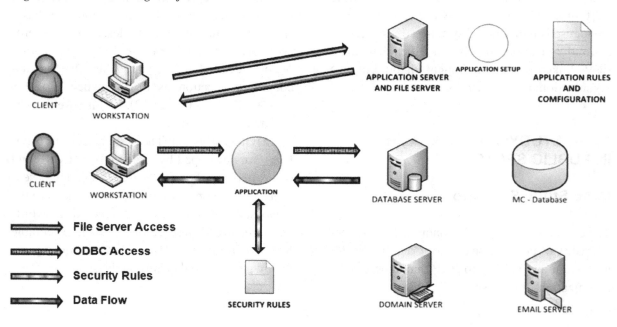

Key Point 1: All workstations inside the municipality network have access to the applications executable, because these files are stored in a file server, and the user only needs one domain account to have access;

Key Point 2: Inside the file server, in the same directory as the application executable, we have the local file with the data for connecting the database. This file has the username and password to connect to ERP database;

Key Point 3: All devices inside the infrastructure have one ODBC connection to the database. To have one SQL (Structured Query Language) console, the user only needs the username and password, and this information is inside the local file, stored together with the application executable on the file server.

Another issue in this institution is the lack of records for remote connections to the infrastructure. In the network of the municipality we have remote buildings with fibre optics connections, remote buildings with Microsoft Remote Desktop Connections (MS-RDP) and users with Virtual Private Network (VPN) connections. In the IT (Information and Technology) Department there isn't any records for these remote connections and the global IT infrastructure don't have one centralized logging system to control and monitor the activity from remote connections.

The final issue in this scenario is the root and administrator accounts. These accounts are shared by users of the IT Department, outsourcing human resources and suppliers. In case of one security incident it's impossible to isolate the access to core systems and functions, because many people know the root and administrator access. These accounts are responsible for managing the infrastructure.

Problems in ERP Systems for Public Institutions

In this municipality two major security incidents happened in the past related to the ERP and core functions for the organization.

First Problem

The security incident was located in ERP and in their servers without affecting other software, not the normal operation of other services within the network of the municipality. Even other computer systems that were within the same database server, but in different instances, were not affected by this security incident. With the scenario presented in this municipality, it was impossible to identify the origins of the incident due to lack of records and liberalized access to the computer system without any control. The only variable was the common focus on ERP supplier Medidata which was used by more than 80% of human resources of the municipality. Another factor was the randomness of the occurrence of the abnormality of the system, i.e. the system was retrieved based on a policy backup of 30 to 30 minutes but the abnormalities computer hour took place in completely separate within working hours. This problem was an additional factor, which increased the complexity of forensic analysis, remote access to the information system. The origin of security incidents could be inside the network of the city, one of the remote buildings or any of the clients who had access VPN. These remotes were not recorded or monitored.

A Step to Solving

After the analysis of the technological infrastructure of the municipality and the lack of control of key points in the information system and computer network, we began a process of reconfiguration of the infrastructure to isolate the source of the problem and ensure the existence of records and evidence in case security incident. We have performed several operations:

- Revoke all remote access to the network of the municipality.
- Encrypt files from local users and passwords.
- Increase the frequency of backups to minimize the impact of data destruction.

- Change the passwords of users (root and administrator) of systems administration from infrastructure, ensuring that only administrators had knowledge.
- Remove all ERP applications for administration, who were on the network shares that users had access.
- Ensure that no system administration task would cause a security incident.

The Problem of Software Development without Security Concerns

In the scenario presented is an instance of the database within an Oracle database, where all ERP has its applications. This ERP comprises several applications and application modules and each has a table structure itself. As previously stated, the division of these tables is done with the structure that Oracle provides owners, or each application has an owner in the database and those are within this owner tables and views the application operation. The problem with this approach is the connection method, ie, is the owner of the tables used to connect to the database; it is not possible to restrict the privileges of the user before the database objects, because he owns the objects. The operations that were to be performed on the database were DROP TABLE and DROP VIEW, destroying the structure of the database without leaving operation records. By destroying the structure, data were also deleted, causing the collapse of the information system. Analysing in detail, the user only requires access to one of the network devices in the municipality to obtain a SQL console to the database and cause the shutdown of the system.

Change System Security

After analysing the operation method of the ERP software that supports the municipality, it was possible to increase the security level of the data layer with changes in the structure of the database.

Example of behaviour of an ERP application:

- **Application:** OBP
- **Owner:** OBP
- **Connection User:** OBP
- **Table:** OBP.TABLE_A
- **View:** OBP.VIEW_A
- **Call Method (Path):** SELECT * FROM TABLE_A

After analysing application behaviour, we learn that all objects (tables and views) are called by the local name, i.e., the user connection is always the owner of the objects and these are never called by full path, only for short name or short path.

With this analysis, we create the structure of the database, ie by each owner (owner A) (user) from database, we will create a new user (owner B) with the suffix _USER. Then we will ensure that the new user can only perform the four operations to the old SELECT, UPDATE, INSERT and DELETE.

After removing the ability to connect with the owner (owner A) of the tables and added a synonym for each object from owner A to the owner B, simulating the local existence of tables and views.

Example of behaviour of an ERP application:

- **Application:** OBP
- **Owner:** OBP
- **Connection User:** OBP_USER
- **Table:** OBP.TABLE_A
- **View:** OBP.VIEW_A
- **Synonymous:** OBP.TABLE_A -> OBP_USER.TABLE_A
- **Synonymous:** OBP.VIEW_A -> OBP_USER.VIEW_A
- **Call Method (Path):** SELECT * FROM TABLE_A
- **Operations between Both:** SELECT, UPDATE, DELETE and INSERT

Following this transaction in the database, we changed the local file where the data connection to the application are stored, and put the information for the new database users. With this change, we guarantee that the applications can only perform basic operations over the data in the database (SELECT, UPDATE, INSERT and DELETE).

Second Problem

After the improvements made in the previous paragraph the information system found a point of stability and finished security incidents that caused the collapse of the system and stopped the services. The improvements applied to the information system were designed to stabilize the system information and then identify the source of the problem. After stabilizing the system, there were no more anomalies or security incidents, therefore it was not possible to identify the source of the problem. After some time of normal system operation, reoccurred anomalies and security incidents, but now with a different pattern. With the restrictions described in the preceding paragraph, it was not possible to destroy the information system, however this has entered a new cycle of problems but located in two ERP applications, application OBP (processes of construction works) and CTA (accounting processes and financial movements). The fact that the incidents are located allowed to isolate the problem and conducted to a more detailed audit.

The Problem in the System

Some system tables were subject to DELETE operations, eliminating all the records inserted. These tables were system tables and do not exist in the application functions or options that allowed a user to manipulate existing data. The elimination of these data caused the shutdown of the system because they were essential to the creation and manipulation of active processes in ERP. Despite the anomaly is found, the system does not hold any registration mechanism that allows analysing and auditing functions or users who were manipulating the data that were deleted.

Nor was it possible to associate with the users of ERP because they were based on the application structure itself without any connection to objects in the database.

Data transactions are recorded by the system database and it was necessary to create a mechanism to register for these operations their audit logs, it was possible to analyse operations and identify the cause of the problem.

From the analysis of the entire information system, described over the various points of this document, we know that we cannot rely on the analysis of ERP users; we also know that all equipment is in the area of the county and that each person has a domain user only. Within the database, we could know the user connection, the table involved, the operations performed and the data manipulated. With all this information, a system was designed to record necessary data, to correlate the operations performed within the database, the domain user and the device.

We created a database of independent ERP where all records of data manipulation in the system were sent. This database had a table with the following structure:

- Domain user
- Device Internet Protocol
- Device Name
- Date and time for the operation
- Table
- Operation
- Owner
- Database user
- An application used for the operation

The structure of the log table aims to cross the operations performed on the database with the source outside the network, the execution of operations. After the creation of this system, it was added a Trigger on each table allowing the ERP to record this data for any operation performed on the tables. Not to cause delay or influence the normal operation of ERP and its applications, it was chosen non intrusive method for the execution of operations, so the system works silently without jeopardizing the work of users and making it impossible to be detected by the attacker, if it is a person.

After several days of monitoring and various anomalies caused by security incidents, we audited records of monitoring and auditing system, where it was possible to perform a forensic analysis and identify how the security incident was caused by a computer user. After crossing with the attendance system and collecting testimonials from other human resources of the municipality confirmed the presence in the place and time of the attacker thus triggering the legal process for such situations.

Solutions and Recommendations

The first problem stems from the gap between the various fields of work within the information technology, ie, the lack of computer security concerns of software development companies, creates a huge hole between the mechanisms implemented in the application and the real security needs a technology infrastructure needs, when analysed as a whole. The solution to this problem goes through a concrete analysis on the architecture of ERP in order to find possible faults that might cause problems for organizations. Furthermore the integration of objects from multiple layers of an information system is essential to ensure interoperability mechanisms that allow objects and enhance the security of applications. Lastly IT departments must have a critical analysis about the implementations made by software vendors, creating an environment of continuous improvement analysis and ensuring the development of applications and increase the security level of information system.

In the case study presented must be made to work together with the ERP supplier, the IT department and a security specialist to ensure the evolution of the computer security to levels that ensure the proper functioning of the municipality.

This work will approach software security needs of the market in which it operates and to increase product quality and may be a differentiating quality factor in a market with a lot of competitors.

The existence of systems for monitoring, control and audit of information systems installed in organizations is essential to ensure the smooth functioning of the organization in case of computer security incident. To some extent, the audit system has the same importance as the information system itself, as it is this that will monitor and ensure that the policies and processes of the organization are executed within the ERP as expected. The audit systems are the ultimate weapon against fraud and misuse of information systems, making independent audit function to the management function of the system.

FUTURE RESEARCH DIRECTIONS

The software security is a field of information and technology that connects software development and computer security, this is a growing field and hard work to develop. The study of the problem of security information at the source, i.e. producing software in order to increase the final quality of the product development is a focal point for the new generation of software, especially with the generation of cloud computing closer, the home user. The search methodologies and standards that define best practices for companies to follow software development will be a differentiating factor for professionals. The education sector will also have to evolve in this direction, so that professionals are aware of the concerns of the market and what paths they can choose to find solutions to this problem.

Typically the management persons are not alerted towards the security problems and their knowledge about computer security is based on common sense. These concerns arise when the first security incidents in the organizations they manage. Even if the management is alerted to the problems of computer security is a big gap between technical knowledge and concerns. The implementation of methodologies such as segregation of duties enables security specialist communicate with the design and management of organizations audit and control processes that have a focus on the real concerns of the organizations. This is a field of study course, since the establishment of formal methodologies that allow communicating with decision elements that have no technical knowledge is essential. The next step in the creation of formal models, for enabling communication with people management organizations, is creating methodologies for implementation and execution. You cannot create a model for control and audit information security, such as segregation of duties, if it has not at the level of implementation. The ability to execute the model in real and practical cases is critical to success and growth. The study of mechanisms for implementing these models is a growing field of computer security.

Monitoring systems, control and audit information systems are an essential tool, even if there is already on the market something that allows multiple systems to collect and correlate logs, these are not oriented information systems, particularly for ERP. The study of the adaptation of existing methodologies and mechanisms for the collection and correlation of data from network equipment and its adaptation to the information systems (ERP) is still an unexplored field. Another factor that is important, is the ability to treat large volumes of data collection systems have the ability to timely analyse and detect anomalies within defined policies and anomalies that escape the normal functioning of the systems. Fields of study such as artificial intelligence are the future (and present) of data correlation and in particular in supporting the identification of problems or anomalies.

CONCLUSION

This work is based on a practical approach to security issues in information systems, in particular ERP systems in the public sector in Portugal. The scenario presented, the problems identified the solutions adopted and the paths taken are based on a real case study. The problems presented are common to many organizations that have the feeling that the information system is safe, even if they have a lot of money invested in technology infrastructure and information system. The problems of computer security should be constant concern, which must be analysed in terms of management of the organization and operated by IT departments and suppliers. The management level is important because it is in this dimension that we can understand what areas and processes are important for the organization, so that investments are invested in the areas of information systems that are important to business.

The case study presented also indicates that huge investments are not generally required to increase the security level of an organization. To understand this dimension, it is necessary to analyse the information system as a whole and with concerns in the field of computer security. Bearing in mind this, we will see where and how we should improve the information system and the organization's policies. The involvement of technology providers is a key to success, but must be available to effect changes in the systems they sell. On the other hand, we realized that it is necessary to perform a job structuring at the level of culture of software houses and the internal staff, normally the developers. This work should be initiated by the education system, because the new generation of developers should be awoken to these concerns and the needs of organizations. Education institutions should look at these concerns as a challenge and not as a problem, because there is a window of opportunity to increase the quality of professionals, if synergies of collaborative work between programmers and computer security experts are converged.

REFERENCES

Alexander, C., & Ayers, A. (2011). *ERP security & continuous controls monitoring (CCM)*. RSM Tenon.

Goel, S., Kiran, R., & Garg, D. (2012). Vulnerability management for an enterprise resource planning system. *International Journal of Computers and Applications*, 19–22.

Hertenberger, M. (2005). *Issues in information systems issues in information systems*. Johannesburg, South Africa: University of Johannesburg.

Lane, A. (2012, April 30). *Understanding and selecting SIEM/LM: Use cases*. Retrieved 11 01, 2012, from http://securosis.com/blog/understanding-and-selecting-siem-lm-use-cases-part-1

Marnewick, C., & Labuschagne, L. (2006). *A security framework for an ERP system*. Auckland Park, South Africa: University of Johannesburg.

Saharia, A., Koch, B., & Tucker, R. (2008). ERP systems and internal audit. *Issues in Information Systems*, 578–586.

Swart, R., Marshall, B., Olsen, D., & Erbacher, R. (2007). ERP II system vulnerabilities and threats: An exploratory study. In *IRMA International Conference* (pp. 925-929). Idea Group Inc.

Tie, W., & Cheng, W. (2011). Study on enterprise information security in the ERP conditions. In *Proceedings of the International Conference on Computer Science and Network Technology* (pp. 332-335). IEEE.

van Wyk, K., & McGraw, G. (2005). Bridging the gap between software development and information security. *IEEE Security & Privacy*, 75-79.

Wolf, P., & Gehrke, N. (2009). *Continuous compliance monitoring in ERP systems - A method for identifying segregation of duties conflicts*. Hamburg, Germany: Wirtschaftinformatik.

Yu, X., & Wen, Q. (n.d.). *A view about cloud data security from data life cycle*. Beijing, China: IEEE.

ADDITIONAL READING

Christian, W., & Probst, R. R. (2007). *Where can an insider attack*. Berlin: Springer.

David Hendrawirawan, H. T. (2007). ERP security and segregation of duties audit: A framework for building an automated solution. *Information Systems Control Jornal, 2*(4).

Fuchs, L. (2012). Minimizing insider misuse through secure identity management. *Security and Communication Networks, 16*.

Juergens, M. (2006). *Global technology audit guide management of IT auditing*. Altamonte Springs, Florida: The Institute of Internal Auditors.

Kotiranta, J. (2012). *Preparing for ERP implementation*. Helsinki, Finland: Helsinki Metropolia University of Applied Sciences.

Madapusi, A. (2008). *Post-implementation evaluation of enterprise resource planning (ERP) systems*. Denton, TX: University of North Texas.

Panda, G. (2011). ERP implementations and its major challenges in auditing security issues for SME. *IARS International Researche Journal, 1*(14).

Skielse, G. J. (2006). *ERP adoption in small and medium sized enterprises*. Stockholm, Sweden: Universitetsservice US AB, Kista.

Song, Y. (2011). Enterprise internal controlling risks and prevention within ERP system. In *Proceedings of the International Conference on Information Management, Innovation Management and Industrial Engineering* (p. 4). IEEE.

Stijn, E. v. (2001). *Sharedness of and commitment to the ERP vision in an ERP envisioning context.* Enschede, The Netherlands: University of Twente, Department of Business Information.

Umble, E. J. (2002). Enterprise resource planning: Implementation procedures and critical success factors. *European Journal of Operational Research*, 17.

KEY TERMS AND DEFINITIONS

Audit System: The set of computerized mechanisms and processes within an organization to ensure the ability to audit a computer system in the event of computer incident or audit process analysis.

Computer Security: Field study on the protection of information in organizations against unauthorized access, misuse or destruction of information. Its basic principles of confidentiality, integrity, availability and authenticity and is not only related with computer mechanisms, but also people and processes.

Data Breach: A data breach is the theft or accidental loss of sensitive information. Usually involves important personal information that can lead to identity theft or fraud of computer systems or personal information.

Enterprise Resource Planing: Set of software modules integrated into a unified platform and interconnected processes, focused on the business of the organization. It is the main source of data and information management for an organization.

Security Incident: It is an event that occurs in an organization and that undermines your business, your services, customer data management or information that is confidential.

Security Information and Event Management: It is the combination of solutions that add the capabilities of various systems to ensure the collection, correlation and alerting timely information about events or incidents of security in an organization.

Segregation of Duties: Basic principle of an internal control system that is the separation of potentially conflicting roles, including authorization, approval, execution, control and accounting of operations.

Software Security: It is a field of computer security that studies the mechanisms and good practices to enhance security in software development.

Compilation of References

18, USC § 1030 - Fraud and related activity in connection with computers. (2012). Retrieved March 21, 2013, from http://www.law.cornell.edu/uscode/text/18/1030

Abeyratne, R. (2010). The deepwater horizon disaster - Some liability issues. *Tulane Maritime Law Journal, 125*(35).

ACM. (n.d.). Retrieved 11 22, 2012, from http://www.acm.org

Adams, G. B., & Ingersoll, V. H. (1989). Painting over old works: The culture of organisations in an age of technical rationality. In Turner, B. A. (Ed.), *Organisational Symbolism.* Berlin: Walther De Gruyter.

Adhikari, S. (2012). *Time for a big data diet.* Retrieved August 12, 2012, from http://technologyspectator.com.au/emerging-tech/big-data/need-big-data-speed?

AIP. (2011). Retrieved July 4, 2013 from http://www.cgu.gov.br/acessoainformacao/acesso-informacao-brasil/index.asp

AIVD. (2013). Retrieved July 4, 2013 from https://www.aivd.nl/english/publications-press/@1587/three-publications/

Alexander, C., & Ayers, A. (2011). *ERP security & continuous controls monitoring (CCM).* RSM Tenon.

Al-Qawabah, M. (2012). *Assessing transformational leadership components as drivers in learning organisations.* (Doctor of Philosophy Dissertation). University of Technology, Sydney, Australia.

AMCAT. (2013). *Remote infrastructure management.* Retrieved from https://www.myamcat.com/aspiration/featured_sector/featured_sector_remote_infrastructure_management.php

Amidon, D. (1997). Dialogue with customers: Secret to innovation strategy. *International Journal of Innovation Management, 1*(1), 73–87. doi:10.1142/S136391969700005X.

Anderson, A., & Lockhart, H. (2004, September). *SAML 2.0 profile of XACML.* OASIS Standard.

Anderson, R. (2001). Why information security is hard? An economic perspective. In *Proceedings of the Computer Security Applications Conference, 2001,* (pp. 358-365). ACSAC.

Anderson, J. M. (2003). Why we need a new definition of information security. *Computers & Security, 22*(4), 308–313. doi:10.1016/S0167-4048(03)00407-3.

Anderson, N. (2012). *Cisco bring your own device - Device freedom without compromising the IT network.* Cisco.

Anderson, R. (2001). *Security engineering: A guide to building dependable distributed systems.* New York: Wiley Publishing.

Andrade, M. C. (1992). *Sobre as proibições de prova em processo penal.* Coimbra, Portugal: Coimbra Editora.

Anttila, J., Kajava, J., & Varonen, R. (2004). Balanced integration of information security into business management. In *Proceedings of the 30th EUROMICRO Conference,* (pp. 558 – 564). EUROMICRO.

APC. (2012). *Association for progressive communication with its APC internet rights charter.* Retrieved October 13, 2012, from http://www.apc.org/en/node/5677/

Argyris, C. (1976). *Increasing leadership effectiveness.* New York: John Wiley and Sons.

Asch, S. E. (1952). *Social psychology.* Englewood Cliffs, NJ: Prentice-Hall. doi:10.1037/10025-000.

Ashraf, A., & Helal, A. (2012). Measuring the latency of semantic message oriented middleware system. *Contemporary Engineering Sciences, 5*(7), 307–313.

Associated Press. (2003). *German parliament sends Google tax to committee.* Retrieved November 30, 2012, from http://www.myfoxdc.com/story/20245195/german-parliament-sends-google-tax-to-committee

Avizienis, A., Laprie, J.-C., Randell, B., & Landwehr, C. E. (2004). Basic concepts and taxonomy of dependable and secure computing. *IEEE Transactions on Dependable and Secure Computing, 1*(1), 11–33. doi:10.1109/TDSC.2004.2.

Aytes, K., & Connolly, T. (2004). Computer security and risky computing practices: A rational choice perspective. *Journal of Organizational and End User Computing, 16*(3), 22–40. doi:10.4018/joeuc.2004070102.

Baker, B. (2001). *Security education for users: A starting place for network administrators.* SANS Institute InfoSec Reading Room.

Balfanz, D., Durfee, G., Shankar, N., Smetters, D., Staddon, J., & Wong, H. C. (2003). Secret handshakes from pairing-based key agreements. In *Proceedings of the IEEE Symposium on Security and Privacy*, (pp. 180-196). IEEE.

Bandeira, G. M. (2011). Abuso de informação, manipulação do mercado e responsabilidade penal das "pessoas colectivas" – "Tipos cumulativos" e bens jurídicos colectivos na "globalização." Lisboa, Portugal: Editorial Juruá. Guinter, J. (2009). Criminal liability of legal persons in Estonia. Juridica International, 16. Retrieved from http://www.juridicainternational.eu/public/pdf/ji_2009_1_151.pdf

Bandeira, G. M. (2004). *Responsabilidade penal económica e fiscal dos entes colectivos, à volta das sociedades comerciais ou sociedades civis sob a forma comercial.* Coimbra, Portugal: Editora Almedina.

Bandeira, G. M. (2011). *Abuso de mercado e responsabilidade penal das pessoas (não) colectivas, "contributo para a compreensão dos bens jurídicos colectivos e dos "tipos cumulativos" na mundialização.* Curitiba, Brazil: Editora Juruá.

Bandmann, O., Dam, M., & Firozabadi, B. S. (2002). Constrained delegation.[IEEE.]. *Proceedings of Security and Privacy, 2002,* 131–140.

Barber, B. (1959). *The logic and limits of trust.* New Brunswick, NJ: Grammercy Press.

Bartoletti, D., & Reichman, A. (2012). *How will you save money in the cloud: Understanding the true cost of cloud computing.* Retrieved from http://www.forrester.com/Will+You+Save+Money+In+The+Cloud+Understanding+The+True+Cost+Of+Cloud+Computing/-/E-WEB11443?objectid=WEB11443&cmpid=mkt:ema:forrWebinaralert

Becker, H. S., & Geer, B. (1970). Participant observation and interviewing: A comparison. In Filstead, W. (Ed.), *Qualitative methodology* (pp. 133–142). Chicago: Rand McNally.

Belenkiy, M., Camenisch, J., Chase, M., Kohlweiss, M., Lysyanskaya, A., & Shacham, H. (2009). Randomizable proofs and delegatable anonymous credentials. In *Proceedings of Advances in Cryptology - CRYPTO 2009 (LNCS)* (Vol. 5677, pp. 108–125). Berlin: Springer. doi:10.1007/978-3-642-03356-8_7.

Bergeron, F., & Begin, C. (1989). The use of critical success factors on evaluation of information systems: A case study. *Journal of MIS, 5*(4), 111–124.

Bertino, E., Squicciarini, A. C., Paloscia, I., & Martino, L. (2006). Ws-ac: A fine grained access control system for web services. *World Wide Web (Bussum), 9*(2), 143–171. doi:10.1007/s11280-005-3045-4.

Bhargavan, K., Corin, R., Fournet, C., & Gordon, A. D. (2007). Secure sessions for web services. *ACM Transactions on Information and System Security, 10*(2), 8. doi:10.1145/1237500.1237504.

Bhatti, R., Joshi, J. B., Bertino, E., & Ghafoor, A. (2003). Access control in dynamic XML-based web-services with x-rbac. In *Proceedings of the International Conference on Web Services,* (Vol. 3, pp. 23-26). ICWS.

Biggs, P. (2009). *Voice over the internet protocol: Enemy or ally?* GSR Discussion Paper. Retrieved October 17, 2012, from http://www.itu.int/ITU-D/treg/Events/Seminars/GSR/GSR09/doc/GSR09_VoIP-Trends_Biggs.pdf

Bingham, T. (2005). The Alabama claims arbitration. *The International and Comparative Law Quarterly, 54*, 1–25. doi:10.1093/iclq/54.1.1.

Birnie, P. W., Boyle, A. E., & Redgwell, C. (2009). *International law & the environment*. Oxford, UK: Oxford University Press.

Blakley, B., McDermott, E., & Geer, D. (2001). Information security is information risk management. In *Proceedings of the 2001 Workshop on New Security Paradigms NSPW '01*, (pp. 97 – 104). ACM. doi:10.1145/508171.508187

Bontis, N., Dragonetti, N., Jacobsen, J., & Roos, G. (2003). The knowledge toolbox: A review of the tools available to measure and manage intangible resources. *European Management Journal, 17*(4), 1–23.

Bookman, S. (2011). Going mobile: hosted VoIP extends PBX mobile functionality to the SMB. *Fierce Enterprise Communications*. Retrieved January 17, from http://www.fierceenterprisecommunications.com/special-reports/going-mobile-hosted-voip-extends-pbx-mobile-functionality-smb

Boyce, J., & Jennings, D. (2002). *Information assurance: Managing organizational IT security risks*. London: Butterworth-Heinemann.

Boyle, A. E. (1990). State responsibility and international liability for injurious consequences of acts not prohibited by international law: A necessary distinction? *The International and Comparative Law Quarterly, 39*(1), 21–24. doi:10.1093/iclqaj/39.1.1.

Boynton, A. C., & Zmud, R. W. (1984). An assessment of critical success factors. *Sloan Management Review, 25*(4), 17–27.

Bradshaw, R. W., Holt, J. E., & Seamons, K. E. (2004). Concealing complex policies with hidden credentials. In *Proceedings of the 11th ACM Conference on Computer and Communications Security (CCS'04)*, (pp. 146-157). ACM.

Brands, S. A. (2000). *Rethinking public key infrastructures and digital certificates: Building in privacy*. Cambridge, MA: MIT Press.

Braun, D. A., & Castle, C. L. (2004). The phonograph record industry. In *Entertainment Law* (3rd ed., pp. 3–75). New York: New York State Bar Association.

Brill, K. (2007). The invisible crisis in the data center: The economic meltdown of Moore's law. *Uptime Institute White Paper, 7*, 1-8.

Brownlie, I. (2008). *Principles of public international law*. Oxford, UK: Oxford University Press.

Bryman, A. (1988). *Quantity and quality in social research*. London: Unwin Hyman. doi:10.4324/9780203410028.

Burgess, M., & Koymans, K. (2007). Master education programmes in network and system administration. In *Proceedings of the 21st conference on Large Installation System Administration Conference* (pp. 215-229). Dallas, TX: USENIX Association.

Business Software Alliance. (2012, April 17). *BSA's guide to software piracy and the law*. Retrieved March 21, 2013, from http://sc-cms.bsa.org/~/media/10A2E6D161594C499AC16F68C7E57A65.ashx

Bussard, L., Nano, A., & Pinsdorf, U. (2009). Delegation of access rights in multi-domain service compositions. *Identity in the Information Society, 2*(2), 137–154. doi:10.1007/s12394-009-0031-5.

Cantor, S. (2005). *Shibboleth architecture: Protocols and profiles*. Retrieved from http://shibboleth.Internet2.edu/shibboleth-documents.html

Castelfranchi, C., Falcone, R., & Pezzullo, G. (2003). Belief sources for trust: some learning mechanisms. In *Proceedings of the 6th Workshop on Trust, Privacy, Deception and Fraud in Agent Societies*. IEEE.

Castellanos, M., Simitsis, A., Wilkinson, K., & Dayal, U. (2009). Automating the loading of business process warehouses. In *Proceedings of International Conference on Extending Database Technology (EDBT)*, (pp. 612-623). Saint-Petersburg, Russia: EDBT.

CEBR. (2012). Data equity: Unlocking the value of big data. *Centre for Economics and Business Research White Paper, 4*, 7-26.

Chadwick, D. W., & Otenko, A. (2003). The PERMIS X. 509 role based privilege management infrastructure. *Future Generation Computer Systems, 19*(2), 277–289. doi:10.1016/S0167-739X(02)00153-X.

Chadwick, D., Zhao, G., Otenko, S., Laborde, R., Su, L., & Nguyen, T. A. (2008). PERMIS: A modular authorization infrastructure. *Concurrency and Computation, 20*(11), 1341–1357. doi:10.1002/cpe.1313.

Chahino, M., & Marchant, J. (2010). *CIS conference presentation.* Paper presented at the CIS Conference. Washington, DC.

Chalupa, S. R. (2007). Systems administration as a self-organizing system: The profissionalization of the SA via Interest and advocacy groups. In Bergstra, J., & Burgess, M. (Eds.), *Handbook of network and system administration* (pp. 961–968). London: Elsevier Science.

Cherdantseva, Y., & Hilton, J. (2012). *The evolution of information security goals.* Retrieved from http://users.cs.cf.ac.uk/Y.V.Cherdantseva/publications.html

Cherdantseva, Y., Rana, O., & Hilton, J. (2011). Security architecture in a collaborative de-perimeterised environment: Factors of success. In *Proceedings of the ISSE Securing Electronic Business Processes*, (pp. 201-213). ISSE.

Cherdantseva, Y., & Hilton, J. (2013). Information security and information assurance: The discussion about the meaning, scope and goals. In Almeida, F., & Portela, I. (Eds.), *Organizational, Legal, and Technological Dimensions of Information System Administrator.* Hershey, PA: IGI Global Publishing.

Cherdantseva, Y., & Hilton, J. (2013). The survey of information security and information assurance professionals 2011. In Almeida, F., & Portela, I. (Eds.), *Organizational, Legal, and Technological Dimensions of Information System Administrator.* Hershey, PA: IGI Global.

chillingeffects.org. (2012, September). *German police ask Twitter to close account -- Chilling effects clearinghouse.* Retrieved November 30, 2012, from https://www.chillingeffects.org/notice.cgi?sID=625342

CIO. (2009). Retrieved July 4, 2013 from http://www.cio.com.au/article/296892/nick_carr_ways_cloud_computing_will_disrupt_it/

Cisco. (n.d.). *Network management system: Best practices white paper.* Retrieved October 24, 2012, from http://www.cisco.com/en/US/tech/tk869/tk769/technologies_white_paper09186a00800aea9c.shtml

Clark, D., & Wilson, D. (1987). A comparison of commercial and military computer security policies. In *Proceedings of the IEEE Symposium on Security and Privacy*, (pp. 184-195). IEEE.

Clark, J., & Soliman, F. (1997). Application of scoring method for measuring the value of knowledge based systems to key employees. *Journal of Systems and Information Technology, 2*, 23–40.

Clifford, M. (Ed.). (1998). *Environmental crime: Enforcement, policy and social responsibility.* Gaithersburg, MD: Aspen.

CloudGov. (2012). Retrieved from http://www.siia.net

CNET. (2009). Retrieved July 4, 2013 from http://news.cnet.com/8301-13772_3-10353479-52.html

CNPD. (2013). *National commission of data protection.* Retrieved from http://www.cnpd.pt/english/index_en.htm

COE. (2010). *International and multi-stakeholder co-operation on cross-border internet.* Retrieved from http://www.coe.int/t/dghl/standardsetting/media/mc-s-ci/Interim%20Report.pdf

COE. (2012). On the definition of CIRs see generally: CoE internet governance and critical internet resources. *Council of Europe.* Retrieved October 13, 2012, from http://www.umic.pt/images/stories/publicacoes5/Internet%20governance_en.pdf

Collins English Dictionary Online. (2012). Retrieved from http://www.collinsdictionary.com

Collins, G. (2012, June 13). *Five steps to simplify software asset management | Guest opinions.* Retrieved November 30, 2012, from http://www.itbusinessedge.com/cm/community/features/guestopinions/blog/five-steps-to-simplify-software-asset-management/?cs=50612

Combacau, J., & Alland, D. (1988). Primary and secondary rules in the law of state responsibility: Categorizing international obligations. *Netherlands Yearbook of International Law, 81*, 95–107.

Combacau, J., & Alland, D. (1995). Primary and secondary rules in the law of state responsibility: categorizing international obligations. *Netherlands Yearbook of International Law, 16*(81), 88–107.

Computerwold. (2009). Retrieved July 4, 2013 from http://www.computerworld.com/s/article/9131998/Cloud_computing_a_security_nightmare_says_Cisco_CEO

CORDIS. (2013). Retrieved July 6, 2013 from http://cordis.europa.eu/fp7/ict/pcp/home_en.html

CORDIS: FP6. (n.d.). Retrieved 10 22, 2012, from http://cordis.europa.eu/fp6/fp6keywords.htm

COURT. (2011). Retrieved July 6, 2013 from http://www.courtofaudit.nl/english/Publications/Audits/Introductions/2011/03/Open_standards_and_open_source_software_in_central_government

Cox, S., & Cox, T. (1996). *Safety systems and people*. Oxford, UK: Buttherworth Heinemann.

CRISTAL. (1970/71). Contract regarding an interim supplement to tanker liability for oil pollution (CRISTAL) 1971. *Journal of Maritime Law & Commerce, 2*, 705.

Croteau, A.-M., & Li, P. (2003). Critical success factors for CRM technological initiatives. *Canadian Journal of Administrative Sciences, 20*(1), 21–34. doi:10.1111/j.1936-4490.2003.tb00303.x.

CRP. (2013). *Constituição da República Portuguesa*. Retrieved from http://dre.pt/comum/html/legis/crp.html

CSIA. (2007). *A national information assurance strategy*. New York: Crown.

Custy, J. (n.d.). *Practical IT service management: Rapid ITIL without compromise*.

Cuzzocrea, A., & Mansmann, S. (2009). OLAP visualization: Models, issues and techniques. In Wang, J. (Ed.), *Encyclopedia of Data Warehousing and Mining* (pp. 1439–1446). Academic Press.

da Silva, G. M. (2009). *Curso de processo penal*. Lisboa, Portugal: Editora Verbo.

Damanpour, F. (1991). Organizational innovation: A meta-analysis of effects of determinants and moderators. *Academy of Management Journal, 34*(3), 555–590. doi:10.2307/256406.

Daniel, D. R. (1961). Management information crises. *Harvard Business Review, 39*(5), 111.

Dark, M., Ekstrom, J., & Lunt, B. (2005). Integration of information assurance and security into the IT2005 model curriculum. In *Proceedings of the 6th Conference on Information Technology Education*. ACM.

Das, S. R., & Joshi, M. P. (2007). Process innovativeness in technology services organizations: Roles of differentiation strategy, operational autonomy, and risk-taking propensity. *Journal of Operations Management, 25*(3), 643–660. doi:10.1016/j.jom.2006.05.011.

Davenport, T. H. (1999). *Think tank: Making the most of an information-rich environment: The future of knowledge management*. Retrieved from http://www.it-consultancy.com/extern/articles/futurekm.html

Davenport, T., & Prusak, L. (2000). *Working knowledge: How organizations manage what they know* (p. 240). Cambridge, MA: Harvard Business School Press. doi:10.1145/347634.348775.

DBR. (2009). Retrieved July 6, 2013 from http://www.official-documents.gov.uk/document/cm76/7650/7650.pdf

De Albuquerque, P. P. (2010). *Comentário do código penal à luz da constituição da república e da convenção europeia dos direitos do homem*. Lisboa, Portugal: Universidade Católica Editora.

De Pous, V. (2011). *Open source computing and public sector policy*. Retrieved July 6, 2013 from http://www.depous.nl/DEPOUS-OPEN-SOURCE-COMPUTING-AND-PUBLIC-SECTOR-POLICY.pdf

De Pous, V. (2012). *Cloud computing en het nieuwe Amerikaanse overheidsbeleid (executive update)*. Retrieved July 4, 2013 from http://www.forumstandaardisatie.nl/english/

Department for Transport. (2004). *Safety culture and work-related road accidents*. Road safety Research Report No. 51. Washington, DC: Department of Transport.

Deutsch, M. (1962). Cooperation and trust: Some theoretical notes. In *Nebraska Symposium on Motivation*. Nebraska University Press.

Dias, R. (n.d.). Aplicações do ITIL. *TechNet Blogs*. Retrieved November 23, 2012, from http://blogs.technet.com/b/rodias/archive/2007/03/05/aplica-ccedil-otilde-es-do-itil.aspx

Dias, J. F. (1974). *Direito processual penal.* Coimbra, Portugal: Coimbra Editora.

Dias, J. F. (2007). *Direito penal, parte geral, tomo I: Questões fundamentais, a doutrina geral do crime.* Coimbra, Portugal: Coimbra Editora.

Dias, J. F., & Andrade, M. C. (1984). *Criminologia: O homem delinquente e a sociedade criminógena.* Coimbra, Portugal: Coimbra Editora.

DL. (2008). *Decree law 143-A / 2008, of July 25.* Retrieved from http://www.wipo.int/wipolex/en/details.jsp?id=5461

DL. (2012). *Decree-law No. 197/2012 of August 24.* Retrieved from http://dre.pt/pdf1sdip/2012/08/16400/0465604666.pdf

Dlamini, M. T., Eloff, J. H. P., & Eloff, M. M. (2009). Information security: The moving target. *Computers & Security, 28*(3-4), 189–198. doi:10.1016/j.cose.2008.11.007.

Domino. (2012). Retrieved July 4, 2013, from http://www.itworld.com/cloud-computing/251214/dominos-pizza-finishes-last-piece-cloud-computing-move

Dowling, D. C. Jr. (2012). English is not your exclusive company license. *NYSBA Journal, 84*(9), 46–51.

Drucker, P. F. (1992). *Managing for the future: The 1990s and beyond.* New York: Truman Talley Books.

DT Knowledge. (2012). Retrieved July 4, 2013, from http://www.datacenterknowledge.com/archives/2012/01/04/feds-now-plan-to-close-1200-data-centers/

Dubois, E., Heymans, P., Mayer, N., & Matulevicius, R. (2010). A systematic approach to define the domain of information system security risk management. In *Intentional Perspectives on Information Systems Engineering* (pp. 289–306). London: Springer. doi:10.1007/978-3-642-12544-7_16.

EC. (1995). *Directive 95/46/EC of the European parliament and of the council of 24 October 1995 on the protection of individuals with regard to the processing of personal data and on the free movement of such data.* Retrieved from http://ec.europa.eu/justice/policies/privacy/docs/95-46-ce/dir1995-46_part1_en.pdf

EC. (1999). *Decision 1999/1720/EC of the European parliament and of the council of 12 July 1999 to adopt a series of actions and measures in order to ensure interoperability of, and access to, trans-European networks for the electronic interchange of data between administrations (IDA).* Retrieved from http://www.etsi.org/about/our-role-in-europe/public-policy/ec-decisions

EC. (2004). *Decision 2004/387/EC "decision of the European parliament and of the council on interoperable delivery of pan-European services to public administrations, businesses and citizens (IDABC).* Retrieved from http://www.etsi.org/about/our-role-in-europe/public-policy/ec-decisions

EC. (2006). *The council directive 2006/112/EC of 28 November 2006 on the common system of value added tax.* Retrieved from http://eur-lex.europa.eu/LexUriServ/LexUriServ.do?uri=OJ:L:2006:347:0001:0118:en:PDF

EC. (2008). *Status report from the expert group on e-invoicing.* Retrieved from http://ec.europa.eu/enterprise/sectors/ict/documents/e-invoicing/index_en.htm

EC. (2010). The council of the European Union, council directive 2010/45/EU of 13 July 2010 amending directive 2006/112/EC on the common system of value added tax as regards the rules on invoicing. Official Journal of the European Union, 189(1).

Edlund, S., & Lövquist, A. (2012). *The role of system administrators in information systems success.* (MSc Thesis). Uppsala University, Uppsala, Sweden.

Ehlert, S., Geneiatakis, D., & Magedanz, T. (2010). Survey of network security systems to counter SIP-based denial-of-service attacks. *Computers & Security, 29*(1), 225–243. doi:10.1016/j.cose.2009.09.004.

EIF. (2004). *European interoperability framework for pan-European e-government service.* Retrieved from http://ec.europa.eu/idabc/en/document/3761/5845.html

Electronic Privacy Information Center. (2012). *Children't online privacy proteciton act.* Retrieved November 30, 2012, from http://epic.org/privacy/kids/

Ellison, C., Frantz, B., Lampson, B., Rivest, R., Thomas, B., & Ylonen, T. (1999). *SPKI certificate theory.* IETF RFC 2693.

ENISA. (2011). Retrieved July 4, 2013, from http://www.enisa.europa.eu/activities/risk-management/emerging-and-future-risk/deliverables/security-and-resilience-in-governmental-clouds

Erica, D. (2013). *Mobile VoIP users will reach 1 billion by 2017?!* Retrieved January 19, from http://blog.voxox.com/the-future-of-voxox-and-the-global-voip-revolution/8623

EU Justice. (2012). Retrieved July 4, 2013, from http://ec.europa.eu/justice/newsroom/data-protection/news/120125_en.htm

EU. (2012). *European commission, justice*. Retrieved October 30, 2012, from http://ec.europa.eu/justice/newsroom/data-protection/news/120125_en.htm

EURLex. (1995). Retrieved October 30, 2012, from http://eur-lex.europa.eu/LexUriServ/LexUriServ.do?uri=CELEX:31995L0046:en:HTML

EURLex. (2000). Retrieved October 30, 2012, from http://eur-lex.europa.eu/LexUriServ/LexUriServ.do?uri=CELEX:32000L0031:En:HTML

EURLex. (2003). Retrieved October 30, 2012, from http://eur-lex.europa.eu/LexUriServ/LexUriServ.do?uri=CELEX:32003L0098:EN:NOT

EURLex. (2009). Retrieved October 30, 2012, from http://eur-lex.europa.eu/LexUriServ/LexUriServ.do?uri=OJ:L:2009:111:0016:01:EN:HTML

European Parliament and Counsel of the European Union. (1995, October 24). *Directive 95/46/EC*. Retrieved November 30, 2012, from http://eur-lex.europa.eu/LexUriServ/LexUriServ.do?uri=CELEX:31995L0046:en:NOT

Evans, M. (2010, March 8). Cyberwar declared as China hunts for the west's intelligence secrets. *The Times*. Retrieved October 13, 2012, from http://technology.timesonline.co.uk/tol/news/tech_and_Web/article7053254.ece

Evans, R., & Lindsay, W. M. (2011). *The management and control of quality* (8th ed.). Cincinnati, OH: Thomson, South-Western.

Fagernes, S., & Ribu, K. (2007). Ethical, legal and social aspects of the systems. In Bergstra, J., & Burgess, M. (Eds.), *Handbook of network and system administration* (pp. 969–999). London: Elsevier Science.

Falcone, R., & Castelfranchi, C. (2001). Social trust: A cognitive approach. In *Trust and deception in virtual societies* (pp. 55–90). Dordrecht, The Netherlands: Kluwer Academic Publishers. doi:10.1007/978-94-017-3614-5_3.

Federal Trade Commission. (2009, October 5). *FTC publishes final guides governing endorsements, testimonials*. Retrieved November 30, 2012, from http://www.ftc.gov/opa/2009/10/endortest.shtm

FedRAMP. (2013). Retrieved July 4, 2013, from http://www.gsa.gov/portal/category/102371

Feng, X., Guoyan, L., Hao, H., & Li, X. (2004). Role-based access control system for web services.[IEEE.]. *Proceedings of Computer and Information Technology, 2004*, 357–362.

Ferraiolo, D., Kuhn, D. R., & Chandramouli, R. (2007). *Role-based access control*. Artech House.

Ferrarini, E. (2002). *Want to control network storage space? Put a policy in place and SRM it*. Retrieved 10 April 2002 from http://www.101com.com/solutions/storage

Flanagan, J. C. (1954). The critical incident technique. *Psychological Bulletin*, *51*(4), 327–359. doi:10.1037/h0061470 PMID:13177800.

FOIA. (1967). Retrieved July 4, 2013, from http://en.wikipedia.org/wiki/Freedom_of_Information_Act_(United_States)

Frank, S. (2011). IT organization assessment—Using COBIT and BSC. *Cobit Focus, 1*.

FRC. (2004). *The Turnbull guidance as an evaluation framework for the purposes of Section 404(a) of the Sarbanes-Oxley Act*. Retrieved from http://www.frc.org.uk/documents/pagemanager/frc/draftguide.pdf

Freudenthal, E., Pesin, T., Port, L., Keenan, E., & Karamcheti, V. (2002). dRBAC: Distributed role-based access control for dynamic coalition environments.[IEEE.]. *Proceedings of Distributed Computing Systems, 2002*, 411–420.

Frisch, A. (2002). *Essential system administration: Tools and techniques for linux and unix administration* (3rd ed.). Sebastopol, CA: O'Reilly Media, Incorporated.

Gambetta, D. (2000). Can we trust trust? In *Trust: Making and breaking cooperative relations*. Academic Press.

Gansle, G., & Garber, J. R. (2012, July 26). Non-compete provisions in California: Unenforceable and affirmative liability for unfair business practices I News & events. *Dorsey & Whitney*. Retrieved November 30, 2012, from http://www.dorsey.com/eU_LE_noncompete_california_072612/

Gartner, Inc. (2012). *Forecast overview: Security infrastructure, worldwide, 2010-2016, 2q12 update*. Washington, DC: Gartner, Inc..

Garvin, D. A. (1993). Building a learning organization. *Harvard Business Review*, *71*, 78. PMID:10127041.

Gehring & Jachtenfuchs. (1960). Convention on third party liability in the field of nuclear energy. *European Yearbook*, *6*, 268.

Gehring & Jachtenfuchs. (1977). Convention on civil liability for oil pollution damage resulting from exploration for and exploitation of seabed mineral resources. *ILM*, *16*, 1451.

Gehring, T., & Jachtenfuchs, M. (1993). Liability for transboundary environmental damage towards a general liability regime. *European Journal of International Law*, *4*, 92–106.

Godt, C. (1997). *Haftung für ökologische schäden: Verantwortung für beeinträchtigungen des allgemeingutes umwelt durch individualisierbare verletzungshandlungen*. Berlin: Duncker & Humblot.

Goel, S., Kiran, R., & Garg, D. (2012). Vulnerability management for an enterprise resource planning system. *International Journal of Computers and Applications*, 19–22.

Goldsmith, N. (1991). Linking IT planning to business strategy. *Long Range Planning*, *24*(6), 67–77. doi:10.1016/0024-6301(91)90045-P.

Golfarelli, M., & Rizzi, S. (2009). *Data warehouse design: Modern principles and methodologies*. Columbus, OH: McGraw-Hill.

Gomi, H., Hatakeyama, M., Hosono, S., & Fujita, S. (2005, November). A delegation framework for federated identity management. In *Proceedings of the 2005 Workshop on Digital Identity Management* (pp. 94-103). ACM.

Google-hosted blog content to be censored on country-by-country basis. (2012, February 6). Retrieved March 21, 2013, from http://www.out-law.com/en/articles/2012/february/google-hosted-blog-content-to-be-censored-on-country-by-country-basis/

Gordon Training International. (n.d.). Retrieved from http://www.gordontraining.com/free-workplace-articles/learning-a-new-skill-is-easier-said-than-done/

Gordon, A. (2005). *Privacy and ubiquitous network societies*. Paper presented at the Workshop on ITU Ubiquitous Network Societies. Geneva, Switzerland.

Gordon, L., & Loeb, M. (2002). The economics of information security investment. *ACM Transactions on Information and System Security*, *5*(4), 438–457. doi:10.1145/581271.581274.

GSA. (2012). *What are the services?* Retrieved October 18, 2012, from http://info.apps.gov/content/what-are-services

GSA. (2013). Retrieved October 30, 2012, from http://www.gsa.gov/portal/category/102371

Guerra, C. (2013). *A spokesman for the national commission on data protection, Clara Guerra, confirms the Antena 1 that several complaints have been received and that the commission is already on the ground to investigate*. Portugal: Antena 1.

Haber, E. M., Kandogan, E., & Maglio, P. P. (2011). Collaboration in system administration. *Communications of the ACM*, *1*(54), 46–53. doi:10.1145/1866739.1866755.

Haefliger, S., Von Krogh, G., & Spaeth, S. (2008). Code reuse in open source software. *Management Science*, *54*(1), 180–193. doi:10.1287/mnsc.1070.0748.

Hair, J. F., Anderson, R. E., Tatham, R. L., & Black, W. C. (1998). *Multivariate analysis* (5th ed.). Englewood Cliffs, NJ: Prentice-Hall International.

Hallam-Baker, P., & Maler, E. (2002). *Assertions and protocol for the oasis security assertion markup language (saml)*. OASIS Committee Specification.

Hamel, G., & Prahalad, C. K. (1985). Do you really have a global strategy? *Harvard Business Review, 63*(4), 139–148.

Handl, G. (1980). State liability for accidental transnational environmental damage by private persons. *The American Journal of International Law, 74*, 525–535. doi:10.2307/2201649.

Health and Safety Executive Core Topics. (n.d.). *Core topic 2: HF in accident investigations*. Retrieved from http://www.hse.gov.uk/humanfactors/topics/core2.pdf

Hertenberger, M. (2005). *Issues in information systems issues in information systems*. Johannesburg, South Africa: University of Johannesburg.

Hislop, D. (2003). The complex relations between communities of practice and the implementation of technological innovations. *International Journal of Innovation Management, 7*(2), 163–188. doi:10.1142/S1363919603000775.

HMG. (2010). *HMG information assurance maturity model and assessment framework*. New York: Crown.

HMG. (2011). *HMG security policy framework*. Boston: Crown Copyright.

Hondo, M., Maruyama, H., Nadalin, A., & Nagaratnam, N. (2006). *Web services federation language*. WS-Federation.

Howe, A., Ray, I., Roberts, M., Urbanska, M., & Byrne, Z. (2012). The psychology of security for the home computer user. In *Proceedings of IEEE Symposium on Security and Privacy*. IEEE.

HP. (2013). *Unleash the full potential of BYOD with confidence*. HP.

Hung, P., & Martin, M. (2006). Security issues in VoIP applications. In *Proceedings of Canadian Conference on Electrical and Computer Engineering*, (pp. 65-71). Ottawa, Canada: IEEE.

Hunt, D. P. (2003). Hunt the concept of knowledge and how to measure it. *Journal of Intellectual Capital, 4*(1), 100–113. doi:10.1108/14691930310455414.

Hunter, R., & Westerman, G. (2009). *The real business of IT: How CIOs create and communicate value*. Boston: Harvard Business School Press.

IDC. (2009). As the economy contracts, the digital universe expands. *IDC White Paper, 5*, 12-18.

IEEE. (n.d.). Retrieved 10 29, 2012, from http://www.ieee.org

ILC. (2001) II (2) *yearbook of the international law commission* 31 ff. Draft Articles on State Responsibility: Titles and texts of articles adopted by the Drafting Committee, International Law Commission, UN Doc. A/CN.4/L.472, hereinafter cited as *2001 ILC Draft Articles*.

ILM. (1984). Draft convention on liability and compensation in connexion with the carriage of noxious and hazardous substances by sea. *ILM, 23*, 150.

Imoniana, J. (2006). Workability of a management control model in service organizations: A comparative study on reactive, proactive and coactive philosophies. *Journal of Information Systems and Technology Management, 3*(1), 35–52. doi:10.4301/S1807-17752006000100003.

Information Assurance Advisory Council (IAAC) & Microsoft. (2002). Benchmarking information assurance. Washington, DC: Information Assurance Advisory Council (IAAC) & Microsoft.

Information Assurance Collaboration Group (IACG). (2007). *Industry response to the HMG information assurance strategy and delivery plan*. IACG Working Group On The Role Of Industry In Delivering The National IA Strategy (IWI009).

Internal Revenue Service. (2010, January 13). *Independent contractor (self-employed) or employee?* Retrieved March 21, 2013, from http://www.irs.gov/Businesses/Small-Businesses-&-Self-Employed/Independent-Contractor-(Self-Employed)-or-Employee%3F

IRP. (2012). *Internet rights and principles coalition with its charter of human rights and principles for the internet*. Retrieved October 13, 2012, from http://Internetrightsand-principles.org/node/367

ISA. (2010). Retrieved July 4, 2013, from http://ec.europa.eu/isa/documents/isa_annex_ii_eif_en.pdf

ISACA. (2008). *Glossary of terms, 2008*. Retrieved from http://www.isaca.org/Knowledge-Center/Documents/Glossary/glossary.pdf

ISACA. (2009). *An introduction to the business model for information security*. ISACA. (ISC)². (2011). *The 2011 (ISC)² global information security workforce study*. (ISC)².

ISACA. (2012). *Calculating cloud ROI: From the customer perspective*. Cloud Computing Vision Series, White Paper. ISACA.

ISACA. (2012). *Guiding principles for cloud computing adoption and use*. Cloud Computing Vision Series, White Paper. ISACA.

ISACA. (2012). *COBIT 5: Enabling processes*. ISACA.

ISACA. (2012). *COBIT 5: A business framework for the governance and management of enterprise IT*. ISACA.

ISC. (2011). *International strategy for cyberspace*. The White House. Retrieved October 17, from http://www.whitehouse.gov/sites/default/files/rss_viewer/international_strategy_for_cyberspace.pdf

ISO/IEC 13335-1:2004. (2004). *Information technology - Security techniques - Management of information and communications technology security: Concepts and models for information and communications technology security management*. ISO/IEC.

ISO/IEC 15408-1:2009. (2009). *Information technology- Security techniques: Evaluation criteria for IT security: Introduction and general model*. ISO/IEC.

ISO/IEC 27000:2009 (E). (2009). *Information technology - Security techniques - Information security management systems - Overview and vocabulary*. ISO/IEC.

ISO/IEC. (2005). *ISO/IEC 27000, information technology -- Security techniques -- Information security management systems -- Overview and vocabulary*. Retrieved October 30, 2012, from http://www.iso.org/iso/catalogue_detail?csnumber=56891 ISO/IEC. (2008). *ISO/IEC 38500: IT governance standard*. Retrieved October 30, 2012, from http://www.38500.org

IT Governance Institute (ITGI). (2007). *COBIT 4.1: Excerpt*. ITGI.

IT Knowledge Exchange. (2011). Retrieved October 30, 2012, from http://itknowledgeexchange.techtarget.com/cloud-computing/ex-fed-cio-vivek-kundra%E2%80%99s-cloud-first-policy-trashed/

ITS. (2012). *IT systems administrator," " systems administrator," or "sysadmin"*. Retrieved from http://www.standalone-sysadmin.com/blog/2012/01/it_system_admin.htm

IVIR. (2013). Retrieved October 30, 2012, from http://www.ivir.nl/legislation/nl/copyrightact.html

Jaffe, A. B., & Lerner, J. (2006). *Innovation and its discontents: How our broken patent system is endangering innovation and progress, and what to do about it*. Princeton, NJ: Princeton University Press.

Jahanirad, M., Al-Nabhani, Y., & Noor, R. (2011). Security measures for VoIP application: A state of the art review. *Scientific Research and Essays*, 6(23), 4950–4959.

Jamoo, G. (2008). *Operational implementation of storage area networks as strategic knowledge management tools*. (PhD Dissertation). University of Technology, Sydney, Australia.

Jericho Forum (JF). (2007). *Jericho forum commandments*. Retrieved from https://collaboration.opengroup.org/jericho/commandments v1.2.pdf

Jericho Forum. (2007). *Jericho forum commandments*. Retrieved April 5, 2012, from https://collaboration.opengroup.org/jericho/commandments_v1.2.pdf

Jerico Forum (JF). (2011). *The what and why of deperimeterization*. Retrieved from http://www.opengroup.org/jericho/deperim.htm

Jih, W.-J. K., & Owings, P. (1995). From in search of excellence to business process re-engineering: The role of information technology. *Information Strategy*, 11, 6–19.

Joint Pub 3-13. (1998). *Joint doctrine for information operations*. USA.

Jorg, T., & Dessloch, S. (2010). Near real-time data warehousing using state-of-the-art ETL tools. In Castellanos, M. et al. (Eds.), *Enabling Real-time for Business Intelligence* (pp. 100–117). Heidelberg, Germany: Springer-Verlag. doi:10.1007/978-3-642-14559-9_7.

Juiz, C., Gómez, M., & Barceló, M. I. (2012). Business/IT projects alignment through the project portfolio approval process as IT governance instrument. In *Proceedings of ICIBSoS 2012*, (vol. 65, pp. 70-75). Amsterdam: Springer.

Juiz, C. (2011). New engagement model of IT governance and IT management for the communication of the IT value at enterprises.[). Berlin: Springer.]. *Proceedings of Digital Enterprise and Information Systems*, *194*, 129–194. doi:10.1007/978-3-642-22603-8_13.

Junipter. (2006). Enterprise VoIP security best practices. *Junipter Networks*. Retrieved March 18, from http://netscreen.com/solutions/literature/white_papers/

Kaufman, C. (2008). *The benefits of business VoIP*. Teledata White Papers. Retrieved October 17, 2012, from http://www.teledata.com/PDF_Resources/Resources/Not%20ShoreTel%20-%20Why%20VOIP%20makes%20Business%20Sense.pdf

Kazemi, M., Khajouei, H., & Nasrabadi, H. (2012). Evaluation of information security management system success factors: Case study of Municipal organization. *African Journal of Business Management*, *6*(14), 4982–4989.

Keil, M. (1995). Pulling the plug: Software project management and the problem of project escalation. *Management Information Systems Quarterly*, *19*(4), 421–447. doi:10.2307/249627.

Kelly, J., Vellante, D., & Floyer, D. (2012). *Big data market size and vendor revenues*. Retrieved October 10, 2012, from http://wikibon.org/wiki/v/Big_Data_Market_Size_and_Vendor_Revenues

Kelly, G. (1955). *Principles of personal construct psychology*. New York: Norton.

Kerravala, Z. (2010). Demystifying VoIP for business. *Yankee Group Research*. Retrieved January 19, from http://www.windstreambusiness.com/media/1015/voip_Webinar.pdf

Keulen, B. F., & Gritter, E. (2010). Corporate criminal liability in The Netherlands. Electronic Journal of Comparative Law, 14(3). Retrieved from http://www.ejcl.org/143/art143-9.doc

Khare, R., & Rifkin, A. (1997). Weaving a web of trust. *World Wide Web Journal*, *2*(3), 77–112.

Khripunov, I., Nikonov, D., & Katsva, M. (2004). *Nuclear security culture: the case of Russia*. The University of Georgia. Retrieved from http://www.uga.edu/cits/documents/pdf/Security%20Culture%20Report%2020041118.pdf

Kichel, M. (n.d.). *Administração de sistemas de informação I*. Retrieved November 11, 2012, from http://d.yimg.com/kq/groups/22104202/1070702132/name/SI01+-+Conceitos+Basicos.PDF

King, G., & Powell, E. (2008). *How not to lie without statistics*. Boston: Harvard University. Retrieved August 12, 2012, from http://gking.harvard.edu/gking/files/nolie.pdf

Kora, A., & Soidridine, M. (2012). Nagios based enhanced IT management system. *International Journal of Engineering Science and Technology*, *4*(3), 1199–1207.

Kotter, J. P., & Heskett, J. L. (1992). *Corporate culture and performance*. New York: Free Press.

Kroeber, A. I., & Kluckhohn, C. (1952). *Culture: A critical review of concepts*. Academic Press.

Kroes. (2011). Retrieved October 30, 2012, from http://europa.eu/rapid/pressReleasesAction.do?reference=SPEECH/11/50&format=HTML&aged=0&language=EN&guiLanguage=en

Kroes. (2012). Retrieved October 30, 2012, from http://europa.eu/rapid/pressReleasesAction.do?reference=SPEECH/12/490&format=HTML&aged=0&language=EN&guiLanguage=en

Kuhn, M. H., & McPartland, T. S. (1954). An empirical investigation of self attitudes. *American Sociological Review*, *19*, 68–76. doi:10.2307/2088175.

Kulesza, J. (2012). *International internet law*. London: Routledge.

Kumar, A. (2010). *Network security administrator responsibilities*. Retrieved from http://www.brighthub.com/computing/smb-security/articles/71358.aspx?cid=parsely_rec

Kumar, A. (2011). Security and risk challenges of VoIP over IP telephony. *International Journal of Electronics*, *3*(1), 85–87.

Labio, W., & Garcia-Molina, H. (1996). Efficient snapshot differential algorithms for data warehousing. In *Proceedings of the 22nd International Conference on Very Large Data Bases*, (pp. 63-74). Bombay, India: IEEE.

Lacey, D. (2009). *Managing the human factor in information security*. New York: J. Wiley and Sons Ltd..

Lane, A. (2012, April 30). *Understanding and selecting SIEM/LM: Use cases*. Retrieved 11 01, 2012, from http://securosis.com/blog/understanding-and-selecting-siem-lm-use-cases-part-1

Latif, T. (2007). *Adoption of VoIP*. (Master thesis). Department of Business Administration and Social Sciences, Lulea University, Lulea, Sweden.

Lazzarotti, J. (2012, September 30). *California becomes third state to limit access to employees and students' social media accounts: Workplace privacy, data management & security report*. Retrieved November 30, 2012, from http://www.workplaceprivacyreport.com/2012/09/articles/workplace-privacy/california-becomes-third-state-to-limit-access-to-employees-and-students-social-media-accounts/

Lee, A. J., & Winslett, M. (2008). Towards standards-compliant trust negotiation for web services. In *Proceedings of the Joint iTrust and PST Conferences on Privacy, Trust Management, and Security (IFIPTM 2008)*. IFIPTM.

Lehdonvirta, V., & Ernkvist, M. (2011). Converting the virtual economy into development potential: Knowledge map of the virtual economy. *InfoDev/World Bank White Paper, 1*, 5-17.

Leidecker, J. K., & Bruno, A. V. (1984). Identifying and using critical success factors. *Long Range Planning, 17*(1), 23–32. doi:10.1016/0024-6301(84)90163-8.

Lenzerini, M. (2002). Data integration: A theoretical perspective. In *Proceedings of the 21st Symposium on Principles of Database Systems (PODS)*, (pp. 233-246). PODS.

Li, J., & Li, N. (2005). OACerts: Oblivious attribute certificates. In *Proceedings of the 3rd Conference on Applied Cryptography and Network Security (ACNS) (LNCS)*, (vol. 353, pp. 3010-3017). Berlin: Springer.

Li, N. (2000). Local names in SPKI/SDSI. In *Proceedings of Computer Security Foundations Workshop, 2000* (pp. 2-15). IEEE.

Li, N., Du, W., & Boneh, D. (2005). Oblivious signature-based envelope. *Distributed Computing, 17*(4), 293–302. doi:10.1007/s00446-004-0116-1.

Li, N., Grosof, B. N., & Feigenbaum, J. (2000). A practically implementable and tractable delegation logic. [IEEE.]. *Proceedings of Security and Privacy, 2000*, 27–42.

Li, N., Grosof, B. N., & Feigenbaum, J. (2003). Delegation logic: A logic-based approach to distributed authorization. *ACM Transactions on Information and System Security, 6*(1), 128–171. doi:10.1145/605434.605438.

Lock, M. (2012). Data management for BI: Big data, bigger insight, superior performance. *Aberdeen Group White Paper, 1*, 4-20.

LOPSA. (n.d.). Retrieved 11 17, 2012, from https://lopsa.org/

Loudcher, S., & Boussaid, O. (2012). OLAP on complex data: Visualization operator based on correspondence analysis. *IS Olympics: Information Systems in a Diverse World, 107*, 172–185. doi:10.1007/978-3-642-29749-6_12.

LPD. (1991). *Lei no 10/91 da lei da proteção de dados pessoais face à informática*. Retrieved from http://www.cnpdpi.pt/Leis/lei_1091.htm

Luhmann, N. (1979). *Trust and power*. New York: Wiley.

M, E. (2012, October 9). *FTC's greenwashing guidance*. Retrieved November 30, 2012, from http://westreference-attorneys.com/2012/10/ftcs-greenwashing-guidance/

Maconachy, W., Schou, C., Ragsdale, D., & Welch, D. (2001). A model for information assurance: An integrated approach. In *Proceedings of the 2001 IEEE Workshop on Information Assurance and Security*. West Point, NY: IEEE.

Mahmud, H., Didar-Al-Alam, S. M., Morshed, M. S., Haque, M. O., & Hasan, M. K. (2010). Designing access control model and enforcing security policies using permis for a smart item e-health scenario. *International Journal of Engineering Science, 2*(8).

Malanczuk, P. (1997). *Akehurst's modern introduction to international law*. London: Routledge.

Maniatis, A., Vassiliadis, P., Skiadopoulos, S., Vassiliou, Y., Mavrogonatos, G., & Michalarias, I. (2005). A presentation model & non-traditional visualization for OLAP. *International Journal of Data Warehousing and Mining, 1*(1), 1–36. doi:10.4018/jdwm.2005010101.

Manyika, J., Chui, M., Brown, B., Bughin, J., Dobbs, R., Roxburgh, C., & Byers, A. (2011). Big data: The next frontier for innovation, competition, and productivity. *McKinsey Global Institute Reports, 5*, 15–36.

Marcus, J., & Elixmann, D. (2008). The future of IP interconnection. *Wik-Consult*. Retrieved January 23, from http://ec.europa.eu/information_society/policy/ecomm/doc/library/ext_studies/future_ip_intercon/ip_intercon_study_final.pdf

Marnewick, C., & Labuschagne, L. (2006). *A security framework for an ERP system*. Auckland Park, South Africa: University of Johannesburg.

Martin, E. W. (1982). Critical success factors of chief MIS/DP executives. *Management Information Systems Quarterly, 6*(2), 1–19. doi:10.2307/249279.

Martin, J., & Siehi, C. (1983). Organizational culture and counterculture: An uneasy symbiosis. *Organizational Dynamics, 12*(2), 52–64. doi:10.1016/0090-2616(83)90033-5.

Mathiyalakan, S. (2006). VoIP adoption: Issues & concerns. *Communications of the IIMA, 6*(2), 19–24.

Maxwell, W., et al. (2012). *A global reality: Government access to data in the cloud*. A Hogan Lovells White Paper, 23 May 2012. Retrieved October 30, 2012, from http://computer3.org/a/a-global-reality-governmental-access-to-data-in-the-cloud-e157-book.pdf.html

McCarthy, S. (n.d.). *Icelandic modern media initiative*. Retrieved March 21, 2013, from https://immi.is/index.php/projects/immi

McCredie, J., & Updegrove, D. (1999). Enterprise systems implementation: Lessons from the trenches. *Cause/Effect, 22*(4), 1-10.

McCumber, J. (1991). Information systems security: A comprehensive model. In *Proceedings of the 14th National Computer Security Conference*. Baltimore, MD: NIST.

McKnight, W. (2002). What is information assurance? CrossTalk. *The Journal of Defense Software Engineering*, 4-6.

McNutt, D. (1993). Role-based system administration or who, what, where, and how. In *Proceedings of the Seventh System Administration Conference (LISA '93)* (pp. 106-112). Monterey, CA: USENIX.

Mell, P., & Grance, T. (2011). *The NIST definition of cloud computing: Recommendations of the national institute of standards and technology*. Retrieved October 30, 2012, from http://csrc.nist.gov/publications/nistpubs/800-145/SP800-145.pdf

Mellinkoff, D. (1963). *The language of the law*. Boston: Little, Brown.

Mobile Applications. (2013). *Final version definition published*. Retrieved July 4, 2013 from http://en.wikipedia.org/wiki/Mobile_apps

Murrey, P. (2005). Fundamental issues in questionnaire design. *Accident and Emergency Nursing, 7*(3), 148–153. doi:10.1016/S0965-2302(99)80074-5.

Na, S., & Cheon, S. (2000). Role delegation in role-based access control. In *Proceedings of the Fifth ACM Workshop on Role-Based Access Control* (pp. 39-44). ACM.

National Computer Security Center (NCSC). (1991). *Integrity in automated information systems*. C Technical Report 79-91 Library No. S-237, 254 (IDA PAPER P-2316). NCSC.

Nelson, K., & Somers, T. (2001). The impact of critical success factors across the stages of enterprise resource planning implementations. In *Proceedings of the 34th Annual Hawaii International Conference on System Sciences*. IEEE.

Network Administrators Past, Present, and Future. (2011). *Simple talk: SQL server and. net articles, forums and blogs*. Retrieved November 7, 2012, from http://www.simple-talk.com/sysadmin/general/network-administrators-past,-present,-and-future/

Neumann, P. (1995). *Computer-related risks*. New York: ACM Press/Addison Wesley.

Newman, M. E. J. (2004). Who is the best connected scientist? A study of scientific co-authorship networks. In Ben-Naim, E., Frauenfelder, H., & Toroczkai, Z. (Eds.), *Complex networks* (pp. 337–370). Berlin: Springer. doi:10.1007/978-3-540-44485-5_16.

News, B. B. C. (2012, April 3). *Credit card data breach contained, says global payments*. Retrieved from www.bbc.co.uk/news/technology-17596394

Nimmer, R. T. (1985). *The law of computer technology*. Warren Gorham & Lamont.

NIST. (2002). *Risk management guide for information technology systems (Special Publication 800-30)*. NIST.

NIST. (2011). *Final version of NIST cloud computing definition published*. Retrieved July 4, 2013, from http://www.nist.gov/itl/csd/cloud-102511.cfm

NMILCW. (2012). *NATO tallinn manual on the international law applicable to cyber warfare*. Retrieved October 13, from http://www.ccdcoe.org/249.html

Nonaka, I., & Von Krogh, G. (2009). Tacit knowledge and knowledge conversion: Controversy and advancement in organizational knowledge creation theory. *Organization Science, 20*(3), 635–652. doi:10.1287/orsc.1080.0412.

Nonaka, I., Von Krogh, G., & Von Hippel, S. (2006). Organizational knowledge creation theory: Evolutionary paths and future advances. *Organization Studies, 27*(8), 1179–1208. doi:10.1177/0170840606066312.

Nuclear Threat Initiative. (2005). *Global nuclear security culture needed, experts say*. Retrieved from http://www.nti.org/d_newswire/issues/2005/3/21/18cd7338-c686-42c1-aa46-68b39c511622.htm

Nunn, L., McGuire, B., & Crowe, B. (2010). VoIP cost efficiencies and the decision to implement. *Review of Business Information Systems, 14*(1), 1–14.

O'Dell, C., & Grayson, C. J. (1998). *If only we knew what we know*. New York: The Free Press.

OE. (n.d.). Retrieved 11 11, 2012, from http://www.ordemengenheiros.pt

Office of Patent Legal Administration. (2009, November 7). *Laws, regulations, policies & procedures*. Retrieved November 30, 2012, from http://www.uspto.gov/patents/law/index.jsp

OJL. (2001). *101/1 - Council decision of 19 March 2001 adopting the council's security regulations (2001/264/EC)*. Retrieved from http://www.etsi.org/about/our-role-in-europe/public-policy/ec-decisions

OJL. (2001). 137/1 - Commission decision of 29 November 2001 amending its internal RULES OF PROCEDURE (notified under document number C (2001) 3031) (2001/844/EC, ECSC, Euratom).

Okowa, P. N. (2000). State responsibility for transboundary air pollution. In *International Law*. Oxford, UK: Oxford University Press.

O'Leary, M., & Chappell, S. (1996). Confidential incident reporting systems create vital awareness of safety problems. *ICAO Journal, 1*, 11–13, 27. PMID:11541832.

OMB. (1998). Retrieved July 4, 2013, from http://www.whitehouse.gov/omb/circulars_a119/

Oppenheim, A. (1992). *Questionnaire design, interviewing and attitude measurement*. London: Pinter.

Oracle. (2009). *ITIL best practices with oracle enterprise manager 10g and oracle siebel help desk*. Oracle.

Oxford Dictionaries Online. (n.d.). Retrieved from http://oxforddictionaries.com

Park, P. (2009). Voice over IP security: Security best practices derived from deep analysis of the latest VoIP network threats. *CISCO White Paper*, 7-43.

Parker, D. (1998). *Fighting computer crime*. New York, NY: John Wiley and Sons.

Patterson, D. (n.d.). *I/O 2: Failure terminology, examples, gray paper and a little queueing theory*. Retrieved November 3, from http://www.cs.berkeley.edu/~pattrsn/252S01/Lec06-IO2.pdf

Pedersen, T. (1991). Non-interactive and information-theoretic secure verifiable secret sharing. In *Proceedings of Advances in Cryptology — CRYPTO '91 (LNCS)* (Vol. 576, pp. 129–140). Berlin: Springer.

Pedler, M., Burgoyne, J., & Boydell, T. (1991). *The learning company: A strategy for sustainable growth.* Maidenhead, UK: McGraw-Hill.

Pereira, M., & Neves, R. (2010). *Aplicação do cobit em empresas de médio porte.*

Pidgeon, N. F. (1991). Safety culture and risk management in organisations. *Journal of Cross-Cultural Psychology, 22,* 129–140. doi:10.1177/0022022191221009.

Pipkin, D. (2000). *Information security: Protecting the global enterprise.* New York: Hewlett-Packard Company.

Pisillo-Mazzeschi, R. (1992). The due diligence rule and the nature of international responsibility of states. *Jahrbuch fur Internationales Recht. German Yearbook of International Law, 35*(11), 9–51.

Poggi, A., Tomaiuolo, M., & Vitaglione, G. (2005). A security infrastructure for trust management in multi-agent systems.[LNCS]. *Proceedings of Trusting Agents for Trusting Electronic Societies, 3577,* 162–179. doi:10.1007/11532095_10.

Pollalis, Y. A., & Frieze, I. H. (1993). A new look at critical success factors. *Information Strategy,* 24-34.

Porter, M. E. (1980). *Competitive strategy.* New York: The Free Press.

Price Waterhouse Coopers. (1999). *Inside the mind of the CEO: The 1999 global CEO survey.* Paper presented at the World Economic Forum 1999 Annual General Meeting. Davos, Switzerland.

Prince, M. (2012, November 29). How Syria turned off the internet. *CloudFlare blog.* Retrieved November 30, 2012, from http://blog.cloudflare.com/how-syria-turned-off-the-Internet

Public Law 112 - 29 - Leahy-Smith America Invents Act. (2012). Retrieved November 30, 2012, from http://www.gpo.gov/fdsys/pkg/PLAW-112publ29/content-detail.html

PwC. (2010). *Information security breaches survey 2010* (Technical report). PwC.

QS World Universities Ranking. (n.d.). Retrieved 11 12, 2012, from http://www.topuniversities.com/university-rankings/world-university-rankings/2012/subject-rankings/technology/computer-science-information-systems

Radding, A. (1992). Dirty downsizing. *Computerworld, 26*(29), 65–68.

Rahm, E., & Hai Do, H. (2000). Data cleaning: Problems and current approaches. *A Quarterly Bulletin of the Computer Society of the IEEE Technical Committee on Data Engineering, 23*(4), 3–13.

Ransome, J., & Rittinghouse, J. (2005). *VoIP security.* Burlington, UK: Elsevier Digital Press.

Reason, J. T. (1997). *Managing the risks of organizational accidents.* Aldershot, UK: Ashgate.

Reddy, V., & Jena, S. (2010). Active datawarehouse loading by tool based ETL procedure. In *Proceedings of International Conference on Information and Knowledge Engineering (IKE'10),* (pp. 196-201). Las Vegas, NV: IKE.

Rivest, R. L., & Lampson, B. (1996). *SDSI - A simple distributed security infrastructure.* Crypto.

Robertson, M., & O'Malley Hammersley, G. (2000). Knowledge management practices within a knowledge-intensive firm: The significance of the people management dimension. *Journal of European Industrial Training, 24*(2/3/4), 241-253.

Rockart, J. F. (1979). Chief executives define their own data needs. *Harvard Business Review, 57*(2), 81–93. PMID:10297607.

Rockart, J. F. (1979). The changing role of the information systems executive: A critical success factors prospective. *Sloan Management Review, 23*(1), 3–13.

Rodrigues, R. (2010). *Integração das ferramentas nagios e cacti como solução de monitoramento de recursos computacionais em redes.*

Rogers, E. (1995). *Diffusion of innovations* (4th ed.). New York, NY: The Free Press. Retrieved from http://www.personal.psu.edu/users/w/x/wxh139/Rogers.htm

Rossebo, J., & Sijben, P. (2006). Security issues in VoIP. *Telektronikk, 2,* 130–145.

Rousseau, D. M. (1990). Assessing organisational culture: The case for multiple methods. In Schneider, B. (Ed.), *Organisational Climate and Culture* (pp. 153–192). San Francisco, CA: Jossey-Bass.

Ruighaver, A. B., Maynard, S. B., & Chang, S. (2007). Organisational security culture: Extending the end-user experience. *Computers & Security*, *26*, 56–62. doi:10.1016/j.cose.2006.10.008.

Rush, M. A., & Paglia, L. G. (2002). Balancing privacy, public safety, and network security concerns after September 11. *Information Systems Security*, *11*(2), 15–24. doi:10.1201/1086/43320.11.2.20020501/36765.4.

SA-BOK, Systems Administration Body of Knowledge. (n.d.). Retrieved 11 24, 2012, from http://www.sysadmin.com.au/sa-bok.html

Sabre Computer System. (2012). *Final version definition published*. Retrieved July 4, 2013, from http://en.wikipedia.org/wiki/Sabre_(computer_system)

Saharia, A., Koch, B., & Tucker, R. (2008). ERP systems and internal audit. *Issues in Information Systems*, 578–586.

Sandhu, R. S., Coyne, E. J., Feinstein, H. L., & Youman, C. E. (1996). Role-based access control models. *Computer*, *29*(2), 38–47. doi:10.1109/2.485845.

SANS Institute. (2004). *An overview of Sarbanes-Oxley for the information security professional*. Retrieved from http://www.cs.jhu.edu/rubin/courses/sp06/Reading/soxForInfoSec.pdf

Sata Technologies. (2011). *Reactive versus proactive management*. Sata Technologies.

Schedule of Ethics. (2005). Retrieved 11 24, 2012, from http://www.sage-au.org.au/sites/sage-au.org.au/files/attachments/SAGEAU/schedule_of_ethics-2005-10-03.pdf

Schein, E. (1986). What you need to know about organizational culture. *Training and Development Journal*, *40*, 30–35.

Schneier, B. (2000). *Secrets and lies*. New York: John Wiley and Sons.

Schneier, B. (2008). *Schneier on security*. New York: Wiley Publishing.

Schuk, C. (2010). The future of consumer VoIP. *Business Insights*. Retrieved January 17, 2013, from http://www.globalbusinessinsights.com/content/rbtc0141t.pdf

Seamons, K. E., Winslett, M., & Yu, T. (2001). Limiting the disclosure of access control policies during automated trust negotiation. In *Proceedings of the Network and Distributed Systems Symposium*. IEEE.

Section 153A - Indian Penal Code (IPC). (n.d.). Retrieved November 30, 2012, from http://www.vakilno1.com/bareacts/IndianPenalCode/S153A.htm

Seibt, C. H. (1994). *Zivilrechtlicher ausgleich ökologischer schäden*. Tubingen: Mohr Siebeck.

Seltzer, W. (2010, March 30). *Free speech unmoored in copyright's safe harbor: Chilling effects of the DMCA on the first amendment*. Retrieved November 29, 2012, from http://papers.ssrn.com/abstract=1577785

Senge, P. M. (1990). *The fifth discipline: The art and practice of the learning organization*. New York: Doubleday.

Senge, P. M. (2006). *The fifth discipline: The art and practice of the learning organization*. Currency.

Shaw, A. (2010). Data breach: From notification to prevention using PCI DSS. *Columbia Journal of Law and Social Problems*, *43*(4), 517–562.

Shaw, M. N. (2003). *International law*. Cambridge, UK: Cambridge University Press. doi:10.1017/CBO9781139051903.

She, W., Thuraisingham, B., & Yen, I. L. (2007). Delegation-based security model for web services. In *High Assurance Systems Engineering Symposium, 2007* (pp. 82-91). IEEE.

Sherwood, J., Clark, A., & Lynas, D. (2005). *Enterprise security architecture: A business-driven approach*. New York: CMP Books.

Shin, D., Ahn, G. J., & Shenoy, P. (2004). Ensuring information assurance in federated identity management. In *Proceedings of the Performance, Computing, and Communications*, (pp. 821-826). IEEE.

Shoemaker, D., Bawol, J., Drommi, A., & Schymik, G. (2004). A delivery model for an information security curriculum. In *Proceedings of the Third Security Conference*. Las Vegas, NV: Information Institute.

Slack, E. (2012). *What is big data?* Retrieved September 23, 2012, from http://www.storage-switzerland.com/Articles/Entries/2012/8/3_What_is_Big_Data.html

Smith, D. (2012). *Big data to add £216 billion to the UK economy and 58,000 new jobs by 2017*. Retrieved August 3, 2012, from http://www.sas.com/offices/europe/uk/press_office/press_releases/BigDataCebr.html

Smith, J. (2003). *Qualitative psychology: A practical guide to research methods*. Thousand Oaks, CA: Sage Publications.

Smith, R., & Shao, J. (2007). Privacy and e-commerce: A consumer-centric perspective. *Electronic Commerce Research, 7*(2), 89–116. doi:10.1007/s10660-007-9002-9.

Sofaer, A. (2012). A proposal for an international convention on cyber crime and terrorism. *Hoover Institute*. Retrieved October 13, 2012, from: http://iis-db.stanford.edu/pubs/11912/sofaergoodman.pdf

Soliman, F. (1997). Role of information technology in business process re-engineering. In *Proceeding of Australasia on Conference Technology for Manufacturing*. IEEE.

Soliman, F. (2009). Modelling the appraisal of quality management programs. *The Employment Relations Record, 9*(2), 73–83.

Soliman, F. (2011). Could one transformational leader convert the organisation from knowledge based into learning organisation, then into innovation? *Journal of Modern Accounting and Auditing, 7*(12), 1352–1361.

Soliman, F. (2011). Modelling the role of HRM in the innovation chain. *The Employment Relations Record, 11*(2), 1–20.

Soliman, F. (2012). Business excellence and business innovation: Should HRM play different roles? *The Employment Relations Record, 12*(2), 55–68.

Soliman, F. (2012). How good is your organisational knowledge? *Academy of Taiwan Business Management Review, 8*(3), 28–35.

Soliman, F. (2012). Could innovation be driven by globalization? *Journal of Modern Accounting and Auditing, 8*(12), 1848–1860.

Soliman, F. (2012). Modeling the appraisal of cloud systems' implementation. *Journal of Modern Accounting and Auditing, 8*(12), 1888–1897.

Soliman, F. (2013). Does innovation drive sustainable competitive advantages? *Journal of Modern Accounting and Auditing, 9*(1), 131–144.

Soliman, F., & Spooner, K. (2000). Strategies for implementing knowledge management: Role of human resources management. *Journal of Knowledge Management, 4*(4), 337–345. doi:10.1108/13673270010379894.

Soliman, F., & Youssef, M. (2003). The role of critical information in enterprise knowledge management. *Industrial Management & Data Systems, 103*(7), 484–490. doi:10.1108/02635570310489188.

Somers, T. M., & Nelson, K. (2001). The impact of critical success factors across the stages of enterprise resource planning implementation. In *Proceedings of the 34th Hawaii International Conference on Systems Sciences* (HICSS-34). Maui, HI: IEEE.

Sony Computer Entertainment America. (2011). *Letter to the subcommittee on commerce, manufacturing, and trade of the U.S. House of Representatives*. New York: Sony Computer Entertainment America.

SOPHOS. (2012). *Sophos survey reveals need for IT security education within organizations: Antivirus, endpoint, disk encryption, mobile, UTM, email and web security*. Retrieved November 1, 2012, from http://www.sophos.com/en-us/press-office/press-releases/2012/04/sophos-survey-reveals-need-for-it-security-education-within-organizations.aspx

Spadaccini, M. (2007). *Forming an LLC*. Irvine, CA: Entrepreneur Press.

Spaeth, S., Stuermer, M., & Von Krogh, G. (2010). Enabling knowledge creation through outsiders: Towards a push model of open innovation. *International Journal of Technology Management, 52*(3/4), 411–431. doi:10.1504/IJTM.2010.035983.

Spiceworks. (n.d.). *Free help desk software, helpdesk support & help ticket tools from spiceworks*. Retrieved October 24, 2012, from http://www.spiceworks.com/free-help-desk-software/

Stoneburner, G., Goguen, A., & Feringa, A. (2012). *Risk management guide for information technology - Recommendations of the national institute of standards and technology.*

Strauch, C. (2011). *NoSQL databases.* Retrieved March 16, 2013, from http://www.christof-strauch.de/nosqldbs.pdf

Sutija, D., Thorsen, T., Wilson, T., Cammarano, J., & Seres, S. (2007). Business intelligence built on search: The adaptive information warehouse. *Fast White Paper*, 1-9.

Sveiby, K. E. (1997). *The new organizational wealth: Man-aging and measuring knowledge based assets.* San Francisco, CA: Barrett-Kohler Publishers Inc..

Swart, R., Marshall, B., Olsen, D., & Erbacher, R. (2007). ERP II system vulnerabilities and threats: An exploratory study. In *IRMA International Conference* (pp. 925-929). Idea Group Inc.

System Administrators' Code of Ethics. (n.d.). Retrieved 11 15, 2012, from https://www.usenix.org/lisa/system-administrators-code-ethics

Tawileh, A., & McIntosh, S. (2007). Understanding information assurance: A soft systems approach. In *Proceedings of the United Kingdom Systems Society 11th International Conference*. Oxford, UK: Oxford University.

Thadani, R. (2010). Advantages of VoIP. *Buzzle.com.* Retrieved January 19, from http://www.buzzle.com/articles/advantages-of-voip.html

The U.S. Joint Staff (JS). (2000). *Information assurance through defense in depth.* US Joint Staff.

Theoharidou, M., Kokolakis, S., Karyda, M., & Kiountouzis, E. (2005). The insider threat to information systems and the effectiveness of ISO17799. *Computers & Security, 24*, 472–484. doi:10.1016/j.cose.2005.05.002.

Thorp, J. (2005). *Rethinking IT governance - Beyond alignment to integration.* The Thorp Network.

Tie, W., & Cheng, W. (2011). Study on enterprise information security in the ERP conditions. In *Proceedings of the International Conference on Computer Science and Network Technology* (pp. 332-335). IEEE.

Tiller, J. S. (2010). *Adaptive security management architecture.* Boston: Auerbach Publications.

Title 16: Commercial Practices, Part 313—Privacy of Consumer Financial Information. (n.d.). Retrieved November 30, 2012, from http://www.ecfr.gov/cgi-bin/text-idx?c=ecfr,sid=1e9a81d52a0904d70a046d0675d613b0,rgn=div5,view=text,node=16%3A1.0.1.3.37,idno=16,cc=ecfr

Tobin, P., & Bidoli, M. (2006). Factors affecting the adoption of VoIP and other converged IP services in South Africa. *South African Journal of Business Management, 37*(1), 31–40.

Toomey, M. (2009). *Waltzing with the elephant: A comprehensive guide to directing and controlling information technology.* Infonomics Pty Ltd..

Trademark Electronic Search System (TESS). (2013, March 21). Retrieved March 21, 2013, from http://tess2.uspto.gov/

Trouwborst, A. (2006). *Precautionary rights and duties of states.* The Hague, The Netherlands: Brill. doi:10.1163/ej.9789004152120.i-352.

Trustwave Holdings, Inc. (2012). *The trustwave 2012 global security report.* Trustwave Holdings, Inc..

Tsou, C.-W. (2012). Consumer acceptance of windows 7 and office 2010 – The moderating effect of personal innovativeness. *Journal of Research and Practice in Information Technology, 44*(1).

TSU. (2012). *Bits & bytes.* Retrieved from http://www.cis.txstate.edu/Resources/Newsletters/May2012.html

U. S. Bureau of Industry and Security - Policies and Regulations. (1918, December 1). Retrieved November 29, 2012, from http://www.bis.doc.gov/policiesandregulations/index.htm#ear

U.S. Copyright Office. (1998). *Circular 92: Appendix B.* Retrieved November 30, 2012, from http://www.copyright.gov/title17/92appb.html

U.S. Copyright Office. (2011). *Copyright law of the United States.* Retrieved November 30, 2012, from http://www.copyright.gov/title17/

U.S. Department of Commerce. (2012, April 11). *Export.gov - Main safe harbor homepage.* Retrieved December 1, 2012, from http://export.gov/safeharbor/

U.S. Department of Defense (DOD). (2007). *Directive number 8500.01E October 24, 2002: Certified current as of April 23, 2007*. Washington, DC: DOD.

U.S. Trademark Law. (2012, August 9). Retrieved November 30, 2012, from http://www.uspto.gov/trademarks/law/Trademark_Statutes.pdf

UIB. (2013). Retrieved February 28, 2013, from http://governti.uib.es

Understanding Health Information Privacy. (2007, August 13). Retrieved November 30, 2012, from http://www.hhs.gov/ocr/privacy/hipaa/understanding/index.html

UNESCO. (2007). *Revised field of science and technology (FOS) classification in the frascati manual* (OECD). Retrieved 11 20, 2012, from http://www.uis.unesco.org/ScienceTechnology/Documents/38235147.pdf

USCPR. (2011). *The US cyberspace policy review*. Retrieved from http://www.whitehouse.gov/assets/documents/Cyberspace_Policy_Review_final.pdf

USCPR. (2011). *International strategy for cyberspace*. Retrieved from http://www.whitehouse.gov/sites/default/files/rss_viewer/international_strategy_for_cyberspace.pdf

USENIX. (n.d.). Retrieved 11 15, 2012, from https://www.usenix.org/

Uttal, B. (1983, October 17). The corporate culture vultures. *Fortune*.

Van Maanen, J., & Schein, S. (1979). Toward a theory of organizational socialization. *Research in Organizational Behavior*, *11*, 209–259.

Van Roekel. (2011). Retrieved July 4, 2013, from http://www.whitehouse.gov/sites/default/files/svr_parc_speech_final_0.pdf

van Wyk, K., & McGraw, G. (2005). Bridging the gap between software development and information security. *IEEE Security & Privacy*, 75-79.

Varshney, U., Snow, A., McGiven, M., & Howard, C. (2002). Voice over IP. *Communications of the ACM*, *45*(1), 89–95. doi:10.1145/502269.502271.

Vassiliadis, P., Simitsis, A., Georgantas, P., Terrovitis, M., & Skiadopoulos, S. (2005). A generic and customizable framework for the design of ETL scenarios. *Information Systems*, *30*(7), 492–525. doi:10.1016/j.is.2004.11.002.

Venkatesh, P., & Nirmala, S. (2012). *NewSQL – The new way to handle big data*. Retrieved March 16, 2013, from http://www.linuxforu.com/2012/01/newsql-handle-big-data/

Venter, H. S., & Eloff, J. H. P. (2003). A taxonomy for information security technologies. *Computers & Security*, *22*(4), 299–307. doi:10.1016/S0167-4048(03)00406-1.

Viscusi, S. (2010). Business VoIP penetration to grow rapidly. *TMCNet*. Retrieved January 17, 2013, from http://www.tmcnet.com/channels/business-voip/articles/74242-business-voip-penetration-grow-rapidly-report.htm

VIT. (2013). *System administration*. Retrieved from http://venturait.com/system-administration

Von Krogh, G., Roos, J., & Kleine, D. (Eds.). (1999). *Knowing in firms: Understanding, managing, and measuring knowledge*. Altamira Press.

Von Krogh, G., & Von Hippel, E. (2006). The promise of research on open source software. *Management Science*, *52*(7), 975–983. doi:10.1287/mnsc.1060.0560.

Von Solms, B. (2001). Information security - A multidimentional discipline. *Computers & Security*, *20*(6), 504–508. doi:10.1016/S0167-4048(01)00608-3.

Wallingford, T. (2005). Switching to VoIP. Sebastopol, CA: O' Reilly Media.

Wasilko, P. J. (2011). Law, architecture, gameplay, and marketing. In Business, Technological, and Social Dimensions of Computer Games: Multidisciplinary Developments (pp. 476–493). Academic Press.

WCD. (2012). *Declaration by the committee of ministers on internet governance principles*. Retrieved October 13, 2012, from https://wcd.coe.int/ViewDoc.jsp?id=1835773

Webhosting Help Guy. (n.d.). *Support ticket systems: 5 tools for managing customer support*. Retrieved November 23, 2012, from http://Webhostinghelpguy.inmotionhosting.com/Website-optimization/support-ticket-systems-5-tools-for-managing-customer-support/

Weill, P., & Ross, J. W. (2004). *IT governance: How top performers manage IT decision rights for superior results.* Boston: Harvard Business School Press.

Welch, V., Foster, I., Kesselman, C., Mulmo, O., Pearlman, L., & Tuecke, S. ... Siebenlist, F. (2004). X.509 proxy certificates for dynamic delegation. In *Proceedings of the 3rd Annual PKI R&D Workshop.* Gaithersburg MD: NIST Technical Publications.

Welch, V., Siebenlist, F., Foster, I., Bresnahan, J., Czajkowski, K., & Gawor, J. ... Tuecke, S. (2003). Security for grid services. In Proceedings of High Performance Distributed Computing, 2003 (pp. 48-57). IEEE.

Whitman, M. E., & Mattord, H. J. (2012). *Principles of information security* (4th ed.). Course Technology, Cengage Learning.

Wilber, L. (2012). A practical guide to big data: opportunities, challenges & tools. *Dassault Systems White Papers*, 4-36.

Wilson, C., & Kerber, J. (2011). Demystifying big data: A practical guide to transforming the business of government. *TechAmerica Foundation White Papers*, 6-37.

Winsborough, W. H., & Li, N. (2000). Automated trust negotiation. In *Proceedings of DARPA Information Survivability Conference and Exposition*, (vol. 1, pp. 88-102). IEEE Press.

Winslett, M., Yu, T., Seamons, K. E., Hess, A., Jacobson, J., & Jarvis, R. et al. (2002). Negotiating trust in the Web. *IEEE Internet Computing*, 6(6), 30–37. doi:10.1109/MIC.2002.1067734.

Wolf, P., & Gehrke, N. (2009). *Continuous compliance monitoring in ERP systems - A method for identifying segregation of duties conflicts.* Hamburg, Germany: Wirtschaftinformatik.

World e.gov. (2011). Retrieved July 4, 2013, from http://wegf.org/en/2011/02/uk-universities-to-adopt-cloud-shared-services/

Yu, X., & Wen, Q. (n.d.). *A view about cloud data security from data life cycle.* Beijing, China: IEEE.

Yu, T., Winslett, M., & Seamons, K. E. (2003). Supporting structured credentials and sensitive policies through interoperable strategies for automated trust negotiation. *ACM Transactions on Information and System Security*, 6(1), 1–42. doi:10.1145/605434.605435.

Zar, A., Stewart, K., Tate, L., Cheyne, A., & Cox, S. (2002). *Development and trials of tools to assess safety culture: Final technical report. QinetiQ Report: QinetiQ/CHS/CAP/TR020057.* QinetiQ..

Zhang, R., Wang, X., Farley, R., Yang, X., & Jiang, X. (2009). On the feasibility of launching the man-in-the-middle attacks on VoIP from remote attackers. In *Proceedings of ASIACCS*, (pp. 61-69). Sydney, Australia: ASIACCS.

Zhang, L., Ahn, G. J., & Chu, B. T. (2003). A rule-based framework for role-based delegation and revocation. *ACM Transactions on Information and System Security*, 6(3), 404–441. doi:10.1145/937527.937530.

About the Contributors

Irene Portela is professor at IPCA, and she is the ombudsman person of the students at IPCA. Her current research focus is Information Communication Technologies and Law. She lectures in Human Rights and Civil Liberties and the use of ICT. Irene holds a Master in Public Administration and a PhD in Public Law and European Institutions. She is the co-editor of the book edited by IGI Global en 2010 titled *Information Communication Technology Law, Protection, and Access Rights: Global Approaches and Issues*.

Fernando Almeida holds a PhD in Computer Science and Informatics Engineering and he is currently a Coordinator Professor in the School of Science and Technology at Polytechnic Institute of Gaya, Portugal. He is the Director of the BSc. degree in Computer Science Engineering and MSc. degree of Network Administration and Information Systems. He is also a consultant and R&D engineer in FP7 European Projects in the field of Information and Communication Technologies (ICT), and he has over 10 years of experience in the Information Systems in the private and public sector. His research interests are mainly in Information Security, Information Systems, Software Engineering, Enterprise Architectures, and Entrepreneurship and Innovation.

* * *

Gonçalo N.C.S. de Melo Bandeira, Professor in the E.S.G.-I.P.C.A., Management SchoolPolytechnic Institute of Cávado and Ave, Barcelos, Portugal, Professor of the Portucalense University I.D.H., Porto, Portugal, Professor at I.D.C.C., Brazil, Associated Investigator of the C.I.C.F.-I.P.C.A. (Research Centre on Accounting and Taxation), Associated Investigator of the I.J.P. ("Portucalense" Legal Institute)-Portucalense University, Investigator of the C.I.J.A. (Center of Applied Legal Inquiry)-I.P.C.A., Doctor in Legal-Criminal Sciences for the Faculty of Law of the University of Coimbra, Master in Law for the Faculty of Law of the Portuguese Catholic University, Law Graduated for the F.L.U. of Coimbra, Researcher-guest in the MaxPlanck-Institut für ausländisches und internationales Strafrecht, Freiburg im Breisgau, BadenWüttemberg, Deutschland-Germany (2005, 2006, and 2011). Diverse publications in the different publishing companies: Juruá, Almedina, Coimbra Editora, Vida Económica, among others. Founder and Member of diverse Portuguese and foreign Publishing Advice. Winner of International Scholarship-Prize Juruá in 2011, 2012 (I.D.C.C., Brazil) and 2013, for merit of Legal Author in Brazil and Latin America, including one scientific voyage of conferences already programmed under the form of invitations and to carry through in Brazil. Author of diverse conferences in Portugal and the foreigner, nominated in Germany and Legal Professor-Guest of diverse Universities and Institutions in Brazil. Member of a series of national and international scientific and politician Associations. Lawyer.

Yulia Cherdantseva is a PhD Research Student at the School of Computer Science and Informatics, Cardiff University of the UK. Yulia is interested in Information Security Management. Her current research focus is the integration of Information Security and Business Process Modelling. Yulia holds an MSc (Hons) in Design of Information Systems and has over 6 years of experience in industry.

José Costa was born in a village called Vila Fria's municipality of Viana do Castelo, northern Portugal, on 12 December 1984. He has a degree in Information and Technology in the School of Technology and Management of the Polytechnic Institute of Cavado e do Ave and he is finishing his Masters in Network Administration and Systems at School of Science and Technology of the Polytechnic Institute of Gaya. He works in the IT department of public company called SMSBVC, and he is the systems and network administrator. The core business of his company is water supply.

José Magalhães Cruz is a full professor at FEUP in the department of Informatics Engineering. His current researches focus in the field of open source operative systems and distributed computation. He lectures in Operative Systems, Distributed Systems and Cryptography, and Security. He is one of the founders of Linux FEUP initiative and an enthusiast of open source projects between academic and business fields.

Jeremy Hilton is a Principal Research Fellow at Cranfield University, Defence Academy of the UK. He has over 25 years of experience in Information Security in the private and public sector, particularly in the design and implementation of Public Key Infrastructures. His research focus is currently in the area of resilience of organisations and communities and the integration of Information Security with Enterprise Systems Engineering. He lectures in Cyber Defence, Systems Thinking, and the application of systems methods within systems engineering. He is a Chartered Engineer, holds a BSc in Mechanical Engineering and an MSc in Design of Information Systems.

Carlos Juiz (1966) received the B.Sc., M.Sc., and Ph.D. degrees in Computer Science from the University of the Balearic Islands (UIB), Spain. He has a postgraduate degree on Office automation from the Polytechnic University of Madrid. Before joining to the Department of Computer Science at UIB, he had several positions related with the computer systems industry. He was visiting researcher at University of Vienna (2003) and Visiting Associate Professor at Stanford University (2011). Carlos Juiz is heading the ACSIC research group and his current research interest mainly focuses on IT governance. He is co-author of more than 150 international papers and one university textbook. Carlos Juiz is senior member of the IEEE and the ACM. He is also member of ARTEMISIA, NESSI, and IFIP. He is an invited expert of the International Communication Union (ITU) and member of the IT Governance committee at AENOR. He is also Academic Advocate of ISACA. Currently, he is Vice rector for Information Technologies at University of the Balearic Islands.

Joanna Kulesza is assistant professor in the Department of International Law and International Relations, Faculty of Law and Administration, University of Lodz, Poland. She holds a M.A. in law (2002) and a Ph.D. in international law (2008) from the University of Lodz. She has been a visiting professor at the Oxford Internet Institute, University of Oslo, Universität Münster, Justus-Liebig-Universität Gießen, and a visiting researcher at the University of Cambridge. She was awarded scholarships from the Foundation for Polish Science, Polish Ministry of Foreign Affairs, Internet Governance Project, and Robert Bosch Stiftung. She serves as an expert for the Council of Europe and had worked for the European Parliament and the Polish Ministry of Foreign Affairs. Currently, she is the Membership Committee Chair of the Global Internet Governance Academic Network. Kulesza is the author of over 30 peer-reviewed articles and three monographs on international Internet governance including the pioneering *International Internet Law* (Routledge 2012). Her research interests cover limits of state competence in cyberspace, human rights in information society and international cooperation on Internet governance.

Mário Lousã is a coordinator professor at Polytechnic Institute Gaya (ISPGaya), Portugal. He received his MSc in Management Informatics from Portuguese Catholic University and the PhD in Technology and Information Systems from Minho University, Portugal. He lectures courses on Computer Science. He is Effective Member of the Portuguese Order of Engineers and professionalized teacher by the group of IT since 2001. His primary area of research is information systems, namely in the domain of the automation of the business process management, as well as knowledge and organizational learning. He is author or co-author of several books, papers, proceedings of events, and software, as well as consultant in the area of IT. He participated in several academic and professional juries. He is a member of the Scientific Commission of the journal *Politécnica* since 2007. He participated in the Technical Vocational Education reform in Angola, as coordinator of the training area of "Computer and Multimedia."

Joel Luz is a System and Network administrator at Ordem dos Advogados and also teacher in Polytechnic Institute of Gaya. He earned his degree in Telecommunications and Computers Engineering in 2006 in Portugal. He is currently at Vigo University, Spain, getting his PhD in Telecommunications Engineering. He is also the CEO at TakeKey – Digital Systems. Joel Luz's interests are in systems and network administration and teaching. As a researcher, he has been working on projects about corporate TV, ITED, and ITUR.

Jo Malcolmson is an experienced psychologist with a track record of successful delivery of research work on organisational culture and its impact for CPNI, the Home Office (OSCT), MOD, and commercial organisations. Jo had overall responsibility for a 2-year project to define and provide a measure of security culture. This work included a detailed comparison of safety and security culture, and has led to the development of a tool used in organisations where security is critical. Jo led a project to measure safety culture for MOD's flying training personnel. She led a project for the Home Office OSCT assessing those aspects of organisational culture that facilitate and act against interoperability in the emergency services. Jo is a visiting lecturer for King's College London, and previously lectured on Organisational Culture and Change for the Open University. Her IEEE Carnahan Security Conference paper, "Security Culture: How it Differs from Organisational Culture," has attracted significant interest.

Vitor Manso was born in a village called Mazarefe's municipality of Viana do Castelo, northern Portugal, on 6 December 1984. He has a degree in Information and Technology in the School of Technology and Management of the Polytechnic Institute of Cavado e do Ave, and he is finishing his Masters in Network Administration and Systems at School of Science and Technology of the Polytechnic Institute of Gaya. He works in Polytechnic Institute of Cavado e do Ave in the IT department as a system and network administrator, and he is the COO (Chief Operating Officer) in a company called DIGIHEART.

José Augusto Monteiro has MSc on Information Management from 'FEUP - Faculdade de Engenharia da Universidade do Porto' (2009). He is MCP - Microsoft Certified Professional, and has CAP - Certificado de Aptidão Pedagógica from IEFP - Instituto de Emprego e Formação Profissional. He has started his professional career on mechatronics and industrial equipment at Cimertex SA, has served in Portuguese Air Force as an operational in Radar Maintenance area, and he has been working in IT Systems area and office automation at Beltrão Coelho (Porto) for over 10 years. Since 2004, he teaches and researches at ISPGaya - Instituto Superior Politécnico Gaya. Also, he plays the role of the coordinator of the Course of Computer Science for Management and is responsible for the IT Systems that support academic activities. Now, he is a PhD candidate on Informatics Engineering (ProDEI) at FEUP - Faculdade de Engenharia da Universidade do Porto.

Filipe Moreira is a System and Network administrator at Decunify, SA. He earned his Bachelor of Arts in Information Science from Oporto University in 2010 and his Master's Degree in Network and Informatics Systems Administration from Polytechnic Institute of Gaya in 2013 both at Portugal. He is a Cisco Certified Network Associate and a WatchGuard Certified System Professional. Filipe Moreira started his professional career as a BPM consultant but soon derived his path to networks and system's administration. His research interests are network and system's administration, information management, end-users training and social skills. He has been involved in both private and public sectors being part of process re-engineering, network redesign, and system's administration projects.

Victor Alexander de Pous (1955) studied law at the Law School of the VU University Amsterdam (Master of Laws). He has been working in the domain of the business and legal aspects of IT and Telecom. During the last 30 years, he wrote articles, books, white papers, commentaries and analyses. Victor de Pous is the co-founder of the Section on Computer Law of the Dutch Society for Informatics NGI and a past executive Member of the Board. In addition, he is the co-founder and a Member of the Board of the International Telework Foundation, a non-profit organization which stimulated academic research in the domain of virtual organizations and smart working. He is the co-founder and a Member of the Board of EuroCloud Netherlands, responsible for legal and public policy affairs. In 2010, he joined the International Federation for Information Processing (IFIP) as their Legal Counsel. From January 2002 until April 2007 Victor de Pous was the pro bono General Counsel and Secretary of the Board of Directors of the Foundation Relatives Victims Tenerife, a non-profit organization for survivors and surviving relatives of the largest air crash in the history of civil aviation. On April 25, 2008, he was knighted by HM Queen Beatrix for his social responsibility work.

Mário Santos is engineer and professor at ISPGaya. He has over 20 years of experience on Software Engineering, Enterprise Resource Planning Software Systems, Object-Oriented Programming, Knowledge-Based Systems, Electrical and Communications Engineering, mainly in the private sector. His present research focus is the Building Information Modelling applied to Transport Systems Engineering. He currently lectures in Software Engineering, Databases, Software Project Management, Complements of Engineering (Building-Information Modelling/Knowledge-Based-Systems), Electrical Circuits, Operational Research, Production Management and Logistics. Mário holds a BSc in Electrical and Computer Engineering specializing in Digital Systems, MSc in Electrical and Computer Engineering specializing in Industrial Computer Systems, and is a PhD Student in Industrial Management and Engineering with a focus on BIM and Transports.

Fawzy Soliman has a Doctorate degree from University of New South Wales, and he is the course director and senior lecturer in Management at University of Technology Sydney. He is also the editor of *International Journal of Electronic Business* and *Journal of Knowledge Management*. Fawzy has been a Chartered Corporate Engineer since 1979. He has more than 20 years experience in the manufacturing industry. Fawzy managed large projects worth millions of dollars and has acquired hands on knowledge of the manufacturing and electronic industry. Fawzy's expertise resulted in substantial savings in the cost of operations and production to many of his clients. Fawzy has been appointed a consultant to many large corporate organizations. He is credited for many of their successful projects. Some of his main clients include Electric Power Transmission, Thiess Bros, Pacific Power, International Combustion Australia, CSIRO, General Electric Australia, Wormald International, Department of Health, Intergraph Corporation, Siemens, Plessey, and 3M Australia and British Aerospace.

Pedro Sousa was born in a village called Torre's municipality of Viana do Castelo, northern Portugal, on 16 January 1985. Pedro Sousa is a computer engineer with a degree in the School of Science and Technology of the Polytechnic Institute of Gaya and he is finishing his Masters in Network Administration and Systems at the same school. He works in a university in north of Portugal as CTO (Chief Technology Officer) and he is the CEO (Chief Executive Officer) in a company called DIGIHEART. He has some hobbies that are beyond professional areas of technology. He is professional guide of canyoning and performance related activities outdoor sports. Like other hobbies, he likes to play football, travelling, movies, and all sorts of activities that allow join with his friends.

Michele Tomaiuolo received a M.Eng. in Computer Engineering and a PhD in Information Technologies from the University of Parma. Currently, he is an assistant professor at the Department of Information Engineering, University of Parma. He has given lessons on Foundations of Informatics, Object-Oriented Programming, Software Enigineering, Computer Networks, Mobile Code, and Security. He participated in various national and international research projects, including the EU funded @lis TechNet, Agentcities, Collaborator, Comma, and the national project Anemone. His current research activity is focused on peer-to-peer social networking, with attention to security and trust management, multi-agent systems, Semantic Web, rule-based systems, peer-to-peer networks.

Peter J. Wasilko, Esq., is an attorney licensed to practice law in New York State, holding at J.D. (Juris Doctor), LL.M. (Masters of Law), and certificate in Law, Technology, and Management from Syracuse University's College of Law. He is active in the New York State Bar Association and its Intellectual Property Section. He is also a member of the Association for the Advancement of Artificial Intelligence, The Association for Computing Machinery, and The IEEE Computer Society. His primary technical interests are Law and AI, Human Computer Interaction, and End User Programming. He has served as Executive Director of the Institute for End User Computing, Inc.—a 501(c)(3) Public Charity—from his founding of the organization in 2002 through the time of this writing in early 2013 as the organization is winding down. More about Mr. Wasilko can be found online at: http://peter.wasilko.info.

Index